OLD TESTAMENT

STUDY GUIDE

GENESIS THROUGH MALACHI verse by verse

CHUCK SMITH

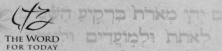

THE WORD
FOR TODAY

P.O. Box 8000, Costa Mesa, CA 92628 • Web: www.twft.com • E-mail: info@twft.com
1-800-272-WORD (9673)

OLD TESTAMENT STUDY GUIDE
by Chuck Smith

© 2006 The Word For Today
Published by The Word For Today
P.O. Box 8000, Costa Mesa, CA 92628
1-800-272-WORD (9673)

Web Site: www.twft.com
E-mail: info@twft.com

ISBN: 978-1-932941-83-8

Second Printing, 2012

CONTENTS

CONTENTS CONTINUED

THE OLD TESTAMENT
STUDY GUIDE

INTRODUCTION

Pastor Chuck Smith has been teaching the Bible for more than fifty years, and the Old Testament study guides collected in this book are based upon his Bible commentaries delivered at Calvary Chapel of Costa Mesa.

These Old Testament commentaries have also been broadcast on radio and the internet worldwide on *The Word For Today*, and were designed to help students of the Bible enhance their knowledge of the Scriptures.

As you read the Bible, we hope that this Old Testament survey will help you grow in your personal understanding of God's Word.

KEYS TO THE

OLD TESTAMENT

STUDY GUIDE

The *Old Testament Study Guide* is designed as a commentary outline to be read with a Bible.

The following icons will aid in your study of the Old Testament.

HEBREW KEY WORD

Definitions of Hebrew words found in the Old Testament.

CALVARY DISTINCTIVE

Excerpts taken from the book *Calvary Chapel Distinctives* by Chuck Smith.

A CLOSER LOOK

Helpful charts or diagrams clarifying certain portions of the Bible.

BIBLE MAP AREA

Area maps relating to Scripture.

STUDY QUESTIONS

Questions pertaining to specific books of the Old Testament.

THE BOOK OF
GENESIS

AUTHOR OF THE BOOK:
Moses

PERIOD OF WRITING:
It was written in the 15th century BC.

TYPE OF BOOK:
Book of the law; first book of the Pentateuch.

THEME:
From the beginning of man to the founding of the Hebrew nation.

INTRODUCTION:
The word "Genesis" in Hebrew means beginning. Genesis is the book of beginnings: the beginning of creation, the beginning of man, the beginning of sin, and the beginning of God's plan for the redemption of sinning man.

CHAPTER 1:
CREATION

•VERSE 1 "In the beginning God." The subject of the Bible is God. The purpose of the Bible is the knowledge of Him and His love.

 HEBREW KEY WORD

> The Hebrew word for God is *Elohiym*, which is plural, indicating the Trinity acted together to create the world (1:1).

Doesn't nature reveal God to us? Nature reveals God's power, greatness, and wisdom, but we need the Bible to provide a unified body of knowledge concerning God.

God is the Creator of all things, the object of creation—the Sustainer of creation.

"God created the heavens and the earth." Men who do not accept God as the Creator must find other theories for our existence.

Problems with the theory of evolution:

(1) No new creation taking place.

(2) Matter is constantly changing but the trend is downward (deterioration), not upward.

(3) The earth would have to be much older than it is to provide time for simple cells to evolve to the complexity of the cells we see today.

Complexity of cells is not synonymous with higher life forms. Frog cells are more complex than human cells.

(4) The dating of fossils is often inaccurate.

(5) Mutations occur within a species but do not cross over to another species.

(6) The population of earth would be greater if man were as old as the evolutionists claim.

(7) Suggested reading: *Evolution: The Fossils Say No* by Duane Gish and *Twilight of Evolution* by Henry Morris.

•**VERSE 2** There could be a gap in time between the first verse and the rest of the chapter.

"But the earth became wasteful and desolate" is another reading of the second verse.

•**VERSE 3** Light is needed for life.

•**VERSES 6-8** The blanket of moisture that surrounded the earth protected men from cosmic radiation and cell damage so that lifespans were much longer.

•**VERSES 11-12** God created plant life that can reproduce itself.

•**VERSES 20-25** God created the families of living things, the species.

•**VERSES 26-28** Man is created in the image of God. The order to "replenish the earth" could indicate a preexistence upon the earth.

CHAPTER 2:
DETAILS OF CREATION

•**VERSE 2** "Rested" indicates that God was finished, not tired.

•**VERSE 13** The Ethiopia referred to is not the area we know as Ethiopia today.

•**VERSE 21** "Rib" actually means curved section in the Hebrew. God may have made an incision in Adam and used his blood or a clone cell to create Eve.

HEBREW KEY WORD

tsalah = rib, curved section, side (2:21).

•**VERSES 21-24** The woman was created to complete the man. The marriage relationship should be a building up and complementing of one another.

CHAPTER 3:
THE FALL

•**VERSE 1** The word "serpent" here is not the Hebrew word commonly used for snake. It could be translated dragon, especially since snakes are reptiles, not "beasts of the field."

•**VERSE 5** Satan implies that God is not fair in withholding the knowledge of good and evil.

•**VERSE 6** Eve was deceived by the serpent, but Adam willfully transgressed when he ate the fruit. She was led into sin by the lust of the flesh, the lust of the eyes, and the pride of life.

•**VERSE 9** "Where art thou?" is the cry of a heartbroken Father. God knew that Adam and Eve were the victims of their choices and that they were now in bondage to death and darkness.

•**VERSES 12-13** Adam and Eve tried to shift the blame for their sin onto others.

•**VERSE 15** The first promise of the Messiah. Jesus, the seed of the woman (Mary), destroyed the "head" or authority and power of Satan by His redemptive death on the cross. The cross is the second tree established by God whereby men might leave the government of death and darkness and go back into the government of life and light.

•**VERSE 21** The concept of a blood sacrifice to cover sin is first introduced here as the animals are slain to provide clothing for Adam and Eve. This event foreshadows Christ's eventual death on the cross, which put an end to blood sacrifice.

•VERSES 22-24 God was merciful, not harsh, when He sent Adam and Eve away from the tree of life because He knew they would not want to have to remain forever in their earthly, aging bodies.

CHAPTER 4:
CAIN'S SIN

•VERSE 3 "In process of time." Adam could have had four generations of children during the time lapse indicated by these words.

Usually a man's entire lineage was not listed in the Bible; only those children relevant to the story are named.

•VERSE 5 Cain's offering did not please God.

•VERSE 7 God explained to Cain that sin in his life had caused his offering to be rejected.

CHAPTER 5:
THE PATRIARCHS FROM ADAM TO NOAH

•VERSES 21-24 The deaths of men are recorded in an unbroken chain until Enoch. Enoch was taken from the earth by God.

Enoch, as a man of faith, represents the church, which will also be taken out of the world (raptured).

Noah symbolizes the 144,000 Jews who will have to go through the tribulation here on earth, but will be protected by God.

•VERSES 25-27 It appears that perhaps Methuselah died in the flood.

CALVARY DISTINCTIVE

And Enoch walked with God: and he was not; for God took him" (Genesis 5:24).

Enoch is an interesting picture of the church. He was translated or raptured.

CHAPTER 6:
THE STORY OF NOAH

•VERSE 3 God cut the life span from an average of 912 years to an average of 120 years.

•VERSE 4 The "sons of God" may refer to fallen angels who married the "daughters of men" and produced giant offspring.

•VERSE 6 "Repented" is our way of describing God's response to the evil in the world He had created, though He actually does not "repent" as we do.

•VERSE 14 "Pitch" is tar.

•VERSE 15 A cubit is 18 to 24 inches. The ark had the square footage of 1,000 boxcars.

•VERSES 19-21 Noah had room for the animals since he only had to take one pair from each species.

God sent the animals to the ark, so Noah did not have to search them out.

CHAPTER 7:
THE FLOOD

•VERSE 6 It took Noah and his sons about 120 years to complete the ark.

•VERSE 11 "Fountains of the deep" are underground reservoirs.

A legend of a flood was part of the mythology of all the ancient cultures, confirming the common origin of man.

•VERSE 12 Forty is the number of judgment in the Bible.

CHAPTER 8:
NOAH LEAVES THE ARK

•VERSE 21 God's evaluation of man: "for the imagination of man's heart is evil from his youth."

CHAPTER 9:
THE COVENANT

•VERSES 9-11 God promised that He would not destroy the earth with a universal flood again.

•VERSE 19 The peoples of the world are divided into three ethnic groups after Noah's three sons.

CHAPTER 10:
THE TABLES OF NATIONS

•VERSE 2 The sons of Japheth are the Caucasians who settled in Russia and the European continent.

•VERSE 6 Ham's descendants populated the African continent.

•VERSE 21 Shem was the father of Eber, where the word *Hebrew* originates (the children of Eber) and Asian people.

CHAPTER 11:
THE TOWER OF BABEL

•VERSE 4 The tower was a ziggurat, where people worshiped the stars.

•VERSE 26 Since Shem and Abram were contemporaries, Shem may have given the details of the ark and the flood to Abram.

CHAPTER 12:
THE PROMISE OF BLESSING

•VERSES 2-3 The promise of blessing God gave to Abram included the promise of the Messiah that was to come from Abram's line: "and in thee shall all families of the earth be blessed."

•VERSE 5 Abram and Sarai had the same father; she was his half-sister. Abram was 75 and Sarai was in her 60s.

•VERSES 11-20 Though Abram is considered to have been a great man of faith, it was not always constant, and here is a lapse of faith.

CHAPTER 13:
ABRAM AND LOT DIVIDE

•VERSES 14-18 God promised the land to Abram and to his descendants forever.

God told Abram to look at the land with the eyes of faith and then to walk in faith all over the land.

CHAPTER 14:
THE KING OF SALEM

•VERSE 18 Salem is thought to be Jerusalem. The term *El Elyon*, "most high God," is first used here.

Some scholars think Melchizedek may have been Shem, who was still alive at that time, while others believe that Melchizedek was a theophany, an appearance of God in human form, which would be Christ.

•VERSE 20 Abram tithed to Melchizedek.

•VERSE 22 Abram used the same term Melchizedek had used—"most high God."

CHAPTER 15:
GOD'S COVENANT WITH ABRAM

•**VERSE 1** Abram had not taken any spoil from the battle, so God told him that He would be his shield and reward.

•**VERSE 13** The 400 years of bondage of the Hebrews in Egypt is prophesied.

•**VERSE 14** The Hebrews "borrowed" from their Egyptian neighbors when they left Egypt.

CHAPTER 16:
SARAI AND HAGAR

•**VERSE 2** Sarai had a lapse of faith when she tried to help God to produce an heir for Abram. Though this lapse was forgiven, the descendants of Ishmael have caused problems for the sons of Abram since these early days.

•**VERSE 11** "Ishmael" means God shall hear.

•**VERSE 14** "Beerlahairoi" means the well of Him that liveth and seeth me.

CHAPTER 17:
THE COVENANT OF CIRCUMCISION

•**VERSE 1** God reveals Himself further as *El Shaddai* meaning Almighty God.

•**VERSE 5** "Abram" means high father. "Abraham" means father of many nations.

•**VERSES 10-14** Circumcision was a symbol of the cutting away of the flesh to pursue the things of God and of His Spirit.

•**VERSE 15** "Sarai" means contentious. "Sarah" means princess.

•**VERSE 16** Romans 4 lists the four keys to Abraham's faith as:

(1) Not considering human difficulty.

(2) Not staggering at the promises of God.

(3) Giving glory and thanks to God for what He will do.

(4) Knowing that God can fulfill His promises.

•**VERSES 17-18** A second lapse of faith: Abraham laughed and wondered inwardly when God told him that Sarah would bear a son.

Then Abraham told God that he would be satisfied with Ishmael.

•**VERSE 19** God told Abraham to call his son Isaac, which means laughter.

CHAPTER 18:
THE LORD VISITS ABRAHAM

•**VERSES 13-17** When LORD is written with all capital letters, it signifies the Hebrew *Yahweh* (YHVH) when it is used in the text.

The Jews do not speak His holy name.

•**VERSE 22** The men (angels) went on to Sodom, but the Lord (Jesus, as a theophany) stayed with Abraham.

•**VERSES 23-32** The concept that the Lord would not destroy the righteous with the wicked was argued by Abraham as the "right" way to act.

According to this concept, God will not destroy His church in the tribulation, but will take it out before His judgment begins, as He removed Lot from Sodom.

CHAPTER 19:
THE ANGELS VISIT SODOM

•**VERSE 1** The two angels had gone on to Sodom. The judges of Sodom sat in the gate.

•**VERSE 5** The men of Sodom wanted homosexual relations with the angels.

•**VERSES 6-8** Lot's offering of his virgin daughters to the wicked men of Sodom is difficult to comprehend unless one understands the mindset of the times:

women were considered chattel. This attitude changed after the advent of Christianity.

•VERSE 10 The angels pulled Lot back into the house.

•VERSE 14 Though Lot was righteous, his compromises in moving into the wicked city cost him his children. Only his two daughters who remained at home escaped with him.

•VERSE 31 The daughters thought they were the only survivors on the earth, so they acted to preserve life.

•VERSES 37-38 The Moabites and Ammonites were the result of these unions and have caused continual problems for the Hebrews.

CHAPTER 20:
ANOTHER LAPSE OF FAITH

•VERSE 2 Sarah was in her 90s at this point.

Abraham had a lapse of faith again, which only confirms that he was a man just as we are. The gift of faith that God gave Abraham is available to us too.

CHAPTER 21:
THE BIRTH OF ISAAC

•VERSES 1-7 The birth of Isaac was a source of awe at God's power and joy in His blessing.

•VERSE 12 God promised Abraham that "in Isaac shall thy seed be called." This promise was to help Abraham in a later trial.

•VERSE 31 "Beersheba" means the well of oath or swearing.

CHAPTER 22:
THE FELLOWSHIP OF HIS SUFFERING

God's fellowship with Abraham was progressive.

Each new revelation of Himself led Abraham to a deeper knowledge of the heart of God.

First appearance: fellowship of the discontent of God with the worldly society (Genesis 12:1).

Second appearance: fellowship with the plans and methods of God (Genesis 13:14-18).

Third appearance: fellowship with the patience of God (Genesis 15:1-11).

Fourth appearance: fellowship of the hope of God (Genesis 15:12-21).

Fifth appearance: fellowship of the sufficiency of God (Genesis 17).

Sixth appearance: fellowship with the justice of God (Genesis 18:23-33).

Seventh appearance: fellowship of His suffering (Genesis 22).

•VERSE 1 "Test" is a better word than "tempt" to describe the experience God planned for Abraham.

•VERSE 2 This verse compares to John 3:16 where God the Father sacrificed His beloved Son. Calvary is located right on the crest of Mount Moriah.

•VERSES 3-10 Repetition of the word "and" denotes consistent, deliberate action.

•VERSE 5 The plural verb was used when Abraham said, "I and the lad will go yonder and worship and [we will] come again to you."

•VERSE 6 Isaac had to carry the wood for the sacrifice even as Christ had to carry the cross.

•VERSE 8 Abraham prophesies, "My son, God will provide Himself a lamb for a burnt offering [sacrifice]."

•VERSES 8-10 Hebrews 11:17-19. Abraham had the promise of God that his descendants would come through Isaac (Genesis 21:12).

And since Isaac had no children when God asked for the sacrifice, Abraham knew that, if necessary, God would raise Isaac from the dead.

Like Christ, Isaac was a willing sacrifice, for he was about 30 years old and could easily have overpowered his aged father.

•VERSE 14 "Jehovah-jireh" means God sees, God provides. "In the mount of the Lord it shall be seen" was a prophecy of the sacrifice of Jesus by the Father on the same mount.

•VERSES 16-18 When Abraham gave his best to God, God rewarded him doubly. Abraham was allowed to enter into a deep, intimate fellowship with God in suffering over the sacrifice of a beloved only son.

CHAPTER 23:
SARAH'S BURIAL

•VERSES 3-20 This chapter provides insight into the dealings of Abraham with the Canaanites.

CHAPTER 24:
A BRIDE FOR ISAAC

The story of Isaac and Rebekah is a beautiful love story that symbolizes the Holy Spirit wooing a bride (the church) for the Son (Christ).

•VERSE 27 Throughout this story, Eliezer is a selfless individual, speaking more of Abraham and Isaac than of himself, just as the Holy Spirit glorifies the Father and the Son without drawing attention to Himself.

•VERSES 29-31 Laban hurried to greet Eliezer when he sensed there could be a profit.

•VERSE 53 The Holy Spirit gives glorious gifts to us.

•VERSE 58 Rebekah was drawn by the Spirit to her bridegroom.

CHAPTER 25:
JACOB AND ESAU

•VERSES 25-26 "Esau" means hairy. "Jacob" means heel-catcher, supplanter.

•VERSE 27 "Plain man" means that Jacob was delicate.

•VERSE 30 "Edom" means red. This was Esau's nickname.

•VERSE 34 Esau did not care about his birthright, for he went on his way after eating the lentils; but to Jacob the birthright was something to be desired.

CHAPTER 26:
ISAAC'S LAPSE OF FAITH

•VERSES 1-11 Isaac said his wife was his sister to protect himself, just as his father had done with his wife.

•VERSE 20 "Esek" means strife.

•VERSE 21 "Sitnah" means contention.

•VERSE 22 "Rehoboth" means room for us all.

•VERSE 23 "Shebah" means seventh.

CHAPTER 27:
THE SUBSTITUTION

•VERSE 38 Esau wept for the loss of the material blessings, but he did not seek the blessing of God on his life (Hebrews 12:17).

•VERSE 40 Esau's descendants were the Edomites who were under the dominion of the Israelites for a time but finally revolted. The Herodian kings in the New Testament were the last known Edomites.

CHAPTER 28:
JACOB IS SENT AWAY

•VERSE 11 Jacob was at Bethel, the same spot where the Lord had shown to Abraham all the land that He would give to him and to his seed.

•**VERSES** 20-21 Jacob was such a scheming man that even his vow to God was basically a bargain with God rather than a loving consecration.

CHAPTER 29:
JACOB MARRIES

•**VERSE 17** "Tender-eyed" means blue-eyed. Blue eyes were considered a weakness then.

•**VERSES** 23-27 Laban was just as scheming as Jacob in giving his older daughter to Jacob in place of his beloved Rachel, for whom Jacob had worked seven years.

•**VERSE 27** The seven years' work for each daughter was a dowry paid to Laban by Jacob.

•**VERSES 30-31** Jacob made his preference of Rachel over Leah obvious.

•**VERSE 32** "Reuben" means see, a son.

•**VERSE 33** "Simeon" means heard

•**VERSE 34** "Levi" means joined.

•**VERSE 35** "Judah" means praise the Lord.

CHAPTER 30:
THE BIRTH OF JOSEPH

•**VERSE 6** "Dan" means judging.

•**VERSE 8** "Naphtali" means wrestling.

•**VERSE 11** "Gad" means a troop.

•**VERSE 13** "Asher" means happy.

•**VERSE 18** "Issachar" means hired.

•**VERSE 20** "Zebulun" means dwelling.

•**VERSE 24** "Joseph" means adding.

•**VERSE 35** Laban removed all the speckled and ring-streaked animals from the herd so that only solid-colored animals would be born and he would have Jacob's labor for free.

•**VERSES 37-43** Jacob devised a system that caused the offspring of the stronger animals to be marked so that only the weaker animals were solid-colored.

CHAPTER 31:
JACOB DEPARTS

The three basic principles of God's guidance are illustrated in this chapter:

(1) Desire—God placed the desire to return home in Jacob's heart.

(2) Uncomfortable circumstances—the situation at Laban's house was getting unbearable.

(3) Direct word—the Lord told Jacob to return to his home.

•**VERSE 7** Laban had tried to outwit Jacob.

•**VERSE 13** God reminded Jacob of the vow he had made to Him at Bethel.

•**VERSES 26-30** Laban was a hypocrite; in verse 29 we can see what was in his heart. It is sad that a man's gods can be stolen.

•**VERSE 47** "Jegarsahadutha" and "Galeed" both mean the witness.

•**VERSE 49** "Mizpah" means the Lord watch between you and me when we are absent one from another.

•**VERSES 50-53** The intent of Mizpah was negative because Laban and Jacob did not trust each other. They wanted God to watch between them since they could not constantly see each other.

CHAPTER 32:
JACOB BECOMES ISRAEL

•**VERSE 2** "Mahanaim" means two hosts.

•**VERSE 12** Jacob reminded God of His promise.

•**VERSES 13-21** After his prayer, Jacob started planning ways to win his brother's forgiveness.

•VERSES 24-26 Though he was 90, Jacob wrestled with the Angel all night and would not submit until he was crippled.

Why did God cripple Jacob? Jacob was a man of faith. He trusted God and believed in His purposes. However, Jacob thought that God needed his help to get things done, and God knew that Jacob had to be defeated so that he would rely on God instead of his own resourcefulness.

God crippled Jacob in order to crown him with His glory. When Jacob surrendered, God's power could begin to be manifested to him.

•VERSE 26 Hosea 12:4 tells us that Jacob was pleading with tears when he cried, "I will not let thee go, except thou bless me."

•VERSE 28 "Israel" means governed by God.

•VERSE 30 "Peniel" means the face of God.

CHAPTER 33:
THE REUNION

•VERSE 4 Perhaps it was when Esau saw Jacob limping that he decided to be reconciled with him. The moment Esau had planned for vengeance became a moment of beauty as the two brothers wept and embraced.

•VERSES 12-18 Jacob had not become fully Israel (God-governed) yet, because when Esau offered to accompany him to Seir, Jacob told him he would follow Esau there. However, when Esau left, Jacob went in the opposite direction to Shechem.

•VERSES 19-20 God had told Jacob to go back to the land of his father and to his family, but Jacob disobeyed and went to Shechem and the Lord allowed him to have serious problems there.

•VERSE 20 "Elelohe Israel" means God, the God of Israel.

CHAPTER 34:
TROUBLE AT SHECHEM

•VERSE 13 Jacob's sons were also deceitful.

•VERSES 16-21 It was not the will of God that the children of Israel be mixed with other people, so this plan was not carried out.

•VERSE 30 Jacob was not so upset by the injustice of what his sons had done as by the dangerous position their actions had put him in.

CHAPTER 35:
JACOB MOVES TO BETHEL

•VERSES 1-6 This time Jacob obeyed God when He told him to go to Bethel.

•VERSE 7 "El bethel" means the God of Bethel. "Bethel" means the house of God.

•VERSE 8 "Allonbachuth" means the oak of weeping.

•VERSES 10-12 In Bethel there was a renewal of commitment—not of Jacob to God, but God confirming His promises to Jacob.

•VERSE 18 "Benoni" means the son of my sorrow. "Benjamin" means son of the right hand.

CHAPTER 36:
THE GENERATIONS OF ESAU

•VERSE 1 Edom was Esau's nickname.

•VERSE 12 Though Esau did not strike Jacob, when the children of Israel came out of Egypt, the first people they fought were the Amalekites—the descendants of Esau.

•VERSE 15 "Duke" means prince, chief of thousands.

Eliphaz was the name of one of Job's comforters; the events in the book of Job may have taken place during the time of Jacob and Esau.

CHAPTER 37:
JOSEPH'S BROTHERS SELL HIM

•**VERSE 3** Jacob showed favoritism to Rachel's son, Joseph, by giving him the coat of many colors, signifying that he had chosen Joseph for his heir.

•**VERSES 5-9** Joseph's prophetic dream that his brothers would bow down to him made them even angrier.

•**VERSE 12** Shechem was about 90 miles from Hebron. They had to go far from home to find pastures for their flocks.

•**VERSE 22** Reuben, the eldest child, planned to rescue Joseph and send him back to his father.

•**VERSE 28** Joseph is a type of Christ: hated and sold by his brothers but eventually becoming their ruler.

CHAPTER 38:
THE DECEPTION OF JUDAH

Apparently the Lord allowed this story to be included in the Bible because Judah was to play an important part in the lineage of Christ. Christ was the lion of the tribe of Judah.

This story also demonstrates the grace of God because He even used a corrupt man rather than only saintly men.

•**VERSE 29** "Perez" means breach.

•**VERSE 30** "Zerah" means sunrise.

CHAPTER 39:
JOSEPH SENT TO PRISON

•**VERSE 6** "Well-favored" means handsome.

Joseph was a beautiful person inside and out.

•**VERSE 9** Joseph recognized that all sin is against God and is in rebellion to His laws.

•**VERSE 20** Joseph was put into the prison where the pharaoh's prisoners were kept.

CHAPTER 40:
JOSEPH INTERPRETS TWO DREAMS

•**VERSE 3** God wanted Joseph to meet the butler of the pharaoh.

•**VERSE 7** Joseph was a man of keen insight since he noticed the depression of the butler and the baker.

•**VERSE 8** Joseph had not become bitter against God over the trials he had to endure.

•**VERSES 20-22** Within three days, the interpretations of the dreams of the butler and the baker became reality.

•**VERSE 23** Once he was back in his comfortable position, the butler forgot about Joseph.

CHAPTER 41:
PHARAOH HAS A DREAM

•**VERSE 1** It is hard to understand why Joseph had to spend two more years in prison after his meeting with the pharaoh's butler. God was probably refining Joseph so He could use him.

The experiences of life can make us a bitter person or a better person. God wanted to make Joseph a better person.

•**VERSE 16** Joseph gave God the credit for interpreting the dreams.

•**VERSE 38** Pharaoh recognized that the Spirit of God was in Joseph.

•**VERSE 45** Pharaoh called Joseph "Zaphnathpaaneah," which means the man to whom secrets are revealed.

•**VERSE 51** "Manasseh" means forgetting.

•**VERSE 52** "Ephraim" means fruitful.

•**VERSES 54-57** The famine that Joseph predicted brought people from the surrounding countries to buy food in Egypt.

CHAPTER 42:
JOSEPH SEES HIS BROTHERS

•**VERSES 6-7** It had been about twelve years since Joseph's brothers had sold him. He dressed and looked Egyptian and spoke to his brothers through an interpreter, so they did not recognize him.

•**VERSES 21-22** Though twelve years had passed since the brothers had sold Joseph, they were still feeling guilty about the way they had treated him.

Sin has a way of causing people to carry an increasing load of guilt that can negatively affect their lives.

Jesus died to cleanse us from our sins and to obtain eternal forgiveness for us.

•**VERSES 23-24** It was not easy for Joseph to be stern with his brothers.

•**VERSE 36** The cry of Jacob came from nearsightedness. He thought everything was going against him when actually God was moving in his life to give him his heart's desire.

Sometimes we think God is not working in our lives when He is quietly doing miraculous things for us.

•**VERSE 38** Jacob was willing to let Simeon stay in prison in Egypt rather than let Benjamin go.

CHAPTER 43:
BENJAMIN GOES TO EGYPT

•**VERSES 11-12** Jacob was scheming again to help his sons to find favor in the Egyptian ruler's (Joseph's) eyes.

•**VERSE 14** "If I be bereaved of my children, I am bereaved." Jacob had been put in circumstances where his own resources were so limited that he had to make a total commitment to God.

Sometimes God puts us in a place that He knows will cause us to rely on Him.

•**VERSE 33** Joseph had his brothers seated around the table according to age, from the eldest to the youngest. They were amazed that he could do this.

•**VERSE 34** "Mess" means portion of food.

CHAPTER 44:
JUDAH'S PLEA

•**VERSE 15** Joseph pretended that he had powers of divination that could tell him when people were trying to steal from him.

•**VERSE 33** Judah had led the attack on Joseph years before. He had changed enough to be willing to take Benjamin's place as a servant in Egypt.

CHAPTER 45:
THE BROTHERS REUNITED

•**VERSE 3** "Troubled" means terrified.

•**VERSE 8** Joseph recognized that God's overall plan to save his family was the reason that he was sent to Egypt, so he did not blame his brothers.

•**VERSE 12** Joseph spoke directly to his brothers in Hebrew so that they would believe him.

CHAPTER 46:
JACOB MOVES TO EGYPT

Jacob's family accompanied him to Egypt. The various members are listed with their mothers.

•**VERSES 8-15** Thirty-three descendants from Leah.

•**VERSES 16-18** Sixteen descendants from Zilpah.

•**VERSES 19-22** Fourteen descendants from Rachel.

•**VERSES 23-25** Seven descendants from Bilhah.

•**VERSE 27** Seventy members of Jacob's family went into Egypt.

•**VERSES 31-34** Joseph encouraged his brothers not to become urbanized but to stay out in the country in Goshen and to continue to be shepherds.

CHAPTER 47:
THE FAMINE WORSENS

•**VERSES 1-12** Jacob and his family had settled in the country and were cared for by Joseph.

•**VERSES 13-17** The people spent all their money for food, so they had to sell their cattle to Joseph to buy food.

•**VERSES 18-26** The next year the people sold their lands and themselves to buy food. Joseph set up a twenty percent tax to be paid into the pharaoh's storehouse from the produce of his farms.

•**VERSE 30** Jacob wanted to be buried in the land that God had promised to him.

CHAPTER 48:
MANASSEH AND EPHRAIM

•**VERSE 5** Jacob (Israel) laid claim to Joseph's two sons and made them part of the tribes of Israel. When the twelve tribes of Israel are listed, Joseph and Levi are often omitted, and Ephraim and Manasseh are included, though the listings vary.

Twelve is always the number listed, however, for it is the number of divine guidance in the Bible.

•**VERSES 13-20** Jacob purposely gave the preference to Joseph's younger son, reminiscent of his own past as the younger son who was told that he would rule over his older brother.

CHAPTER 49:
JACOB BLESSES HIS SONS

In this chapter Jacob called his sons to his deathbed and prophesied over each one.

•**VERSE 4** Reuben lost the good opinion of his father when he took Jacob's concubine.

•**VERSES 5-7** Simeon and Levi always seemed to work together. They had violent, ungoverned tempers.

•**VERSES 8-9** The lion became the symbol of the tribe of Judah.

•**VERSE 10** After God rejected Saul, who was from the tribe of Benjamin, as king over Israel, He placed David, who was from the tribe of Judah, on the throne. The throne of Israel was to belong to Judah until the Messiah (Shiloh) came.

•**VERSE 13** Zebulun's tribe was to dwell by the sea along the northern coast of Israel.

•**VERSE 16** Dan's tribe produced the judges.

•**VERSE 19** Gad's tribe produced the troops, the soldiers.

•**VERSE 20** Asher was the baker for the tribes.

•**VERSE 22** Joseph could enjoy the fruit of his godly life and others were blessed by his life too, as passersby enjoy fruit that hangs over the wall.

God wants our lives to be fruitful and to overflow with the blessings He bestows on us so that we share His goodness with others.

•**VERSE 23** Most of the arrows were shot by Joseph's brothers. There were various trials he had to endure:

(a) Arrows of doubt and scorn sent when he tried to share his dreams (Genesis 37:8).

(b) Arrows of hatred because the ten older brothers knew he was their father's favorite (Genesis 37:4).

(c) Arrows of treachery when his brothers decided to kill him (Genesis 37:18).

(d) Arrows of temptation as Potiphar's wife tried to seduce him (Genesis 39:7).

(e) Arrows of false accusations as she accused him of trying to attack her (Genesis 39:13-18).

(f) Arrows of forgetfulness when the butler forgot Joseph for two years (Genesis 40:23).

•**VERSE 24** It takes greater strength to hold back from taking revenge when it is in our power to do it. Though the arrows were shot at him, Joseph did not shoot back.

The Father had His arms around Joseph's arms, holding the bow for him and giving him His strength to draw upon.

•**VERSES 29-32** Jacob asked his sons to bury him with his fathers back in the Promised Land.

CHAPTER 50:
A BURIAL AND A DEATH

•**VERSES 2-3** Perhaps Jacob's body is well-preserved even now since the Egyptian physicians embalmed him.

•**VERSE 11** "Abelmizraim" means the mourning of the Egyptians.

•**VERSE 19** Joseph realized that God does not want us to retaliate for wrongs done to us. When He is our shield and defender, no weapon that is formed against us shall prosper.

•**VERSE 20** The providence of God caused the plots of his brothers and Potiphar's wife to turn out to be good for Joseph and his family. Their motives did not matter, for God still brought good out of it.

"And we know that all things work together for good to them that love God, to them who are the called according to His purpose" (Romans 8:28).

🔍 THE SONS OF JACOB	
NAME	**MEANING**
REUBEN	BEHOLD A SON
SIMEON	HEARD
LEVI	JOINED
JUDAH	PRAISE
DAN	JUDGE
NAPHTALI	WRESTLING
GAD	FORTUNE/TROOP
ASHER	HAPPY
ISSACHAR	HIRED/WAGES
ZEBULUN	DWELLING
JOSEPH	INCREASE
BENJAMIN	SON OF MY RIGHT HAND

STUDY QUESTIONS FOR GENESIS

1. The first chapter of Genesis covers the creation. According to verses 26 and 27, what did God say when He created man?

_____

_____

_____

2. After Adam and Eve disobeyed by eating the forbidden fruit, how did God take care of their sin according to Genesis 3:21? What does this act introduce to us?

_____

_____

_____

3. What was God's promise to Abraham in Genesis 12:2-3? What else did this promise include?

_____

_____

_____

4. In chapter 32, we read that Jacob wrestled with the Angel all night. When Jacob ultimately surrendered, the Angel gave him a new name. What was this name, and what does it mean? (Genesis 32:28).

_____

_____

_____

5. After all that Joseph had been through, he did not blame his brothers. Compare Genesis 45:8 and Romans 8:28. What do you see?

_____

_____

_____

THE BOOK OF
EXODUS

AUTHOR OF THE BOOK:
Moses

PERIOD OF WRITING:
Approximately a period of about 300 years from the end of Genesis to the start of the book of Exodus. Some time in 15th century BC.

TYPE OF BOOK:
Book of the law; second book of the Pentateuch.

THEME:
God's deliverance of the children of Israel from their slavery in Egypt.

INTRODUCTION:
The first five books of the Old Testament (Genesis, Exodus, Leviticus, Numbers, and Deuteronomy) are just one book divided into five and are called "The Pentateuch." They comprise approximately one-seventh of the entire Bible, and are almost two-thirds longer than the New Testament. Exodus is a continuation of Genesis and begins with the story of Moses. It is named after the central event in the book, when God delivered the children of Israel from their slavery in Egypt.

CHAPTER 1:
OPPRESSION IN EGYPT

•**VERSE 7** There was a population explosion. Seventy originally came to Egypt; but 300 years after Joseph's death, when the Jews made the exodus out of Israel, there were 600,000 adult males. They were doubling their population every 25 years.

•**VERSES 11-12** Nations seem to become strong and grow under adversity. However, prosperity can often be the cause of a nation's decline. The same seems to be true of the church. Early in its history, the Roman government severely persecuted the church, but instead of weakening it, it grew by leaps and bounds.

CHAPTER 2:
MOSES

•**VERSE 2** The word "goodly" is beautiful.

•**VERSE 3** She was fulfilling Pharaoh's command to cast the child in the river, putting him in a waterproof basket.

•**VERSES 4-6** We see the beautiful story of God's preservation.

•**VERSE 7** Wet nursing was common in those days.

•**VERSES 8-9** During his formative years, Moses received the strong inculcating of the Hebrew traditions, and was endowed with a sense of a nation of destiny.

It's a tremendous example of what Proverbs 22:6 declares, "Train up a child in the way he should go: and when he is old, he will not depart from it."

•**VERSE 10** "Moses" means to be taken out of the water.

•**VERSE 12** He looked this way and that way, but he didn't look up. We make that mistake so often. We look this way and that way, and then we act, not realizing that God sees us.

Moses got ahead of God. He tried to fulfill God's will in the ability and power of his flesh. The work of the Spirit can never be accomplished in the ability of our flesh. To do the work of the Spirit, I must be anointed, empowered, and directed by the Spirit of God.

•**VERSE 22** "Gershom" means stranger.

•**VERSES 22-23** Between verses 22 and 23 there is a period of about 40 years.

CHAPTER 3:
MOSES AND THE BURNING BUSH

•**VERSE 1** Moses was learning the lay of the land: where the wells were, the weather patterns, and wilderness or desert survival, which would prove to be very handy later.

•**VERSE 7** "Seeing, I have certainly seen, knowing, I have certainly known, hearing, I have certainly heard." It's an emphatic in the Hebrew. God declares the fact that He has seen, He has heard, He knows. These are the characteristics

of God emphasized by Jesus Christ in the New Testament, "Your Father sees, your Father hears, your Father knows."

•**VERSE 10** After 40 years the fire is gone. He's not that short-tempered, ready to go to battle any more. In fact, he has become very meek.

•**VERSE 11** Everyone who is called of God probably asks that question, "Who am I, Lord, that I should be the one to do this?" It is imperative that we have a sense of our unworthiness in being an instrument through which God might do His work.

•**VERSE 12** He was at Mount Horeb, where he later received the Ten Commandments.

•**VERSE 14** The name of God is a verb, "to be." "The Becoming One" is named *Yahweh*, as God becomes to you whatever your need might be. "I am your peace, your strength, your help. I am your guide. I am your righteousness. I am your salvation. I am your hope."

•**VERSES 21-22** They were taking the back wages that were due to them through the years of slavery in which they were not paid.

CHAPTER 4:
MOSES' RESPONSE TO GOD'S CALL

•**VERSE 2** A rod is a walking stick.

•**VERSE 11** God has declared that in certain cases He has created certain physical infirmities. If I only believe what I can understand, that doesn't take faith. That only takes intellect. Believing what I can't understand is that step of faith which honors God. "Without faith it is impossible to please Him" (Hebrews 11:6).

•**VERSES 14-15** That wasn't God's direct will; it was permissive. Aaron became a stumbling block. God will lift you to the highest level that you will allow Him.

CALVARY DISTINCTIVE

"...but I am slow of speech, and of a slow tongue" (Exodus 4:10).

God is able to overcome our disabilities. He's the one who created our mouths.

"O my Lord, send, I pray thee, by the hand of him whom thou wilt send" (Exodus 4:13).

Here the Lord used Aaron to be Moses' spokesman, but that was God's alternate plan. We often miss God's best and force Him to choose Plan B.

•**VERSE 16** In other words, "You'll be the go-between. I'll speak to you and give you My words, and you give My words to Aaron." So now you've got a step-between.

Who made the golden calf out there in the wilderness? Aaron brought a snare upon Israel. Moses is insisting that God come down to his level rather than he arise to God's level.

•**VERSE 20** "Sons" here is plural, so it doesn't tell us when the other son was born.

•**VERSE 21** "Harden" in Hebrew literally means strengthen. "I will make strong his heart." As we read of Moses' dealings with Pharaoh in chapter 8, we read, "Pharaoh hardened his heart."

The word "hardened" there is a different Hebrew word. In other words, Pharaoh set his heart and God strengthened him in that set.

•**VERSES 24-25** God had commanded that the Hebrew children should be circumcised on the eighth day as a mark of the covenant relationship of these people with God. They were to be walking after the Spirit, not after the flesh, thus the cutting away of the flesh. It was a symbolic action by which these people were identified as God's people.

•**VERSE 26** Moses was going to lead God's people out of the land, and he had not even fulfilled that covenant mark in his own sons. Because of Moses' failure, God was just impressing on him that He meant business.

HEBREW KEY WORD

chazaq = harden, strengthen (4:21).

CHAPTER 5:
ISRAELITES' BURDENS INCREASE

•**VERSES 20-21** Thus begins Moses' problems with the children of Israel. They are complainers and grumblers from the word "go."

Here they're crying unto God, "Oh God, deliver us." Now God sends a deliverer, and the first thing they do is give him a bad time.

•**VERSES 22-23** Moses went to the Lord and began to pour out his complaint to Him, "Lord, why did You send me? Things aren't getting better; they're getting worse!"

Quite often, when you embark on a work of God, Satan throws so many obstacles in the way that things look like they've just gotten worse. He does his best to discourage you right at the onset of an endeavor for God. So the secret is just keep going. If God has called you to a task, just do it.

CHAPTER 6:
GOD'S RESPONSE TO HIS PROPHET

•**VERSE 1** Pharaoh is not just going to let them go, he's going to drive them out. By the time they go, he's going to be glad to see them leave.

•**VERSE 2** "I am the Lord." Many times we try to take that position away from Him, so He reminds us who He is. We are so prone to exalt ourselves or to exalt man, and we forget that He is the Lord and He is in control.

When we forget that He is the Lord, then we fall into the category that Paul referred to in Romans 1:21, "When they knew God, they glorified Him not as God." They began to take things in their own hands. They began to live as though God was their servant rather than they were God's servants.

We need to be reminded that He is the Lord, and we need to remember the greatness of His power, His wisdom, and His glory.

•**VERSE 3** Abraham, Isaac, and Jacob called Him "Jehovah," but not in the sense of "The Becoming One." They knew God, but their relationship was less intimate than what Moses would experience.

God said, "They've not known Me by My name Jehovah. You, Moses, are going to know Me in a closer, more intimate way."

God wants to relate to you in this way, so He sent His only begotten Son that you might relate to God as a father with his child, that you might boldly come into His presence, and that you might receive mercy in your time of need.

•**VERSES 4-5** "I know, I heard, and I have remembered My covenant." Sometimes because of time delays, we feel that God has forgotten His promises to us.

"In the last days," the Bible says, "scoffers will say, 'Where is the promise of the coming of Jesus Christ?'" (2 Peter 3:3-4). Because of the time delay men will scoff, but "God is not slack concerning His promises as some men count slackness, but is faithful" (2 Peter 3:9).

•**VERSES 6-8** Here God states what He will do for His people—seven "I wills" that they can be sure will come to pass.

Symbolically, Israel's journey typifies the experience of the child of God. We come out of bondage through the Red Sea, baptism, into a new relationship of faith with God in the wilderness and on in through the death of the old life and the old self into the Land of Promise, a life of richness and fullness.

•**VERSE 9** They were so discouraged because of these things the Egyptians were laying upon them, that even when Moses came with these glorious promises and declarations of God, the people just couldn't believe it.

•**VERSE 12** Moses is still dragging his heels at the call of God, at the commission of God upon his life.

•**VERSES 14-25** At this point there is inserted a little genealogy of the first three sons of Jacob. With Reuben and Simeon, Israel's first two sons, it lists just the names of their sons, as seen in Genesis.

However, Levi's genealogy lists the sons, grandsons, and great-grandsons in order to bring us down to Moses and Aaron.

•**VERSES 28-30** A recap is inserted after the genealogy to bring us to chapter 7.

CHAPTER 7:
SIGNS FOR PHARAOH

•**VERSE 4** God is speaking by foreknowledge. He knew the decision that Pharaoh was going to make. God strengthened Pharaoh in his position.

•**VERSE 5** This is the purpose, in order that the Egyptians—and that all the world may know: "I am the Lord."

•**VERSES 10-12** The magicians of Pharaoh were able to duplicate the feats of Aaron and Moses. The powers of darkness are often able to counterfeit the work of God. Satan is a great counterfeiter.

However, just because a particular situation seems miraculous does not ensure an actual legitimate work of God.

One of the marks of the Antichrist will be his tremendous ability to work miracles, signs, and wonders in the eyes of the people. We are told concerning Satan that he is able to transform himself into an angel of light in order to deceive (2 Corinthians 11:14).

•VERSES 13-16 Pharaoh had said, "Who is the Lord? I don't know Him." The purpose of this episode is that he might get acquainted with Him and find out who He is.

•VERSES 17-22 We find here a counterfeit once more. But how does that help Pharaoh? The magicians are adding to the plagues. It would be better if they purified the rivers rather than polluting them.

CHAPTER 8:
PLAGUES OF FROGS, LICE, AND FLIES

•VERSES 1-2 The Egyptians worshiped the snakes; and thus, when his rod turned into a serpent, they couldn't kill it. They also worshiped the Nile River as one of their gods because of its life-sustaining forces.

When it turned to blood, God is striking out at another one of their gods. They also worshiped frogs, and they couldn't kill them because they were held to be sacred.

•VERSE 9 In other words, "Tell me when you want the frogs gone, so that when it comes to pass, you will know that God did it."

•VERSES 13-14 He didn't send them back to the river, He just let them die.

•VERSE 15 "Hardened" in the Hebrew is *kabad*. He stiffened or heavied his heart.

•VERSE 16 It's either lice or mosquitoes.

•VERSE 18 The magicians weren't able to duplicate this plague because life was being created. This was their limit.

•VERSES 21-23 From this point on, God is going to make a distinction between the Egyptians and the children of Israel. The plagues are going to come upon the Egyptians, but the children of Israel are going to be spared.

•VERSE 25 Here Pharaoh is offering the first of the compromises. Satan often offers us compromises.

•VERSES 26-27 Because the Egyptians held certain animals to be sacred, Moses knew that if they sacrificed in the land, the Egyptians would be angered and they would be stoned.

•VERSE 28 The second compromise.

HEBREW KEY WORD

kabad = hardened, stiffened, or heavied (8:15).

CHAPTER 9:
LIVESTOCK DISEASE, BOILS, AND HAIL

•VERSE 1 The sixth demand.

•VERSE 3 "Grievous murrain" is a type of boil.

•VERSE 6 Only the Egyptian's cattle died; however, this verse doesn't necessarily mean that their entire stock was wiped out.

•VERSE 8 This is another plague that comes on the pharaoh unannounced.

•VERSE 13 The seventh demand.

•VERSE 16 This verse speaks of the sovereignty of God. Even though God is sovereign, we are also responsible for our actions.

•VERSES 27-28 We have now a confession of sin, but it was insincere.

With a confession of sin there must be a real repentance, a turning away from sin in order that there be forgiveness. Confession in and of itself is not enough.

CHAPTER 10:
LOCUSTS AND DARKNESS

•**VERSES 1-2** The Lord's been doing these things up to this point to let Pharaoh know who He is. But here's an interesting twist: God wanted Moses and Aaron to know that He was Lord, that they might rehearse these things to their children.

•**VERSES 10-11** Pharaoh is offering another compromise. "Look, you can go, but let your children stay. It's going to be tough out there in the wilderness and all. Don't subject your children to that."

How many times Satan says, "Hey, you don't want to rob your kids from fun. If you want to make your commitment to the Lord and you want to live a life of dedication to God, that's all right for you if you're going to do it. But don't put that kind of a trip on your kids. You don't want them to be thought of as weird or whatever. So let them go ahead and do the things with the other kids so that they're not thought of as different. Go, but don't take your children with you."

•**VERSES 16-17** The confession of sin, and asking them to pray for him. Again, an insincere confession of sin.

•**VERSE 24** The last compromise that he suggests, "Go serve God, but don't take your possessions; let your flocks and herds remain. Give yourself, but don't give your possessions to God."

•**VERSE 26** In other words, "We don't know what the Lord our God will ask us to give to Him. We don't know what sacrifice He's going to require in the future, so we've got to take everything

in order that we might be prepared for whatever God might call upon us to sacrifice unto Him."

THE PLAGUES OF EGYPT

1. NILE TURNED TO BLOOD
2. FROGS
3. LICE
4. FLIES
5. DISEASE OF LIVESTOCK
6. BOILS
7. HAIL
8. LOCUSTS
9. DARKNESS
10. DEATH OF FIRSTBORN

CHAPTER 11:
ANNOUNCEMENT OF THE LAST PLAGUE

•**VERSE 2** The word "borrow" here is unfortunate and is better translated as let them ask. In a sense, these are back wages. They had been serving the Egyptians as slaves for many years without pay, so they are asking for the compensation due to them.

•**VERSE 5** The eradication of the first-born was to be complete from the least to the greatest in the land, and even to include their own animals.

CHAPTER 12:
THE PASSOVER

•**VERSES 1-2** God is going to bring them into a new relationship with Himself, and they're going to start counting their life from this point.

•**VERSE 7** Notice the blood was to be stricken on the side posts and on the upper doorposts—not on the threshold. The blood of this lamb is actually symbolic of the blood of Jesus Christ, which is never to be trampled under foot (Hebrews 10:29-30).

•**VERSES 8-11** They were to stuff themselves when they ate this lamb. They're going to make their flight and are going to need all of the reserve, strength, and energy that they can store up. So they're to eat the whole thing.

•**VERSE 12** God is declaring that the purpose of these plagues has been that He might execute His judgment against all of the gods of Egypt.

•**VERSES 13-14** The blood was protective—a seal for that house, a token. When God saw the blood on the doorposts, He would pass over that house and the firstborn would not die.

However, whatever house did not have the blood over the doorposts and on the side posts of the house, the firstborn in that house would be slain. The only protection and the only salvation was through the blood: no other hope, no other way, no other salvation except through the blood applied by faith.

God is saying that to us today, as far as life and death is concerned. When He sees the blood of Jesus Christ applied to your heart, He passes over you. You've passed from death unto life. "Whosoever liveth and believeth in Me," Jesus said, "shall never die" (John 11:26).

No longer does the Feast of Passover carry you back to Egypt. This feast now carries you back to the cross of Jesus Christ. And as often as you eat this bread and drink this cup, you show the Lord's death—not the death of the lamb in Egypt, but the death of the Lamb of God.

•**VERSE 15** Leaven is yeast. It is decomposition, the breaking down of substance.

Any sin tolerated or allowed has a way of just expanding until it takes over and controls your life. So leaven is to be excluded; they were to eat the unleavened bread, a memorial.

In the Passover meal, there are three wafers of unleavened bread in a little napkin. The middle wafer is broken, hidden, and then the children have to find it.

Jesus said, "I am the bread of life" (John 6:35). "This [bread] is My body" (Mark 14:22). And even as He was in the grave for three days, hidden, when discovered, there is great rejoicing!

•**VERSE 22** As long as you were in the house where the blood was applied, you were safe. If you went out of the house then you were no longer safe.

The only place of safety is in Jesus Christ. He said, "Abide in Me, and let My words abide in you. And if any man abide not in Me, he is cut off like a branch, and withers and dies, and men gather them and throw them into the fire. Abide in Me" (John 15:4-7).

•**VERSE 25** "Service" is celebration, feast, or festival.

•**VERSES 26-27** The purpose of the feast was a memorial, a reminder of what God had done, but it was also to create a question in the mind of the children.

God deliberately creates questions in their minds to give you an opportunity to teach them the things of God, to make them conscious and aware of the presence of God.

•**VERSE 38** A mixed multitude is always a weakening element among the people of God. This mixed multitude got them into trouble later on. "The mixed multitude began to lust after the things of Egypt, began to complain unto Moses" (Numbers 11:4).

Whenever God is doing a marvelous work and gathering His people, and there's a real excitement over the things of God—a genuine revival of the Spirit—there are always those who just come along for the ride who haven't made a true commitment. They are part of a mixed multitude.

•**VERSE** 40 God had prophesied this to Abraham in Genesis that they would be in the land for four hundred years.

•**VERSES** 42-45 No stranger is to eat of the Passover. Paul the apostle also warned against unbelievers partaking of communion. "For he that eateth unworthily eateth and drinketh damnation to his own body" (1 Corinthians 11:29).

•**VERSE** 46 They weren't to break the bones of the lamb.

Jesus, of course, was to be the sacrificial Lamb. And that is why His legs weren't broken to hasten His death, unlike the other prisoners. Because He was a sacrificial Lamb, not a bone of Him could be broken.

•**VERSE** 48 If a person wanted to proselytize into the Jewish faith, there were three things that were necessary: (1) baptism; (2) circumcision; (3) the partaking of Passover. Until you had gone through these three things, you were not considered a Jew.

CHAPTER 13:
SANCTIFICATION OF THE FIRSTBORN

•**VERSES** 1-2 God spared the firstborn. The firstborn child always belonged to God and was set apart for God.

•**VERSES** 11-14 The firstborn son or animal had to be redeemed. If you wanted to keep the animal, then you purchased it from God. If you didn't redeem it, you had to kill the animal. To redeem the firstborn child, you needed to offer a sacrifice unto the Lord.

•**VERSES** 17-20 The easiest, closest route to Israel would be right up the coast, through the land of the Philistines, actually making the journey within a week or so. But if the Philistines were to come out to meet them with war, their faith in God was not yet strong enough. Fear would grip their hearts and they would seek to return to Egypt.

Their journey in the wilderness is necessary in order that they might have the experience of trusting God, learning what it is to have faith in God, and learning the power of God.

CHAPTER 14:
CROSSING THE RED SEA

•**VERSE** 15 In other words, there's a time to move. There's a time when we get off of our knees and start moving. God, of course, desires us to pray at times, but there's also the time when we need to start moving. That's what God said, "Hey, why are you crying unto Me? Now's the time to move."

•**VERSE** 19 The cloud had been leading them, and now the Lord puts it behind them, and settles it down so that the Egyptians find themselves in a heavy fog. They can't see a thing.

The children of Israel are still walking in the light of the pillar of fire, but the cloud is settled on the Egyptians so they don't know what's going on in the camp of Israel.

•**VERSES** 20-22 God deliberately led them into a trap in order that He might manifest unto them His power of delivering them when there was no way of deliverance. God can make a way where there is none.

It's marvelous to be led by God. He will never take you down a seemingly dangerous path and desert you, but will provide the way out. "There is no temptation taken unto you but what is common with all men, and God with the temptation will provide the way of escape" (1 Corinthians 10:13).

•**VERSE** 25 They begin to get bogged down in the mire.

•**VERSE** 31 We find here the purposes of God. "The people feared the Lord," or reverenced the Lord, "and they believed in the Lord." Their faith is growing.

CHAPTER 15:
THE SONG OF MOSES

•**VERSE 1** The song of Moses of God's deliverance and victory.

•**VERSES 9-15** The experiences I am going through now are preparing me for future victories, future conquests.

"We are His workmanship, created in Christ Jesus, unto good works, which God has before ordained that we should walk in them" (Ephesians 2:10). God already has the plan for your life, and He's preparing you for that plan.

•**VERSES 16-18** The acknowledgment of God's power, glory, and purposes that He shall bring to pass. Praise that He shall reign forever and ever.

•**VERSE 20** Miriam was the older sister of Moses, and was called a prophetess.

•**VERSE 23** "Marah" means bitter.

•**VERSE25** God can take the bitter experiences of your life and bring sweetness out of them.

The difference was the tree cast in the water. That tree, in our case, is the cross of Jesus Christ, which transforms everything in our lives and makes the bitter to become sweet.

•**VERSE 26** They have a covenant. The promise being; if you keep the law then I will keep you. "I'm the Lord who heals you." But the healing is so often through preventative measures of proper diet, proper sanitation and so forth.

As we get into the law of Moses, we find that much of it deals with health and healthy practices. God wants you to be healthy, and He's given you the rules. "Jehovah-rapha": the Lord who heals.

CHAPTER 16:
MANNA

•**VERSE 1** They have been journeying for 45 days.

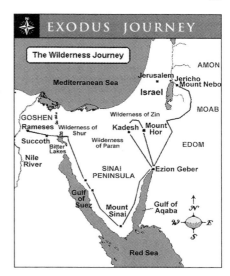

•**VERSES 2-3** They quickly forgot the misery and cruel bondage of Egypt. Oftentimes after coming out of the bondage of sin, a person will look back on those experiences as more glamorous than they were in reality. We forget the emptiness, the pain, the hurt, and the suffering. All we remember is the full stomach.

So as the children of Israel look back on their experiences in Egypt, all they remember are the full stomachs as they sat by the flesh pots.

•**VERSES 6-8** Any complaining that I do is complaining against God. For God is the one who has brought me to these circumstances. God is the one who has placed me here, unless I've been disobedient to Him.

•**VERSE 10** Suddenly in this cloud that had been leading them, the glory of the Lord appeared. It doesn't declare how and in what manner, but it was no doubt an awesome kind of a display or demonstration.

One of these days very soon God is going to demonstrate His glory in the clouds, as Jesus comes with clouds and great glory, demonstrating His glory in the clouds.

•**VERSE 15** "Manna" means What is it?

•**VERSE 23** They would grind the manna into flour and bake it into bread, or they would boil it and eat it like a cereal.

•**VERSES 23-30** The Sabbath was established and practiced before the law was given. The idea of six and one—six days of labor and one day of rest—had been established in their national life.

CHAPTER 17:
WATER FROM THE ROCK

•**VERSES 1-2** We are warned in the New Testament concerning the failure of the children of Israel because they were guilty of tempting God, proving Him, and murmuring against Him.

•**VERSES 3-4** Their first complaint was that of hunger; the second was that of thirst. These are man's two necessities, food and drink, especially in the wilderness.

It's important to notice that though Moses was upset with the people, there's no indication that God was upset. Their accusatory manner was extreme and wrong; yet, their need was natural. God recognized that.

•**VERSES 5-6** Jesus, on the last day of the Feast of Tabernacles, cried, "If any man thirst, let him come unto Me and drink. And he who drinks of the water that I give, out of his innermost being, there will flow rivers of living water" (John 7:37-38).

They were celebrating how God preserved their fathers through the 40 years of wandering in the wilderness. A part of the preservation was the providing of the water out of the rock.

We are told by Paul in the New Testament that that rock was Christ. He is the rock from which the living waters flow.

The final invitation of Revelation is "Him that is athirst, let him come and drink of the water of life freely" (Revelation 22:17).

Partake of Christ, the rock from which the water flows, the water of life, by which we might have life.

•**VERSE 7** "Massah" means temptation, and "Meribah" means chiding or striving.

•**VERSE 8** Amalek was the grandson of Esau and symbolizes the flesh. In Scripture Amalek is always a type of the flesh. There's a spiritual side of my nature and a fleshly side of my nature, and the spirit and the flesh are in constant conflict and warfare.

Here God's people, the spiritual seed, came in to take the land, but the flesh stopped them from possessing that which God had promised to give them. Our flesh is often the biggest barrier to experiencing the fullness of God's promises.

•**VERSE 13** "Joshua" is the name Jesus in Greek, which means Jehovah is salvation. Joshua was put over the servants of God and fought against Amalek, the picture of the flesh, and prevailed.

•**VERSE 14** Have you met an Amalekite lately? No. God has wiped them out just as He said He would.

•**VERSE 15** "Jehovah-nissi" means the Lord has become our banner.

•**VERSE 16** The Lord has sworn that you're going to have a battle with your flesh from generation to generation.

CHAPTER 18:
JETHRO'S ADVICE TO MOSES

•**VERSE 1** The same Hebrew word for father-in-law could be translated brother-in-law, for we remember earlier the father-in-law of Moses was called Reuel. Jethro could be another name for Reuel, or Jethro could be Moses' wife's brother.

•**VERSE 2** Zipporah quickly circumcised their boy, but accused Moses of being a bloody man. Evidently Moses sent Zipporah and their two sons, Gershom and Eliezer, back to Zipporah's father, Jethro. But now as Moses comes back into the area of Midian, Jethro comes out and brings them back.

•**VERSE 12** Jethro built an altar and sacrificed a burnt offering to God. He was a priest, but he wasn't one of the children of Israel.

•**VERSES 14-20** Persons of Moses' caliber and strength often become over-burdened with things that don't always pertain to just leadership. It's possible to find yourself so engaged in little non-essentials that you don't have time to do the essentials. Priorities are vital!

•**VERSE 21** The men who were chosen revered God, hated covetousness, and loved truth.

•**VERSE 27** Evidently Moses' wife and children stayed with him at this point, and his father-in-law returned home.

CALVARY DISTINCTIVE

"And Moses chose able men out of all Israel, and made them heads over the people" (Exodus 18:25).

We believe the pastor is ruled by the Lord and aided by the elders to discover the mind and will of Jesus Christ for His church.

CHAPTER 19:
MOUNT SINAI

•**VERSES 5-6** A priest was a man who stood before God representing the people, but he also stood before them representing God. They were to be a special people who would represent God before the world. God is looking for people to represent Him.

•**VERSE 10** The people were to cleanse themselves before God. Washing their clothes symbolized their need for thorough cleansing: heart, soul, mind, and strength. God called them to sanctification, set apart for His use.

•**VERSE 15** They were to refrain from sexual relations, setting themselves aside for God for three days.

•**VERSE 17** They stood away from the mountain.

•**VERSE 22** Some of the priests apparently didn't sanctify themselves. In the book of Hebrews we read where some of the priests died on this day (Hebrews 12:25-26).

Moses is told to tell the priests that they're not excluded from this.

CHAPTER 20:
THE TEN COMMANDMENTS

•**VERSE 2** "I am [Jehovah] thy God." The word *Jehovah* is a verb, which means the Becoming One. God chose this word to express Himself because He would become for them whatever their need might be.

•**VERSE 3** That's not "before" in a sense of precedence. It doesn't mean that you can have all other kinds of gods as long as God is first in your life. You're not to have any other gods. He is to be the exclusive God of your life.

•**VERSE 4** Man loses the consciousness of God's presence in his life when he makes an idol. Whenever I make an idol, a reminder, it is indicating that I need this little relic as a reminder of God because I've lost the consciousness of His presence.

If I'm living in the consciousness of the presence of God, I don't need any relic to remind me of God. Idols are always an indication of a degraded spiritual state.

•**VERSE 5** God prohibits the making of any likenesses, because once you've made them, the next thing is so often the bowing down to them—which leads to serving them.

So the progression. You make a god, then you worship your god, finally you're serving your god. "But no man can serve two masters" (Matthew 6:24).

•**VERSE 7** It means more than just using the name of God in a profane way. If you take the name of Jehovah, it means that you have placed Him as the Lord, the guide, the director of your life.

If you don't give Him the chance to guide and direct your life, you've taken His name in vain.

Jesus said, "Why do you say 'Lord, Lord,' and you don't do the things that I command you?" (Luke 6:46).

If you're not obeying Him, you've taken His name in vain.

•**VERSES 8-11** For man's sake, God established a pattern of six and one. "The Sabbath was made for man, not man for the Sabbath" (Mark 2:27).

God has ordained for the body's sake one day of rest for the purpose of recuperation.

"Hallowed it" means honored it.

•**VERSES 12-17** To covet is to desire earnestly. Paul the apostle said this is the law that wiped him out. He said, "I didn't know that coveting was sin except the law said, 'Thou shalt not covet'" (Romans 7:7).

He had been righteous to the law, and he wrote to the Philippians concerning his past experience as a Pharisee and said, "And concerning the righteousness which is of the law, I was blameless" (Philippians 3:6).

But then he saw that the law was spiritual. That was the whole basis of the teaching of Christ—that the law is spiritual. "Thou shalt not kill." What does that mean? It means you're not to have hatred for anybody because hatred is the seedbed of murder.

Thus you can violate that law and never club a fellow at all. But if you have a hatred for him, animosity against him, you've violated the law.

The law was intended as a schoolmaster to drive us to Jesus Christ, to make us realize that we were spiritually bankrupt.

•**VERSE 20** That you might reverence God.

A person who truly reverences God has no need to fear.

God outlined what constitutes sin. The Law of God shows us how to have a right relationship with God and a right relationship with our fellow man. And if you don't have a right relationship with God, then you're not going to have a right relationship with your fellow man.

•**VERSES 24-25** Notice the Lord disallows building ornate altars. God doesn't want anything to distract from Him, not even a glorious, fancy altar. He doesn't want man glorying in the works of his own hands.

•**VERSE 26** In other words, don't go up steps and stand high above where people can look up and see your bare legs. God wants attention drawn to Him when we are worshiping. He wants your heart and your mind to be centered upon Him, not to be distracted.

CHAPTER 21:
LAWS ABOUT SERVANTS AND INJURIES

•**VERSE 1** These guidelines were to be followed by the judges in Israel in the matters that were brought before them.

•**VERSE 4** The slave had no rights at all, no rights of possession.

•**VERSE 6** The word "judges" here is the Hebrew word *elohiym*, which is the word for gods. The judges were called gods because they brought His judgment upon man and enforced it. *Elohiym* is not a term used exclusively for the God who created the heavens and the earth.

•**VERSES 7-8** Men bought their wives and they became like a servant, or like a slave practically. If you took a wife, you paid the dowry.

A dowry was alimony in advance. If the husband didn't like her, then she could be redeemed. She didn't have to stay, but he didn't have any right to sell her to a strange nation. She had the right of her dowry and could live off of the dowry.

•**VERSE 10** In other words, he paid her alimony in advance.

•**VERSES 12-13** If you were guilty of murder, you were to receive capital punishment. But if it was accidental then God was going to appoint a place where you could flee and be safe. You could flee to a city of refuge and remain safe from the avenger.

•**VERSE 14** If it was premeditated murder, then even if you flee to the altar of God, they can kill you.

•**VERSES 20-21** If he lingers before he dies then you won't be punished—actually you've lost your own money; he belongs to you. This indicates what little rights the maids and servants had.

•**VERSE 22** If the woman has a miscarriage.

•**VERSES 23-25** This was to put a limitation. An eye for an eye, not two eyes for an eye. The purpose of the law was so that it wouldn't exceed, but they had begun to interpret it as an obligation.

Jesus said, "I say unto you if a man smites you on one cheek, turn the other" (Matthew 5:39). Don't seek retribution or to get even. Christ was showing that the law was intended to curb man's spirit, and to curb that spirit of retaliation.

•**VERSE 29** If you've been told that your ox is goring people and you do nothing to corral or to restrain it, then you are responsible for what your ox did.

•**VERSE 30** So you could buy your way out of that one.

CHAPTER 22:
LAWS CONCERNING PROPERTY

•**VERSE 8** The judges, *elohiym*, or the gods.

•**VERSE 14** If I borrow your horse and I overwork him in the heat, then I've got to pay you for your horse.

•**VERSES 26-27** If you borrow money from me and you give me your coat for a pledge, before the sun goes down I have to give you the coat back.

In those days they didn't have blankets; they used their clothing to wrap themselves up. The coat was their covering.

•**VERSE 28** "Pray for those who are in authority over us" (1 Timothy 2:1-2).

CHAPTER 23:
LAWS ABOUT OBEDIENCE AND VICTORY

•**VERSE 2** Do not get into a riotous situation.

•**VERSES 3-6** Judgment was to be fair. No advantages should be given to the poor nor should they be disadvantaged because of their poverty. Financial status was not to be considered.

•**VERSES 4-5** God wants us to be merciful toward animals.

•**VERSE 8** Judges weren't to receive gifts lest they would be influenced and wouldn't give true judgment.

•**VERSES 11-12** The seventh year is just for the poor people. Whatever grows up naturally, whatever seeds were left in the ground, let it grow, and let the poor go out and gather it.

•**VERSE 13** "Be circumspect" means be careful, keep it carefully.

•**VERSES 20-23** The Angel is Jesus Christ.

•**VERSES 24-30** In this we find the principles of God's victory and how He brings it forth in our lives.

The Jebusites and Hivites are a type of giant in our flesh; coming into the Promised Land is coming into the life of the Spirit and victory of the Spirit.

The overcoming life is coming out of the wilderness, out of the yo-yo Christian experience—where you're up and down—into a beautiful, victorious life in Christ Jesus.

A life of victory is a life after the Spirit, not after the flesh. The enemies who were in the land represent those aspects of our flesh that have so often defeated us and conquered us. But God is promising victory over anger, anxiety, fears, or temper—over any area that has held you in bondage.

God is promising you the victory, but it comes one area at a time. God doesn't just give you instant perfection. Instead, we're growing in the grace and in knowledge of our Lord and Savior Jesus Christ.

•**VERSE 31** The sea of the Philistines would be the Mediterranean.

CHAPTER 24:
GOD'S GLORY REVEALED

•**VERSES 9-10** What does this verse mean, "They saw God"?

In the gospel of John, he declares, "No man hath seen God at any time; the only begotten Son, which is in the bosom of the Father, He hath declared Him" (John 1:18).

We have to compare Scripture with Scripture. Exodus 33:20 also declares that you cannot see God and live. Therefore, I must conclude that "they saw the God of Israel" in a vision, much as Isaiah, Ezekiel, and others saw Him. But they did not actually see God Himself, because Scripture says it is impossible.

"And there was under his feet as it were a paved work of a sapphire stone, and as it were the body of heaven in his clearness." These men saw the glassy sea before the throne of God. John describes it, "And before the throne there was a sea of glass like unto crystal" (Revelation 4:6).

•**VERSE 11** Fellowship with God.

CHAPTER 25:
FURNISHINGS FOR THE TABERNACLE

•**VERSE 2** The people were to make an offering willingly (2 Corinthians 9:7). Giving is never to be by constraint or pressure. God never wants to hear you gripe over what you've given to Him.

•**VERSE 9** The tabernacle is a model of heaven. That's why He says, "Be careful you make it exactly as you were told."

As God gives to him the design, He starts with the furnishings within, not with the tabernacle itself.

•**VERSES 10-22** The ark is to be placed in the Holy of Holies, the center place of the tabernacle where they're going to meet with God. The ark of the covenant will be made with acacia wood and overlaid with gold. It was to be 45 inches long, 27 inches wide, and 27 inches tall—a box of sorts.

The lid on the box was called the mercy seat. Within it were placed the two tables of stone where God etched the Ten Commandments, a jar of manna signifying God's sustenance for them in the wilderness, and Aaron's rod that budded, signifying the Aaronic priesthood. These were the only furnishings allowed in the Holy of Holies.

•VERSES 23-25 The table was to be 36 inches long, 18 inches wide, and 27 inches tall, with a crown gold ornamentation around the top. It also was to be made with acacia wood and overlaid with gold.

The table was part of the outer room's furnishings with twelve loaves of bread upon it constantly that were changed once a week. The twelve loaves represented the twelve tribes of Israel.

•VERSES 26-28 On the ark and the table were put gold rings on each corner, and then they took these sticks, overlaid them with gold, and ran them through the rings.

Whenever they moved the ark or the table, four men carried them using the sticks overlaid with gold, so that no one would actually touch them.

•VERSES 31-36 As the priest would enter the tent, on his righthand side was the golden table with twelve loaves of bread, and on his lefthand side was the candlestick with seven oil-filled golden cups. The priest's daily job was to fill these cups with oil to make sure that the candlestick remained lit constantly.

The candlestick was the tent's source of light, but it was also a symbol of God's desire for the nation of Israel to be the light of the world.

CHAPTER 26:
INSIDE THE TABERNACLE

•VERSE 2 Twenty-eight cubits, or 42 feet. Four cubits, or six feet.

•VERSE 3 A curtain of 30 feet by 42 feet.

•VERSES 4-6 You ultimately end up with one curtain that can be taken apart and folded into two.

•VERSES 7-13 The second curtain of goat's hair was to be bigger than the first; it's to drape down further over the linen one. Again, the length would be 30 cubits, or 45 feet, instead of 42 feet.

•VERSE 14 Then the third covering was of badger's or ram's skin dyed red. This is the outer covering and it's waterproof. There are actually three coverings over the tabernacle.

•VERSES 18-26 This describes the tabernacle's front entrance. The boards were set in sockets of silver, side-by-side. Over the top hung the linen curtain, the hanging goat hair curtain, and the badger's skin. The boards were 27 inches wide and 15 feet high. Rings were necessary so the entrance could stand upright, and the curtains draped over the top.

This is a rectangular shape, 45 feet by 15 feet. The tabernacle had two rooms. The outer room was 30 by 15, and then the Holy of Holies was a 15-foot cube.

•VERSES 31-35 A veil separated the rooms on the inside. Some records indicate that this veil was 18 inches thick, woven together—a very heavy, thick veil.

This same veil was torn from top to bottom when Jesus was crucified, symbolizing that through Him, God had opened the door for all men to come to Him freely. Access to the Father is no longer limited to just the high priest, but is now open to everyone.

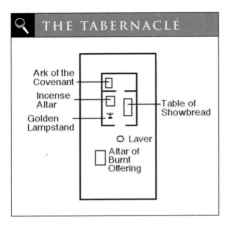

THE TABERNACLE

Ark of the Covenant

Incense Altar

Golden Lampstand

Table of Showbread

Laver

Altar of Burnt Offering

CHAPTER 27:
THE BRONZE ALTAR AND OUTER COURT

•**VERSES 1-2** It is 7.5 feet square on top and 4.5 feet high, overlaid with brass—symbolizing judgment—where sacrifices were to be burnt unto the Lord.

•**VERSES 3-19** These are the furnishings of the outer court and a description of how the outer court was made.

CHAPTER 28:
THE PRIESTLY GARMENTS

•**VERSE 3** God was going to fill men with the spirit of wisdom, giving them the skill to make these robes.

•**VERSE 4** A miter is a crown. A girdle is a sash.

•**VERSE 6** The ephod was a coat worn over the shoulders and down.

•**VERSE 16** A span is the length between your thumb and little finger.

•**VERSE 29** As Aaron comes into the presence of God, he bears the names of the tribes of Israel on his shoulders and on his heart.

•**VERSE 30** Some believe that the Urim and the Thummim were actually two stones—one black and one white—that were used in the inquiring of the Lord.

The priest would reach in and pull out one of the stones.

If he pulled out the white stone, it was God saying "yes." If he pulled out the black stone, it was God saying "no."

HEBREW KEY WORDS

Urim and Thummim =
light and perfections (28:30).

•**VERSES 33-35** When the priest was ministering in the area of God's presence, things had to be just right or it could mean death for the high priest.

The purpose of the little golden bells around the hem was to let the people know he was alive. If they didn't hear the bells, they would pull on the rope tied to his foot and drag him out.

•**VERSES 39-40** The priests were very ostentatious and awesome in these robes. The robes were made entirely of linen. No woolen garment could be worn by a priest. Wool causes perspiration and God didn't want a priest laboring for Him.

God wants our service to be inspired service rather than perspired service. If you have the inspiration, it doesn't take the perspiration. If you don't have the inspiration, even the perspiration's not going to do it.

CHAPTER 29:
CONSECRATION OF PRIESTS & OFFERINGS

•**VERSES 1-14** For the priest to serve God, his own sin had to be forgiven. Aaron is consecrated, the oil signifying the anointing of God, then the sacrifice of the sin offering.

Aaron and his sons were to put their hands on the head of the bullock, symbolizing the transfer of guilt onto the ox.

As that oxen had his throat slit, it is dying for their sin. It brings the awareness of the awfulness of sin and that sin brings death.

•**VERSES 15-22** The ram was a burnt offering unto God, a gift to God. The next ram was offered for consecration, and thus the blood was placed upon Aaron and his sons on the tip of their right ear, their right thumb, and upon their big toe of their right foot.

Remember it's the consecration, "I consecrate my ear to hear the voice of God. I consecrate my hands to do the work of God. I consecrate my feet to walk in the path of God."

•**VERSE 28** The priests could eat that portion themselves and it became theirs.

•**VERSE 33** "Atonement" is the word *kaphar*, which is to cover.

In the New Testament the word "atonement" means becoming one with God, possible only through Jesus Christ. It was impossible that the blood of goats and bulls could put away sins. It was only covering for sin, but it could not put them away. These things were all testifying of Jesus Christ, our great sacrifice, the One who was sacrificed for our sins.

•**VERSE 34** What wasn't eaten was to be burned in the fire.

•**VERSE 42** Here we see the purpose of the tabernacle: a place where God would come and meet with them and speak to them.

CHAPTER 30:
THE ALTAR OF INCENSE

•**VERSES 1-8** This little gold altar was set in the holy place, before the veil that separated the holy place from the Holy of Holies, and it was to burn incense, a sweet smelling savor before God perpetually.

•**VERSE 10** Yom Kippur is the Day of Atonement.

•**VERSES 12-16** They did not actually take a census, as such; they were forbidden by God to number the people.

Once a year, every man over the age of 20 had to give a half shekel. Counting the half shekels allowed them to know how many people there were.

•**VERSES 23-25** This refers to the anointing oil and how they were to make it. A hin is about six quarts, and a shekel is about 65 cents worth of myrrh.

The apothecary is the druggist.

CHAPTER 31:
THE SABBATH

•**VERSES 1-8** God gave these fellows abilities and wisdom.

•**VERSES 12-18** The Sabbath day was a covenant between God and the nation of Israel, signifying that God wanted His people to rest in Him. They never did rest in Him, even though they did nothing on the Sabbath day.

Today Christ is the fulfillment of the Sabbath day, for Christ is our rest. We who are in Christ have entered into His rest, so we have a perpetual Sabbath. I have ceased from my own labors; I have entered into the finished work of Jesus Christ. And even as God is now resting in the finished work of Jesus Christ, as far as my salvation, I must rest and realize that there is no work that I can offer to God of my hands that can save me.

CHAPTER 32:
GOLDEN CALF AND MOSES' INTERCESSION

•**VERSE 1** Moses has been gone now for almost 40 days.

•VERSES 2-4 Remember Aaron is the high priest, which might be a warning that not all who are in the ministry are totally honest in all their dealings.

•VERSE 7 The Lord isn't claiming them at this point. "Thy people, which you brought out of the land of Egypt, corrupted themselves."

•VERSES 11-12 Now Moses says, "Thy people." Nobody wants to claim them at this point.

•VERSE 14 The obvious reading of the Scripture looks like God is angry, ready to destroy the children of Israel, and Moses uses sound logic and reason with God to spare them.

"Repent" means to change or to turn from. The actions of an infinite God cannot adequately be described in human language. But since we have to describe the activities of God in human terms, we use the phrase "God repented." In reality God has no need to change or to repent. "God is not a man that He should lie, nor the son of man that He should repent."

The inspiration of Moses' prayer came from God Himself. All true prayer begins with God. Thus God was the inspiration behind the prayer. What God has purposed, He will fulfill. Had He purposed their extermination, God would have done it.

•VERSE 17 Joshua was Moses' servant.

•VERSE 27 That is, those who were leading in this blasphemous sacrilege.

•VERSE 31 We see Moses offering intercessory prayer before God. He first confesses the sins of the people.

Confession of sin is so important because without it there can be no forgiveness. Unless you confess your sins to God, there's no way God can forgive your sins. "Whoso seeks to cover his sin shall not prosper, but whoso shall confess his sin, the same shall be forgiven" (Proverbs 28:13).

•VERSE 32 That dash with the semicolon indicates a passing of time. How much time, we don't know, but an interim of time passed as Moses was waiting for God to answer.

This certainly shows a depth of love that very few of us can comprehend or understand. Where did this love come from? God had placed compassion and love for these people in the heart of Moses. That is why it is sheer folly for us to try to generate compassion. It has to come from God.

CHAPTER 33:
THE PLACE OF MEETING

•VERSES 2-3 People read this as a harshness from God, being very hard on Moses and on the people. In reality, it's a sign of God's grace, as we read the reason why they were so stiff-necked.

Because the people were so rebellious and so prone toward sin, God said He wasn't going to go up in the midst of them lest they be consumed for their sinfulness by His holiness. Rather than being a statement of judgment on God's part, it was an outpouring of grace.

•VERSE 4 They took their jewelry off and mourned before God.

•VERSE 7 This is not the tabernacle that was to be built. This is prior to the actual building of the tabernacle.

•VERSE 11 When Moses talked to God "face to face" it doesn't mean he was looking at God's face.

Rather this indicates a complete and total communication between God and Moses. It was a dialogue rather than a monologue. No other man has had this experience of being on such a conversational basis with God.

•VERSE 14 Moses recognized their absolute need: the presence of God. He knew what God could do—he wasn't sure what the angels could do.

Knowing the power of the presence of God, he didn't want to accept any substitute.

•**VERSE 15** Moses did the wisest thing: he stayed where he was until he had the promise of God's presence. You're foolish to venture anywhere apart from the presence of God.

•**VERSE 19** God is going to proclaim to Moses a name highly revered by the Jews—they didn't even attempt to pronounce it. The name of God became unpronounceable. There was probably nothing that was held in higher respect than the name of God.

Yet God declared, "I will honor My Word above My name" (Psalm 138:2).

•**VERSE 23** Sort of the afterglow, the hinder part, just that glow that is left from having passed by.

CHAPTER 34:
THE NEW TABLES OF STONE

•**VERSES 6-7** There isn't one God of the Old Testament and a different God of the New Testament. He is revealed in both Testaments as gracious, loving, kind, merciful, and forgiving. He is also revealed in both Testaments as a God of judgment and wrath, that is, to those without repentance.

•**VERSE 7** People are troubled with the fact that the Bible declares, "visiting the iniquity of the fathers upon the children, and upon the children's children unto the third and to the fourth generation." That is clarified a little bit more in the commandments, adding "to those that continue in them."

•**VERSE 10** The word "terrible" is an old English word, and should be translated awesome.

•**VERSE 11** There's a difference between seeing and observing. When God says observe, it means see and live in harmony with it.

•**VERSE 18** This is a Feast of Passover.

•**VERSE 19** The firstborn of everything belongs to God.

•**VERSE 22** The Feast of Weeks is similar to our Thanksgiving.

•**VERSE 25** Leaven is a type of sin.

•**VERSE 26** God demands the "first of the firstfruits" from you, not the leftovers.

Cooking a lamb in his mother's milk was thought to increase fertility, and it was a part of the practice of the land.

•**VERSE 28** God was able to sustain him without food and water. Though physically it is impossible, God has miraculous power and He can set aside certain laws of nature.

•**VERSES 29-35** In Corinthians we are told that the reason for the veil over his face was so that they would not see the shining go away, fading. The shine that faded indicated that the law given was to fade away when God established the new covenant with man through Jesus Christ.

Paul goes on to say, "But even today their faces are still veiled when it comes to the Word of God" (2 Corinthians 3:15). They can't see the truth of God in Jesus Christ. They still have that veil over their face as God speaks to them today, and they deny that Jesus Christ is indeed the Messiah whom God had promised to the nation of Israel.

CHAPTER 35:
OFFERINGS FOR THE TABERNACLE

•**VERSE 5** He has commanded to take an offering, but there was one requirement—you did it with a willing heart.

Paul the apostle says when we give to God, it should never be by constraint, but "as every man has purposed in his own heart so let him give, for God loves a cheerful (literally, hilarious) giver" (2 Corinthians 9:7).

God doesn't want anything from you that you grudgingly give to Him, whether it's money, time, or service.

•VERSES 21-22 Notice the giving came from a person's heart being stirred. That is always the secret of true giving: God stirring your heart.

CHAPTER 36:
BUILDING THE TABERNACLE

•VERSES 1-2 God stirred their hearts. The work of God is always accomplished through willing hearts.

CHAPTER 37:
MAKING THE ARK

As you read through the descriptions here, it notes the sizes, the dimensions, and how everything was put together.

CHAPTER 38:
MATERIALS USED FOR THE TABERNACLE

•VERSE 8 In Egypt, the mirrors were made of highly polished bronze. When the children of Israel left Egypt, every woman took their mirror. But needing the bronze now to make this laver for the washing of the priests, the women donated their mirrors.

•VERSE 24 At $400 an ounce—about $10 million worth of gold was used for the overlaying of the tables, making of the mercy seat, and the cherubim.

•VERSE 25 At $1.84 per ounce of silver—about $194,000. This was a beautiful and expensive tabernacle that they were building for God, where they might meet God in the wilderness.

CHAPTER 39:
MOSES INSPECTS THE WORK

•VERSE 42 Everything was done according to the blueprints, just as the Lord had ordered; to be a model of things in heaven (Hebrews 8:5).

CHAPTER 40:
THE TABERNACLE INDWELT BY THE LORD

•VERSE 17 The second year, in the first month when they came out of Egypt, was the celebration of the Passover, and they raised up this tabernacle there in the wilderness.

•VERSE 20 The "testimony" referred to the two tables of stone containing the Ten Commandments.

•VERSES 34-38 Imagine what that would be like as you are constantly reminded of the presence of God, having the tabernacle in the midst of the Israelites encamped around it.

At night they would see the fire of God hovering over the tabernacle. During the day they would see the cloud resting there. When the cloud lifted and moved, the people would fold the tabernacle and carry it off. They would follow the cloud until it stood still.

STUDY QUESTIONS FOR EXODUS

1. The book of Exodus is all about the exodus of the Israelites from Egypt. Why did they need to leave? (Exodus 1:8-14). What effect did this have on the children of Israel? (Exodus 1:12).

_____

_____

_____

2. The name of God is a verb meaning "to be" (Exodus 3:14). He is "The Becoming One," as He becomes to you whatever your need might be. What did God become to the children of Israel in Exodus 15:26 and 17:15? What do you need Him to be in your life today?

_____

_____

_____

3. List the ten plagues that God brought upon Egypt. What was significant about those specific things that were affected? (Exodus 8:1-2).

_____

_____

_____

4. During the last plague that God was to bring upon the Egyptians, God instituted a way of protection for the Israelites that their firstborn would not perish (Exodus 12:3-12). How was the Passover a shadow of things to come for the protection of our lives today? (Exodus 12:13-14 and 1 Corinthians 5:7).

_____

_____

_____

5. What does the Sabbath symbolize for Christians today? (Hebrews 4:9-11; Exodus 31:12-18).

_____

_____

_____

THE BOOK OF
LEVITICUS

AUTHOR OF THE BOOK:
Moses

PERIOD OF WRITING:
Some time in the 15th century BC.

TYPE OF BOOK:
Book of the law; third book of the Pentateuch.

THEME:
God's desire for fellowship with the children of Israel and His instructions to live a blessed life.

Since Adam and Eve sinned, something had to be done about the law in order for God to restore man into fellowship. Thus, God established in the Old Testament this system of sacrifices where the animal became man's substitute and where the animal was slain for man's sin.

The people would lay their hands on the animal, transferring their sin to it, and the animal would die in their place. It became their substitute. And through the death of the animal, their sin was covered, and they could have fellowship with God—until they sinned again, and then they had to sacrifice another animal.

INTRODUCTION:
The book of Leviticus, which means "pertaining to Levites," concerns how the Levitical priests conducted the sacrifices and supervised the worship of the nation of Israel.

This system is foreign to us, because this covenant has now been set aside that God might establish a better covenant with us. This covenant of the sacrifice of the animals could never make anything perfect; it can only point ahead to the one and only sacrifice, Jesus, whereby we could be brought into full perfection before the Lord.

The offerings that were given to the Lord were divided into the sweet savor offerings and the sin offerings. There were three basic sweet savor offerings:

(1) The burnt offering, which was for consecration.

(2) The meal offering is translated as "meat," however it was made of fine flour and oil, which was a sacrifice of service unto God.

(3) The peace offering, which was for fellowship and communion with God.

Then there were the two sin offerings:

(1) The sin offering.

(2) The trespass offering.

Paul tells the Ephesians that they are to be followers of God as dear children. "Walk in love as Christ also hath loved us and hath given Himself for us an offering and a sacrifice to God for a sweet-smelling savor" (Ephesians 5:2).

Christ is more than just our sin offering; He is also the sweet savor offering.

CHAPTER 1:
THE BURNT OFFERING

Chapter 1 deals with the burnt offering. It was an offering of consecration. If I wished to consecrate my life completely to God, I would signify this desire by bringing an ox to the priest, laying my hand upon its head and slaying it.

"I beseech ye therefore, brethren, by the mercies of God that you present your bodies holy and acceptable unto God, which is your reasonable service" (Romans 12:1).

God wants you to present yourself completely to Him, not reserving or holding back anything but consecrating yourself totally.

•VERSE 3 Any sacrifice or offering to the Lord had to be voluntary. God does not force you to love, to serve Him.

•VERSE 4 In the case of the sin or trespass offering, it was the laying of your hand upon the head of the animal in order that your guilt and your sin might be transferred onto the animal, and thus it was slain for your sins.

In the case of the burnt offering, your consecration, the laying on of your hand symbolized the animal taking your place as a complete offering unto God, a total consecration unto Him.

"Atonement" in the Old Testament comes from the Hebrew word *kaphar*, meaning to cover.

It was impossible that the blood of bulls or goats could put away our sin, but they did make a covering for sin, so that the guilt of the person was covered but it wasn't put away.

•VERSES 5-9 The priest took the blood in and put it on the horns of the altar, and then the ox was to be burnt entirely. The whole thing was to be consumed on the altar as a sweet smelling savor unto God.

This speaks of the fact that my consecration to God needs to be not holding back any area for myself.

•VERSE 14 You could use an ox, a sheep, or if you were poor, you could use turtledoves for this offering.

CHAPTER 2:
THE MEAL OFFERING

•VERSE 1 Translated as "meat," but it should be meal offering.

•VERSE 2 Fine flour would be mixed with oil and frankincense and made into a dough and baked unto the Lord.

HEBREW KEY WORD

kaphar = atonement, to cover (1:4).

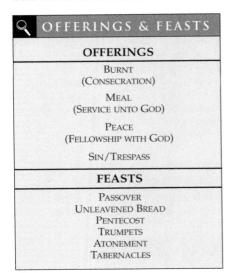

🔍 OFFERINGS & FEASTS
OFFERINGS
BURNT (CONSECRATION) MEAL (SERVICE UNTO GOD) PEACE (FELLOWSHIP WITH GOD) SIN/TRESPASS
FEASTS
PASSOVER UNLEAVENED BREAD PENTECOST TRUMPETS ATONEMENT TABERNACLES

These things bespeak the work of man's hand. I am bringing flour, mixing it with oil. In order to get the flour, I had to till the soil, plant the seed, and harvest the seed. I had to thresh the seed, and I had to grind the seed into flour itself. So it was the work of my hands.

I picked the olives, pressed them, and got the oil. So in the meal offering, I am offering to God my service, dedicating the work of my hands unto God.

And thus, this meal offering again was a sweet smelling savor because what smells better than home-baked bread?

• **VERSE 11** There were two things that were never to be mixed with the flour; one was leaven and the other was honey. The leaven is always a type of sin through the Scripture; and thus, it was never to be mixed.

Leaven actually causes a putrefaction or a decay. Honey can also have that same effect, but honey represents a natural sweetness.

It is interesting that being naturally sweet doesn't buy you any points with God. It is only the sweetness that comes from Him that is acceptable.

• **VERSE 13** Salt was used in those days as a preservative and, of course, to make things more tasty. So the salt was to give the flavor.

CHAPTER 3:
THE PEACE OFFERING

• **VERSES 1-17** The final of the sweet savor offerings was the peace offering. This is the offering of communion and fellowship with God.

In this offering, a part of it would be returned to the person to eat. Part of it is burned for God, but then part of it is given back so the person can sit down and eat, actually fellowshiping with God. God is eating part of it and I am eating part of it. I am becoming one with God.

CHAPTER 4:
SIN OFFERINGS

• **VERSE 2** Sins of ignorance needed forgiveness. Transgression is never related to ignorance. Sin is related to ignorance because there is a vast difference between sin and trespass; and thus, the difference between the sin offering and the trespass offering.

In Greek *hamartia* is missing the mark. Now, I could try to hit the mark and still miss. That is still sin.

Trespass is missing the mark deliberately. I know what I am doing and I know that God doesn't want me to do it. I do it anyhow. That's a trespass. It's a deliberate, willful act against God.

• **VERSES 11-12** Everything of the animal was taken outside of the camp and burnt with fire.

Going back to the first offering, the offering of consecration, the animal hides could be kept by the priest. They would make them into coats and wear them.

But with a sin offering, the priest could not keep the hides. They were to be taken out and burnt completely with fire outside of the camp.

•VERSES 27-28 The rulers brought the male kid of the goats, and the commoners brought a female kid of the goats.

CHAPTER 5:
CONFESSION

•VERSE 5 Even though you were to bring a sacrifice, the confession of your guilt was still necessary. "Whoever seeks to cover his sin shall not prosper; but whoso will confess his sin shall be forgiven" (Proverbs 28:13).

God cannot deal with sin in your life as long as you're trying to hide it.

HEBREW KEY WORD

asham = trespass, a fault (4:2, 5:7).

CHAPTER 6:
THE PRIESTS' PORTION

•VERSE 13 God was the one who was to kindle the fire on the altar, but the priests weren't to let it go out. Once God kindled the fire, it was the priests' duty to keep it lit.

•VERSES 22-23 If the priest offered the meal offering for himself, it could not be eaten.

•VERSE 26 The priest got a part of the offering when the people brought it. This was a payment to the priest, but later became corrupted.

CHAPTER 7:
FELLOWSHIP OFFERINGS

•VERSE 12 It was fellowship with thanksgiving unto God.

•VERSE 14 The heave offering is the offering that was lifted up in a heaving motion before God. The wave offering was moved back and forth and waved before God.

CHAPTER 8:
CONSECRATION OF AARON AND HIS SONS

•VERSES 7-9 Aaron is being dressed for the first time in the garments of the high priest.

•VERSE 10 The tabernacle is now set up and it's time to dedicate and sanctify it unto God.

The word "sanctify" means to set apart for exclusive use. This was to be a single-use building. It was only for the purpose of man having a place to meet God.

•VERSE 12 Aaron was to be used only for God as God's instrument; thus he was anointed with the oil.

•VERSES 13-14 Before they could serve the Lord and act as God's representatives to the people, there had to be a sin offering.

•VERSES 15-17 The sin offering was the first offering in this new tabernacle, that Aaron and his sons might be sanctified for the ministry unto the Lord.

•VERSE 18 First was the atoning of the sins for the priests, and then a total consecration of their lives to God.

•VERSE 23 Consecration of a man's ears, hands, and feet—a total dedication of himself unto the Lord.

CHAPTER 9:
AARON BEGINS THE SACRIFICES

•VERSE 5 Moses instructed Aaron step by step how the sacrifices were to be made.

•VERSE 22 We see the twofold function of the priests going before God to represent the people. They then returned to bless the people on God's behalf.

CHAPTER 10:
NADAB AND ABIHU OFFER STRANGE FIRE

•VERSE 1 God has prescribed the way that we are to worship Him. I am not free to worship God any way I feel or want.

They were coming in a way in which God didn't command them—taking this fire and offering the incense. This was totally done on their own part, maybe to show their importance to the people.

•VERSES 2-3 It is always tragic when the instrument of God receives more attention than giving the glory to God, or seeks to draw attention to himself.

We are to be a mirror reflection of the Lord before the world. The only time a mirror attracts attention to itself is when it is dirty.

☟ CALVARY DISTINCTIVE

"Nadab and Abihu...offered strange fire before the Lord, which he commanded them not" (Leviticus 10:1).

I'm very leery of strange fire, the kind of service that doesn't originate with God. It's an endeavor to draw attention to the instrument rather than to the Master.

•VERSES 4-7 Aaron was not to mourn for his sons publicly as that would indicate an unfairness on God's part. What God had done to his two sons was just.

•VERSES 8-10 God commanded no wine or strong drink when serving God, in order to discern between the holy and the unholy, between the clean and the unclean.

Perhaps Aaron's sons were inebriated when they offered the false fire, thus not able to clearly discern their own actions or respond to God in the right way. Perhaps that was what caused them to be wiped out.

God wants your mind to be perfectly clear when you worship and serve Him. He doesn't want you to be under a false stimulant.

CHAPTER 11:
CLEAN AND UNCLEAN ANIMALS

•VERSE 6 This animal in the Hebrew is *arnebeth*. We don't know what kind of animal it is, but the King James translators think it may be a rabbit. However, just lately they discovered that a rabbit does chew a cud.

There's a danger with wild rabbits of carrying the yellow fever disease.

•VERSE 7 We know that if we eat pork, it is important that we cook it well-done because of the danger of getting trichinosis from rare pork.

God is protecting them rather than telling them how to cook. He just put it on one of the forbidden lists.

•VERSES 9-11 Crab and clams were forbidden. Shellfish during certain months of the year are deadly and poisonous.

God, again, was protecting the people with these laws in regards to these things that are in the water.

•VERSES 25-40 The care and washing yourself after touching dead carcasses. God is teaching good hygiene.

CHAPTER 12:
PURIFICATION AFTER CHILDBIRTH

•VERSE 6 She brought a lamb for a burnt offering the first year, which was an offering of consecration and a sin offering.

•**VERSE 8** "Turtles" would be turtle-doves.

If someone could not afford to bring a lamb, the poor were allowed to bring two turtledoves.

It is interesting after the birth of Jesus, when Mary and Joseph came for this purifying rite, Mary brought two turtledoves, indicating that they were poor.

CHAPTER 13:
DIAGNOSING LEPROSY

•**VERSES 1-8** A careful examination was performed to make sure a person was truly a leper, so he wasn't isolated unfairly.

God wanted them to isolate the leper from the people to keep this disease from spreading. It was like a quarantine.

CHAPTER 14:
CLEANSING FOR LEPROSY

•**VERSES 1-2** Leprosy is incurable. So in His grace, God made a provision in the law—apart from a human instrument.

•**VERSES 3-10** He is to offer a trespass offering, a sin offering, and then a burnt offering of consecration.

Leprosy has often been used to symbolize sin because of the mystery of its origin and of its transmission. We don't know how leprosy is transmitted from one person to another, even as we don't know how sin is actually transmitted from one to another.

Leprosy by all human standards is incurable. Sin is also incurable, as far as man is concerned. Leprosy is deadly; sin is deadly in its result.

Leprosy is insidious in its development within the body, destroying first the nerves and progressing until it hits a vital area.

Sin seems to be progressive and insidious in that it destroys man's will to resist.

•**VERSES 35-45** There was a plague that would also get in the houses, probably like mildew. If this growth was in the house, they were to scrape the rocks and re-plaster them.

If it broke out again, they tore down the house completely. If it didn't break out again, the house was considered clean, and they could live in it.

CHAPTER 15:
UNCLEANNESS

•**VERSE 31** It is important that we realize that this was a ceremonial uncleanness, in which they were not allowed to come to the tabernacle of God.

If you had a running sore, you were not allowed to come to the tabernacle of God until you had gone through the seven days of washing: your clothes, your body, everything. After the running sores had scabbed and healed, then you could come to the tabernacle.

CHAPTER 16:
THE DAY OF ATONEMENT

•**VERSES 1-4** On the Day of Atonement, the high priest would do all the work. If you count the number of animals that he had to kill and butcher, it comes to over thirty, plus he had to bathe five times.

On this day, he did not wear the beautiful garments of the high priest, the ephod, or the blue mitre. He wore just the plain linen robes of the priesthood.

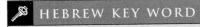
HEBREW KEY WORD

tumah = uncleanness;
a religious impurity (15:31).

First, he sacrificed an offering for his own sins, then he would offer for the sins of the people.

This is looking forward to Jesus Christ. This is a beautiful symbolism all the way through, except that there is no equivalent in Christ for the sin offering that the high priest offered for himself. Jesus did not have to offer any sacrifice for Himself, as He is sinless.

Christ has become our High Priest, entering into the heavens, of which the earthly tabernacle was only a model. Jesus once and for all was our sacrifice, not with the blood of goats, but with His own blood.

His was not an annual affair, as the high priest was required to offer each year, but is forever sitting down now at the right hand of the Father, until His enemies are made His footstool.

CHAPTER 17:
LAWS REGARDING SACRIFICES

•**VERSES 1-9** There was only one place for sacrifice, and that was the temple. You brought your animals to the temple and offered them unto the Lord as a peace offering, or a communion with God.

After you would offer it, you would get a part of the meat back for yourself, and as you ate, you communed with God. I'm eating with God and having fellowship with God, this was the peace offering.

•**VERSES 10-14** This showed respect for life, and signified that it was the blood that covered their sins.

CHAPTER 18:
MORAL LAWS

•**VERSES 1-5** His people are to be a pure people. His people are to be representatives before the world.

You're not to be as the world. "Everybody's doing it" is no excuse for the child of God. You're to be separate and different from everybody else. He is the Lord your God.

•**VERSE 22** This prohibits homosexual relationships.

CHAPTER 19:
LAWS ON DAILY LIFE

•**VERSE 5** Man's free will is important in his service and worship to God.

•**VERSE 17** The Jews forgot that the law was dealing with the spirit and heart of man. They started to observe it as an outward thing.

When Jesus came He pointed out where they misinterpreted the law completely as governing outward activities. The law is spiritual, and God is concerned with the attitude.

•**VERSE 26** Do not follow horoscopes.

•**VERSE 32** In other words, when the old, gray-haired man (hoary head) comes in, you're supposed to stand.

CHAPTER 20:
PUNISHMENTS FOR VARIOUS SINS

•**VERSES 2-15** It gives you an idea of what God thinks of sin. God is not very soft and easy. God ordered severe punishment in order that they might remain clean and pure—in order that they might not be polluted.

CHAPTER 21:
RULES FOR PRIESTS

•**VERSE 5** Many times people would shave their heads when making a vow. A priest was not to make that vow.

His body was to be unblemished. He wasn't to defile or mark up his body, because the priest was standing before God.

•**VERSE 6** The word "holy" is actually separated.

•**VERSE 7** He was not to marry a divorced woman.

•**VERSE 18** He couldn't have any weird growth on his body.

CHAPTER 22:
EATING AND GIVING SACRIFICES

•**VERSES 17-24** When you give something to God, you give of your own free will, offering God an unblemished animal. You weren't to offer the cast-offs, animals of no value, or deformed animals to God.

CHAPTER 23:
THE FEASTS

•**VERSE 4** There are seven feasts listed here.

•**VERSE 5** The month of April.

•**VERSE 6** The fourteenth day is Passover. The next day begins a seven-day period of the Feast of Unleavened Bread in which they cleansed their house of all leavened bread. They were to have this week of vacation, resting, feasting unto the Lord. No work was done. They were like vacations.

•**VERSES 9-14** This was the offering of firstfruits unto God (the Feast of Firstfruits), separate from the Feast of Pentecost. When they came into the land, they brought God the firstfruits of the harvest, recognizing that the firstfruits are God's—not leftovers, but that which is first.

•**VERSE 15** Count from the final Sabbath of the Feast of Unleavened Bread to get the day to begin the Feast of Pentecost.

•**VERSE 22** The welfare program in the state of Israel wasn't a give-away. If you were poor, you gathered from the corners of the fields.

•**VERSES 24-25** This was a holiday, the first day of the seventh month, the Blowing of the Trumpets (the Feast of Trumpets), actually marking the most holy month of the calendar.

•**VERSE 27** Yom Kippur, the Day of Atonement, the day that the priest was to make an offering before the Lord for the sins of the people.

•**VERSE 32** That is why the Jews don't count the days from midnight, but from sundown to sundown. They celebrate their Sabbaths from Friday sundown to Saturday sundown.

•**VERSES 42-43** They moved into these booths and lived in them for eight days as a reminder of the hardships that their ancestors went through coming out of Egypt and coming into the land that God had promised to them.

It was rugged living for one week a year during the Feast of Tabernacles.

CHAPTER 24:
OIL, BREAD, AND AN EYE FOR AN EYE

•**VERSES 2-4** God commanded olive oil to keep the lamps burning continually in the tabernacle.

•**VERSES 5-9** God explains the shewbread. It should be laid in two rows of six upon the golden table in the tabernacle. Each loaf represented one of the tribes of Israel. It was to be changed once a week, and when it was removed, it was eaten only by the priests.

It was a holy bread because it was before the Lord.

•**VERSE 12** They waited upon the Lord for His guidance.

•**VERSE 20** These are the limitations—never more than a breach for a breach, an eye for an eye, or a tooth for a tooth.

Forgiveness with love is better.

•**VERSE 22** No favoritism was shown in the justice system; it was one law for all.

CHAPTER 25:
THE YEAR OF JUBILEE

•**VERSE 9** This is also called Yom Kippur.

•**VERSE 10** They would count seven Sabbath years. The next year, the fiftieth year, was the Year of Jubilee.

All debts were canceled, all mortgages were canceled, and all the slaves were set free. This was a real celebration.

•**VERSE 15** You never bought the land; you leased the land and the lease would end at the Year of Jubilee. So you always figured the price by the number of years until the Year of Jubilee.

•**VERSE 23** God is saying, "You're My guests. This land is Mine."

•**VERSE 25** It stayed within the family.

CHAPTER 26:
BLESSINGS OF OBEDIENCE

•**VERSE 3** God lays out the conditions of blessings: walk, keep, do.

Some of the commandments of God involve our walk, some command our actions, and some are things that we are to keep and to keep from.

•**VERSE 10** Your crops will last and you'll still be eating from last year's crops when you've already harvested this year's.

•**VERSE 11** God's presence is promised.

God is promising prosperity, peace, and power. Men are not seeking these things today. But we've got it reversed: we are seeking these things, but we don't have time to seek God.

If I would give God my heart, the first-fruits of my life, and worship, follow, and obey Him, He would do all these things for me.

•**VERSE 13** They walked humped over after carrying these heavy loads for years.

•**VERSES 14-15** So the conditions; "Keep the commandments, I'll bless you. Break the commandments, I'll break you."

•**VERSE 19** He promised earlier that He'd give them power; now He's going to break the pride of their power.

He was going to cause the land to bring forth abundantly, but now He's going to make the earth as hard as brass.

•**VERSE 26** "You're going to experience constant hunger."

•**VERSE 31** "I'll not accept your sacrifices any more."

•**VERSE 33** As long as they sought the Lord, God prospered and blessed them. They were strong, had plenty, and dwelt in peace.

But when they forsook the Lord, God forsook them. All of these things that God had said, happened—even eating their own children during a siege of Samaria by Benhadad.

Finally, God dispersed them into all the nations of the world. God literally fulfilled those things that He said He would do to them. Their land lay desolate for centuries.

•**VERSE 44** "I will preserve them as an ethnic group," which God has done. He kept His promise and His Word.

No other nation has had that same fate. Every other nation who has been without a homeland has disappeared as an ethnic group.

CHAPTER 27:
VOWS AND TITHES

•**VERSE 2** If you made a vow unto God and said, "God, I'm going to give You my life," and now you want to take your life back, you had to buy yourself back from the Lord.

Anything that you vowed or promised to God, if you wanted to take it back, then God charged you. He doesn't just give it back to you.

Be careful what you promise God. The Bible says, "When you come into the presence of God don't be swift to speak; weigh your words."

The psalmist prayed, "Lord, don't let me sin with my lips" (Psalm 34:13). I think of how many times we actually sin with our lips when we're making promises and vows to God.

The Bible says, "It's better not to make a vow at all" (Ecclesiastes 5:5). God doesn't require you to make vows. So it's better that you don't make any vow at all than to break it, because God takes you seriously.

•**VERSE 9** The firstborn of anything automatically belonged to God. If you wanted to keep it, you could buy it from God. You even had to buy your firstborn son from God.

•**VERSE 11** If a horse or an animal was considered unclean, you couldn't offer it to God. Since it's still the firstborn, you'd have to give the money instead of the horse.

•**VERSE 13** If it was not to be redeemed, you sold it for the estimated price.

•**VERSE 28** Once you devote it to the Lord, it belongs to the Lord.

•**VERSE 29** If you try to do it, you'll be put to death.

•**VERSE 30** He laid claim to a tenth of everything. The first tenth of firstfruits belongs to God.

If you held back that tenth, then you had to add twenty percent. Whatever is left is yours.

•**VERSES 32-33** When the flock was brought in, every tenth animal belonged to God. It was to be done honestly.

•**VERSE 34** God is asking quite a bit, but He's giving three, seven-day vacations during the year, every seventh year off, plenty of food, plus His presence.

I'd say that you're getting a pretty good deal. If you do your part, God does His part.

STUDY QUESTIONS FOR LEVITICUS

1. The Lord described to Moses the specifications for bringing offerings to Him. What are the five different types of offerings, and what do they represent?

_____

_____

_____

2. Leviticus 1:3 and 19:5 discuss bringing offerings to the Lord. What is the requirement to bring an acceptable offering to the Lord?

_____

_____

_____

3. During the sacrifices, laying hands on the animal's head represented the transference of sins to the animal, and the animal dying in their place. This was "atonement" for their sins. What does this mean? (Leviticus 1:4).

_____

_____

_____

4. God prescribed the way in which worship was to occur. According to Leviticus chapter 10, what happened to Nadab and Abihu, and why?

_____

_____

_____

5. God appointed feasts for celebration and remembrances for Israel. What are the seven feasts described in Leviticus chapter 23? Choose one of these feasts and explain why it was celebrated.

_____

_____

_____

THE BOOK OF
NUMBERS

AUTHOR OF THE BOOK:
Moses

PERIOD OF WRITING:
Around 1500 BC.

TYPE OF BOOK:
Book of the law; fourth book of the Pentateuch.

THEME:
The tragedy of unbelief.

INTRODUCTION:
The book of Numbers is so named because the children of Israel were numbered—once at the beginning of wandering in the wilderness for 40 years and then again when entering into the Promised Land.

The journey from Egypt to the Promised Land should have taken 40 days, yet it took them 40 years. Their unbelief caused their delay. The people were afraid to enter the Promised Land, as a result of bad reports given by most of the spies. They were doomed to wander around until the entire generation died off.

The wilderness experience was tough, and many died. There was a population depletion during this period.

CHAPTER 1:
THE CENSUS

•**VERSE 1** This is the second year after coming out of Egypt. The tabernacle was set up on the first day of the first month of the second year. This is one month after the tabernacle had been established.

•**VERSES 2-3** The women and the children were not counted in this census; only those men who were above the age of 20.

•**VERSE 5** "Elizur" means my God is a rock.

•**VERSE 6** "Shelumiel" means at peace with God.

•**VERSE 7** "Nahshon" means a diviner.

•**VERSE 8** "Nathaneel" means the gift of God.

•**VERSE 9** "Eliab" means my God is Father.

•**VERSE 10** "Elishama" means God has heard. "Gamaliel" means my God is a rewarder.

•**VERSE 11** "Abidan" means my Father is judge.

•**VERSE 12** "Ahiezer" means brother of health.

•**VERSE 13** "Pagiel" means event of God.

•**VERSE 14** "Eliasaph" means God addeth.

•**VERSE 15** "Ahira" doesn't have a good name. It is his brother is evil.

•**VERSES 20-21** In the second numbering, after the end of the 40 years, there were only 43,730, and so there was a diminishing of almost 3,000 men in the tribe.

•**VERSES 22-23** At the end of the 40 years, there were only 22,200 in the tribe of Simeon.

•**VERSES 24-25** Of the tribe of Gad, 45,650. At the end of the 40 years, there was a loss of 5,150.

•**VERSES 26-27** The tribe of Judah increased during the wilderness wanderings to 76,500.

•**VERSES 28-29** At the end of the wandering, there were 64,300. There was an increase of Issachar of almost 10,000.

•**VERSES 30-31** The tribe of Zebulun was 57,400 and increased to 60,500.

•**VERSES 32-33** The tribe of Ephraim was cut down to 32,500, a loss of 8,000.

•**VERSES 34-35** The tribe of Manasseh was 32,200 and increased to 52,700.

•**VERSES 36-37** The tribe of Benjamin was 35,400 and increased to 45,600.

•**VERSES 38-39** The tribe of Dan was 62,700 and increased to 64,400.

•**VERSES 40-41** The tribe of Asher was 41,500 and increased to 53,400.

•**VERSE 46** Those are the men above 20 years of age that were able to bear a spear and go to war, who entered into the 40 years of wilderness wandering.

CHAPTER 2:
ARRANGEMENT OF THE CAMP

•**VERSE 2** The center of the entire camp was the tabernacle: the place of meeting. The cloud rested on the tabernacle during the day and the pillar of fire rested on the tabernacle at night.

It is very significant that the tabernacle set right in the center of the camp of Israel, because God was desiring to be at the center of the nation, the center of the hearts of these people.

Every man in Israel would rise in the morning and be looking to the center of the camp, and would see the cloud resting upon the tabernacle. This reminded him of the centrality of God among the people.

•**VERSES 3-9** The tribes of Judah, Issachar, and Zebulun were to set forth first. These tribes had a lion as their ensign and their color was green. They encamped on the east side of the tabernacle.

•**VERSES 10-16** The tribes of Reuben, Simeon, and Gad were on the south side of the tabernacle. The ensign of this tribe had the face of a man and their distinguishing flag color was red.

•**VERSES 18-24** The tribes of Ephraim, Manasseh, and Benjamin were on the west side of the tabernacle. Their ensign had on it the head of a calf, and their flag color was golden.

•**VERSES 25-31** The tribes of Dan, Asher, and Naphtali were on the north side. Their ensign was an eagle and their flag colors were red and white.

•**VERSE 34** With these ensigns, we have a lion, the face of a man, the head of a calf, and an eagle.

As we read the description of the cherubim in Ezekiel and in Revelation, we realize that these are the faces that are on the face of the cherubim—the concept of the angels of the Lord encamping around His people.

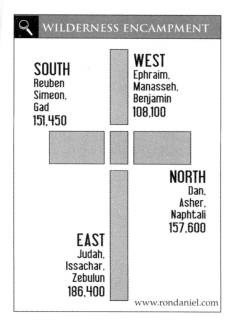

WILDERNESS ENCAMPMENT

SOUTH
Reuben
Simeon,
Gad
151,450

WEST
Ephraim,
Manasseh,
Benjamin
108,100

NORTH
Dan,
Asher,
Naphtali
157,600

EAST
Judah,
Issachar,
Zebulun
186,400

www.rondaniel.com

CHAPTER 3:
THE LEVITES

•**VERSES 12-13** After God destroyed the firstborn in Egypt, He said, "All of the firstborn are Mine; they belong to Me." Now God has chosen the tribe of Levi.

Instead of every family committing their firstborn unto the priesthood, now God has chosen the tribe of Levi. It is to be the priestly tribe.

•**VERSE 15** They were to count all of the males from a month old and older, instead of the 20 years of age like in the other tribes.

•**VERSE 17** God had Moses set out the tribe of Levi into three major families: Gershon, Kohath, and Merari.

•**VERSE 38** The family of Gershon was west of the tabernacle. Immediately south was the family of Kohan. The family of Merari was to the north, and right in front of the entrance to the east side was Moses, Aaron, and his sons.

The tabernacle is in the center. The tribe of Levi encamped immediately around it, and then the 12 tribes surrounding the camp were further out.

•**VERSES 40-49** They numbered 22,000 male Levites, but there were 22,273 firstborn throughout Israel. God told Moses to charge five shekels of silver for each of the additional 273 males and give it to Aaron.

CHAPTER 4:
THE FAMILIES OF THE LEVITES

•**VERSE 3** The tribe of Kohath was to do the service of carrying. It's obvious that little kids couldn't carry these heavy boards, so they were to begin the ministry at 30 years old and retire at 50 years old.

•**VERSES 5-20** Aaron and his sons were to cover all these things, wrap them up, get them ready to carry, and then the Kohathites would come in and just pick up the sticks and carry them as porters with staves without touching or seeing the instruments, lest they die.

•**VERSES 24-28** All the curtains were to be carried by the family of Gershon.

There were four curtains over the top of the tabernacle, the hangings over the door, and a curtain that went around the tabernacle.

•**VERSES 48-49** The tabernacle was quite portable. They could move in, collapse it, carry it off, and then set it up again.

When they came to the place where the cloud was resting, they would set up the tabernacle. When the cloud moved, they moved. So the tribe of Levi, by these families, each had their own duty in the carrying of the tabernacle. There were 8,580 men involved in this task.

CHAPTER 5:
PURITY IN THE CAMP

•**VERSES 2-4** God didn't want defilement in the camp where He dwelt. The children of Israel had to put out of the camp those that were leprous, those that had any runny type of sores, and those who had been defiled by touching dead bodies.

•**VERSE 15** This was a couple of quarts.

•**VERSES 16-21** The woman would have to drink the bitter water and wait for the consequences. If her stomach swelled, she was considered guilty and was put out. But if there was no ill effect, she was considered to be innocent, and her husband's jealousy was unfounded.

CHAPTER 6:
THE NAZARITE VOW

•**VERSE 2** The vow of a Nazarite was a vow of consecration unto God. During that time you were not to drink any wine, grape juice, or eat any grapes—even raisins. During the time of the vow you didn't shave or cut your hair.

This is the vow that Samson was to have from his birth. There are many people who have a false concept that Samson's long hair attributed to his strength. False. Hair cannot make you strong and the lack of hair doesn't make you weak. His strength lay in his consecration to God, and the absence of his hair was the sign of his broken commitment.

Any man who will consecrate his life to God has a source of strength and power. But a broken vow or a broken covenant makes you weak as any other man.

•**VERSES 12-14** The threefold offering: a burnt offering, consecrating yourself; the sin offering; and the peace offering, the offering of fellowship or communion with God.

•**VERSE 23** The priests' ministry was twofold: representing the people unto God, and representing God unto the people. The priest was to represent God with this threefold blessing.

•**VERSE 24** God wants to bless His people.

•**VERSE 25** The shining face always speaks of hope, goodness, and grace.

•**VERSE 26** The smiling face means your countenance is lifted up. A fallen countenance is a scowl or a frown. Many people imagine God scowling at them or frowning at them.

•**VERSE 27** God wanted His name to be put upon the people.

CHAPTER 7:
OFFERINGS OF THE PRINCES

•**VERSE 5** Offerings were given to the tribe of Levi in order to help them, as they carried the curtains and all that went with the tabernacle.

•**VERSE 84** Each of the princes of Israel brought the same offering to the Lord.

CHAPTER 8:
CLEANSING THE LEVITES

•**VERSES 7-11** This was an ordaining for the ministry.

•**VERSE 20** The tribe of Levi was brought before the tabernacle and the congregation of Israel gathered around them and laid their hands upon them.

CHAPTER 9:
CELEBRATING THE PASSOVER

•**VERSE 7** They were ceremonially unclean and couldn't participate.

•**VERSES 11-13** The Lord said that if they were ceremonially unclean and could not observe the Passover in the fourteenth day of the first month, or if they were out of the country, then they could observe it in the fourteenth day of the second month.

But if you were not ceremonially unclean or you weren't away, then there was no excuse for not observing the fourteenth day of the first month. And if you failed to observe it then you were to be cut off from the camp of Israel.

•**VERSES 15-20** God controlled when they moved and stayed. They were obedient unto the Lord.

CHAPTER 10:
CALLING ASSEMBLY FOR THE JOURNEY

•**VERSES 2-9** When you have 500,000 adult males plus women and children, you've got to keep the camp in order. If you're attacked on the east side, the people on the west side wouldn't know what was going on.

From the years of warfare up until modern communication, the bugle was blown to instruct the troops of various things.

•**VERSES 11-12** God is beginning to move them toward the land that He has promised. The cloud was lifted, moving from the wilderness area of Mount Sinai toward the Promised Land into this area of Paran.

•**VERSES 29-30** Rather than journeying toward the Promised Land, Hobab just wanted to go back to his own home and family.

•**VERSE 31** Hobab had that desert savvy, that desert knowledge. Moses desired that he stay with them because of his knowledge.

CHAPTER 11:
LESSONS FOR COMPLAINING AND LUST

•**VERSE 1** A pattern of chronic complaining is beginning to emerge. Inasmuch as God is in control of the circumstances of our lives, any com-plaining against our circumstances is a complaint against the Lord.

If I'm a child of God and have been called according to His purpose, then I must believe that "all things are working together for good for those who love Him and are called according to His purpose" (Romans 8:28).

HEBREW KEY WORD

anan = to complain, to mourn (11:1).

•**VERSE 3** "Taberah" means burning.

•**VERSE 4** The mixed multitude were not full covenant people of God; they were part Egyptian, part Israeli. They didn't have a real commitment to the purposes of God, but they were just coming along for the ride or the adventure.

•**VERSE 5** The appetite of Egypt was still in their hearts. Egypt represents the world, the life of the flesh, which always leads to bondage. They forgot the horrors of slavery and only remembered the excitement of their flesh being satisfied.

•**VERSE 8** They would grind up the manna and make little wafers out of it, having an oily taste. No doubt nutritious, but very bland to eat.

•**VERSE 15** Moses was at the end of his rope.

•**VERSES 21-23** How big is your God? So many times we limit God to our own mental capacities. "My ways are not your ways," saith the Lord, "My ways are beyond your finding out" (Isaiah 55:8; Romans 11:33).

•**VERSES 24-25** They began to speak forth the word of the Lord. Prophecy is not always predictive, but for the most part it is speaking forth the word of the Lord to the church for edification, comfort, and exhortation.

•**VERSE 29** Moses wanted to see God's Spirit fall on the entire camp of Israel. It would make his job so much easier if they were all walking in the Spirit.

The prophets foresaw that day. "It shall come to pass in the last days I'll pour out My Spirit upon all flesh" (Joel 2:28).

In the Old Testament it was limited; only certain men at certain times had the anointing of the Spirit upon their lives. In the camp of Israel, it was limited to 70 men.

•**VERSES 33-34** "Kibrothhattaavah" is the grave of lust. This is an ugly sight in Israel, as the people were giving themselves over to unbridled lust.

Psalm 106:14-15 speaks of this experience in the wilderness, "He gave them their request; but sent leanness to their soul." They desired flesh; He gave them the flesh, but there was a leanness in their experience.

Paul was referring to this in 1 Corinthians 10:6 when he said, "These things all happened to them as examples unto us," that we would learn not to lust after the old life, the things of the life of bondage and sin.

CHAPTER 12:
MIRIAM AND AARON MURMUR

•**VERSES 6-7** God spoke to the prophets, as a rule, by visions or by dreams. God spoke directly to Moses.

•**VERSE 8** They should have respected his position as God's servant and the anointing of God that was upon his life.

CHAPTER 13:
SPYING OUT THE LAND

•**VERSES 1-2** They're entering and possessing the land that God had promised. They chose one man from each tribe, and thus there were twelve spies who entered the land.

•**VERSE 16** "Jehoshua" was later contracted to Joshua. "Oshea" means deliverer or salvation, and "Yeh" is the contraction for Jehovah, the name of God.

The name "Joshua" is one of the compound names of Jehovah, meaning, "God is salvation," or, "the Lord is salvation."

•**VERSE 23** The grapes were so large that they cut a bunch of grapes and carried it on a staff between them.

HEBREW KEY WORDS

Oshea = deliverer or salvation.
Joshua = The Lord is salvation (13:16).

CHAPTER 14:
THE PEOPLE REBEL

•**VERSES 1-10** Here is the tragic failure of the people. God had brought them right to the border of entering full blessing, the abundant rich life. All they had to do was go in and possess it. God had already promised, "I will drive out the inhabitants from before you. I'll send hornets before you to drive out the inhabitants. Just go in and take the land."

The people failed to enter because they allowed fear to dominate their hearts instead of faith.

Whenever you allow fear to dominate your life instead of faith, the fear brings unbelief and that will rob you from that which God has already made available to you.

There are so many Christians today who have failed to enter into the full, rich life that God has for them. They are living a yo-yo Christian experience.

Egypt represents the old life of bondage in sin; passing through the

Red Sea represents the baptism and a new relationship with God through Jesus Christ; and the wilderness represents the normal growth of the believer. The Promised Land represents the full, rich life that you can have in Christ.

•**VERSE 11** It was their lack of belief and trust in God that kept them out.

•**VERSE 20** God wanted to pardon them, and He answered the prayer of Moses.

 CALVARY DISTINCTIVE

"How long shall I bear with this evil congregation, which murmur against Me?" (Numbers 14:27).

I can find no scriptural example of effective congregational rule. So woe to the man who pastors a congregational church. Like Moses, the pastor will only find murmuring and uprisings.

CHAPTER 15:
VARIOUS LAWS

•**VERSES 2-18** God is more or less just confirming the fact that He's going to keep His word and bring them into the Promised Land.

•**VERSE 24** The sins of ignorance need attention. It wasn't a deliberate, willful thing; it was just ignorance, and yet it needs forgiveness.

•**VERSES 32-36** As a violation of the law they didn't know what to do. They put him in jail and the Lord said, "Stone him." So the man was put to death.

•**VERSE 39** The blue ribbons are reminders to the people to follow the commandments of the Lord, and not to follow their own hearts.

CHAPTER 16:
THE REBELLION OF KORAH

•**VERSES 38-40** Brass plates over the altar were a continual reminder that God had anointed and appointed the family of Aaron to the priesthood and no man takes that office unto himself or presumptuously.

•**VERSE 41** The anger of God was kindled against the people as they tried to blame Moses.

•**VERSES 47-48** Moses grabbed the incense and stood between the living and the dead to stop the plague of God because of the people's murmuring. This is a beautiful picture of intercession: standing between the living and the dead.

CHAPTER 17:
AARON'S ROD BUDS

•**VERSE 10** They put Aaron's rod into the ark of the covenant signifying that God had chosen the family of Aaron for the priesthood.

CHAPTER 18:
WAGES FOR THE PRIESTS

•**VERSE 8** The people were to give a tenth to the temple and a tenth of that was to go to Aaron's family as the ministering priests within the temple. The remainder was divided among the rest of the Levites.

•**VERSE 20** The Lord said, "You're not going to inherit any of the land, because I am your inheritance." That's beautiful to me.

CHAPTER 19:
LAWS OF PURIFICATION

The orthodox point out they cannot enter into the priesthood without the cleansing rites, in which they need the ashes of the red heifer.

They can take the ashes of the last red heifer that was sacrificed and mix it with the new; so, it might carry back to the original one sacrificed here in Numbers.

So there is an interesting search today for the ashes of the red heifer.

CHAPTER 20:
WATER FROM THE ROCK

•VERSES 6-13 Moses acted as God's representative to the people. God said, "Go out and speak to the rock."

Remember the first time around God said, "Take your rod and smite the rock."

In the New Testament we read that this rock was Jesus. Christ was smitten in order that the water of life might flow from Him to all of us. The Shepherd was smitten but out of the smiting came forth life-giving water, salvation to all. But once smitten, He never needed to be smitten again.

Moses is breaking the whole analogy. In the second time around, smiting the rock twice is breaking the analogy because Christ was smitten once.

This was a misrepresentation of God, and so Moses was refused the privilege of taking the people into the Promised Land for his failure to represent God before the people.

CHAPTER 21:
THE BRASS SERPENT

•VERSE 4 The children of Israel have been in the wilderness for 39 years and they are now beginning to make their move toward the Promised Land. Miriam and Aaron are dead. Those who came out of Egypt who were 20 years old at the time they left Egypt are now dead.

They went around Edom and are circling in and coming in above—the area of Galilee, the Golan Heights. It was a long, hard route, and they were discouraged.

•VERSES 5-7 They are complaining against God again. You can gripe about any situation that you face—and you can be thankful for a situation.

God wants you to live a thankful life and appreciate what He has done for you. "In everything give thanks, for this is the will of God concerning you in Christ Jesus" (1 Thessalonians 5:18).

Because of their complaining, God sent fiery serpents among them.

•VERSES 8-9 God gave them a choice, you can live or die.

God gave a foreshadowing of the cross of Jesus Christ. The serpent is always a symbol for sin, remembering Satan came in the form of a serpent in the garden of Eden.

Brass is always a symbol of judgment. They confessed, "We have sinned." The brass serpent on the pole was a symbol that your sin has been judged.

This is looking forward to God judging man's sins upon the cross, as God laid upon Him the iniquities of us all and bore the sins of the world.

"For as Moses lifted up the serpent in the wilderness, so must the Son of man be lifted up; that whosoever believeth in Him shall not perish, but have eternal life" (John 3:14-15).

And now you who are dying from this deadly affliction of sin, just now look to the cross of Jesus Christ and see that God has judged your sin and believe in Him.

•VERSE 16 "Beer" means well.

•VERSE 20 From the top of Mount Pisgah they were able to look over the land that God had promised.

•**VERSE 23** Israel sent messengers to the king of the Amorites, asking permission to pass through his land, just as they did to Edom. The king refused and came down to meet them with his army.

Since the Edomites were actually relatives, they went away peacefully. But they weren't related to the Amorites, so they fought against them.

•**VERSE 35** They're beginning to possess that land on the northern end of Israel, the eastern banks of the Sea of Galilee, and the Jordan River.

CHAPTER 22:
BALAAM

•**VERSE 7** The king sent rewards of divination. When they'd go to a prophet seeking advice from God, they'd take a gift for the prophet. That was the custom of the day.

•**VERSE 8** It would definitely appear that he was a prophet of God, though he was not from Israel.

•**VERSE 12** God's direct command.

•**VERSE 15** Men of greater stature, as far as the government was concerned.

•**VERSES 19-20** I can imagine Balaam was laying it upon the Lord, because he was thinking about these great rewards that had been offered to him by the king. I assume that this was the case because the Lord gave him permission to go, but it wasn't God's will for him.

It is possible for us to enter into a gray area of what is termed the "permissive will of God." Yes, God will permit you to do it, but it isn't His perfect will for you.

•**VERSE 28** Some people have great pride because God has spoken through them. God spoke through a donkey, and that should deflate anybody who thinks they're something special.

It's amazing how angry we get when we want to do our own thing and God puts a block in our way. We become upset because God is blocking that which I've got in my mind to do.

•**VERSE 39** "Kirjathhuzoth" means the city of the streets.

CHAPTER 23:
BALAAM BLESSES ISRAEL

•**VERSE 10** People want to die the death of the righteous but they don't want to live the life of the righteous.

•**VERSE 19** God has spoken his blessing upon the nation Israel, but Balaam wants God to curse the people that God has blessed. The immutability of God's Word—He doesn't change; He's not a man. If God has declared His blessing, His blessing shall come.

•**VERSE 21** Jacob had iniquity, but God chose not to see it. That is what David meant when he said, "Oh how happy is the man to whom the Lord imputeth not iniquity" (Psalm 32:2). That's grace.

•**VERSE 23** As God brings the people into the land, establishing the nation, they're going to say, "Oh, look what God has wrought!"

There's no divination, no enchantment, no hex that can be put on you that will have any effect because you're God's child and God has chosen to bless you as His child. It can't be reversed.

CHAPTER 24:
BALAAM CONTINUES TO COUNSEL

•**VERSE 7** The king and kingdom looking ahead in prophecy to Jesus Christ.

•**VERSE 11** You don't want the honor that the Lord holds back.

•**VERSE 14** He prophesied once more concerning Jesus Christ, and it's a beautiful prophecy concerning the Lord.

•**VERSE** 20 Amalek in Scripture is always a type of the flesh. This is God's Word against the flesh: it's going to perish forever.

•**VERSE** 25 Balaam, greedy for the rewards offered by the king, began to give the king evil counsel.

In Numbers 31:16 we are told, "Behold, these caused the children of Israel, through the counsel of Balaam, to commit trespass against the Lord in the matter of Peor." It doesn't tell us immediately in our text that this is what happened, but by looking at other Scriptures (Numbers 31:16; 2 Peter 2:1-3,15; Jude 1:11; Revelation 2:14), we understand the next chapter.

He probably advised the king that God wouldn't allow him to bring a curse. But the people's strength lies in the fact that they worship God and God honors them as His people. But God is a very jealous God, and if they start worshiping other gods, His wrath will come and destroy them.

He advised to take the beautiful young girls to flirt with the young men, enticing them into acts of fornication. Then the girls brought out their gods, and said, "These are the gods that we worship." And their gods were worshiped in sex acts.

CHAPTER 25:
ISRAEL WORSHIPS BAALPEOR

•**VERSE** 3 Baalpeor, or the lord of Peor. Peor was the name of the mountain there.

•**VERSE** 6 They were weeping and repenting before God for what was done, and here comes this guy with a prostitute where they could all see him.

•**VERSE** 7 Phinehas was the grandson of Aaron.

•**VERSE** 9 Balaam was successful in bringing a curse by his advice to the king in laying a stumbling block before God's people.

When Moab was conquered and the Midianites were conquered and slain, Balaam was slain with them.

CHAPTER 26:
CENSUS OF THE NEW GENERATION

•**VERSES** 1-2 The tribes are numbered at the end of wandering 40 years.

•**VERSE** 51 There's approximately 2,000 less at the end of the forty years of wandering, yet some of the tribes actually grew in number through the wilderness wanderings.

•**VERSES** 64-65 There's no one left from that generation except for Moses, Joshua, and Caleb. Those who came out of Egypt who were 20 years old or older have died, with the exception of these three men. Moses is soon to die before they go into the land.

CHAPTER 27:
THE LAW OF INHERITANCE

•**VERSES** 1-3 They were dividing the land and giving the sons their portions.

•**VERSES** 8-11 He gave the law of the inheritance. If there isn't a son then it goes to the daughters.

If there aren't daughters or sons, then a man's brothers inherit. If he doesn't have brothers, then his father's brothers inherit. And if his father doesn't have brothers, then the next of kin inherits.

•**VERSE** 21 Joshua is to lead the people and to come before Eleazar, the priest, to inquire of the Lord.

The priest sought counsel from God through the Urim and the Thummim.

Urim and Thummim mean light and perfections—a pouch with a white and black stone inside.

When they asked the Lord a question, if the priest would pull out a white stone, God's answer was "yes;" if it was black, the answer was "no."

CHAPTER 28:
VARIOUS OFFERINGS

•VERSE 2 Moses gave the various sacrifices to be offered every day, sacrifices for the Sabbath day, sacrifices for the first day of every month, and sacrifices for the Feast of the Passover and the Feast of Pentecost.

CHAPTER 29:
OFFERINGS IN THE SEVENTH MONTH

•VERSE 1 The number seven is a significant number meaning perfection in the Bible. Thus, the seventh month was special. It is the month of October approximately on our calendar.

•VERSE 39 The burnt and peace offerings were individual and commanded here in chapter 29.

CHAPTER 30:
VOWS

•VERSE 2 A promise unto God is serious, and He expects you to keep your vow. God doesn't want you to make a vow and then break it. "It's better not to vow at all than to vow and to break it" (Ecclesiastes 5:5).

God doesn't require you to make vows. A person does so voluntarily.

•VERSE 3 If a young girl living in her father's house makes a vow unto God, and her father hears, he has the capacity of disallowing it. But if he doesn't disallow it, then the vow is to stand; it is binding, and she must keep that vow to the Lord.

•VERSES 6-15 If a girl is engaged or married to a husband and he hears the vow that she makes, he is able to dis-

allow that vow. But if a widow or a divorced woman makes a vow, then she is bound to that vow.

CHAPTER 31:
CONQUERING THE MIDIANITES

•VERSE 2 This was one of Moses' final acts. They are ready to enter into the Promised Land, and God orders avenging against the Midianites, who caused the children of Israel to commit fornication and idolatry. Now God is judging the Midianites.

•VERSE 8 This also included the prophet Balaam, who was guilty of greed. He allowed greed to master him, thus removing himself from the place of God's blessing. Rather than dying the death of the righteous, he was slain.

•VERSES 15-17 In order to understand these commands, it would be necessary to understand a little bit about the culture and their religious practices.

In all the history of the world these people had the lowest kind of morals. Every kind of sin imaginable was practiced. Marriage vows were nothing. They lived as animals, to the point of bestiality as a common practice.

Their manner of living was so polluted and corrupted that it was impossible for their survival. They believed in human sacrifice and offered their children as sacrifices unto their gods.

God ordered their extermination lest their pollution infect His children. God is bringing them into a land, using them as a tool of judgment because of their horrible, abominable practices.

•VERSE 27 Half the spoil is to go to all of Israel, and half the spoil will go to the 12,000 men who went to battle.

•VERSES 28-29 Eleazar the high priest became a very wealthy man overnight. Of the 12,000 men who went to battle and received the spoil, one-twenty-fourth of the spoil went to Eleazar.

There were about 337,500 sheep for those who went to battle.

•**VERSE 30** From the spoil that went to Israel, one in five was to go to the Levites.

•**VERSE 49** When they came back from war, there wasn't one man missing.

•**VERSE 50** The captains brought offerings of gold, silver, and brass to the Lord as thanksgiving for His preservation of their troops in the battle.

CHAPTER 32:
SOME TRIBES SETTLE OUTSIDE

•**VERSE 5** They were content to stay in the territory that they had conquered—the area that is presently Jordan.

•**VERSE 23** "Everything is open and naked before Him" (Hebrews 4:13). There is no secret sin; that's a delusion. You can be sure your sin will find you out. "Whatsoever a man soweth, that shall he also reap" (Galatians 6:7).

CHAPTER 33:
POSSESSING THE LAND

•**VERSES 1-2** This is a summary of their exodus out of Egypt. Moses wrote down all the places where they had stopped as they made this journey from Egypt to the Promised Land.

•**VERSES 51-53** God wanted all the artifacts destroyed because the pictures were extremely lewd and lascivious. The molten images were their gods that they worshiped, which were grotesque and exaggerated sexual features.

The high places, where they offered the sacrifices unto their gods, were ordered utterly destroyed lest there remain that polluting influence in the land.

•**VERSE 54** This is giving a portion of the land to everybody, each family getting its own land grant. This land was to remain in those families perpetually.

•**VERSES 55-56** Israel failed to obey the Lord. A lot of times we think we know better than God. We think that we can handle it. We learn, to our own dismay, the folly of disobedience discovering that God knew us better than we knew ourselves.

 HEBREW KEY WORD

yarash = possess, seize, occupy (33:53).

CHAPTER 34:
BORDERS OF THE PROMISED LAND

•**VERSE 2** This is the land that God promised to Abraham, but now it belonged to these people. It was theirs; God had given it to them. There was only one thing—they had to go in and possess it.

God has given to you so many rich and precious promises. All you have to do faithfully claim that which God has promised to you.

•**VERSE 6** The Mediterranean was the border on the west side.

•**VERSE 11** "Ain" means fountains, which no doubt is a reference to the headwater of the Jordan River at the base of Mount Hermon.

CHAPTER 35:
CITIES OF REFUGE

•**VERSES 3-5** Extending out from the city was a thousand cubits for their farm area, and another two thousand cubits for their cattle.

•**VERSE 11** A part of their culture was revenge killing. God placed restrictions upon it rather than seeking to totally root out the tradition, though He wasn't in favor of it.

Revenge killing was so deep that even if it was an accident, the avenger of blood was prone to catch the guy and kill him. In order to modify this deeply ingrained practice, God established the cities of refuge so that if you killed someone by accident, you could flee to somewhere safe.

The Levites would shelter and protect you, and guarantee a fair trial. If you didn't make it to the city, your trial was unfair.

• **VERSE 14** Cities of refuge were placed strategically throughout the land so that you'd only need to run a half-day's journey.

• **VERSES 16-21** If it could be proven that it was not an accident, and that you had hatred and animosity, then you were delivered from the city of refuge and the avenger would put you to death.

• **VERSES 31-33** There wasn't a ransom for the guilty. In other words, he was not able to buy his way out. The guilty were put to death to free the land from pollution.

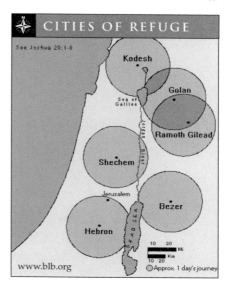

CHAPTER 36:
INHERITANCE OF WOMEN

• **VERSE 8** Whenever girls inherited the land, then it was necessary for them to marry someone from that tribe in order to keep the inheritance.

STUDY QUESTIONS FOR NUMBERS

1. The book of Numbers is so named because of the two censuses that transpired. After studying chapters 1 and 26, describe how and when the censuses took place and why.

_____

_____

_____

2. Where was the tabernacle placed in the Israelites' campsite? (Numbers 1:52-2:2). Why do you think God wanted it in that particular place?

_____

_____

_____

3. God had direct control when the Israelites moved and when they stayed. According to Numbers 9:15-23, how did they know God's will concerning their movements?

_____

_____

_____

4. The journey to the Promised Land only took two years. According to Numbers 14:1-11, why didn't the children of Israel go into the Promised Land and what was the result? (Numbers 14:22-25).

_____

_____

_____

5. We read in Numbers chapter 11 about the Israelites complaining. Why do you think the Lord is displeased when we complain? (Numbers 11:1).

_____

_____

_____

THE BOOK OF
DEUTERONOMY

AUTHOR OF THE BOOK:
Moses wrote the book of Deuteronomy, except for the last few verses about his death. It is believed that these were written by Joshua.

PERIOD OF WRITING:
As the children of Israel were in the wilderness between Egypt and the Promised Land.

TYPE OF BOOK:
Book of the law; fifth book of the Pentateuch.

THEME:
Love and obedience.

INTRODUCTION:
The word "Deuteronomy" means the second law. This is Moses' final address to the people. It probably covers the last month-and-a-half of Moses' life. He is about 120 years old.

Before he died, Moses wanted the next generation to understand the importance of obedience to God's commandments. Many had been born in the wilderness, so Moses communicates God's words, God's faithfulness, and exhorts the people to obedience.

Many didn't see the miracle of the Red Sea being parted or remember the horrible bondage in Egypt. Growing up as children, they weren't aware of the hazards of the wilderness, so he wanted to give a good history lesson. These are his final exhortations prior to their crossing the Jordan and entering into the land. He is encouraging them to go in and take the land that God had promised.

CHAPTER 1:
MOSES ADDRESSES THE PEOPLE

•**VERSE 1** These words of encouragement recount what God has done.

•**VERSE 2** The journey from Horeb to Kadesh-barnea (about 126 miles), the entrance to the Promised Land, takes 11 days, but they have been journeying for 40 years and 11 months.

We recognize to get from the Red Sea to the Promised Land it was necessary to go through the wilderness. So, there was a legitimate wilderness experience, but most of the journey was illegitimate.

•**VERSE 22** The request for spies came from the people and it seemed good unto Moses.

•**VERSE 27** "God hates us." That borders on blasphemy. In reality God loved them and wanted to give them a land that they might dwell in, that it might be their land. God wanted to free them from the horrible bondage of Egypt, yet now they are accusing God of hating them.

•**VERSE 28** The Anakims were giants.

•**VERSE 30** God had been with them through the wilderness experience.

•**VERSE 33** If we only realized how all-encompassing the work of God is that surrounds our lives. God went before them, prepared the place, and then led them.

CHAPTER 2:
WANDERING IN THE DESERT

•**VERSE 7** Moses speaks of God's miracles: over one million people traveled through the wilderness for 40 years, yet lacked nothing.

•**VERSES 11-12** This area of Moab was once inhabited by the Emims, relatives of the Anakims.

The Israelites feared going into the Promised Land because of the giants there. But Moses gives them a history lesson: the giants were driven out of other territories that God had promised to His people. He will do the same for them.

•**VERSES 20-23** Again, Moses recounts history, letting them know that they don't have to worry about giants.

CHAPTER 3:
MOSES FORBIDDEN TO CROSS JORDAN

•**VERSE 5** During their journey, they had conquered 60 walled cities of Basham. Moses says, "Look, it is noth-

ing with God. You don't have to worry about the walled cities or the giants. If God be for us, who can be against us?"

"God has promised to go before you and drive out your enemies, and thus, the things that cause terror and fear in your heart and destroy your faith need not stop you. Go in."

•**VERSE 26** The first time they asked for water, God told Moses to smite the rock. But the second time he was to speak to the rock only. In his anger, Moses smote the rock again.

Moses misrepresented God as he portrayed God as being angry. Therefore, God did not allow Moses to go into the Promised Land.

God wanted to impress the importance of obedience, and in this case, proper representation of Himself. We, too, are God's representatives in the world today.

God always answers prayer: sometimes the answer is yes, sometimes the answer is no. In this case Moses' request was not granted by God in order that He might teach the nation the importance of obedience.

CHAPTER 4:
THE CALL TO OBEDIENCE

•**VERSE 1** Moses is making application.

•**VERSE 2** The people are forbidden to add or take away from the commandments, from the word that God had spoken through Moses.

•**VERSE 9** Teach these commandments to your children and grandchildren. Moses reminds them of the exclusive privilege as a nation so near to God and giving them righteous laws.

•**VERSE 12** When they heard the voice of God they didn't see any form at all—deliberately. God did not want them making any likeness of Him.

•**VERSES 16-19** There is something within man that drives him to worship. It is tragic when men leave the worship and service of the true and the living God, the Creator of the universe, and begin to worship idols.

•**VERSES 21-22** Moses recognizes that it was for their sakes that God was sticking to His Word.

•**VERSE 24** The fire of God will consume His enemies.

But the same fire also consumes the impurities from our lives. His refining fire burns within our hearts, consuming the dross and transmitting purity into permanency.

•**VERSES 25-27** This passage is prophetic: "In generations to come, your children's children are going to start making graven images." Moses is prophesying the failure of the nation, which will cause them to be driven out and dispersed into all the world; yet, a remnant will remain.

•**VERSE 32** In essence, "Look back in your history books and see."

•**VERSES 37-38** Moses said God didn't do this because of their greatness or goodness, but because of His love for their fathers.

CHAPTER 5:
REPEATING THE TEN COMMANDMENTS

•**VERSE 1** The children of Israel were to learn these commandments, then keep and do these commandments.

•**VERSE 29** This is God's cry, God's lamentation. God cries over the failure of the people, and thus, His inability to bless them as He desires.

CHAPTER 6:
LOVE THE LORD YOUR GOD

•**VERSES 4-5** This is called the Shema, the great commandment.

•**VERSES 6-9** God wanted His Word to permeate their very lives.

CHAPTER 7:
COMMAND TO OBEY GOD

•**VERSE 6** A "holy people" means a separated people.

•**VERSES 12-13** God elected these people, not because they were great or faithful, but because of His love for their fathers, the faithfulness of Abraham, and his promise to Abraham that through his seed would the Messiah come (Genesis 18:18). Therefore, they are actually reaping the benefits of the faith of Abraham.

The covenant that God made was conditional: "If you will obey." As you read the commandments in Exodus and Leviticus, they are health codes: laws for diet and sanitation. If they keep the laws, they will be kept from the diseases of the Egyptians.

CHAPTER 8:
COMMAND TO REMEMBER GOD

•**VERSE 2** They had to wander in the wilderness to be proven.

Many times God tests us, not to prove anything to Him, but to show us what's inside. God puts us through tests to show our weaknesses and to remind us to depend upon Him. We can't depend or rely upon ourselves; we must rely upon the Lord.

THE TEN COMMANDMENTS

I. THOU SHALL HAVE NO OTHER GODS BEFORE ME	VI. THOU SHALL NOT KILL
II. THOU SHALL NOT MAKE ANY GRAVEN IMAGES	VII. THOU SHALL NOT COMMIT ADULTERY
III. THOU SHALL NOT TAKE GOD'S NAME IN VAIN	VIII. THOU SHALL NOT STEAL
IV. THOU SHALL KEEP THE SABBATH	IX. THOU SHALL NOT BEAR FALSE WITNESS
V. HONOR THY FATHER AND MOTHER	X. THOU SHALL NOT COVET

•**VERSES 11-14** A warning that national peril will come, not during the conquest, not during the development, but in times of prosperity. We may forget God, and we are prone to attribute our success to our own works.

CHAPTER 9:
REMEMBERING ISRAEL'S REBELLION

•**VERSES 1-3** If they do not enter in at this point, it will mean disaster. Moses is seeking to encourage them. He is presenting the upcoming obstacles realistically, yet seeking to encourage their hearts by reminding them of the greatness of God.

•**VERSE 4** Self-righteousness is terrible, and attaches to us so easily. Our very nature is perverse, causing us to desire others to think that we are more righteous than we really are.

CHAPTER 10:
ENCOURAGEMENT TO REVERENCE GOD

•**VERSES 12-13** What does God require? Reverence Him, walk in all of His ways, love and serve Him with all your heart and soul, and keep all of His commandments and statutes.

What does God actually require of me? That I believe in His Son Jesus Christ. As I believe in Jesus, I receive His indwelling power and His presence begins to give me the strength and ability to live according to God's divine ideal.

•**VERSE 14** "The earth is the Lord's, and the fullness thereof; the world, and they that dwell therein" (Psalm 24:1).

•**VERSE 16** The rite of circumcision was given to Abraham and was intended to be spiritual: the cutting away of the fleshly life. You weren't to live after the flesh, but after the Spirit. They kept the covenant physically, but not spiritually.

•**VERSE 17** The word "terrible" is better translated awesome.

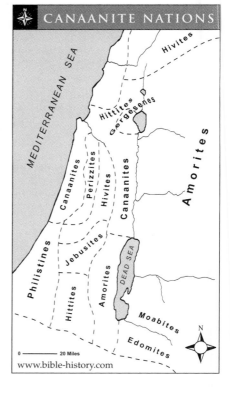

www.bible-history.com

CHAPTER 11:
REWARDS OF OBEDIENCE

•**VERSES 13-15** Upon entering the land, the Jews were to love and serve God. If they obeyed, they would be blessed.

•**VERSES 18-20** You can get into rituals but forget why you practice them.

Today, the Israelites go through the ritual of binding the law upon their hand, upon their foreheads, placing mezuzahs on their doors, and kissing them upon entry. It's just a ritual—no real serving and loving God with all their hearts and souls. We must beware lest we allow a ritual to substitute for reality.

•**VERSES 26-28** God sets before you the blessing and the curse; it's your choice.

•**VERSE 29** Shechem was the area Abraham first came to and the place Jacob lived for a time and dug a well.

South of Shechem is Mount Gerizim and north is Mount Ebal. When they came into the land, men were to go to the top of Mount Gerizim and shout the conditions of blessings to the people in the valley. But on Mount Ebal, they shouted the curses if they disobeyed. It was meant to be impressed in their minds so that they wouldn't forget, but unfortunately, they did just that.

CHAPTER 12:
INSTRUCTIONS FOR WORSHIP

•**VERSE 2** In order for the people to lose interest and forget the foreign gods, everything was to be utterly obliterated.

•**VERSE 5** God said He would choose a place for worship when they came into the land.

•**VERSE 15** They would offer to God what they ate as a peace offering. The fat would be burned unto God as a sweet smelling savor, and then they were free to eat the meat. They'd sit down, eat with God, and have a great time fellowshiping with Him.

Now, they're going to be scattered throughout the land, and they won't be able to bring the ox every time they want to eat meat. So they were told to eat it in their cities, but don't offer it as a sacrifice to God. The burnt offering was to be given only when coming to Jerusalem.

•**VERSE 16** This was to be perpetual, for the life of the flesh is in the blood; and they were to thoroughly bleed the meat before they ate it.

•**VERSES 17-18** An offering, whether a freewill offering or a peace offering, was to be eaten in the specified place that God had commanded.

•**VERSE 30** It's dangerous to inquire into spiritism or spiritualism out of curiosity. This is perilous and can become a snare to you.

•**VERSE 31** Human or infant sacrifice was very common.

CHAPTER 13:
FALSE PROPHETS AND IDOLATRY

•**VERSES 1-5** A phenomenon for which there is no scientific explanation does not necessarily mean it comes from God. Satan is a deceiver and is able to create spectacular phenomena. Thus, phenomena should not draw our attention or be used as criteria for truth.

•**VERSES 6-9** God wanted a spiritual purity among these people, lest they become infected by the lascivious practices of the pagan worshipers, thereby losing the land.

CHAPTER 14:
COMMANDS REGARDING FOOD

•**VERSE 21** They were not to eat anything that died on its own. They were to give it away or sell it to a stranger.

•**VERSES 24-26** If it was too far to go to Jerusalem carrying the offerings, they were to sell them. When they arrived in Jerusalem, they were to buy their meat, offer it in sacrifice, and have a feast before God.

CHAPTER 15:
THE SEVENTH YEAR

•**VERSE 1** All debts were to be forgiven in the seventh year. They were not to demand it again, except if it were from a foreigner or a stranger.

•**VERSE 7** God cares for the welfare of the poor and desires for us to be interested also. Here He is protecting the poor (Proverbs 19:17).

•**VERSE 11** Jesus quotes from Deuteronomy, "The poor you have with you always" (Matthew 26:11). There will always be poor and we should always be concerned for the poor.

•**VERSE 12** Hebrew male or female slaves were to serve for six years; but in the seventh year they were to be freed.

•**VERSE 17** The usual practice was to put a gold ring in the ear, signifying that a man was a slave by choice.

This description of the bondslave provides a beautiful parallel: he is a servant by choice and a servant for life.

Likewise, as a believer, I have become a bondslave of Jesus Christ. He didn't force me. I have chosen to serve Him for life.

CHAPTER 16:
FEASTS

•**VERSES 5-6** They couldn't keep the Passover in any other city except the one God appointed for His place of worship: Jerusalem.

•**VERSES 9-10** Seven weeks after Passover, the next day, they were to keep the Feast of Pentecost.

•**VERSES 11-15** Again we see the commandment to rejoice. God doesn't want any long-faced, griping service. In sacrifice, in worship, and in giving, God wants you to serve Him gladly.

•**VERSES 18-19** When the Jews got into the land, they were to appoint judges in every city, and in the place of judgment, men who were honest and would not take bribes.

HEBREW KEY WORD

samach = rejoice, to be glad (16:11).

CHAPTER 17:
COMMANDS REGARDING FUTURE KINGS

•**VERSE 1** We should never give to God our castoffs. Never give a sacrifice that has blemishes. God isn't honored when we give that which has no value to us.

•**VERSE 2** God was seeking to preserve the nation. Nations must be built upon solid pillars of righteousness, justice, and equity. When these pillars begin to rot, the nation will soon fall. One of the rotten plagues God was guarding them against was idolatrous worship.

•**VERSE 14** God knew that one day these people would insist upon a king. Though it was to be 400 years or so before they would crown Saul, God provided in advance the principles to govern their kings.

•**VERSES 16-17** When Solomon became king, he not only multiplied horses, but he also went to Egypt to horse trade (the second disobedience). Finally, he multiplied wives unto himself.

God said don't multiply wives lest they turn your heart away from Me. Solomon's wives did turn his heart from the Lord and ultimately brought him failure.

CHAPTER 18:
THE PROPHET TO COME

•**VERSE 1** The tribe of Levi was not to be given any portion of the land.

•**VERSE 10** The "observer of times" is actually the practice of astrology, the use of horoscopes.

•**VERSE 13** The word "perfect" here means thou shalt be completely toward the Lord. They were not to have other gods in their lives or have divided hearts with other interests.

•**VERSES 15-18** Here we find a great prophecy concerning the coming of Jesus Christ.

•**VERSE** 20 God doesn't appreciate a person speaking for Him when He hasn't spoken. Thus, the false prophets in those days were to be put to death.

CHAPTER 19:
CITIES OF REFUGE

•**VERSES** 3-9 Three cities of refuge had already been established on the other side of Jordan. God said to appoint three more cities when they came into the land.

•**VERSE** 14 They would set up piles of stones as landmarks. They were not to move their neighbor's landmark. This crime was looked upon with great disfavor.

•**VERSES** 18-19 If a man spoke falsely against his neighbor, his punishment would be the crime leveled against his neighbor.

•**VERSE** 20 God wanted them to have a healthy fear of lying as a witness.

CHAPTER 20:
RULES OF WARFARE

•**VERSE** 1 They had been slaves and feared battle. They weren't trained, fighting men. The children of Israel didn't have horses or chariots for battle. Having a chariot was like having a tank against an infantry.

David said, "Yea, though I walk through the valley of the shadow of death, I will fear no evil: for Thou art with me" (Psalm 23:4). The consciousness of the presence of God dispels fear.

•**VERSE** 5 God knows our frames. If there is any hesitation in warfare, we will be a hindrance rather than a help in battle.

Therefore, in these next few verses, God outlines who should be excused from battle.

•**VERSE** 6 If a man had planted a vineyard but had never eaten of its fruits, he too was to be excused from battle.

•**VERSE** 8 Those who were apt to panic, thus creating more panic among the troops, were to be excused.

•**VERSE** 9 By the end of eliminations, they were left with a pretty good group of fighting men who weren't afraid and didn't have any distractions.

•**VERSES** 16-17 They weren't to make peace treaties, but totally destroy the people.

•**VERSE** 18 Because they were practicing horrible, lascivious acts, God wanted the nations in verse 17 totally eradicated, lest they infect the Israelites. They didn't obey the Lord, sparing some cities, and thus became polluted.

This ultimately led to being driven out of the land because they had practiced after the manner of the nations that they should have destroyed.

•**VERSES** 19-20 During a siege, they were not to cut down any fruit trees to use as a bulwark against the city, thus providing food for them in the future.

CHAPTER 21:
DOMESTIC LAWS

•**VERSES** 10-14 They usually sold the captives as slaves. If someone had taken a captive as a wife, they could put her away, but couldn't sell her as a slave.

•**VERSES** 15-17 A man couldn't reverse the inheritances on his sons. The first-born son was given the inheritance.

•**VERSES** 22-23 Any man hung on a tree was cursed of God. Paul tells us that Christ became a curse for us (Galatians 3:13). Paul was referring to these verses from Deuteronomy.

CHAPTER 22:
VARIOUS LAWS

•**VERSE 1** If a man saw another's ox or sheep going astray, and ignored it and didn't retrieve it, then he was at fault.

•**VERSES 2-3** If someone found a lost item, they were to seek to restore it to its proper owner. They were not to hide it for themselves.

•**VERSES 13-21** After a marriage was consummated, a cloth that proved the woman's virginity was given to the parents. Later, if the man lied about his wife, the parents would have evidence of her virginity to give to the elders, and the husband could be found a liar and had to pay the father 100 shekels of silver for bringing evil upon a virgin in Israel.

If the woman couldn't prove her virginity, she was put to death.

•**VERSE 23** "Betrothed" means engaged.

CHAPTER 23:
EXCLUSION FROM THE TEMPLE

•**VERSE 1** Eunuchs were forbidden in the temple.

CHAPTER 24:
SOCIAL LAWS

•**VERSE 1** God gave certain conditions for the law of divorce.

Jesus declared, "The law was given for the hardness of your hearts," because man couldn't achieve God's divine ideal.

After marriage, if they realized they made a mistake then they're allowed a bill of divorcement.

•**VERSES 3-4** If a man has already put away his wife, he was not to take her back again.

•**VERSE 6** They couldn't take a millstone as a pledge for debts because it was their livelihood—to grind their wheat. Without a millstone, there's no bread.

•**VERSE 7** Capital punishment was the penalty for kidnappers.

•**VERSE 9** This refers back to Miriam coming against Moses; the lesson: leaders should be honored.

•**VERSES 17-18** God watches out for the stranger, the fatherless, the downcast, and the outcast.

•**VERSES 19-21** Whatever was left on the vines was for the poor people. It was an excellent welfare program.

CHAPTER 25:
LAWS REGARDING BUSINESS DEALINGS

•**VERSES 1-3** Forty is the number of judgment, and they weren't to give more than 40 stripes. The sentence was often 39, offering justice tempered with mercy.

•**VERSE 13** "Divers weights" was a common practice, having two weights for the balances: a lighter one for buying, a heavier one for selling. So, here we see the establishment of God's national standard of weights and measures for Israel. They were not to have different weights for buying or selling. Diverse weights are an abomination to God.

•**VERSES 14-15** God desires honesty, not cheating or treating others deceitfully.

•**VERSE 19** Amalek used dirty tactics against Israel; therefore, they were to remember Amalek's actions, knowing one day they would get revenge. When this occurred, they were to wipe out Amalek completely.

In biblical typology, Amalek is a type of the flesh. God's edict for our flesh is that we wipe it out utterly—don't leave any remnant or it will cause trouble. See 1 Samuel 15:2, 3.

HEBREW KEY WORD

tsedeq = honest, just, right (25:15).

CHAPTER 26:
BRINGING FIRSTFRUITS AND TITHES

• **VERSE 3** The Jews acknowledge God's faithfulness to keep His promise.

• **VERSE 5** This verse speaks of Jacob, calling him a Syrian.

• **VERSES 6-10** They were to rehearse God's great work in bringing them from the bondage of Egypt into the blessings of God, giving the firstfruits unto God of the glorious land He had given.

• **VERSE 11** God commands them to rejoice. What kind of a witness is it to God if His people are always sour and dour? God wants you to rejoice.

CHAPTER 27:
MOUNT EBAL

• **VERSE 5** God commanded that the altars be built just out of earth. God didn't want them building ornate places of worship, distracting them by the surroundings. They would glory in the beauty of the place rather than worship Him undistracted.

• **VERSE 6** The burnt offerings were the offerings of consecration, symbolizing the consecrating of their lives to God.

• **VERSE 7** The peace offerings were the offerings of communion, symbolizing their desire to fellowship with God.

• **VERSES 12-13** Certain tribes were to pronounce the blessings upon the people from Mount Gerizim. And on Mount Ebal other tribes were to pronounce the curses.

• **VERSE 15** "Amen" means so be it.

CHAPTER 28:
BLESSINGS AND CURSES

• **VERSE 1** God's promise was conditional: they would only possess and dwell in the land if they were obedient to the commandments of God.

• **VERSE 15** "Righteousness exalts a nation: but sin is a reproach to any people" (Proverbs 14:34). If a nation places God at the center, it shall be blessed of God abundantly.

• **VERSE 37** That verse has been literally fulfilled. In being driven into the other nations, the Jews have become a byword. And today, they are often hated by people without cause.

• **VERSE 47** We have so much to be thankful for, we should be serving God with joyfulness and gladness of heart. If you can't serve God without griping, then don't serve.

• **VERSE 49** This is a reference to the Roman Empire.

• **VERSE 53** They will be so hungry that they will eat their own children. This horrible curse was fulfilled in 2 Kings, chapter 6.

CHAPTER 29:
THE COVENANT

• **VERSES 1-8** They witnessed the works of God but they were blind to it.

After 40 years their clothing and shoes hadn't worn out. They hadn't been able to plant or harvest, yet God had given them food.

When they battled King Sihon and King Og, God gave them victory and gave the land to the Israelites as an inheritance.

• **VERSE 9** Their prosperity was tied directly to their keeping and doing the commandments of God. This was the condition of God's covenant.

• **VERSES 19-20** When God pronounces a curse, they smile within themselves and say, "It won't happen to me." God's Word will be fulfilled. Don't be deceived, God is not mocked.

CHAPTER 30:
CHOOSE LIFE

•**VERSE 6** God will deal with a man's heart and take away the fleshly desires out of his heart.

•**VERSES 11-14** God has given His Word in understandable terms. He has put it in your heart and in your mouth.

Paul the apostle quotes this passage in Romans 10:6-9, showing how close every man is to salvation. Salvation is just as near as your heart and your mouth.

•**VERSE 19** Life or death, blessing or cursing: it's your choice. God doesn't make that choice and He has always known the choice you are going to make.

CHAPTER 31:
MOSES WRITES THE LAW

•**VERSE 2** Moses, representing the Law, could not lead them into the Promised Land. It was up to Joshua to take them into the land.

The same is true for you: the law cannot bring you into that glorious rich life in the Spirit, it can only lead you to it. But you must enter in by faith (Galatians 3:24-25).

•**VERSES 10-11** Every seven years at the Feast of Tabernacles, the law of Moses was to be read before the people.

The book of Ezra records when Ezra returned from captivity, they found the law and read it to the people for several days. The people would stand there from morning until evening as the law was read and explained to them.

•**VERSE 12** The people were to learn the law, to reverence God, and to do the law.

•**VERSES 19-21** The song was to remind them of the reason why the calamities had befallen them: because they had forsaken God.

CHAPTER 32:
THE SONG OF MOSES

•**VERSES 11-12** These verses beautifully describe God figuratively as an eagle. This symbolizes God, as He develops our walk and relationship with Him.

•**VERSE 15** "Jeshurun" is Israel.

•**VERSE 17** They who sacrifice to idols are actually sacrificing to devils (1 Corinthians 10:19-21). Many idols representing the pagan gods actually have demons associated with them.

•**VERSE 29** God wants you to be wise and look ahead to the end of the lifestyle you've chosen. God's crying over man's ignorance and folly.

•**VERSE 35** Jonathan Edwards used this text for his sermon, "Sinners in the Hands of an Angry God." He said, "A sinner is like a man walking over a fiery pit on an icy plank. Your footing is so unsure at any moment you can slip into the abyss."

•**VERSES 46-47** Set your heart to the words of God. They are not empty—they are your life.

•**VERSES 48-51** Moses' time has come. What a heavy responsibility Moses had being God's representative. His failure at the waters of Meribah cost him the privilege of leading God's people into the Promised Land. We too have a heavy responsibility, for we are God's representatives to the world.

CHAPTER 33:
THE BLESSINGS OF MOSES

•**VERSE 6** Notice the word "not" is in italics, which means it was added. It should read, "let his men be few." As they took the land, Reuben was one of the smaller tribes.

•**VERSE 9** Aaron was not to mourn for his sons when they died. His service to God was more important.

•**VERSE 12** A map of Benjamin looks like shoulders, and right between the shoulders is the city of Jerusalem. "And so the Lord shall dwell between his shoulders." Here is the first hint that Jerusalem will be the place where the temple will be built and the people will worship the Lord.

•**VERSES 13-14** Jacob said Joseph was a "fruitful bough" (Genesis 49:22). Moses described the fruitfulness of Ephraim and Manasseh, the sons of Joseph.

•**VERSE 24** A map of Asher looks like a leg from the knee down with a foot, and the toe of Asher is Haifa. "He shall dip his foot in oil." The first major oil pipeline in the Middle East was built from Iraq to the city of Haifa. Through Haifa, Asher had his foot in the oil just as Moses predicted 4,000 years ago.

•**VERSE 25** God's grace is sufficient for you. And whatever you are facing, God will give you strength.

•**VERSE 27** With His hands, God stretched out the heavens like a curtain (Psalm 104:2). If He could stretch out the heavens, His everlasting arms can hold you through any problem you might be facing.

CHAPTER 34:
THE DEATH OF MOSES

•**VERSE 1** This was probably written by Joshua. Surely Moses didn't write the account of his own death.

•**VERSE 3** Zoar is thought to be the bottom part of the Dead Sea area.

•**VERSE 6** "[God] buried him." We are told in the book of Jude that Satan and Michael had a dispute over the body of Moses. God buried him, but not before this dispute occurred. His body has never been found—the sepulcher remains a mystery.

STUDY QUESTIONS FOR DEUTERONOMY

1. Moses was reminding the people of their recent history and what God had done for them. According to Deuteronomy 1:30-33, what did the Lord do for them?

_____

_____

_____

2. We read in Deuteronomy 3:25-27 that Moses prayed to the Lord that he would be able to lead the Israelites into the Promised Land. Why was he forbidden access? (Numbers 20:9-13 and Deuteronomy 32:48-52). What lesson can we learn from this?

_____

_____

_____

3. Why does the Lord say He is a consuming fire and a jealous God?

_____

_____

_____

4. The Israelites were going to have to fight when they came into the land, but their enemies were stronger in battle. What encouraging words did Moses say to lessen their fear? (Deuteronomy 20:1, 4).

_____

_____

_____

5. Deuteronomy 10:16 says, "Circumcise therefore the foreskin of your heart, and be no more stiffnecked." What does this mean? (Deuteronomy 30:6 and Romans 2:29).

_____

_____

_____

THE BOOK OF
JOSHUA

AUTHOR OF THE BOOK:
Joshua

PERIOD OF WRITING:
After Moses' death.

TYPE OF BOOK:
Historical

THEME:
Overcoming the enemy in battle and learning to walk in the Spirit.

INTRODUCTION:
Joshua is the first book of the Bible to be named after a person. Joshua's name means "Yahweh is salvation" and is the same name as "Jesus" in the New Testament. So we find in Joshua a very interesting type of Jesus Christ, as Joshua led the people into the inheritance.

Moses led the Israelites out of Egypt to the border of the Promised Land, but he couldn't lead them in. Moses stands for the law, but the law can't lead you into the fullness of God's blessings for your life. The law can lead you to the border, but it can't take you in. Joshua took the Israelites into the Promised Land and now there is a new relationship based on faith. They're going to have to begin by stepping out in faith, coming into this land that God had promised.

The Israelites' conquest of Canaan is typical of Christians entering into a glorious victory over the flesh in and through Jesus Christ. But Joshua could only lead them so far. He led them into the conquering of the land, but he never brought them into a rest. That is something that was reserved for Jesus Christ. Once Christ made the work of salvation complete through His death upon the cross, He brought rest in our salvation, our eternal life. Jesus has done for us what Joshua could not do. Joshua brought them into the land, not into the rest. Jesus has brought us into a glorious rest.

CHAPTER 1:
GOD ENCOURAGES JOSHUA

•**VERSE 1** The true meaning of the word "minister" is servant. It doesn't mean that Joshua was Moses' pastor. Jesus said, "If any man would be chief among you, let him be the servant of all" (Mark 10:44). A true minister is a man who is there to serve the needs of the people.

HEBREW KEY WORD

sharath = minister or servant (1:1).

•**VERSE 3** "Every place you put your foot, I have already given to you." Notice it's in the past tense. God has already given a glorious, full, rich life of victory. All you have to do is go in and take it by faith.

•**VERSE 4** They only went so far and then they quit. Tragic. They didn't put their foot all the way in. They never did go to the River Euphrates. They never took all that God had given to them.

•**VERSES 5-6** Encouragement for Joshua as God promises His presence and His power.

•**VERSES 7-8** "Blessed is the man who walks not in the counsel of the ungodly, but whose delight is in the law of the Lord; and in His law does he meditate both day and night, he shall be like a tree planted by the rivers of water" (Psalm 1:1-3). These are the conditions upon which you will experience the presence and power of God.

CHAPTER 2:
RAHAB AND THE SPIES

•**VERSE 1** A few women are listed in the genealogy of Jesus Christ. One is this prostitute, Rahab. Another is Ruth, a Moabitess; and the third was Bathsheba,

David's wife. These women were chosen by God to be in the lineage of His Son.

Rather than coming from pure, royal, blue blood lineage, we find very common, sinful people listed in the line of Jesus Christ.

•**VERSES 18-19** This is a beautiful picture of abiding in Him. Those who are within Christ are safe no matter what happens. Outside of Him, I have nothing and I'm open prey.

•**VERSE 22** The mountains are behind Jericho, opposite direction from Jordan.

CHAPTER 3:
ISRAEL CROSSES THE JORDAN

•**VERSE 4** Two thousand cubits is about half a mile. They were to stay behind the ark of the covenant about half a mile or two-thirds of a mile.

•**VERSES 15-16** Even as God parted the Red Sea, God stopped the Jordan River in flood season and they were able to cross. When they came to the Red Sea, Moses stretched forth his rod and the Red Sea was parted. The Lord is testing their faith and developing their faith. The priests stepped into the river, stepping out in faith. This is a new relationship of faith with God.

CHAPTER 4:
MEMORIAL STONES

•**VERSES 6-7** God desires that His power and truth are transmitted to our children. The monument wasn't built for Joshua, but to remind them of God's work. Let's keep our memorials to the Lord for the work that He has wrought.

•**VERSE 9** Two memorials were erected. Stones were piled in the middle of the Jordan River, and piled up on a bank.

•**VERSE 19** It is four days prior to the Feast of Passover.

CHAPTER 5:
CIRCUMCISION AT GILGAL

•VERSES 2-7 Circumcision is a symbolic act of cutting away the flesh. God wanted a person's heart after the Spirit. God said, "Circumcise your hearts" (Deuteronomy 10:16). Cut away that desire after the flesh from your heart.

•VERSE 9 "Gilgal" means rolling, because God rolled away that reproach of Egypt, symbolic of living after the flesh or lusting after the flesh.

•VERSES 11-12 They are leaving the old manna, that monotonous diet, and eating the fruits of the land that God had promised. The life of the Spirit is a life of variety. A life of excitement—thrilling to walk and live after the Spirit. You never know what God has planned for you today.

•VERSES 13-15 Here Joshua met Jesus—Jesus, the Captain of the Lord's host. If it were an angel then He would have refused worship. Several times in the book of Revelation, John tried to worship an angel, and he said, "Stand up; worship the Lord." The Lord said, "Thou shalt worship the Lord thy God and Him only." Therefore, the Captain of the Lord's host is none other than Jesus who is ready to lead him into the Promised Land.

Here is a true picture of leadership. God chose Joshua as a leader to rule over the people of Israel because Joshua was ruled by the Lord; the proper chain of command.

CHAPTER 6:
CONQUERING JERICHO

•VERSES 8-14 I could imagine those in the city of Jericho a little quizzical after a few days. They see an army coming to take their city with these rams' horns and carrying this box between the staves—walking around, not saying a word for six days.

•VERSE 19 This is the first city in the land that they are conquering. Any gold, silver, brass, or iron was given to the Lord's treasury as the firstfruits. The firstfruits always belong to God.

•VERSE 20 You should have no problem with this story if your God is big enough. God brought down the walls of Jericho, and the city was taken by Joshua and the children of Israel.

•VERSE 26 The prophecy of Joshua was literally fulfilled in 1 Kings 16:34, several hundred years later.

CHAPTER 7:
ACHAN'S SIN

•VERSE 1 He took some of the spoil that was only for God.

•VERSE 2 Jericho is 1,200 feet below sea level, whereas Bethel is 2,800 feet above sea level.

•VERSE 7 "Alas" is a term that means "We've had it."

•VERSES 11-12 They are entering a new relationship with God—the life and the walk of the Spirit. God hasn't promised all victory. There are battles, giants in the land. Their flesh has been deeply entrenched for a long time. They had victory over the first battle because they obeyed the Lord's instructions. But a danger arose: self-confidence. Had he prayed before going into battle, he wouldn't be in this predicament.

Beware of self-confidence; you can't conquer the small areas of your flesh without divine guidance and help. We need the Lord's help to have victory over the flesh.

•VERSE 20 His sin cost the lives of 36 men of Israel, those who fell before the men of Ai. A person thinks that his sin only bothers himself, but sin has a bad effect on others.

CHAPTER 8:
CONQUERING AI

•VERSES 26-28 They failed conquering the city by their own ingenuity and abilities, but experienced victory when directed by God.

•VERSE 30 They are in the middle of the land.

•VERSE 34 Joshua told them the conditions to be blessed by God and cursed by God; the conditions to establish the land and how they could be driven from the land. The blessings, the cursings—all conditional upon obedience to the commandment of God.

CHAPTER 9:
DECEPTION BY THE GIBEONITES

•VERSE 2 The kings of Canaan pooled their armies and resources in one massive assault against Israel in hope of stopping this migration of people.

•VERSE 18 They honored the pact they had made with the Gibeonites; however, the people began to murmur against Joshua because of his strategic blunder. They had been deceived.

This is the second mistake Joshua made as a leader. The first mistake was when the men of Ai defeated them; failing to pray and seek counsel from God before deploying the troops to attack the city.

The same problem existed here: failure to pray and inquire of God concerning the Gibeonites. They looked at the outward circumstances—the dry, moldy bread and the ragged clothes—and were deceived. If we would seek God first, we could be spared tragic experiences that we encounter in life.

CHAPTER 10:
THE LONG DAY OF JOSHUA

•VERSES 4-5 When these five kings heard that the Gibeonites had made this league with the children of Israel, they decided to attack the Gibeonites as traitors.

•VERSES 11-13 Skeptics and theologians try to find a plausible explanation or say it didn't happen. But if you believe "In the beginning God created the heavens and the earth," then why should you have a problem with this?

In ancient world history there was a long afternoon or morning as it related to their location at that time of Joshua. The records of the Indians in Central America state there was a strange day when the sun only came to the horizon for a whole day without coming up.

•VERSE 42 God is not remote and far off. He is vitally interested in your life, even those little things troubling you. You're His child. He doesn't like to see you fretting. Don't think of God as untouchable or unapproachable.

Paul said to the Athenian philosophers, the Epicureans, "For in Him we live, we move, and have our being" (Acts 17:28). God wants to demonstrate His presence and His love. "You have not because you ask not" (James 4:2). Realize that God is with you.

God demonstrated to Joshua and the people His interest and presence in a powerful way. They conquered these kings and the major enemies in the land.

CHAPTER 11:
DEFEATING THE NORTH

•VERSES 1-3 These are the kings that are in Galilee and the upper Galilee region up to Mount Hermon.

•VERSE 8 This is to the lower part of Lebanon, the upper part of Israel.

•VERSE 10 Hazor is in upper Galilee, and one of the major cities at that time.

•VERSE 23 He took the land, except where there were pockets of resistance.

The incomplete conquest of the land was tragic. For instance, the Jebusite city of Jerusalem wasn't taken by Joshua—not until the time King David took the city of Jerusalem, hence calling it "The City of David." Also, Gaza and Ashdod were not taken at that time.

CHAPTER 12:
TERRITORY OF REUBEN, GAD, MANASSEH

Joshua dealt with the territories that the tribe of Reuben, Gad, and half of the tribe of Manasseh had settled.

Down in the lower area by the Dead Sea was apportioned to Reuben. This is the area of Jordan today.

Then north of Reuben was where the tribe of Gad had settled and half the tribe of Manasseh, which today is known as the Golan Heights.

CHAPTER 13:
LAND NOT YET CONQUERED

•**VERSE 1** "Stricken in years" refers to the feebleness that accompanies old age.

•**VERSE 2** They failed to take all the land God had promised. There is a sequel in our own spiritual lives—coming into the Land of Promise and taking the spiritual promise of victory, walking in the Spirit, the victory over the flesh.

It's a sign of spiritual stagnation when you've got to look back to relate vital experiences with God. God wants an up-to-the-moment experience of His victory, grace, and love in your life.

They came to the place where they were satisfied and content and didn't press on to the full victory. Beware of spiritual plateaus or complacency where you think you're spiritually satisfied.

CHAPTER 14:
CALEB'S INHERITANCE

•**VERSE 14** Caleb conquered the area around Hebron. He was from the tribe of Judah, that actually had the area south from Jerusalem, east to the Dead Sea, and west toward the Elah Valley.

The reason for Caleb's victory is he wholly followed the Lord God of Israel.

HEBREW KEY WORD

nachalah = inheritance (14:14).

CHAPTER 15:
JUDAH'S PORTION

•**VERSE 62** Engedi is by the Dead Sea, existing today—beautiful waterfall, Fern Grotto, absolutely gorgeous.

CHAPTER 16:
EPHRAIM AND MANASSEH'S PORTION

•**VERSES 1-3** Part of the tribe of Manasseh settled on the east banks of the Jordan River, but the other part settled on the west banks, the area of Jericho, through Bethel, north of Judah.

•**VERSE 10** The book of Judges shows the cost of disobedience, failing to totally take the land and allowing the people to remain. As the Scripture predicted, they were thorns in their sides.

CHAPTER 17:
HALF-TRIBE OF MANASSEH'S INHERITANCE

•**VERSE 1** The land was apportioned by circumscribing an area, and the tribes would draw lots.

•**VERSE 5** Half the tribe of Manasseh was to settle on the western bank, actually the West Bank today.

•**VERSES 12-13** The children of Israel failed to enter the complete victory and conquer of the land.

God desires that we take full victory over every area of the flesh. If we allow strongholds of the enemy to remain, they will be a continual and constant problem in our spiritual growth.

• **VERSE 14** The tribe of Joseph refers to the tribes of Ephraim and Manasseh, Joseph's sons. Joshua agreed that two lots should be given to them, Manasseh dwelling next to Ephraim on the West Bank, and the other part of Manasseh on the east bank of the Jordan River.

CHAPTER 18:
DIVISION OF THE REMAINING LAND

• **VERSE 1** Sacrifices to God only took place at the tabernacle at Shiloh, the spiritual gathering of the people.

• **VERSES 4-6** Three men from each tribe were chosen as a survey team to mark the territory and draw the boundaries. Usually the boundaries were by cities, rivers, valleys, and mountains.

• **VERSES 11-12** Benjamin dwelt around northern Jerusalem, a narrow strip that went from Jordan through Bethel.

CHAPTER 19:
THE OTHER TRIBES' PORTIONS

• **VERSES 1-8** Simeon became the southernmost tribe in Israel, near Kadesh-Barnea and Beersheba, a vast desert area.

• **VERSES 10-16** Zebulun got the Valley of Megiddo, Haifa to Mount Gilboa.

• **VERSES 17-23** Issachar received the area south of the Sea of Galilee.

• **VERSES 24-31** Asher received the beautiful Mediterranean coastal area from Haifa to Sidon.

• **VERSES 32-39** Naphtali received the area around the Sea of Galilee.

• **VERSES 40-46** Dan got the area known as the Hula Valley, before the Sea of Galilee, with the Golan on the right and Lebanese mountains on the left, up to Mount Hermon.

• **VERSES 49-50** Mount Ephraim was in the center part of the land, the ancient city of Samaria or Shechem.

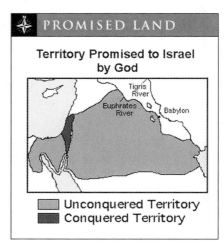

CHAPTER 20:
CITIES OF REFUGE

•**VERSES 4-5** Six cities of refuge were established where you could flee and be safe from the avenger of blood. It was less than a day's run for each city.

CHAPTER 21:
CITIES OF THE LEVITES

•**VERSE 21** The cities of refuge belonged to the Levites.

•**VERSE 43** The Lord gave it all to them, but they didn't take it all. God gave salvation to all, but not all will take it.

CHAPTER 22:
EASTERN TRIBES RETURN

•**VERSE 1** Moses asked them to conquer the land, leaving their wives and children here. The land has been won, and the tribes received their portion.

•**VERSE 12** The house of Israel was ready to attack, already lapsing into idolatry, offering sacrifices to God other than at the tabernacle.

•**VERSES 23-28** A memorial to worship the true and the living God. They had no intention of offering sacrifices there.

CHAPTER 23:
JOSHUA'S FAREWELL

•**VERSE 1** Since conquering the land, Reuben, Gad, and Manasseh had gone back to the other side 17 years later.

•**VERSES 7-12** Joshua commanded to remain separate from these people and refrain from intermarrying. God isn't opposed of mixing races—that's not at all what this is advocating. God was preserving a race in order to bring His Son through them.

Any kind of superior or inferior race is wrong. For in Christ He has made us one, whether Jews or Gentiles,

Barbarian, Scythian, bond or free; we are new creatures in Christ Jesus.

•**VERSE 15** Even as God has watched over you for good, God will watch over you for evil. Cleave to the Lord, love the Lord, and serve the Lord.

CHAPTER 24:
CHOOSE WHOM YOU WILL SERVE

•**VERSE 1** This is in the center of the land between Mount Ebal and Gerizim.

•**VERSE 3** God speaking a word of prophecy through Joshua to the people.

•**VERSE 15** Joshua speaks the marvelous works of God, and challenges them to choose whom they're going to serve, recognizing that God has given man the capacity of choice. Each person chooses—not "if" you will serve, but "whom" you will serve.

Though he's old and stricken in years, he still rules his house. It's marvelous when the husband, the father, can speak for his house.

•**VERSES 19-20** God is a jealous God, and when you turn your back upon Him, He won't take that lightly but will bring His judgments upon you.

☮ CALVARY DISTINCTIVE

"**Choose you this day whom ye will serve**" (Joshua 24:15).

This is the clear teaching of choice given to us by God; He expects us to make a choice.

STUDY QUESTIONS FOR JOSHUA

1. When the Israelites crossed over the Jordan into the Promised Land, we are reminded of their exodus from Egypt when they crossed the Red Sea. How were these events related? (Joshua 3:14-17; Exodus 14:15-29).

2. We all make mistakes in life. Although Joshua was a great leader, what was the mistake he made twice in Joshua 7:11-12 and 9:14-18?

3. Even though Rahab was not an Israelite, her faith earned her a place in the genealogy of Jesus Christ. What was the incredible thing she did, and who did it benefit? (Joshua chapter 2 and Joshua 6:22-25).

4. The children of Israel didn't take all the land promised to them. How is this a lesson in our spiritual walk? (Joshua 13:1-2).

5. At the end of Joshua's life, he exhorts the Israelites to fear the Lord. In Joshua 24:15 he says, "Choose this day whom you will serve." Who will you serve? God is asking this question today. Use the last part of this verse for your answer.

THE BOOK OF
JUDGES

AUTHOR OF THE BOOK:
The author is unknown, but Jewish tradition says it was written by Samuel.

PERIOD OF WRITING:
Exactly when it was written is unknown, but most likely around 1000 BC during the early period of the kings.

TYPE OF BOOK:
Historical

THEME:
Defeat and disappointment.

INTRODUCTION:
The book of Judges covers the historic period of the nation of Israel from the death of Joshua to the beginning of the kings. It is accepted that the time period is about 300 to 400 years.

The book gets its name from the 13 different judges that God chose in the time of spiritual declension. They were leaders but were never fully empowered by the people as rulers. This was an interim period between Joshua and the establishing of a monarchy when Saul became the first king over Israel.

During this time Israel had 13 declensions, 13 revivals, 13 periods of captivity, and 13 periods of deliverance from the oppression of the enemy. It's a sad, tragic story of their failure to consistently worship and honor God.

CHAPTER 1:
CANAANITES LEFT IN THE LAND

NOTE: The book of Judges does not follow a precise chronological order.

•**VERSE 1** The book of Joshua closed with the people in the land but much of the land was not yet conquered. They hadn't completely driven out the enemies or taken the territories that God had promised unto them.

When Joshua died, the people had inquired, "Who shall go first to take the land that God has given?"

•**VERSES 2-3** Judah received land south of Jerusalem. Simeon's lot was south of Judah, toward Beersheba. Judah said to Simeon, "Help us take our portion, and then we'll help you take your portion."

•**VERSES 5-6** "Adoni" means lord. He was the lord of Bezek, or king of Bezek.

•**VERSE** 7 Lord Bezek conquered 70 kings and cut off their great toes and thumbs. He said, "As I have done, now God has requited unto me."

The Scripture declares, "For in the same manner in which ye judge, ye shall be judged: and whatever measure you mete, it shall be measured out to you" (Matthew 7:2).

•**VERSE** 13 Othniel was the nephew of Caleb, or the cousin of Achsah.

•**VERSES** 28-31 "When you come into the land, you're to utterly drive out the inhabitants thereof." Here is a failure on their part to obey the voice of God.

Their rationale was, "We could live peaceably and they can be our servants." Whatever the rationale, it's wrong if it's opposed to God.

So often we're guilty, as the children of Israel, of disobeying the commandment of the Lord because we don't understand why God commanded it.

HEBREW KEY WORD

adoni = lord or master (1:5).

CHAPTER 2:
THE NEXT GENERATION

•**VERSES** 1-2 They broke the covenant. God is always faithful to His side of the covenant. It is man who breaks his promise with God.

•**VERSE** 3 These people that weren't destroyed became a snare. Soon we find them worshiping gods that were left in the land. It was a constant problem through their history.

•**VERSES** 4-5 The people wept and sacrificed unto God, but they didn't change. That is typical of people today. They weep, but they don't change. There's no value to their repentance.

The children of Israel have a form of religion, a form of godliness, but don't have a true repentance.

•**VERSE** 10 The parents failed to pass on to their children the power and work of God. The purpose of the Passover was to relate God's great deliverance out of the hand of the Egyptians. Evidently they had ceased observing the Passover.

Rarely does a powerful work of God continue into a second generation. "God has no grandchildren." Each person must have his own personal relationship with God.

•**VERSE** 13 Ashtaroth is the goddess of heaven, Ashtart to the Greeks, the female deity of ancient history.

•**VERSES** 14-15 The faithfulness of God to keep His word is something that we want to remember—blessings upon those who will obey, curses upon those who will forsake Him.

•**VERSES** 16-19 This is a brief summary of the book of Judges.

CHAPTER 3:
JUDGES OTHNIEL, EHUD, AND SHAMGAR

•**VERSE** 7 The groves were places of extremely licentious worship.

•**VERSE** 9 Othniel married Caleb's daughter since taking the city Kirjath near Hebron. So Othniel became the first judge over Israel.

•**VERSE** 11 Forty years is the time of a generation. So when the judge died, they went back to the old apostasy, not carrying over to the second generation.

•**VERSE** 16 A cubit is about 18 inches.

•**VERSE** 30 The land rested for 80 years.

•**VERSE** 31 Evidently he was plowing with his oxen when the Philistines came over the hill. He goes after them with an ox goad—and killed 600 men. Shamgar was the third judge of Israel. That's about all we know.

CHAPTER 4:
DEBORAH AND BARAK DEFEAT SISERA

•**VERSE 2** Hazor was a large fortified city, 15 miles north of the Sea of Galilee.

•**VERSES 4-5** Deborah, a prophetess, dwelt between Ramah and Bethel, five miles north of Jerusalem. Many exclude women to serve God, but God doesn't.

•**VERSES 11-12** Moses' father-in-law's family dwelt with the children of Israel, but were traitors informing Sisera that they were in Mount Tabor with an army.

CHAPTER 5:
THE SONG OF DEBORAH

•**VERSE 6** Shamgar is mentioned, but no more is written of him in the text.

The people were living in fear, and they wouldn't take the main roads to travel. They were oppressed by their enemies who possessed the land.

•**VERSE 8** They were disarmed and had nothing.

•**VERSE 11** They had forsaken God, so God allowed their enemies to ambush them with bows and arrows as they came to the water.

•**VERSES 16-17** The question: Why didn't other tribes come to help?

•**VERSES 20-22** God fought with them. The mud from the flood bogged down their chariots in the Valley of Megiddo, and they were destroyed.

•**VERSE 23** The curse of Meroz was the curse of doing nothing, taking a neutral position, withdrawing from helping in the work of God. It is tragic that many people today are guilty of the same thing: non-involvement. When God calls, it's our responsibility to respond.

•**VERSE 31** The purpose of these songs were to remember God's delivering power.

CHAPTER 6:
THE CALL OF GIDEON

•**VERSE 4** Gaza is the southernmost point along the Mediterranean. When they got to Gaza, they had gone through the entire land.

•**VERSE 11** Gideon was hiding from the Midianites as he was threshing the wheat. If the Midianites had caught him, they would have taken the wheat.

•**VERSE 15** People have trouble responding to God's call.

God called Moses and he said, "Lord, how can I go before Pharaoh? I'm not eloquent in speech."

The Lord called Jeremiah and he said, "Lord, how can I stand before kings? I'm young, no one's going to listen to me."

God called Gideon and he said, "Lord, how can I deliver? My family's nothing, and I'm the least of my household."

☪ CALVARY DISTINCTIVE

"Behold, my family is poor in Manasseh and I am the least in my father's house" (Judges 6:15).

When we don't have confidence in our own power, we know that if the work is going to be done, it has to be done by the Lord.

•**VERSE 16** God gave to Gideon the key to success, "I will be with thee." That's the key: learning to work together with the Lord.

•**VERSE 24** God called Gideon to deliver Israel from oppression of the Midianites, but he calls the altar Jehovah-shalom, "God our peace." He is looking beyond the battle to God's peace—even in the midst of the conflict.

•**VERSE 25** Gideon's dad worshiped the idol of Baal in a grove.

•**VERSE 32** "Jerubbaal" means let Baal plead for himself.

•**VERSES 33-35** South of Manasseh were the tribes Ephraim, Benjamin, Judah and Simeon; they were not brought into this battle, only the tribes that were around the Valley of Megiddo, known as Jezreel. This is where 132,000 Midianites had encamped.

•**VERSES 36-40** People seek to discern the voice of God by offering a fleece before the Lord, to see if it is truly God speaking to their heart. I don't know how valid fleeces are for children of the Lord to ascertain the will of God.

In the Old Testament they cast lots to ascertain the will of God. In the book of Acts the disciples cast lots to ascertain who should take Judas' place. But this was prior to the descent of the Holy Spirit upon the church.

After the descent of the Holy Spirit, we do not read of casting lots or using fleeces to ascertain the will of God. The Holy Spirit had begun to direct the church; there was a greater certainty in ascertaining the will of God.

CHAPTER 7:
GIDEON DEFEATS THE MIDIANITES

•**VERSE 1** The well of Harod is still there today.

•**VERSE 2** Gideon gathered together 32,000 men against 135,000 Midianites. God doesn't want people praising the instrument, but praising Him.

☙ CALVARY DISTINCTIVE

"... lest Israel vaunt themselves against Me, saying, 'Mine own hand hath saved me'" (Judges 7:2).

God wants to work, but God wants the glory for the work that He does. That's why He uses the simple things of this world to confound the wise.

•**VERSE 3** The reason God relieved the fearful was they were apt to panic and flee, leaving that flank exposed.

•**VERSE 15** There are three confirmations to the call of God to Gideon.

Gideon tested to make sure the angel was real—"Let me bring out an offering," and he saw the miracle there. Then he put out the fleece, and finally, he slips down into the camp to listen, and God confirms once more.

•**VERSE 19** The beginning of the middle watch is about midnight.

•**VERSES 21-22** Gideon's men stood there blowing their trumpets and holding up the pitchers. The Midianites became so startled, they swung their swords at each other in the darkness and then ran. God has interesting ways of turning the enemy on his heel.

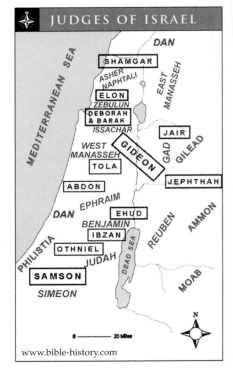

www.bible-history.com

CHAPTER 8:
GIDEON CONTINUES THE CONQUEST

•**VERSES 1-3** The Ephraimites were troublemakers to Gideon, but Gideon was gracious, having a true humility and an admirable quality. When the Lord called him to lead the Israelites against Midian he responded in a very sincere way.

•**VERSE 6** They didn't want to be guilty of helping—just in case they were defeated, they would retaliate. They refused to feed Gideon's men.

•**VERSES 22-23** They wanted the family of Gideon to rule over Israel—thereby his sons and his grandsons, setting up a dynasty and a monarchy.

•**VERSE 27** An ephod is a gold robe, but it became a snare. People traveled to Gideon's house to see this golden ephod that he made from the gold of the Midianites and began to worship it. Gideon made a mistake. When he saw the people worshiping this ephod, he should have melted it down into a gold brick.

•**VERSE 29** "Jerubbaal" is Gideon.

•**VERSE 30** He had 70 sons.

CHAPTER 9:
ABIMELECH'S CONSPIRACY

•**VERSE 7** Mount Gerizim is above the city of Shechem, which is a natural amphitheater. From the top of Gerizim you can be heard clearly in the valley.

Jesus spoke to a crowd of 10,000 people there and they were able to hear Him without amplifying systems.

•**VERSE 20** Let there be strife between the men of Shechem and Abimelech.

•**VERSE 21** Jotham got away from them.

•**VERSE 25** The men of Shechem began to set an ambush for the people at the top of the mountains, and robbed all of those that were going along that way.

•**VERSE 28** In other words, "He's an outsider. We ought to be serving Hamor and his family instead."

•**VERSE 53** Millstones are like lava rock, as big as four feet high, weighing as much as 500 pounds. It is chiseled round, with a hole in the middle, and then the stick goes through the center to roll.

They would hook oxen to it and circle this stone groove. As the oxen would go around, the ladies would pour their wheat in the little groove, and it would grind the wheat into flour.

CHAPTER 10:
THE PHILISTINES AND AMMONITES

•**VERSE 6** This is the sixth recorded time that they forsook God and worshiped and served other gods.

•**VERSES 7-9** Reuben, Gad, and half the tribe of Manasseh were oppressed by the Amorites that were actually in the territory before they had come. Then the children of Ammon passed over the Jordan and began to fight in the land of Judah, Benjamin, and Ephraim.

•**VERSE 14** People say it doesn't matter which god you serve: all roads lead to heaven. False. It really makes a big difference when you're in trouble and need help. God says, "Cry unto the gods that you have chosen to serve." But they can't help.

CHAPTER 11:
JEPHTHAH'S VOW

•**VERSE 39** Some teach that he gave her to God to perpetual virginity—to keep her from ever marrying, because of the vow her father had made.

God forbade human sacrifice. Human sacrifice was a common practice among the pagans, but was strictly forbidden by God. Jephthah did it of his own will, not because God demanded it.

CHAPTER 12:
CONFLICT WITH EPHRAIM

•**VERSE 1** The men of Ephraim came to Jephthah as they did with Gideon years earlier. Gideon was very diplomatic and mild-mannered, but Jephthah was the son of a harlot, a tough cookie.

•**VERSES 2-3** Notice all the I's and the my's in these verses. It demonstrates his egocentricity.

•**VERSE 6** The men from Ephraim couldn't pronounce the "sh" sound and they pronounced it "Sibboleth." By this they knew that they were Ephraimites and they were wiped out.

•**VERSE 8** The tenth judge was Ibzan from Bethlehem.

•**VERSE 11** Elon became the eleventh judge. He was from the tribe of Zebulun.

LIST OF JUDGES

(IN ALPHABETICAL ORDER)

ABDON

DEBORAH

EHUD

ELON

GIDEON

IBZAN

JAIR

JEPHTHAH

OTHNIEL

SAMSON

SHAMGAR

TOLA

CHAPTER 13:
THE BIRTH OF SAMSON

•**VERSE 5** A Nazarite vow required that you refrain from cutting your hair or drinking wine. Samson was to be a Nazarite from his birth, dedicated and committed to God.

•**VERSE 18** That word "secret" in the Hebrew is actually wonderful.

•**VERSE 25** The valleys of Zorah and Eshtaol are eight miles from Jerusalem. It was part of the inheritance of the tribe of Dan. This is where Samson grew up and God's Spirit began to move on him at various times.

HEBREW KEY WORD

piliy = secret, wonderful (13:18).

CHAPTER 14:
SAMSON'S MARRIAGE

•**VERSE 1** Timnath was a Philistine city.

•**VERSE 18** An interesting phrase in those days was calling your wife a heifer.

CHAPTER 15:
SAMSON BURNS THE PHILISTINE CROPS

•**VERSE 1** The chamber is the bedroom.

•**VERSES 2-3** He paid the dowry and his father-in-law offered the younger sister, but Samson didn't appreciate that he gave his bride away. He decided to get even with the Philistines for getting the secret out of his bride.

•**VERSE 5** If you've ever seen a dog with a tin can on his tail, imagine the panic of the jackals with torches on their tails running through the wheat fields, ripe for harvest, golden brown, and then burned to the ground.

•**VERSE 17** "Ramathlehi" means the hill of the jawbone.

•**VERSE 18** It was June, so it was very hot and dry. Samson thought he was going to die of thirst.

•**VERSE 19** He changed the name to "Enhakkore," which is the well of him that cried.

•**VERSE 20** Samson exposed himself to needless kinds of desires and lusts in the camp of the enemy. The Philistines had legalized prostitution and they had loose morals. That's probably what drew him there.

CHAPTER 16:
SAMSON AND DELILAH

•VERSE 3 Hebron is 25 miles from Gaza. He carried these gates to a hill before Hebron. In the morning the men from Gaza sent a regiment to get their gates back. Again, going into the territory of the enemy, setting himself up.

•VERSE 13 Samson is guilty of compromise, which is always dangerous. When she said, "What is the secret of your strength?" he should have said, "I'll never tell." But he thinks he's clever, yet he's getting closer to the truth.

•VERSE 17 The word "Nazarite" is separated. The strength of Samson lay in his commitment of his life to God, which was done before his birth. The law for the Nazarite is described in Numbers chapter 6.

•VERSE 20 The Lord was with Samson as long as he kept that vow, even though he wasn't always doing the right thing. The Lord didn't desert him until he deserted the Lord, when the vow was broken.

He was blind to his own spiritual state. It is possible to be self-deceived about your own spiritual state. "If we say we have no sin, we deceive ourselves, the truth isn't in us" (1 John 1:8).

•VERSE 21 Usually an ox would push the pole around in a circle to roll the millstone to grind the flour. It now became the occupation of Samson.

This is the most colorful picture of giving yourself over to unbridled lust, living in sin. They find themselves bound by the power of sin, ultimately becoming a grind.

•VERSE 22 I see the marvelous grace of God. Even though we fail Him, He will not fail us. If we will just turn back to Him, He will be merciful and gracious.

On a boring job there's plenty of time to think, and I imagine Samson thought of his mistakes as he was pushing that post around. Many times God has to bring us to the bottom so we'll look up.

HEBREW KEY WORD

Nazarite = separated, consecrated (16:17).

CHAPTER 17:
MICAH'S IDOLATRY

NOTE: The remainder of the book of Judges is not in chronological order. Samson is the end of the historical chronology.

The next few chapters are an appendix to the book of Judges examining Israel's moral decay during the period of the judges, giving an insight to the moral corruptness, God's people lacking a real consciousness of God as their King. Some stories take us clear back to the time immediately after Joshua.

•VERSE 5 Micah was making images that represented God to him. God expressly forbids making any graven image of God to bow down and worship—the second commandment. He was not turning away from Jehovah in the sense of making an image of Baal or Molech or the pagan gods.

He seeks to worship Jehovah together with the teraphim and the ephod, making a worship center in his house, having his own little idols where he goes to pray and worship. This was expressly forbidden. He lost the consciousness of God's presence, thus he needed something to remind him.

•VERSE 6 This is an insight to the moral degeneracy. Rather than being ruled by God, they did what was right in their own eyes. It was a period of anarchy.

•VERSE 10 Here is a deterioration in the Levite; a professional religionist, selling himself for an annual salary of ten shekels of silver, a new suit, and his daily food.

•VERSE 13 The only reason Micah wanted the Levite priest was to prosper. He was using God for gain.

CHAPTER 18:
DANITES SETTLE IN LAISH

•VERSES 1-2 They were unable to drive the Philistines out of Ashdod, Ashkelon, and Gaza. They were occupying a small territory 20 miles from Jerusalem in the little Valley of Eshkol. They sent men to look where the tribe of Dan might inhabit for farming.

•VERSE 7 The people in Laish lived carelessly. They didn't have business or trade with anybody as they were over the Lebanese mountain range, isolated and easy prey.

They dwelt in a beautiful section of land, past the city where the Jordan River flowed. The water was clear and it was good farming territory.

•VERSE 29 They captured Laish and destroyed the inhabitants. A good portion of the tribe of Dan inhabited the upper part of the Hula Valley where the headwaters of the Jordan River come out from Mount Hermon. And thus, the city was called Dan. The river was named Jordan, or "out of Dan," because the headwaters of the Jordan River comes from the city of Dan.

CHAPTER 19:
THE LEVITE AND HIS CONCUBINE

•VERSE 1 God intended Israel to be a theocracy. But the people didn't want

to submit to God. Thus there was confusion; everybody was doing what he felt was right.

It's wrong for a priest to have a concubine. This followed the pagan practices of the people.

•VERSE 15 In those days they didn't have hotels. People were gracious and allowed you to stay in their home.

•VERSE 22 God judged and destroyed Sodom and now we see the moral depravity among His own people in the tribe of Benjamin.

•VERSE 24 In Jesus there is neither male nor female, just a beautiful equality. Jesus elevated the woman from this place of the pagan cultures where she was put down and subjugated.

CHAPTER 20:
THE ISRAELITES FIGHT THE BENJAMITES

•VERSES 1-8 The tribes were horrified to get a torso, a leg, an arm, or a head. This man told them the evil that was done by the tribe of Benjamin, the city of Gibeah. And the people of Israel decided to go against them in battle.

CHAPTER 21:
WIVES FOR THE BENJAMITES

•VERSES 1-6 Most vows in the Bible are foolish. The Bible says quite a bit about keeping your mouth shut. When you go into the temple of the Lord, put a lock on your mouth lest you sin with your mouth.

•VERSES 8-12 No one from Jabeshgilead entered the vow, so they wiped out the city, killing the married women and the men. They took the virgins and brought them back, but there still weren't enough. It's covering one stupidity with a greater one.

•VERSES 19-21 Shiloh was the religious center at that particular time.

STUDY QUESTIONS FOR JUDGES

1. After the death of Joshua, there arose a generation which did not know the Lord. According to Judges 2:10-13, what was the result?

_____

_____

_____

2. Judges 2:16-19 gives a summary of the book. Write this summary in your own words.

_____

_____

_____

3. In Judges 16:17 we see Samson finally revealing the secret of his strength to Delilah. What was the secret?

_____

_____

_____

4. Like many who are called of God, Gideon was hesitant about being used as His instrument. What is the key to be successful in your service to God? (Judges 6:16; Exodus 3:12; and Joshua 1:5).

_____

_____

_____

5. Although we see the children of Israel weeping in Judges 2:4 as they were rebuked by the Lord, we still see them continuing their sin. How can we avoid making the same mistake? (2 Corinthians 7:10 and Revelation 2:5).

_____

_____

_____

THE BOOK OF
RUTH

AUTHOR OF THE BOOK:
Unknown, but Jewish tradition attributes it to Samuel.

PERIOD OF WRITING:
During the time of the judges. Others believe it was written during the reign of Solomon because of the references to David's throne and his genealogy.

TYPE OF BOOK:
Historical

THEME:
God's redemptive work in the midst of darkness.

INTRODUCTION:
The story of Ruth is an appendix to the book of Judges, and occurred when the judges were ruling over Israel. It was a time of spiritual confusion, apostasy, and moral declension. Yet, in the midst of it all, God was working out His plan in those hearts and lives that were open to Him.

The book of Ruth gives insight to how God works His purposes on the earth, even under adverse circumstances. It shows us the heart of God, as He desires to reach the whole world, not just the Jewish people.

We see the introduction of the kinsman-redeemer, where a close relative could take over the right of inheritance and redeem it when the heir was unable. We see this love story serving as a bright light in a dark time—God preparing a family through which He could reach out His love for the world to redeem us to Himself.

CHAPTER 1:
NAOMI AND RUTH

•**VERSE 2** They were from Ephra, which was the general area where Bethlehem was situated.

"Elimelech" means my God is King. "Naomi" is pleasantness. "Mahlon" means sickly, and "Chilion" means pining.

Children were named after circumstances of their birth. When Mahlon was born, perhaps he was premature. When his brother was born, he didn't look much better and called him "pining."

•**VERSE 5** Both of the boys died without having any children.

•**VERSE 8** During this family tragedy, these two girls showed a real depth of character. They were very kind to Naomi and comforted her. Naomi declared her wish that they also might receive this same degree of kindness.

•**VERSE 9** She encouraged the girls, "May you both find some good boys and get married. May you have a happy married life. May you find someone else, and may you live at rest in the house of your husband."

•**VERSES 16-17** A beautiful bond was created between daughter-in-law and mother-in-law.

•**VERSE 20** "Mara" means bitter. In other words, "Don't call me pleasant, call me bitter."

She blames the tragedy on God. "The Lord has dealt bitterly with me." We feel bitterness because we see death conceptually as being the end. We are inclined to blame God for tragedies, especially death. We know that man's days are appointed by God.

We are warned to be careful lest any root of bitterness take hold because of its defiling effect on our lives (Hebrews 12:15).

Bitterness is an attitude that I choose because of the circumstances that I face. I don't have to become bitter—I choose to become bitter. Other people might go through similar circumstances, but they become better people because they learn to commit and trust in God all the more.

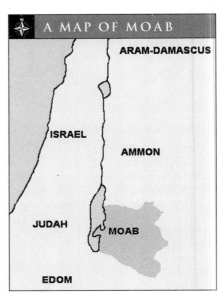

A MAP OF MOAB

HEBREW KEY WORD

mara = bitter (1:20).

CHAPTER 2:
RUTH GLEANS IN THE FIELD OF BOAZ

•**VERSE 1** In the fourth chapter Boaz calls him, "our brother Elimelech," so he's related, perhaps a full or half brother who became a very wealthy man.

•**VERSE 2** In the law, God made a provision for the poor. The law declared that when you had fields, you could only harvest them once. You couldn't go back through to pick the second time.

This commandment was given so the poor of the land could come into your field after your harvesters had gone through.

•**VERSE 3** Instead of "her hap," today we would say, "It so happened." But that's not so. Nothing just so happens; nothing is a coincidence. When you're God's child, and God's hand is on your life, there are no coincidences.

God held Ruth by the hand and directed her to Boaz's field.

•**VERSE 4** Boaz shows characteristics of a godly man. The period of the judges was a time of spiritual declension and apostasy. Here's a man who's walking with God, and greets his servants by saying, "The Lord be with you!" Evidently there's a good management relationship here with the servants.

•**VERSE 12** God is often portrayed as a loving parent who protects His children, similar to a mother hen who lovingly protects her little chicks. When danger threatens, the little chicks run under the mother who ruffles out her feathers and stands to protect them against danger. God is pictured in this way in the Old Testament.

•**VERSE 14** Boaz showed a definite interest in her.

CHAPTER 3:
A KINSMAN-REDEEMER

•**VERSE 9** God loves the family and seeks to preserve it. Therefore, His law stated that if a man married a wife, but died before they had any children, then it was his brother's obligation to take that woman as his wife. The firstborn son would then be named after the dead brother so that the family's name would continue in Israel.

Now, because Elimelech and his two sons had died, the family name was about to be extinguished. So Ruth was actually asking Boaz to take the part of the *goel*, the kinsman-redeemer, and to have a son who could be named after the family of Elimelech.

She was asking, "Cover me with this covering of the family, because you are the kinsman-redeemer."

•**VERSE 10** Boaz was a godly man.

Boaz was probably an older man. He was very flattered that this younger girl would ask him to fulfill this kinsman relationship.

•**VERSE 11** Ruth's reputation had gotten around. She was a virtuous girl, and she worshiped and served God by taking care of her mother-in-law.

•**VERSE 13** They would not always fulfill this part. Sometimes they didn't like the gal. So, if they didn't want her, they would take their shoe and hand it to her. It was almost like saying, "Hey, you're a dirty shoe, as far as I'm concerned." They were giving up their right.

She then would spit in the man's face, and he would be called, "The man from whom the shoe was loosed in Israel." These men were considered contemptible because they didn't fulfill the family obligations—no family loyalty.

•**VERSE 14** It was still so dark you couldn't recognize anybody.

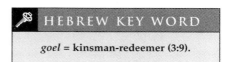

HEBREW KEY WORD

goel = **kinsman-redeemer (3:9).**

CHAPTER 4:
BOAZ'S LOVE FOR RUTH

•**VERSES 1-4** Jewish law declared that whenever a parcel of land was sold, a reversionary clause was included, giving the original owner the right to buy the land back again within a specified period. If they were too poor to buy the land back when the time of redemption came, then one of the family members could buy it so that it could remain in the family.

When Naomi and Elimelech had moved to Moab, they had sold their parcel, and per the reversionary clause, the time to redeem it was now.

•**VERSE 6** The nearest kinsman was already married and had children lined up for the inheritance.

•**VERSES 9-10** Because of Boaz's love for Ruth, he bought the field in order that he might obtain the bride. His primary interest was not the field at all. He was a mighty man of wealth and didn't need another field. He bought the field in order to obtain the bride.

He becomes a very beautiful picture of Jesus Christ, who bought the world in order that He might purchase His bride, the church, out of the world. He was not interested necessarily in the planet earth as such, but interested and in love with His bride. Jesus purchased the world in order to take His treasure (Matthew 13:44).

•**VERSE 12** The story of Tamar, Judah, and Pharez found in Genesis 38:6-29 was a similar situation of the obligation of a kinsman to raise up a child for the dead son. The son who was born was called Pharez. His name is found in the genealogy of Jesus Christ, so he was Elimelech's ancestor. This was a similar situation, an older man fulfilling the kinsman part, raising up a son.

•**VERSE 16** She wet-nursed her grandson, which was very common in those days.

•**VERSE 17** "Obed" means worshiper.

•**VERSES 18-22** Ten generations are listed from Pharez unto David. Herein is the background of the genealogy of David, which also becomes the background to the genealogy of Jesus Christ.

Christ came through David, who came through Pharez, who was born of Tamar by Judah—quite an unsavory situation. Here we see a Moabitess, a people cursed by God, who could not come into the house of God until the tenth generation.

This is the line of Christ, identifying with all backgrounds in life.

STUDY QUESTIONS FOR RUTH

1. Describe what happened to Naomi after she moved to Moab (Ruth 1:2-5). How did these circumstances affect her, according to Ruth 1:20?

_____

_____

_____

2. As a child of God, we desire to be led by the Lord and to do His will in our lives. How did God lead Ruth and how does He lead us today? (Ruth 2:3).

_____

_____

_____

3. Throughout this book, we see that Ruth is a virtuous and hardworking woman. Write out Ruth 2:12 and record how that blessing came true for her.

_____

_____

_____

4. Boaz told Ruth in chapter 3, verse 11, that he would do for her all that she requested. What exactly is she requesting in Ruth 3:9? (Deuteronomy 25:5-10).

_____

_____

_____

5. We read in Ruth 4:9-10 that Boaz agreed to buy Naomi's field and to take Ruth as his wife. How were the actions of Boaz a picture of what Jesus has done for us? (Matthew 13:44).

_____

_____

_____

THE BOOK OF
FIRST SAMUEL

AUTHOR OF THE BOOK:
Samuel; the prophets Nathan and Gad finished it after Samuel's death.

PERIOD OF WRITING:
11th century BC.

TYPE OF BOOK:
Historical

THEME:
Israel transitions into the time of the kings.

INTRODUCTION:
This book presents the personal history of Samuel who was the last of the judges. The book of Samuel is a transitional period in Israel's history. The nation moved from a theocracy to a monarchy. However, it wasn't truly a theocracy because they weren't following God as King. They were moving from an anarchy—quoting the book of Judges, "And every man did that which was right in his own sight"—into a monarchy, having an earthly king. This book ushers in the period of the kings among the children of Israel.

First Samuel covers the life of Samuel, the life of Saul, and the life of David.

This book in the Septuagint is called *The First Book of the Kings*. First and Second Samuel and First and Second Kings in the Septuagint are called *First, Second, Third, and Fourth Kings.*

CHAPTER 1:
HANNAH PRAYS FOR A SON

•**VERSE 1** "Elkanah" means acquired of God.

•**VERSE 3** Shiloh was the religious center and Eli was the high priest at that time.

•**VERSE 7** There was friction between the two wives as they bid for the love of one man.

•**VERSE 11** Hannah had been praying for a son for a long time, yet there was no answer. God delayed the answer, seeking to bring her into alignment with His purposes (2 Chronicles 16:9).

God was waiting to bring Hannah's heart completely toward the things of God, and that which God wanted. God needed a man to lead Israel during these desperate days of transition.

Hannah prayed, "Lord, if You will give to me a son, I will give him back to You all the days of his life." When God brought her to this place of commitment, the Lord answered her prayer.

James says, "You ask, and receive not, because you ask amiss, that you might consume it upon your own lusts" (James 4:3). Prayer can be looking at God as Santa Claus, instead of seeking His will for our lives (1 John 5:14-15).

•VERSE 18 She believed the word of the Lord and had a change of attitude. Herein is one of the marks of faith—acting as though you have it before you actually have it.

•VERSE 19 Ramah; north of Jerusalem, the modern city of Ramallah.

•VERSE 20 "Samuel" means asked of God.

•VERSE 28 This is where we get the dedication of babies, following this same pattern of Hannah. We recognize our children are gifts from God, and we give them back to Him.

HEBREW KEY WORD

Samuel = asked of God, or heard of God (1:20).

CHAPTER 2:
ELI'S WICKED SONS

•VERSE 1 The prayer of Hannah has a depth of spirituality. Mary patterned Hannah when she came to her cousin Elisabeth while expecting Jesus.

•VERSE 3 You can do the right thing with the wrong attitude and it counts for nothing, as God weighs your actions. What motivates your actions?

•VERSE 5 Hannah's prayer seems to gloat a little here over this woman that troubled her for so long.

•VERSE 8 It is foolish to take this picturesque speech of Hannah and say the Bible teaches the ancient theory that the earth was set upon pillars. This is not a divine revelation at all.

•VERSE 9 I am the strongest when I am aware of my weakness, and am weakest when I think I am strong. When we rely and trust in the strength of the Lord, then we are truly strong.

•VERSES 16-17 They were bullying the people, and men began to abhor the offering of the Lord. What a horrible sin when you turn people from God because of your attitude of greed, and you cause people to blaspheme.

•VERSE 22 They were supposedly representing God as the priests, yet were immoral, crooked, and perverse.

•VERSE 25 They had gone too far; the Lord wanted to wipe them out.

•VERSE 35 Here is the prophecy of the new priesthood, Jesus Christ, the High Priest after the order of Melchizedek.

CHAPTER 3:
THE LORD SPEAKS TO SAMUEL

•VERSE 1 "Precious" means scarce.

•VERSE 13 Eli's refusal to discipline his sons brought God's judgment upon his house.

•VERSE 14 They can't offer any sacrifice to cleanse their sin.

CHAPTER 4:
THE PHILISTINES CAPTURE THE ARK

•VERSE 3 They were beginning to look at the ark of the covenant as a good luck amulet.

•VERSE 9 Bringing the ark actually had a reverse effect. It inspired the Philistines so that they attacked.

•VERSE 21 "Ichabod" means the glory is departed.

CHAPTER 5:
PHILISTINES' PROBLEMS WITH THE ARK

•**VERSE 7** They began to relate these things to the ark of the covenant being with them.

•**VERSES 11-12** They were plagued and didn't know exactly what to do with it.

CHAPTER 6:
THE ARK RETURNED TO ISRAEL

•**VERSE 9** If the cows wander in the fields, or turn back for their calves, then it was an accident or a coincidence.

•**VERSE 16** They recognized that it was the hand of the Lord against them.

•**VERSE 19** It was strictly forbidden to look at the ark of God, except for the priests. But these curious men began to peer at it and 70 of them died.

•**VERSE 20** That absolute holiness of God is deadly for sinful man to approach. None of us dare try to stand before a holy God by our righteousness.

On the mount when God gave the law, He said, "Now put a fence around it. Don't let anybody approach lest they be slain by the presence of God."

The high priest could only approach once a year, and that after many sacrifices. Some of the high priests had died. The holiness of God was something that they highly respected. Tragically, we don't respect the holiness of God today.

CHAPTER 7:
REVIVAL AND DELIVERANCE

•**VERSE 3** Ashtaroth was the goddess of sexual love and fertility.

•**VERSE 9** Samuel exercised his ministry of intercessory prayer.

•**VERSE 12** The Ebenezer stone was a stone of memorial.

The help of the Lord in the past is a prophecy to the help of the Lord in the future, giving assurance that God is going to see me all the way. The Lord will complete that which concerns you; having begun a good work in your life, He will finish it (Philippians 1:6).

•**VERSE 13** Up to this point the Philistines had won every battle. Now as they set up the stone, it was the beginning of God's victory over their enemies.

So as God brings victories, set up your Ebenezer stone, "Praise the Lord. He helped me this far," marking the places of victory and God's work in your life.

HEBREW KEY WORD

Ebenezer = **the stone of help (7:12).**

CHAPTER 8:
ISRAEL DEMANDS A KING

•**VERSE 2** Beersheba is in the south.

•**VERSE 3** Samuel was a godly man, yet his sons weren't. They coveted money and perverted judgment for bribes.

•**VERSES 4-5** The elders of Israel demanded they have a king like the rest of the nations.

•**VERSE 7** A nation governed by God is a theocracy. These people rejected a theocratic form of government and demanded a monarchy. However, God was not faithfully represented to the people by their rulers.

CHAPTER 9:
GOD REVEALS THE KING TO SAMUEL

•**VERSE 9** "Seer" implies a man who has spiritual perception. "Seer" was the original name for a prophet.

•**VERSE 15** The Lord speaks in Samuel's ear.

CHAPTER 10:
SAMUEL ANOINTS SAUL AS KING

•**VERSE 6** We see that Saul has many advantages: a good home, security, loving parents, handsome, big—those all mean nothing compared with the Spirit of God anointing him, changing his heart, and turning him into another man.

•**VERSE 26** The potential of men whose hearts have been touched by God is incomprehensible. Men who have committed their lives to Jesus Christ, whose hearts have truly been touched by God, have a potential of turning the world upside down.

•**VERSE 27** The children of Belial objected to Saul's reign. The children of Belial were evil men—Belial being a term for Satan—the children of the Devil. Saul returned to his home and went back to his work of farming.

CHAPTER 11:
SAUL DEFEATS THE AMMONITES

•**VERSE 7** This was a call to battle.

•**VERSE 11** God gave Saul a great victory, and catapulted him into the position of king. The people were looking for a man to lead their armies into battle against their enemies.

•**VERSE 13** At the beginning of Saul's reign, he had marvelous characteristics, such as humility. It is tragic that as Saul's life progressed, he lacked humility and had spiritual pride. But in this particular case he still showed signs of humility.

CHAPTER 12:
SAMUEL'S SPEECH

•**VERSE 1** Samuel's career as judge over Israel is ending, as the reigns of government are turned from a theocracy to a monarchy where Saul is ruling.

This is his farewell speech to the people and then he'll no longer be the leading public figure in Israel.

•**VERSE 2** The people recognized that God's hand was upon this young man, and he naturally grew into the position of a leader and judge over Israel.

•**VERSE 3** He is declaring his innocence before the people. Samuel had a very beautiful and remarkable career as the judge of Israel.

•**VERSE 7** He has justified himself, and now he is seeking to justify God.

•**VERSE 12** When faced with a crisis, rather than crying out unto God for His deliverance, they asked for a king. They were rejecting God as King.

•**VERSE 19** Repentance means a change. If it were true repentance, they would have said, "Get rid of Saul and let God reign over us."

The Lord requires repentance from sin, not just a sorrow for sin. So often we are sorrowful because of sin's consequences, but we go on doing it.

•**VERSE 21** If you are not serving God, you're serving something that can't help or deliver you.

•**VERSE 23** If God has commanded us to pray one for another, then our failure to pray is disobedient and sinful.

CHAPTER 13:
SAUL'S SINFUL OFFERING

•**VERSES 3-4** Jonathan was destroying the Philistines and Saul was blowing the trumpet, taking the glory.

•**VERSES 6-7** A tremendous formidable force of Philistines had come against them. People were deserting, crossing the Jordan, and going over to the other side.

•**VERSE 13** When you willfully disobey the commandment of God, you are doing foolishly.

God's ways are best, and for me to presume that I can improve on God's way is sheer folly.

•**VERSE 14** God rejected Saul as the continuing king.

•**VERSE 15** The Philistines have 30,000 chariots, 6,000 horsemen, and people like the sands of the sea.

•**VERSES 19-21** Although the Philistines and the people of the land had entered into the Iron Age, the Hebrews had not yet developed the capacity for smelting. When they sharpened their farm implements, the Philistines sharpened them since they didn't have blacksmiths in Israel.

The Philistines deliberately kept them from developing these skills and creating swords and fighting devices.

•**VERSE 22** That's not a very well-equipped army—600 men with clubs and sticks—against the 30,000 chariots and horsemen. There's no hope of victory.

CHAPTER 14:
JONATHAN'S VICTORY

•**VERSE 6** If the Lord wants to give the victory to Israel over the Philistines, He doesn't need a whole army. He can give the victory to one man as well as 600.

 CALVARY DISTINCTIVE

"... for there is no restraint to the LORD to save by many or by few" (1 Samuel 14:6).

All God needs is one person in harmony with His purpose and God can accomplish His desires through one man.

•**VERSE 24** Saul was humble in the beginning but is now manifesting real pride. This was a foolish curse and vow.

•**VERSE 27** He'd been chasing Philistines all day and was exhausted physically. Honey is a quick energy source and he was refreshed.

•**VERSE 44** Saul began with tremendous potential, but pride entered in. This man is gradually deteriorating before our very eyes, as he begins to exalt himself and turn from God.

CHAPTER 15:
SAUL'S DISOBEDIENCE

•**VERSE 1** Saul has shown a pattern of disobedience and has become self-willed, so the prophet is warning him.

God seeks to warn us from our self-willed path of destruction. God doesn't let us stumble into destruction; oftentimes there are repeated warnings (Proverbs 29:1).

•**VERSE 3** The practices of the Amalekites were corrupt. God ordered the eradication of a cancer within the society. They were like mad dogs. If you don't destroy them, they're going to hurt innocent people.

The Amalekites are a type of flesh in Scripture; God orders utter destruction of the flesh (Romans 8:13, 13:14).

•**VERSE 9** This is disobedience to God's command to utterly wipe out the Amalekites and their cattle and sheep.

A few hundred years later, when Esther was chosen queen in Persia, Haman sought to destroy the Jews because he hated this Jew, Mordecai, who refused to bow to him. Haman was a descendant of the king of the Amalekites, "Agag."

Saul almost cost Israel its whole national existence because he failed to completely obey the command of God.

If you don't bring your flesh to the cross and mortify the deeds of your flesh, but make allowance for the flesh, it will come back to destroy you.

•**VERSE 13** He's lying but using the spiritual language: "Blessed be thou of the Lord." Often spiritual jargon is used as a disguise.

•**VERSE 15** Saul has developed a pattern of making excuses, rather than repenting. Religious excuses are the most damnable of all.

•**VERSE 20** He was lying; he was not repenting. Now pride has filled his life and it's about to destroy him.

•**VERSE 22** God isn't interested in the sacrifices from a disobedient heart and life. God would rather you obey Him than sacrifice. Many times people are giving to God in order to cover their feelings of guilt. Giving to God isn't a sign of great spirituality.

The fat of rams is that which is burned in the sacrifices.

•**VERSE 23** Rebelling against God is as bad as witchcraft. Rebellion and stubbornness displease God.

•**VERSE 24** He said he feared the people, but he didn't. God wants a straight confession. Repentance is what God is seeking.

•**VERSE 29** The "Strength of Israel" is a reference to God.

•**VERSE 30** He says, "The Lord thy God" and not "The Lord my God."

•**VERSE 35** The word "repent" means change. God is changing His attitude toward Saul.

We have only one word to describe that change, "repent." We just read in verse 29, "God is not a man that He lies or repents."

We have to express the activities of God with human language, but the only word we have is "repent." It isn't a repentance as we think of repent in human terms.

CHAPTER 16:
SAMUEL ANOINTS DAVID

•**VERSE 2** Saul has strayed so far from the Lord that he would actually kill the prophet of God.

•**VERSE 13** Saul was still on the throne, though David is God's anointed choice for king. In the next few chapters Saul is going to do his best to hang on to that which is no longer rightfully his.

Satan, as Saul, seeks to hold on to that which is no longer rightfully his. But when you come against him in the authority of Jesus, he has to yield because he was defeated. You have to deal with him very firmly in prayer. You can have real victory in your life and bring victory to the lives of others through prayer.

•**VERSE 14** Satan couldn't exist unless God allowed him to exist, which means that he must be serving a purpose for God. If it were not for Satan then we would have no power of choice.

God has allowed Satan's rebellion, and for him to tempt us and make it difficult for us to serve God. It is a choice serving God in spite of the difficulties. Thus, God is assured that our love is genuine.

When the Spirit of God departs from our lives, the door is open for evil to come. The Spirit of God had departed from Saul, and God allowed an evil spirit to harass him.

•**VERSE 16** He was mean and sullen.

•**VERSE 21** Saul had always been a hero in David's eyes. David respected Saul right up to his death and thereafter. David never lost respect for this man.

•**VERSE 23** How long this went on we are not told.

CHAPTER 17:
DAVID AND GOLIATH

•**VERSE 2** The Elah Valley is 15 miles southwest of Jerusalem.

•**VERSES 3-11** In those days they'd yell and shout and psyche each other out for battle. The children of Israel had been pretty psyched out by Goliath, who came every day for 40 days.

•**VERSE 20** David went to the battlefield in the Elah Valley, 20 miles from Bethlehem.

•**VERSE 40** There are thousands of smooth round stones in this streambed in the Elah Valley.

•**VERSE 46** David was assured victory not only over the giant, but over the whole host of the Philistines.

CHAPTER 18:
SAUL'S JEALOUSY OF DAVID

•**VERSE 1** A bond between Saul's son Jonathan and David developed. They were two of a kind, both adventuresome and daring. Both had a great love for the Lord.

•**VERSE 2** At this point Saul had an admiration for this brave young kid, so he wouldn't let him go home.

•**VERSE 5** Though he was very young, he was set over a part of the army, which respected him very much.

•**VERSE 7** The women had praised Saul when he had come back from victory. He was used to this. Now in this particular case they praised David, and Saul became extremely jealous of him.

•**VERSE 8** He wasn't aware that God had anointed David to be the king over Israel. He began to suspect that the kingdom was in jeopardy.

•**VERSE 17** If Saul sent David out against the Philistines they'd kill him, and he wouldn't have to do it.

•**VERSE 27** Saul set up a dowry regarding the Philistines, and David went out and gave him double dowry. Saul was surprised. He figured David would get killed going out against the Philistines.

CHAPTER 19:
SAUL ATTEMPTS TO KILL DAVID

•**VERSE 6** Saul manifests schizophrenia. He had great depression. He had remorse and periods of change. He had spoken great words of love, and then tried to ram a javelin through David.

•**VERSE 17** She lied her way out of it.

CHAPTER 20:
DAVID AND JONATHAN'S OATH

•**VERSE 26** Saul didn't say anything the first day because he thought David was ceremonially unclean—perhaps he killed somebody and needed to go through the cleansing rites first before coming home.

•**VERSES 30-31** Saul showed his true feelings and Jonathan saw what was in his dad's heart.

•**VERSE 42** Jonathan had realized God was going to give the kingdom to David. David made an oath to Jonathan that he would treat the house of Saul with respect, kindness, and love.

CHAPTER 21:
DAVID RUNS FROM SAUL

•**VERSE 1** David was a captain over 1,000 men; so where are the troops?

•**VERSE 2** David's saying, "I'm on a secret mission for the king, and no one knows about it. So my men are over here, and I need some bread for them."

•**VERSE 4** It was bread that had been set out before God on the table of shewbread.

•**VERSE 6** The holy bread wasn't lawful for any man to eat but the priests.

Jesus makes reference to this particular incident in Mark 2:25-27. When the Pharisees are trying to accuse Him in some technical aspect of the law, Jesus makes mention of David, showing that human need rises above the law.

•**VERSE 10** He fled to the camp of the enemy, the Philistines in the city of Gath, and to King Achish.

•**VERSE 13** He acted like he was insane.

•**VERSE 15** "The fear of man brings a snare" (Proverbs 29:25). It declares that David was afraid of Achish. David's not afraid of the giant, he's afraid of the king. Acting like a madman, he's reduced to spit running down his beard, but he escaped out of the hand of Achish.

CHAPTER 22:
SAUL KILLS THE PRIESTS AT NOB

•**VERSE 3** He crossed over in the area of the Dead Sea, went over to Moab, and established his family. He knew that Saul's anger would ultimately turn against his family.

•**VERSE 4** "Masada" means hold. Some believe that David was in the fort of Masada, which was later developed by King Herod as a winter palace and fortress. It's possible David was in that area of the Dead Sea and that this is a reference to Masada.

Psalms 57 and 142 were written at this particular time of David's experiences.

•**VERSE 18** Doeg killed 85 priests—a terrible, terrible crime.

•**VERSES 22-23** David felt responsible for the death of all those families. He made a mistake letting Doeg go free instead of killing him.

CHAPTER 23:
SAUL PURSUES DAVID AND HIS MEN

•**VERSE 3** David didn't have a very brave army at this point.

•**VERSE 6** They inquired of the Lord through the ephod.

•**VERSE 12** David delivered the city from the Philistines, yet the men weren't faithful to him.

•**VERSE 17** Saul was aware that God's anointing was gone and knew that David was to be the king. He's trying to hold onto the kingdom that he knows isn't his.

Jonathan recognized David was going to be king, and his love was so great that he let David be exalted. He was willing to just be a helper to David. He was willing to abdicate the throne for David's sake and let David rule.

•**VERSE 21** "Not all who say, 'Lord, Lord' are going to enter into the kingdom of heaven" (Matthew 7:21). A lot of people use the right spiritual jargon, but they're not going to make it.

•**VERSE 28** "Sela-hammahlekoth" means the crag of divisions.

•**VERSE 29** David headed toward the wilderness area of the Dead Sea. Engedi is 20 miles from where the Jordan comes into the Dead Sea. It's a beautiful oasis with a lot of ibex, the wild goats of Israel—a beautiful place to hide out.

 HEBREW KEY WORD

engedi = wild goats, or fountain of a kid (23:29).

CHAPTER 24:
DAVID SPARES SAUL'S LIFE

•**VERSE 3** "Went in to cover his feet" means to go to sleep. Saul came into this very cave where David and his men were hiding.

•**VERSE 13** If you're wicked, wickedness is going to proceed from your life. It doesn't make you wicked; it only proves that you are wicked. Because I'm a sinner, I sin. Sinning doesn't make you a sinner; it only proves that you are one.

Even so in Christ Jesus, I am now righteous. Therefore, the righteousness that I do doesn't make me righteous; I do it because I am righteous. Because of God's work in my life, I now do the deeds of righteousness.

•**VERSE 20** He knew God's will and fought the will of God (Isaiah 45:9).

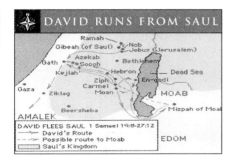

CHAPTER 25:
NABAL AND ABIGAIL

•**VERSE 2** Carmel is the mountain range at the port city of Haifa and Megiddo is in a lower portion of this range of Carmel.

•**VERSE 25** "Nabal" means foolish.

•**VERSES 32-34** This shows the greatness of David. Some men can't take the advice from women, but he saw that it was sound, and he respected and admired her for it.

•**VERSE 37** He was so angry and upset in what she did, he froze. He probably had a heart attack.

> ### 🔑 HEBREW KEY WORD
>
> *Nabal* = **stupid, wicked, or foolish** (25:25).

CHAPTER 26:
DAVID SPARES SAUL'S LIFE AGAIN

•**VERSE 2** The wilderness of Ziph lies between Hebron and the area of the Dead Sea—a vast, barren area.

•**VERSES 3-5** In that wilderness area there are a lot of places to hide and a lot of places to observe the movements of others without being seen.

•**VERSE 9** Even though the anointing of God had left Saul, David had such a high respect because of God's anointing upon his life that he refused to touch him (1 Chronicles 16:22).

•**VERSES 13-14** David called from afar. There are tremendous acoustics so that you can hear for miles. There's something about the atmosphere that causes sound to conduct very easily.

•**VERSE 21** Saul confessed, but he never repented. "Except thou repent," Jesus said, "you're going to perish" (Luke 13:3). Repent means to turn from your sin. Saul many times was rebuked by Samuel the prophet, but there wasn't any sign of repentance.

•**VERSE 25** Saul was trying to protect the throne to pass it on to his own children. Yet in his heart he knew that God had anointed David to be king.

CHAPTER 27:
DAVID DWELLS AMONG THE PHILISTINES

•**VERSE 1** David made a negative confession. There are negative people that have positive things happen, and positive people that have negative things happen (Matthew 5:45).

•**VERSE 2** Gath is one of the five major Philistine cities, ten miles inland from

Ashdod and Ashkelon, making a triangle. David is seeking political asylum because Saul was after him.

•**VERSE 10** He was wiping out these little Philistine and Canaanite villages and inferring to King Achish that he was fighting against Judah.

•**VERSE 11** What David did isn't admirable. There are no excuses for David's actions. Perhaps it says that God can use men who aren't perfect.

CHAPTER 28:
SAUL CONSULTS A WITCH

•**VERSE 2** David was his personal bodyguard.

•**VERSE 4** Gilboa is south of the Sea of Galilee. The Philistines had moved against the Israelites and had taken a lot of territory at this point. Saul was being boxed into a very small area.

•**VERSE 7** "A familiar spirit" means a demon-possessed woman.

•**VERSE 10** He was talking to a witch and swearing by the Lord that no evil will come to her if she proceeds to bring forth a spirit for him.

•**VERSE 12** The witch was shocked and screamed when she saw Samuel. It could be that she had been using, as spirit mediums often do, a particular demonic spirit that gives them information.

There is a reality to the spirit world, but you are warned by the Bible to stay away. It's possible to contact spirit entities, but it's a demon disguised as different people. Demons have lived in various ages and observe many things, and are naturally able to tell you facts about your life and past that nobody else knows. People are drawn into these kinds of things, but we are warned not to dabble with them.

•**VERSE 14** Samuel came up out of the earth. Prior to the resurrection of Jesus Christ, every one who died went into Sheol, which is in the heart of the earth and divided into two separate compartments, as taught by Jesus in Luke's gospel, chapter 16.

So Samuel came up out of the earth and spoke to Saul, telling him that God had departed from him.

CHAPTER 29:
PHILISTINES DISMISS DAVID FROM BATTLE

•**VERSE 1** Jezreel is the area of the plains of Megiddo or Armageddon.

•**VERSE 11** David was divinely protected by God from fighting against Saul and Jonathan.

CHAPTER 30:
DAVID'S VICTORY OVER THE AMALEKITES

•**VERSES 1-2** The Amalekites were to be utterly exterminated by Saul, but he disobeyed God.

Had Saul utterly destroyed the Amalekites, they wouldn't have invaded Ziklag and taken David's wives and the spoil.

•**VERSE 6** David had a rough crew. Everyone who was in debt, in trouble, or fleeing from the law, all came to David. Every renegade and outlaw fled to David.

Sometimes the only place you can find encouragement is in the Lord. David encouraged himself in the Lord (Psalm 42:5). You get strength and courage looking to the Lord and get the proper perspective.

•**VERSE 16** They took advantage that the Philistines and Judah had a battle. They came in with only women and children left, and were able to destroy these towns and take the spoil.

•**VERSE 24** Those who stay back home equally share in the spoil with those who go into battle.

This is also true in the area of missions. If a missionary is out there, how can he go except he be sent? When we support missionaries back at home, we equally share in the rewards of their ministries.

CHAPTER 31:
SAUL'S DEATH

•VERSE 4 Saul fell on his spear, but even then he didn't die.

In 2 Samuel he was lying there, and an Amalekite came by, and Saul pleaded with the Amalekite to kill him, which he did.

•VERSE 5 That is, the armor-bearer thought he was dead.

•VERSE 10 Bethshan is right at the northern edge of Mount Gilboa.

•VERSE 11 Jabesh-gilead was on the other side of the Jordan River.

•VERSE 12 They cremated Saul and his sons.

Saul's career as king began at Jabesh-gilead. There was an invading king who came to Jabesh-gilead and demanded the inhabitants surrender on the basis of plucking out the right eyes of all of the men.

They cried to Saul for help, who came with the men of Israel and destroyed this invading army. So Jabesh-gilead was saved by Saul, and that catapulted Saul into prominence and into acceptance by the people as king over Israel.

It is significant that the men of Jabesh-gilead came and rescued his body, feeling a great obligation and debt to Saul.

•VERSE 13 The end of Saul's career is sad and tragic. He was a man endowed by God who had tremendous abilities, and the anointing of God was upon his life, yet, he rebelled against God and disobeyed His word.

Because he rejected God from ruling over him, God rejected Saul from ruling over Israel.

The sad and the tragic end of the man who played the fool—body mutilated by the Philistines, cremated by his friends and buried.

1. Hannah had desperately sought the Lord for a son. We read in 1 John
5:14 that if we ask anything according to His will, He hears us. What did
Hannah pray in her heart that was according to His will? (1 Samuel 1:11).

_____

_____

_____

2. In 1 Samuel 3:13 the Lord was going to judge Eli's house because his
sons were vile and he didn't restrain them. What were the sins of Eli's
sons according to 1 Samuel 2:12-25?

_____

_____

_____

3. The people came to Samuel demanding a king reign over them. What
were the reasons why Israel wanted a king? (1 Samuel 8:5-7).

_____

_____

_____

4. When Saul disobeyed the Lord by refusing to utterly destroy the
Amalekites, what did Saul say? What does the Lord truly want from us?
(1 Samuel 15:15, 22; Psalm 51:16-17; Hosea 6:6).

_____

_____

_____

5. When David was anointed as God's choice for a king, the Scripture
says, "And the Spirit of the Lord came upon David from that day forward." According to 1 Samuel 16:14, what became of Saul's spiritual
state?

_____

_____

_____

THE BOOK OF
SECOND SAMUEL

AUTHOR OF THE BOOK:
The prophets Nathan and Gad.

PERIOD OF WRITING:
Written in the 10th century BC, during the reigns of David and Solomon.

TYPE OF BOOK:
Historical

THEME:
David's success due to his obedience to God, and David's failure due to his pride and allowing his flesh to rule over the spirit in his life.

INTRODUCTION:
First Samuel dealt with the reign of King Saul over Israel and ends with the death of Saul at the hands of the Philistines. Saul, the tragic story of a man who had many natural abilities and many God-given opportunities; yet, his was a wasted life, never achieving his full potential because he failed to submit totally to God.

Second Samuel begins with the reign of David as he ascended to the throne of Israel. Where Saul was disobedient to the Lord, David had a heart for God. Even when he failed miserably, he repented and sought the Lord's favor.

The first ten chapters speak of David's victories, as God established the nation of Israel under David's leadership. The rest of the book records the decline in his kingdom as a result of his failures.

CHAPTER 1:
DAVID MOURNS SAUL AND JONATHAN

•**VERSE 1** Back in 1 Samuel, chapter 30, the Amalekites came into Ziklag while the men were away, stole everything, burned their city, and took their wives and children captive. Had Saul utterly destroyed the Amalekites as God said, this wouldn't have happened.

•**VERSE 8** He was from the nation that God had ordered Saul to utterly destroy.

•**VERSE 10** Had he utterly wiped out the Amalekites, this young Amalekite boy could have never killed him. But his failure to obey the Lord and utterly wipe out the Amalekites came back on him. It is true that God tells you to put to death the flesh, because if you don't, the flesh will come back to destroy you.

•**VERSE 11** Ripping your clothes was always a sign of great emotion and feeling.

•**VERSE 14** David had tremendous respect for the anointing of God upon a person's life. Because of that anointing upon Saul, David wouldn't touch him.

> *mashiyach* = anointed, consecrated person (1:14).

•**VERSES 15-16** David rewarded him, but not as he thought.

•**VERSE 19** This is the beginning of the lamentation.

•**VERSE 20** Gath and Ashkelon were two of the principal Philistine cities. When men came back from war with victory, the young girls would get their tambourines and dance.

•**VERSE 21** This is a curse upon Mount Gilboa since Saul had fallen there. When you go to Israel today and see Mount Gilboa, it's a rocky, barren mountain. The mountains around are covered with lush trees, beautiful and green. The people of Israel helped this prophecy because in all the reforestation of Israel, they planted millions of trees, but not on Mount Gilboa because of this lament of David.

•**VERSE 26** Some perverted minds say that David and Jonathan had a homosexual relationship because of this declaration of David. This is blasphemous. No such thing is inferred from the Hebrew text at all.

CHAPTER 2:
DAVID ANOINTED KING OVER JUDAH

•**VERSE 1** David doesn't take action without seeking guidance from God (Proverbs 3:5-6).

David had been living in the Philistine city of Ziklag because Saul had been chasing him. He thought Saul wouldn't pursue him there. But now David says, "Lord, shall I go to one of the cities of Judah?"

•**VERSE 8** Abner was the one that David had chided earlier because he failed to guard Saul. Mahanaim is on the other side of Jordan.

•**VERSES 10-11** The kingdom is divided. David ruled only over Judah. The rest of the tribes swore their allegiance to Saul's son Ishbosheth under Abner's instigation.

•**VERSE 12** Abner knew God anointed David to be king. Abner was actually a cousin to Saul and was seeking to reign as king himself, but used Ishbosheth as a figurehead.

•**VERSE 13** Joab was David's general. Joab was very cruel and difficult— tough as nails. David tolerated him because he had such devotion to him and he was a great fighter. But David was never comfortable with Joab because of his nature.

•**VERSES 14-15** Ten of the young men of David and ten from Abner entertain these two generals.

•**VERSE 16** It's hard in our Christian, western culture to imagine such a thing as being a sport, escalating into a real battle.

•**VERSE 18** Asahel was a great runner.

•**VERSE 21** Evidently Asahel didn't have any armor; he was only running after him.

•**VERSE 23** As the men of David came up, they waited and were shocked to see Asahel, the brother of Joab dead.

•VERSES 27-32 Joab and his men went home, however, Joab carried a desire for vengeance against Abner.

CHAPTER 3:
JOAB KILLS ABNER

•VERSES 2-5 Six sons were born to him while in Hebron, and all by different wives. David began to display a weakness that ultimately led to his terrible sin with Bathsheba.

He began to add wives and concubines, which was forbidden by God in Deuteronomy 17:17.

•VERSE 7 This one concubine Rizpah had borne Saul two sons. This was a false and grievous charge. To go into another man's concubine, even though he was dead, was symbolic of taking over his authority.

•VERSE 9 He knew the Lord had sworn that David should be the king, yet he established Ishbosheth upon the throne. He knew it was wrong and yet he did it.

•VERSE 10 Dan is in the furthermost northern part of Israel, where the Jordan River comes right out of the ground going southward. Beersheba was on the southern extreme, just on the border of the wilderness. This covered the northern and southern borders of Israel from Dan to Beersheba.

•VERSES 12-13 Saul promised David his daughter as a wife for killing the Philistine, but gave his daughter Mirab to another man. When Michal fell in love with David, Saul thought she would be an irritant to David. She was probably self-willed. So he let David marry Michal. When David fled from Saul's presence, Saul gave Michal to another man, Phaltiel, and he became her husband—and greatly loved her.

David became vindictive at this point, yet he had already taken other wives and concubines in Hebron. This was pride on his part.

•VERSE 14 That was the dowry he had given to Saul for her.

•VERSE 16 This is a sad scene because evidently he really loved her.

•VERSES 22-25 When Joab came back, he heard that Abner had made a league with David. There was bitterness in Joab's heart against Abner because he killed his brother.

•VERSE 27 The fifth rib is where your heart is positioned.

•VERSES 28-29 David curses Joab and his house for this cruel and vindictive deed.

•VERSES 31-34 David publicly gave his disapproval of Joab's deeds.

•VERSE 37 David behaved wisely, allowing God to establish the kingdom. David isn't trying to do it himself; he's letting God take care of everything.

The people are drawn to David showing his heart, desiring the right thing. He's not out promoting himself (Psalm 75:6-7).

CHAPTER 4:
ISHBOSHETH IS MURDERED

•VERSE 6 These two men came to the palace as though getting wheat, and jumped him while taking his afternoon nap. They smote him under the fifth rib—they ran him through the heart.

•VERSE 12 David showed he wasn't promoting himself, and punished these men who killed Ishbosheth.

CHAPTER 5:
DAVID IS KING OVER ALL ISRAEL

•VERSE 6 The Israelites had never been able to take Jebu, the ancient site of

Jerusalem. It was a walled city and had excellent defenses. They felt that their defenses were so strong that they could actually defend the city with just blind and lame men.

•VERSE 20 "Baalperazim" means the plain of breaches.

•VERSES 23-24 David inquires of the Lord and receives directions from God. Thus, he is very successful, as is any man who will seek guidance from God.

CHAPTER 6:
BRINGING THE ARK TO JERUSALEM

•VERSE 2 Baale of Judah is Kirjath-jearim, eight miles from Jerusalem where the ark of God was located.

•VERSES 6-9 Uzzah reached out his hand to steady the ark and God smote him dead. David became angry with God and this put a fear in David's heart.

Rather than reading the book of the Law to see how God ordered the ark of the covenant transported, David followed the Philistine example: a cart pulled by oxen.

However, the Law said to put staves through the rings and carry it by four priests. David wasn't following God's pattern but the Philistine pattern, and it was disastrous.

•VERSES 12-13 This time he read the Law of the Lord and had the priests bear the ark of the covenant.

•VERSE 14 He only had on a linen robe, a common garment. He had taken off his kingly robes and was dressed as a common person, out with the crowd dancing with all of his might before the Lord, having a hilarious time.

•VERSES 22-23 He disgraced her by refusing relations with her and refused her the honor of having a child—the most important thing for a woman.

CHAPTER 7:
GOD'S PROMISE TO DAVID

•VERSE 13 It was a glorious promise from God to David (Acts 2:30).

•VERSE 19 David asks, "Is this the manner of man, O Lord God?" No, it isn't the manner of man. This is divine grace of which we know so very little.

As His children, God promises eternal blessings in His kingdom, living with Him forever. God has already done so much for us, but then He gives us fabulous promises of the future.

•VERSE 20 David, so gifted in expressing his heart and feelings in the Psalms, is speechless.

•VERSE 21 God's grace is never a reward for your goodness or righteousness—it's because He loves you. That's His nature to show His love and overwhelm you, though you realize how undeserving and how unworthy you are. The hardest thing is to accept grace gracefully.

CHAPTER 8:
DAVID'S VICTORIES

•VERSES 2-3 The Moabites became the tributaries of David; then he moved a little north and came against Hadadezer.

•VERSE 11 Even though God refused David the privilege of building a house for God, he started gathering gold, silver, and brass in abundance. When his son Solomon built the house of God everything was already gathered.

•VERSE 13 The Valley of Salt is south of the Dead Sea.

CHAPTER 9:
DAVID'S KINDNESS TO MEPHIBOSHETH

•VERSE 1 Jonathan and David made a friendship pact to show kindness unto each other and to each other's descendants forever.

So now that David is established, he seeks to find out if there are any left from Saul's house that he might honor and keep this pact made with Jonathan.

HEBREW KEY WORD

chesed = **kindness, mercy (9:1).**

•**VERSE 3** Mephibosheth was only five years old when his father Jonathan and his grandfather Saul were killed when they battled against the Philistines at Mount Gilboa.

When his nurse heard that the Philistines had taken Jonathan and Saul in battle, she grabbed the little boy, seeking to flee. As she did, she dropped him and broke both his legs. Not being set properly, he became a cripple.

CHAPTER 10:
DAVID DEFEATS THE AMMONITES

•**VERSE 2** He greeted them in David's name to express David's sorrow for the death of his father.

•**VERSE 6** When they heard these men were not allowed back into Jerusalem until their beards grew back, they feared an immediate attack by David.

CHAPTER 11:
DAVID'S SIN WITH BATHSHEBA

•**VERSE 6** David sought to cover his sin. His son Solomon later wrote Proverbs 28:13.

•**VERSES 8-9** He thought that Uriah would go home to be with his wife, and later when it was discovered that she was pregnant, no one would ever know the truth except for David and Bathsheba. But Uriah was a very honorable man and didn't go home.

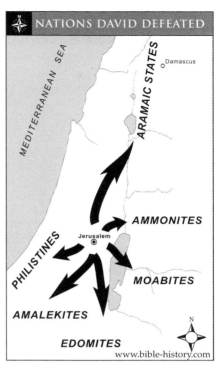

NATIONS DAVID DEFEATED

www.bible-history.com

•**VERSES 14-15** As sin so often does, it leads to something worse. It begins to compound and begins to develop in its insidious manner. So David turned to a second plan, more dastardly than the first. That plan was to deliberately have Uriah killed in battle.

•**VERSE 27** God couldn't allow David's sin to go unnoticed or unpunished.

CHAPTER 12:
NATHAN REBUKES DAVID

•**VERSES 8-9** Why is it that when God has been so good to us that we don't appreciate it and aren't satisfied with what God has done? Why do we reach out for more when we already have more than what we can possibly use or enjoy?

•**VERSE 13** David's judgment for this man was, "He shall surely be put to death." God's judgment for David was you cannot sin with impunity and get off the hook completely.

Sin, though forgiven, leaves its mark. There are certain aspects of sin that cannot be undone. There are certain marks that sin leaves upon your life and the lives of others that remain.

•**VERSES 10-14** One of the tragic byproducts of sin in the life of a believer is the fact that the enemies of God look at it and blaspheme God.

The punishment: the sword was never to depart from David's house; his own children would rebel against him; his own wives would be publicly humiliated; and the child to be born was going to die. This experience took the fire out of David.

It is sad and tragic when the fire is gone out of a person's life.

Psalm 32 was written by David upon hearing the words of the prophet, "Thy sins are forgiven, you will not die." David wrote, "Oh how happy is he whose transgression is forgiven." When trying to cover your sin, you're always living in fear and worried that you're going to get caught. Happy is the man who can be honest and forthright, who doesn't have to deceive, hide, and connive.

•**VERSE 23** David is showing his faith in life after death, showing confidence that his child was saved.

•**VERSE 25** "Jedidiah" means beloved of the Lord.

CHAPTER 13:
AMNON'S SIN AGAINST TAMAR

•**VERSE 3** Any man who would help and advise you in fulfilling a sinful desire isn't a true friend.

•**VERSE 15** Amnon had expressed a tremendous love for his sister, but it wasn't love at all—it was his own personal gratification. He wasn't looking for someone to love and bless with his kindness and goodness. He was seeking to satisfy his own fleshly desires, and discarded her once that had been accomplished.

•**VERSE 21** Amnon was wrong, but the tragedy is that David wouldn't discipline Amnon because of his own past.

Solomon wrote so much about the importance of disciplining children, seeing the lack of discipline in his own family, because his father David was not a disciplinarian.

•**VERSE 37** He went to live with his grandfather, protecting him from David's vengeance.

CHAPTER 14:
ABSALOM RETURNS TO JERUSALEM

•**VERSES 25-26** He was a very beautiful person outwardly, but was cunning and cruel inwardly.

It says that he polled his hair annually. Every year he grew about three to four pounds of hair. They would give them so much per shekel for the polling of their hair. Interesting that it was his hair that led to his death. He was riding through the woods and his hair got caught on a branch. He was hanging there by his hair when Joab came along and threw the dart through his heart.

•**VERSES 29-30** You can't ignore Absalom. He wanted Joab to set up a meeting with his dad, but Joab wouldn't even come to see him.

•**VERSE 33** There was the forgiveness, the weeping, and the rekindling of love, except that Absalom began to conspire against his own father.

CHAPTER 15:
ABSALOM'S CONSPIRACY

•**VERSES 3-5** Absalom would say, "My father's busy; bring the matter to me and let me judge it for you." And the people would bow to him, and he'd take them by the hand, and kiss their hands. He was a shrewd politician, kissing the babies, and saying the things that the people wanted to hear.

•**VERSES 7-10** When Absalom felt that he was in a strong position, he headed for Hebron with some of the key leaders and announced his kingdom there in Hebron.

•**VERSE 12** This desertion of his friend Ahithophel is expressed by David in Psalm 55. Perhaps he deserted David because Bathsheba was his grand-daugher (2 Samuel 11:3; 23:34).

•**VERSE 14** Rather than setting up his troops to defend himself from Absalom's army, David's spirit is gone. He makes no attempt to defend the city or himself. David begins an exodus from the city with his faithful followers and they go over the Mount of Olives toward the wilderness.

•**VERSES 32-34** Hushai was one of David's counselors, an older man. David told him to go to Jerusalem and subvert the counsel of Ahithophel. David began to set up his men to destroy the purposes of Absalom.

CHAPTER 16:
ABSALOM SETS UP IN JERUSALEM

•**VERSE 3** Ziba is lying to David about Mephibosheth, declaring that Mephibosheth was saying that he was going to get the kingdom back.

•**VERSES 10-12** David is broken, realizing this was the fruit of his sin, and yet there is a beautiful submission of David unto the will of God—even the judgment of God, which made David a man after God's own heart—total and complete commitment.

•**VERSES 21-22** A breach was created between Absalom and David that could not be healed. The people would feel secure in following Absalom now because David could never forgive this sin.

One of the acts of taking the kingdom from his predecessor was taking the king's wives.

The prophecy of Nathan was fulfilled, as we find the wives of David being publicly humiliated.

CHAPTER 17:
HUSHAI'S COUNSEL

•**VERSES 10-13** Hushai suggested to wait on the attack and summon all of Israel, that they might have a great invasion against David. Let Absalom lead the armies against David so the people will see Absalom is able to lead them into war.

•**VERSE 23** Absalom didn't follow his counsel, so he set his house in order and committed suicide. Ahithophel probably realized that Absalom would also be destroyed by David for this treacherous turnaround. And realizing that Hushai's counsel was going to lead to disaster, he was only trying to bail out before disaster came.

•**VERSE 26** Gilead is the area around the southern end of the Sea of Galilee over on the Jordanian side.

CHAPTER 18:
THE DEATH OF ABSALOM

•**VERSE 5** Even though Absalom had rebelled against his father, he was still his son, and David had a great love for him.

•**VERSE 9** Hair can be attractive, but it can also be disastrous. For Absalom, his hair got caught in the oak and the donkey kept going, leaving him swinging by his hair from the branch.

•VERSE 18 Absalom had a pillar that he had erected, a monument, and it was set up in a valley. For he said, "I have no son to keep my name in remembrance." The Scripture says he had two sons. Either both of his sons died young, or he built the pillar before his sons were born.

•VERSE 23 Ahimaaz was a faster runner, overtook old Cushi, and left him in the dust.

•VERSE 29 Ahimaaz was a good runner, but he didn't have a message. It doesn't matter how well you run; if you don't have a message to deliver.

CHAPTER 19:
DAVID RETURNS TO JERUSALEM

•VERSE 7 This was actually good advice on Joab's part.

•VERSES 9-10 Israel turned from David, but now they want David back.

•VERSES 19-20 As David was returning to Jerusalem, the first one to meet him was Shimei, who threw rocks and cursed David on his way out. Now that David is coming back, Shimei is welcoming him back.

•VERSE 25 The servants of Mephibosheth had lied to David saying that Mephibosheth had pledged allegiance to Absalom, or was trying to take over the kingdom himself after David fled.

•VERSES 41-43 There was a division between the northern tribes of Israel and the southern tribes of Judah. This division was manifested in the beginning of David's reign for seven years over Judah before he reigned over all of Israel. Now that there is this division, the old rivalry rises again.

Later under David's grandson Rehoboam, there came a complete break;

Jeroboam became the king of Israel, and Rehoboam became the king of Judah. From that time on there were two nations.

In the prophecy of Ezekiel, God promises that they would be united in the restoration of the nation. When Israel was restored in 1948, there were no longer the northern and southern tribes. There is unity in the nation of Israel. The Scripture has been fulfilled as predicted by Ezekiel.

CHAPTER 20:
SHEBA'S REBELLION

•VERSE 1 Sheba blew a trumpet in Israel, signaling the people to gather for a rebellion against David.

•VERSE 3 They were humiliated by Absalom there on the roof.

•VERSE 4 David had asked Amasa to be one of his generals over his army. Amasa was the general under Absalom, but when Absalom was killed, David asked him to be one of his generals. Joab wanted nothing to do with that.

CHAPTER 21:
THE GIBEONITES

•VERSE 1 The Gibeonites fooled Joshua saying they wanted to make a league with the children of Israel. Instead of seeking God's wisdom, Joshua used his own judgment.

Once they made the covenant, God expected them to honor it, even though it was wrong and they made it under deception. God expects us to honor the covenants that we make.

Saul broke the covenant with the Gibeonites, killing them in his reign.

Saul had been dead for 30 years at this point, and they experienced three years of famine because of the broken covenant.

•**VERSE 6** Gibeah was the city where Saul had lived.

•**VERSE 8** We are told earlier in the Scriptures that Michal was childless, as David's punishment for mocking him when he brought the ark of the covenant back from Kirjath-jearim to Jerusalem. She remained childless until the day of her death.

If you will go back in the record, these five sons were the sons of Merab, who was the daughter of Saul—originally given to David for killing Goliath—but Saul gave her to someone else. These sons who were turned over to the Gibeonites to be hung were her five sons. The two others were the sons of Saul from one of his concubines.

•**VERSES 15-17** David's old now. From this point on, they wouldn't allow David to go out into battle.

CHAPTER 22:
DAVID'S SONG OF DELIVERANCE

•**VERSE 1** Here is a psalm that is not in the book of Psalms. It is one of David's psalms of God's deliverance.

CHAPTER 23:
DAVID'S LAST WORDS

•**VERSE 2** David acknowledges that God spoke by him. It was God's word that was in his tongue. These words are confirmed by Peter in the New Testament quoting one of the psalms of David (Acts 1:16). He attributes the words of David to the Holy Spirit, as does Jesus in Mark 12:36.

As you read the Psalms you realize that the worship of God is actually inspired by God.

•**VERSE 3** No man can rule over man unless he is consciously ruled by God, otherwise it is tyranny and slavery. Jesus told the parable of the unjust judge who feared neither God nor man.

A true ruler must think of justice toward men, but he must rule in the fear of God, knowing that he's going to answer to God one day for each decision he makes.

•**VERSE 6** "Belial" is Satan.

•**VERSE 8** This is David's hall of fame. These are the mighty men who fought with David in his armies.

•**VERSE 10** He was fighting so long that he couldn't tell where his hand ended and the sword began. His hand was locked.

CHAPTER 24:
THE CENSUS OF ISRAEL

•**VERSES 3-4** Joab rightfully objected to David executing this numbering process, but David insisted. The Lord opposed the census. God had declared that He was going to multiply Abraham's seed so that it would be as the sands of the seas and the stars of the heavens—innumerable. For David then to seek to count the people was defiance against the promise of God.

But David's pride sought to count the number of fighting men that he had both in Judah and in Israel.

•**VERSE 17** David is seeking the Lord, but back in the first verse, the Lord was angry with Israel for their apostasy.

•**VERSE 24** We don't truly understand what it means to sacrifice unto the Lord. Generally people give from their abundance; it doesn't really cost or take away. In reality, the poor always give much more to God than the rich.

When Jesus and His disciples watched the people casting their money into the treasury, seeing the rich give their great gifts, the people were impressed. This poor little widow came along and gave a mite—one-fortieth of a penny. Jesus said to His disciples, "She gave more than all of the rest" (Mark 12:41-44).

STUDY QUESTIONS FOR SECOND SAMUEL

1. In 2 Samuel 1:1-15 David hears of Saul's death from a young man claiming to have taken his life. What is significant about this man, and what "reward" did David give for this act?

_____

_____

_____

2. According to 2 Samuel 2:1 and 5:19, 23 what was the explanation for David's success?

_____

_____

_____

3. David loved the Lord greatly and wanted to bless Him by building Him a house—but the Lord blessed David! What was God's promise to David found in 2 Samuel 7:13-16?

_____

_____

_____

4. We realize there are consequences to sin even after forgiveness. What were the consequences of David's sin according to 2 Samuel 12:10-14?

If you have sin in your life right now, write a prayer to the Lord asking for forgiveness.

_____

_____

_____

5. We read in 2 Samuel chapter 9 of the great kindness that David showed to Mephibosheth. Who was Mephibosheth, and why did King David bestow such blessings upon him?

_____

_____

_____

THE BOOK OF
FIRST KINGS

AUTHOR OF THE BOOK:
The book of First Kings was traditionally believed to be written by Jeremiah. We're uncertain, but he had the qualifications to do so.

PERIOD OF WRITING:
Around the 6th century BC.

TYPE OF BOOK:
Historical

THEME:
Blessings that come from following and serving God, and the trouble that arises when we ignore or disobey God.

INTRODUCTION:
First Kings is the continuation of the history of the kings of Judah and Israel. First and Second Samuel apply to the time from Samuel through the reign of David. As we get into the books of the Kings, we continue the history of the kings of Israel and Judah after David passes from the scene.

First and Second Kings cover a period of approximately 400 years, and seems to be a compilation from several other documents including: *The Book of the Acts of Solomon, The Book of the Chronicles of the Kings of Israel,* and *The Book of the Chronicles of the Kings of Judah.*

These last two books were the official records of the two kingdoms when Israel was divided into the northern and the southern kingdoms.

CHAPTER 1:
SOLOMON ANOINTED KING

•**VERSE 1** To be old and stricken in years is to be an invalid. For some, like Moses, their strength remained. His sight was excellent right up until the day of his death. As others became old, they became an invalid.

•**VERSE 4** David did not have relations with her.

•**VERSE 5** David's son Adonijah was the full brother of Absalom. He was the son of Haggith, who bore David at least two sons.

•**VERSE 7** Joab was King David's chief general.

•**VERSE 9** Adonijah threw a great party pronouncing himself as king of Judah.

•**VERSE 29** What a glorious testimony that is. Notice he didn't say, "The Lord kept my soul from all distress." A lot of times we have a mistaken notion that God is somehow going to give us divine immunity from problems.

As a child of God, I face many distressing situations, but I know God will deliver me (2 Corinthians 1:10).

•**VERSE 50** He grabbed these little raised areas that looked like horns on the four corners of the altar.

CHAPTER 2:
DAVID'S ADVICE TO SOLOMON

•**VERSE 3** When Moses was giving Joshua the charge, Moses said much of what David is saying to Solomon: keep the commandments, ordinances, and statutes of the Lord (Joshua 1:8).

The key to prosperity is obedience to the Law of God (Psalm 1:3). Excellent advice by David to his son.

•**VERSE 4** David reminds him of God's conditional promise, but notice that it is a conditional promise.

David's descendants did not walk before the Lord in truth and thus there came an end.

Yet the promise to David was fulfilled in and through Jesus Christ, for that everlasting kingdom that was promised to David was fulfilled when Christ came (Isaiah 9:7).

•**VERSE 5** David's advice to Solomon was very good, but then it lapsed into personal vengeance. So typical of David—he had extremely high spiritual characteristics, but had the capacity to be very human.

•**VERSE 6** "Hoar head" means gray head.

•**VERSES 8-9** Shimei the Benjamite was the one who went along the hill cursing and throwing rocks at David.

•**VERSE 17** Abishag was David's concubine, a beautiful girl that was brought in to be with David when he was dying.

•**VERSE 22** A part of the ascension to the throne was receiving the concubines of the previous ruler. Remember when Absalom came into Jerusalem and took the ten concubines that David had left. That was a mark of the ascension to the throne. David had even taken some of Saul's concubines when he came to the throne.

Solomon saw this as a desire of Adonijah to take the kingdom.

•**VERSES 26-27** Abiathar, a descendant of Eli, was the other priest who conspired to put Adonijah on the throne. Solomon banished him from the priesthood. God fulfilled the word concerning the end of the priesthood to the house of Eli in 1 Samuel 2:31-35, because Eli's sons were evil.

•**VERSE 28** Joab ran in and grabbed hold of the horns on the altar. It was a position of real supplication unto God.

CHAPTER 3:
SOLOMON ASKS FOR WISDOM

•**VERSE 1** Solomon begins the gathering of wives. He took the pharaoh's daughter as his wife, and later built her a house in Jerusalem.

•**VERSE 3** He was behaving as the pagans around them.

•**VERSE 4** He had a great sacrifice unto God that were peace offerings and celebrations. The animals were sacrificed and burnt—a great barbecue.

•**VERSE 5** If God should say that to you, what would you ask? Your answer can reveal a lot about you, whether or not you are living for the flesh or the Spirit.

• **VERSE** 13 This is one of those indications of God's grace, giving more than what we ask (Matthew 6:33; Ephesians 3:20).

Let your heart remain set upon the Lord, never upon riches (Psalm 62:10).

• **VERSE** 15 Burnt offerings are offerings of consecration—committing my life to God. The peace offerings are the offerings of communion, entering into communion and fellowship with God.

CHAPTER 4:
SOLOMON'S WEALTH AND WISDOM

• **VERSE** 7 He had 12 men, each responsible to provide food for one month during the year.

They probably tried to gather everything during the 11 months because it took a lot to run his household for one month.

• **VERSE** 21 This was the Nile River.

• **VERSE** 22 A measure is about ten bushels, needing about 300 bushels of fine flour a day, plus 600 bushels of meal.

• **VERSE** 30 Egypt was famous for its wisdom in architecture, mathematics, and magical arts. Solomon's wisdom exceeded that of the Egyptians.

• **VERSE** 31 These men were noted historically; they were the 'Einsteins'— men who had been noted for tremendous brilliance; and yet, it declares that Solomon's wisdom excelled all of them.

• **VERSE** 32 We have a book of Proverbs in which there are only some. The book of Proverbs is probably less than one-third of all of the proverbs which he spoke.

We have three of his songs in the book of Psalms; Psalms 77, 127, and 128 are attributed to him.

CHAPTER 5:
WOOD FOR BUILDING THE TEMPLE

• **VERSE** 1 Tyre was the southern coast of Lebanon. Hiram was a friend of David.

• **VERSE** 5 Solomon wants to fulfill this unfinished dream of his father David.

• **VERSE** 9 They were to float them down the Mediterranean to Joppa, the only seaport on the coast of Israel. From Joppa, they carried these huge timbers 40 miles to Jerusalem for the building of the temple. Quite a monumental task.

• **VERSE** 11 A measure is ten bushels— 200,000 bushels of wheat a year for the servants. A liquid measure was about 85 gallons—16,000 plus gallons of pure olive oil.

• **VERSE** 13 A levy of men means that he drafted men.

• **VERSE** 14 They were in Lebanon working for a month, and then they'd come home for two months.

• **VERSE** 15 Solomon had 70,000 slaves that carried the logs, and 80,000 men who were cutting the logs in the forest.

CHAPTER 6:
BUILDING THE TEMPLE

• **VERSE** 2 A cubit is 18 inches, so the temple was to be 90 feet long, 30 feet wide, and 45 feet tall.

• **VERSE** 7 The cutting of stone was done at the quarry, underneath the city. They would cut the stones to size there, and then bring them to the site. There was no noise of a hammer or any iron tool at the actual construction site of the temple.

• **VERSES** 12-13 God's conditional promise to Solomon that God would dwell in the midst of the people (2 Chronicles 15:2).

• **VERSE** 20 The Holy of Holies was a 30-feet cube.

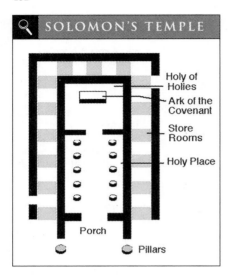

SOLOMON'S TEMPLE

Holy of Holies

Ark of the Covenant

Store Rooms

Holy Place

Porch

Pillars

CHAPTER 7:
SOLOMON'S PALACE AND TEMPLE

•**VERSE 1** This shows his priorities: seven years building the house of God, then 13 years building his own.

•**VERSE 2** A good-sized main house; 75 feet by 150 feet. The height of it was 45 feet, which would give ample room for three stories, 15 feet per floor—around 25,000 square feet within the house.

•**VERSE 15** They were hollow in the center. The brass was about three inches thick. The pillars were about 12 feet around, and 18 feet high.

•**VERSE 21** "Jachin" means He shall establish, and "Boaz" means in it is strength. It is believed that these pillars didn't hold anything up. They were there in the front and spoke of the fact that God had established these people in His strength. They were later carried away to Babylon.

•**VERSE 23** This was for the priests, that they might bathe before they went into the temple to wash off the defilement. It was 15 feet across, and about seven feet deep.

•**VERSE 47** Everything that would apply to the altar on the outside of the temple was brass. Brass is always symbolic of judgment—the cleansing in the brass laver, the necessity of cleansing—judgment.

The animals dying on the altar—judgment. All of the instruments that were used for the sacrifices were all brass.

•**VERSES 48-50** Once you enter into the temple, you're entering into the figure of heaven, and gold is always symbolic of the heavenly scene. Those things that had to do with the fellowship and worship of God inside the temple were of gold, symbolic of the heavenlies.

•**VERSE 48** This is the altar where the incense was offered that stood before the holy place.

HEBREW KEY WORDS

Jachin = He shall establish
Boaz = In it is strength (7:21).

CHAPTER 8:
DEDICATION OF THE TEMPLE

•**VERSE 2** This was taking place during the Feast of Tabernacles.

•**VERSE 9** Originally in the ark were two tablets of stone, representing God's covenant; a golden jar of manna, a reminder of God's miraculous provision through the wilderness; and the rod of Aaron that had blossomed, establishing the priesthood with the house of Aaron.

When the Philistines took the ark of the covenant, they probably took the golden jar with the manna, and the rod of Aaron had disappeared. Now when the ark of the covenant is brought, they only had the two tablets of stone.

•VERSE 10 God's presence, the *shekinah* glory of God, fills the temple.

•VERSES 17-18 God takes your motives usually above your actions. Having the right actions with the wrong motives is not acceptable by God. Man looks on the outward appearance; whereas God looks on the heart.

•VERSE 20 Solomon affirmed God's faithfulness to perform His word. You can be sure that God will perform His word.

•VERSE 27 Solomon recognized the ludicrous situation, knowing that the heaven of heavens couldn't contain God, much less the house that he had built. God couldn't be confined to this house, but it was a place where the people could meet Him.

•VERSE 31 He envisions seven different situations that might drive the people to pray.

•VERSES 33-37 Notice that he attributes the national calamities to the sins of the people (Proverbs 14:34).

•VERSES 46-49 When Solomon prayed, God answered him. The answer is oftentimes quoted by itself and not in context. The Lord's answer to Solomon was, "If My people, which are called by My name, shall humble themselves, and pray, and seek My face, and turn from their wicked ways; then will I hear from heaven, and will heal their nation" (2 Chronicles 7:14).

•VERSE 54 He began by standing, but evidently went down on his knees during the prayer.

•VERSE 63 There is great feasting and rejoicing before the Lord as they have now completed the temple and dedicated it to the Lord.

•VERSE 64 He declared the whole area holy because they didn't have enough room for all the sacrifices.

•VERSE 66 That's the way people should always leave the presence of God—joyful and glad of heart. That's the proper attitude. Fellowship with God should always create that joyfulness and happiness within.

CHAPTER 9:
GOD'S CONDITIONAL PROMISE

•VERSE 2 Solomon asked that the Lord would give him wisdom and understanding that he might govern over this glorious people of God.

•VERSE 3 The Lord is referring to the prayer of dedication of Solomon after he finished the temple.

•VERSE 4 David was far from a perfect person as far as sinlessness is concerned, yet David was never involved in idolatry. He remained true and faithful unto Jehovah.

•VERSE 5 This was a conditional promise of God and they failed to keep it; thus, God was not obligated to keep the promise.

•VERSES 6-9 Because they forsook the Lord, they were cut out of the land. God kept His word given to Solomon.

Whenever God speaks to you about any area of your life, listen carefully, because God doesn't waste words. And if He talks to you about some issue in your life, you can be sure that's the issue you're going to be facing down the road (1 Corinthians 10:12).

•VERSE 13 "Cabul" means displeasing.

•VERSE 25 The three times were the three major feasts of Passover, Pentecost, and Tabernacles.

CHAPTER 10:
SOLOMON'S WEALTH AND SPLENDOR

•VERSE 9 Solomon was still walking with the Lord and honoring God (Matthew 5:16).

Evidently, Solomon was honoring God because she sees the whole thing and praises God.

•**VERSES 11-12** He developed another navy to ply the waters of the Mediterranean. The first navy was in the Persian Gulf and went to the east coast of Africa, the Ivory Coast. This second navy was in the Mediterranean, going as far as England and bringing back peacocks and gold and rare trees.

CHAPTER 11:
SOLOMON'S DOWNFALL

•**VERSE 1** In the Law, God gave certain commandments for the kings (Deuteronomy 17:16-17). Solomon disobeyed in all cases, first going down to Egypt and multiplying horses. Then he loved many strange women. He did exactly those things that God said he should not do.

•**VERSE 3** The reason why the Lord said the king shouldn't do these things— lest their hearts be turned away from the Lord. What happened to Solomon? His heart was turned from God.

•**VERSES 7-8** For each of his wives he built a worship shrine that they might worship the gods that were native to their own ethnic groups.

•**VERSE 25** Hadad gathered men and began to make excursions against the southern borders of Israel and harass Solomon.

Rezon was up in the area of Damascus, and he began to harass Solomon in the northern borders of the land.

•**VERSE 28** The house of Joseph would be the northern part.

•**VERSE 41** We do not have the *Acts of Solomon*. It would be a very interesting book, but we don't need it for God's revelation of His purposes.

CHAPTER 12:
THE KINGDOM DIVIDED

•**VERSE 1** Shechem is in the center of the land, the heart of the country.

•**VERSE 7** The older counselors advised that the people would revolt if he did not give tax relief.

•**VERSES 16-17** The kingdom was divided. This is an important point in the history of the nation.

•**VERSE 19** The northern kingdom was called Israel; the southern kingdom was called Judah.

•**VERSE 25** It says that he built Shechem—but Shechem was already there. It means that he built a wall around Shechem.

•**VERSE 27** He feared that the people's hearts would be drawn back to the king of Judah if they were to go down to Jerusalem for Passover every year.

•**VERSE 28** The worship of the calves was something that came from Egypt. He turned the hearts of the people away from the Lord.

•**VERSE 29** Dan is at the northernmost part of the kingdom. Bethel is 15 or 20 miles from Jerusalem. He set up idols in both ends of the kingdom, the southern and northern parts of Israel.

CHAPTER 13:
DISOBEDIENT PROPHET FROM JUDAH

•**VERSES 2-3** This is before Josiah was ever born, yet he prophesies exactly what Josiah was going to do in the priests' offering upon the high places.

In order that they might know that God had truly spoken, this altar is going to be torn in two and the ashes spilled out, fulfilled in 2 Kings 23:15.

•**VERSES 15-24** Pay attention to what the Lord has to say and not man. You are responsible to listen to God and follow the Lord's command. God will hold you responsible for that.

CHAPTER 14:
AHIJAH PROPHESIES AGAINST JEROBOAM

•**VERSE 4** Ahijah was so old that he had gone blind.

•**VERSE 6** A person cannot disguise the truth from God. People are often in a disguise when they come to the house of the Lord, but God can see through each disguise.

•**VERSE 15** At the beginning of Israel's history, God predicts the judgment that will come 450 years later. Because they worshiped other gods, they're going to be driven out of the land that God has given to them.

•**VERSE 19** We have the chronicles of the kings of Judah. They are known as First and Second Chronicles. However, we do not have the chronicles of the kings of Israel at the present time.

•**VERSE 21** It's going to start bouncing back and forth from the northern kingdom to the southern kingdom.

•**VERSE 27** Solomon had made these gold shields, three pounds of gold per shield. But Rehoboam replaced the shields with brass shields—brass being the symbol of judgment, the beginning of God's judgment for worshiping other gods.

CHAPTER 15:
ASA REIGNS OVER JUDAH

•**VERSE 16** During the time of Asa, Baasha became the king over Israel in the northern tribes.

•**VERSE 17** Ramah is the present-day city of Ramallah, intended to be a fortified city. He was going to cut off all supplies going into Jerusalem.

•**VERSE 21** When Baasha heard they had been invaded from the north, he took his troops from building this fortified city of Ramah and went to face the Syrians.

•**VERSE 22** Asa and his men took all of the materials they had brought for this fortified city and built a couple of cities.

This seems like brilliant strategy, but as we get into Chronicles, we find that God rebuked Asa for this.

•**VERSE 23** In Chronicles there is an implication that because he sought the aid of the physicians and didn't seek the Lord, he died of the disease, but his heart was turned from the Lord in the later years.

•**VERSE 25** This verse speaks of the northern kingdom. Jeroboam was the one that God had prophesied against.

CHAPTER 16:
ISRAELITE KINGS

•**VERSE 3** Baasha's house was utterly wiped out.

•**VERSE 18** He committed suicide after having reigned for a few days.

KINGS OF ISRAEL	
KING	**CHARACTER**
JEROBOAM	BAD
NADAB	BAD
BAASHA	BAD
ELAH	BAD
ZIMRI	BAD
OMRI	VERY BAD
AHAB	VERY BAD
AHAZIAH	BAD
JEHORAM (JORAM)	BAD MOSTLY
JEHU	BAD MOSTLY
JEHOAHAZ	BAD
JEHOASH (JOASH)	BAD
JEROBOAM II	BAD
ZECHARIAH	BAD
SHALLUM	BAD
MENAHEM	BAD
PEKAHIAH	BAD
PEKAH	BAD
HOSHEA	BAD

KINGS OF JUDAH	
KING	**CHARACTER**
REHOBOAM	BAD MOSTLY
ABIJAH	BAD MOSTLY
ASA	GOOD
JEHOSHAPHAT	GOOD
JEHORAM	BAD
AHAZIAH	BAD
ATHALIAH	VERY BAD
JOASH	GOOD MOSTLY
AMAZIAH	GOOD MOSTLY
UZZIAH	GOOD
JOTHAM	GOOD
AHAZ	VERY BAD
HEZEKIAH	VERY GOOD
MANASSEH	VERY BAD
AMON	VERY BAD
JOSIAH	VERY GOOD
JEHOAHAZ	BAD
JEHOIAKIM	VERY BAD
JEHOIACHIN	BAD
ZEDEKIAH	BAD

•**VERSE 21** Divided from the southern kingdom, there was a civil war in the northern kingdom.

•**VERSE 34** The prophecy of Joshua was fulfilled 500 years later (Joshua 6:26).

CHAPTER 17:
ELIJAH AND THE WIDOW

•**VERSES 1-3** Elijah came and said, "It will not rain until I say so." Then he took off and was gone for three and a half years. He went over to the brook Cherith, which is toward Gilead, from which he had come.

•**VERSE 9** Zarephath was near Zidon, which would be in the area of Lebanon today. Zidon is about ten miles north of Accho.

•**VERSE 10** In the more primitive cultures, the ladies go out and gather sticks for their fires.

•**VERSES 13-16** Get your priorities correct and God will take care of the other aspects of your life. The most important relationship that I have in this world is my relationship with God, and nothing should get before it.

CHAPTER 18:
ELIJAH PRAYS FOR RAIN

•**VERSE 1** This is important to the future of the story. He has the promise of God that rain is going to come.

•**VERSE 2** Samaria was in the northern kingdom.

•**VERSE 17** Some people live wicked lives and then when the fruit of their wickedness comes, they blame God for the calamities.

•**VERSES 42-44** His prayer and sending his servant out looking for a cloud is related to the first verse where the Lord promised, "I will send rain."

His prayer was premised upon the fact that he had heard from the Lord and received the promise of God. Prayers that are based upon God's promises and God's Word are going to be answered.

•**VERSE 45** Jezreel is at the other end of the Valley of Megiddo.

CHAPTER 19:
ELIJAH FLEES

•**VERSE 3** Beersheba is about 85 miles south from where they were.

•**VERSE 4** If he truly wanted to die, he didn't have to run. The very fact that he was running showed that he wanted to survive.

•**VERSE 8** Mount Sinai is another name for Mount Horeb; both names are given to this mount, the mountain where Moses met God. It is way down in the barren wilderness.

He's fleeing from Jezebel.

•**VERSE** 9 Elijah didn't understand the question. The question was, "What are you doing here, Elijah?" And Elijah answered why he was there, not what he was doing there.

•**VERSE** 10 Discouragement and despair cause you to overstate the case, and it looks worse than it really is. Elijah was overstating the problems in Israel.

•**VERSES** 11-12 We often miss the voice of God because we are anticipating God to speak in such great thunderous tones or in such mystic ways.

When God is leading your life, He does it in natural ways so that generally you're not even aware of His guidance.

•**VERSE** 13 The Lord got to specifics with this upset prophet. He was hiding. He had put himself out of service.

There was no one to witness to down there, and there wasn't any work for God to be done in that barren wilderness. God doesn't like for us to do nothing.

•**VERSES** 15-16 God got him away from this place of hiding in a cave and doing nothing, and commissioned him back into service.

CHAPTER 20:
AHAB DEFEATS BENHADAD

•**VERSES** 1-4 He asked for complete capitulation. He wanted all of their gold, silver, and wives. Ahab was surrendering, but Benhadad wasn't satisfied.

•**VERSE** 23 They thought of gods in a localized sense. We should never think of God in a localized sense. God is omnipresent; He's everywhere at once.

•**VERSE** 28 Though Ahab had turned against God and was a wicked king, God was continuing to speak to him.

In the same way, God continues to speak to you because He loves you and seeks to draw you unto Himself; and thus, God doesn't cease speaking to man.

CHAPTER 21:
NABOTH'S VINEYARD

•**VERSE** 1 It was an excellent vineyard next to property that Ahab owned, and Ahab desired it.

•**VERSE** 4 He started pouting because he couldn't have his way.

•**VERSE** 13 The penalty for cursing God was being stoned to death.

•**VERSE** 25 There is none any worse than this king.

CHAPTER 22:
AHAB AND JEHOSHAPHAT

•**VERSE** 15 He answered in a very sarcastic way that Ahab realized that this man wasn't sincere.

•**VERSE** 17 He's prophesying the death of Ahab, the shepherd over the people. The people are scattered over the hills because their shepherd has been destroyed.

•**VERSES** 19-23 Micaiah's vision of heaven is very interesting. We don't often consider Satan as a servant of God, serving God's purposes. Satan is acting in the sphere of his own free will, yet the controls are ultimately held by God.

•**VERSE** 34 He just let an arrow fly in the direction of their enemy and it actually hit Ahab.

•**VERSE** 43 Asa was a good king for the most part.

•**VERSE** 47 This area is south of the Dead Sea and on the far bank.

•**VERSE** 48 The ships were probably broken up in a storm.

STUDY QUESTIONS FOR FIRST KINGS

1. God's desire is to give good gifts to His children. In 1 Kings 3:5 God said to Solomon, "Ask what I shall give you." What was Solomon's answer? If God should say that to you today, what would you ask?

_____

_____

_____

2. Although Solomon was wise, wealthy, and had peace in the land, his heart turned from God. What ultimately led him away? (1 Kings 11:1-6).

_____

_____

_____

3. An important point in the history of Israel is when the kingdom was divided. Why was the nation divided? What were the two kingdoms called? (1 Kings 12:1-17).

_____

_____

_____

4. The Bible says, "Seek ye first the kingdom of God, and His righteousness; and all these things shall be added unto you" (Matthew 6:33). How was this demonstrated in 1 Kings 17:10-16?

_____

_____

_____

5. Many times fear can grip our hearts and overwhelm us. This happened to Elijah in 1 Kings chapter 19. How did the Lord show Himself to Elijah in verses 11-12? In what way did Elijah ultimately hear Him?

_____

_____

_____

THE BOOK OF
SECOND KINGS

AUTHOR OF THE BOOK:
Traditionally believed to be written by Jeremiah.

PERIOD OF WRITING:
6th century BC.

TYPE OF BOOK:
Historical

THEME:
God's people turning away from Him.

INTRODUCTION:
At the end of First Kings, God was dealing with the northern kingdom under the reign of Ahab with his wicked wife Jezebel. They had brought the northern kingdom of Israel into its lowest state morally and spiritually as they led the people into idolatry—the worship of Baal—introduced by Jezebel. And thus, Israel was sinking into a state of great spiritual apostasy.

As Second Kings continues, we are told of the divided kingdom of Israel. The various kings of the north and south are depicted, and their reigns are evaluated based on whether or not they were following after God and walking in the way of David, the prototypical righteous king over Israel.

Second Kings ultimately tells the story of God's people turning away from Him and being carried off into captivity. During this time, we see God using various prophets, such as Elisha and others, as He warns them of the consequences of their choices.

CHAPTER 1:
AHAZIAH'S TWO-YEAR REIGN

•**VERSE 1** When David was king, he subdued Moab, and it became a tributary to the nation of Israel. Later, Moab rebelled.

But under Omri, Moab was brought into subjection to Israel again. When-

ever a king died, especially a powerful one, the nation that was a tributary would rebel to see if the yoke could be removed.

With the death of Ahab, and his son Ahaziah ascending to the throne, came the successful rebellion of Moab.

•**VERSE 2** "Baalzebub" means lord of the flies. These people in Ekron were evidently worshiping flies.

HEBREW KEY WORDS

Baal = lord.
zebub = a fly.
Baalzebub = lord of the flies (1:2).

•**VERSE 17** Ahaziah's younger brother Jehoram began to reign over Israel. Because there wasn't a son to pass the throne to, the next oldest son of Ahab took over the throne in Israel. His name was the same as the king of Judah.

The northern and southern kingdoms were both ruled by men whose names were Jehoram.

CHAPTER 2:
ELIJAH IS TAKEN TO HEAVEN

•**VERSE 1** Elijah will be one of two witnesses in Revelation chapter 11 and Malachi 4:5. He also was with Jesus on the Mount of Transfiguration in Matthew 17:3.

•**VERSE 4** From Bethel to Jericho there's a winding valley, downhill 18 miles to Jericho.

•**VERSES 12-14** The anointing of God's Spirit came upon Elisha that he might continue the ministry of Elijah. The same miracle that Elijah had performed is now done by Elisha, indicating the prayer of Elisha was answered.

•**VERSE 15** When a person has the power of God in his life, people want to bow down to them, looking at the instrument rather than to God.

•**VERSE 23** Translated "little children" gives the wrong concept. The Hebrew language indicates a late teenager rather than a child.

•**VERSE 24** It's hard to understand why he would do that, except that they had great irreverence for a man of God.

It doesn't say that they killed them but scratched them up.

•**VERSE 25** Mount Carmel is in the area of Haifa on the coast. Samaria is about nine miles from the Mediterranean, about 25 miles from Mount Carmel.

CHAPTER 3:
MOAB REBELS

•**VERSE 3** He continued in the ways of the first king of Israel, Jeroboam.

•**VERSE 4** Moab was in the area across the Jordan River, the area that is now Jordan. They had been tributaries to Israel, and Moab had to pay 100,000 sheep and 100,000 goats a year.

•**VERSES 8-9** The king of Edom joined them to attack Moab.

•**VERSE 17** The cattle were taken along for food. The beasts were brought with them to carry their supplies.

•**VERSE 20** It can be a hot sunny day, and suddenly you get torrents of water flowing down through the canyon from the rain in the mountains. They didn't see the rain or hear the winds, and yet, the valley was full of water that came from Edom.

•**VERSE 22** The early morning sun rising was a reddish tint that reflected on the water.

•**VERSE 25** The one city they were not able to take was Kirharaseth. It's positioned on a hill making it extremely difficult to capture.

CHAPTER 4:
ELISHA'S MIRACLES

•**VERSE 1** If you borrowed money, you could pledge yourself as security. If you couldn't pay your debt then you were sold into slavery.

"Son of the prophets" was a term that meant he was in the prophets' school.

•VERSE 7 There is a similarity between this miracle and the one with Elijah during the three-year famine, when the oil and the flour never ran out.

•VERSE 19 He probably had sunstroke.

•VERSE 27 Lest people attribute his ability to know things to mind reading, God inserted this that you would know his gift was of God. And when God withheld the gift, he didn't know anything unless God revealed it to him.

•VERSE 29 "Gird up your loins" means pulling up these long robes, tying them with a sash so you could fight or run.

•VERSE 38 In Bethel, Jericho, and Gilgal there were schools for these prophets.

•VERSE 40 These wild gourds were bitter and noxious.

•VERSES 42-44 We are reminded of the miracles of Christ feeding the 5,000 men with the five loaves and two fish.

Elisha was a foretype of Jesus; whereas Elijah was a foretype of John the Baptist.

CALVARY DISTINCTIVE

"...and the LORD hath hid it from me, and hath not told me" (2 Kings 4:27).

Elisha had amazing spiritual insight and such a close communion with God that he was surprised when God didn't show him things.

CHAPTER 5:
NAAMAN HEALED OF LEPROSY

•VERSE 1 Leprosy was a loathsome disease. With all the qualities of this man, this was a black mark upon him.

•VERSE 12 His intellect was insulted; it was illogical that you could be cleansed by dipping seven times in the Jordan River. Also, his pride was offended.

Naaman was a captain used to having people bow down and respect him. His intellect and pride prevented the work that God wanted to do in his life.

•VERSE 13 Because God gives freely and in such a simple way, nobody can take credit for it. Somehow I would like to deserve or earn God's blessings, but I can't. I can only receive the goodness of God by grace (Acts 16:31).

•VERSE 16 People become very excited when they see God work. They want to lavish the servant of God with gifts. But Elisha is refusing the gift—rightfully so. He didn't heal Naaman—the Lord healed Naaman (Matthew 10:8).

Whenever you are in a church where they begin to put an emphasis upon money, red flags should go up in your mind.

•VERSE 26 Elisha discerns what was on his heart. The prophet starts laying out the things that he had in mind to do with this money.

God knows our thoughts and the intents of our hearts. He knows the motives behind the things that we do.

It is sheer folly to think that you can hide your guilt or your sin from God. There is no such thing as a secret sin.

CHAPTER 6:
SYRIANS TRY TO CAPTURE ELISHA

•VERSE 11 Benhadad thought his upper council was leaking the secrets. There was a security leak somewhere.

•VERSES 15-17 Since we live in the physical realm, often we lose sight of the spiritual, and are prone to be filled with fear and despair because it looks like things are hopeless. That's because we're looking at the things which are seen (2 Corinthians 4:18).

Spiritual insight makes a difference on our outlook in life.

•VERSE 20 They were surrounded by the Samaritan army, and the king of Samaria was excited.

•VERSE 22 In the Hebrew, it's "Set a feast before them."

•VERSE 23 They had been on these marauding excursions, harassing and attacking daily. This ended and for a time there was peace.

•VERSES 24-25 To capture a walled city, they would surround it, cut off all supplies, not allowing anyone in or out. After a time, the city would be starved into submission.

•VERSE 31 This king was leading the people into idolatry, they then had these problems; and yet, he wants to blame God and the servant of God for the problems.

CHAPTER 7:
ELISHA PREDICTS GOD'S SUPPLY

•VERSE 2 He mocked the promise of God because of unbelief—which often keeps us from partaking in the blessing.

•VERSE 3 Leprosy was a loathsome disease, the people were ostracized from the community, living outside the city wall, surviving off garbage dumped over the wall.

The famine was so bad in Samaria, they weren't dumping garbage; they were selling it. As they're eating babies in the city, there wasn't much being thrown over the wall to survive.

•VERSES 17-20 The word of the prophet came to pass. He saw it, but he didn't eat of it. The tragic price of unbelief.

CHAPTER 8:
ELISHA PREDICTS EVIL FROM HAZAEL

•VERSE 3 After seven years, she came back from the land of the Philistines and found people had moved into her house and taken over her land.

CALVARY DISTINCTIVE

"Why sit we here until we die?" (2 Kings 7:3)

I think of all of the ventures of faith that have been made on that kind of a promise. Who knows what God might be wanting to do? Let's step out and give God a chance.

•VERSE 8 In 1 Kings 19:15, God had told Elijah to anoint Hazael to be king over Syria.

•VERSE 12 This is much like when Jesus was on the Mount of Olives looking at Jerusalem on the day of His triumphant entry, and He began to weep (Luke 19:42-44).

Here the prophet Elisha could see what this man was going to do, the horrible devastation, the atrocities.

•VERSE 16 Here's when these two Jehorams are reigning at the same time. One is the son of Ahab; the other is the son of Jehoshaphat.

Jehoshaphat and Ahab were co-conspirators. They were friends; perhaps they decided to name their sons the same name.

•VERSE 18 The idolatries of the northern kingdom are now introduced into Judah through Jehoram. He was a wicked, evil king.

CHAPTER 9:
BOTH KINGS AND JEZEBEL KILLED

•VERSE 6 Israel had long ago forsaken Jehovah. Under the influence of Ahab, they were worshiping Baal. But God had not yet forsaken the nation. Though they had forsaken God, He still acknowledged them as His people.

•VERSE 21 Ahaziah was the king of Judah, visiting Jehoram at Ramoth-Gilead because he was sick.

There was a family relationship between the kings at this particular time.

• **VERSE 30** Jezebel was the wicked wife of Ahab, who had led the Israelites into the worship of Baal.

• **VERSE 34** Her father Ethbaal was the king of Sidon.

• **VERSE 35** The dogs had already eaten Jezebel in the street. Even today, when wild dogs devour a body, they don't eat the soles of the feet or the palms of the hands for some strange reason.

CHAPTER 10:
JEHU KILLS AHAB'S FAMILY

• **VERSE 1** Ahab was Jezebel's husband, who was extremely wicked. He had 70 sons; so evidently Jezebel wasn't his only wife. These sons grew up in Samaria and in Jezreel, brought up by tutors. His sons were leaders in these communities.

• **VERSE 10** Again the word of the Lord was fulfilled in that God said He was going to cut off all of the descendants of Ahab. .

• **VERSE 13** Jehu met 42 men from Judah who didn't know King Ahaziah was killed. He ordered them slain.

• **VERSE 28** Baal worship was eliminated out of the kingdom of Israel. It was totally obliterated.

• **VERSE 29** However, Jehu did not destroy the two golden calves that Jeroboam had set up in Dan and Bethel, and still worshiped the golden calves—thus, not serving the Lord completely.

• **VERSES 32-33** The kingdom of Israel began to diminish in its strength. Reuben, Gad, and Manasseh were the first to fall to the enemy since they were on the other side of Jordan and didn't have the defenses of the land that God had promised.

Crossing over the Jordan River, in a spiritual analogy, represents reckoning the old life and old nature to be dead. It's that place of faith where I reckon my old life to be dead, and I enter into that life of the Spirit, the promised life of victory in Christ Jesus.

CHAPTER 11:
ATHALIAH AND JOASH

• **VERSE 1** We go back now 28 years to when Jehu first became king and killed Ahaziah the king of Judah, the southern kingdom. He was the son of Athaliah, who was the daughter of Ahab and Jezebel. Through marriage there was a uniting of the northern and the southern kingdoms.

Athaliah killed all of her grandchildren in order that she might reign as queen.

• **VERSE 4** Jehoiada was the priest who had raised Joash in the temple. Joash was a descendant of David, but Athaliah wasn't.

• **VERSE 18** There came a time of spiritual revival as they now had a king who was raised in the temple under the strong influence of the priest.

CHAPTER 12:
JOASH REPAIRS THE TEMPLE

• **VERSE 1** Jehoash is another name for Joash.

• **VERSE 2** He was a puppet leader; Jehoiada the priest was the influence behind the throne.

• **VERSE 5** The temple had come into a state of disrepair as the people were worshiping Baal on the high places.

• **VERSES 6-7** The priests had done nothing to repair the temple. They were pocketing all the money.

• **VERSE 17** Hazael captured the Reubenites, the Gadites, and the tribe of Manasseh, and had moved his troops into the area between Jerusalem and the city of Gath, which was a Philistine city. He had taken the city of Gath and was moving his Syrian army to besiege Jerusalem.

•VERSE 18 It is recorded in 2 Chronicles that in the meantime, Jehoiada had died, and there was a downward spiritual spiral.

The invasion of Hazael was a judgment of God because the king allowed pagan worship.

CHAPTER 13:
ELISHA DIES

•VERSE 2 The northern kingdom did not have one decent king who followed after the Lord. Jeroboam was the first king who led the people away from Jehovah to the worship of the calves.

•VERSE 6 The grove was the place of pagan worship.

•VERSE 8 His death is recorded here, but in chapter 14 it comes back to Jehoahaz, because Amaziah is related to Jehoahaz.

•VERSE 9 Joash is still the king in Judah, but it's a different Joash here. For three years there were kings by the same name reigning in the north and south.

•VERSE 14 This is what is called a parenthetical. Although it already reported the death of Joash, he is still king during this period of time of Elisha's death.

People of great faith get sick and die. It is folly to believe that sickness or death results from a lack of faith or commitment to God.

CHAPTER 14:
AMAZIAH REIGNS IN JUDAH

•VERSE 8 There is a part of history in Chronicles that isn't recorded here.

We need this portion of the story to understand it fully.

Edom had once been subjugated to Judah, but rebelled 100 years earlier.

Amaziah decided to take Edom again, gathering an army of 300,000 men, and 100,000 mercenaries from Israel to go with them (2 Chronicles 25:7-8).

•VERSE 9 This is a parable where the thistle represents Amaziah and the cedar tree represents Jehoash.

And the desire to have the daughter as the son's bride was setting himself on an equal with Jehoash.

•VERSE 13 About 600 feet of the wall was broken down.

•VERSE 14 His defenses were destroyed and treasures taken because he wouldn't listen, but insisted on meddling.

So often we insist on meddling until we are defeated by the enemy. The result: our defenses are destroyed.

We lose something valuable when we meddle, such as the treasures of purity, innocence, health, and a clear mind.

•VERSE 21 The name Azariah may be more familiar by the name of Uzziah. He is called by both names.

There is a complete history of him in 2 Chronicles.

•VERSE 23 Jeroboam I was the first king over Israel, and now another king is named after him. This is Jeroboam II.

🗝 HEBREW KEY WORDS

Azariah = **The Lord is my help.**
Uzziah = **The Lord is my strength (14:21).**

CHAPTER 15:
AZARIAH (UZZIAH) KING OF JUDAH

•VERSE 3 He was a strong leader and a good king. The people came to trust in him because he had brought the kingdom into a place of prosperity.

•VERSE 5 The full story is in 2 Chronicles 26:16-23. His son Jotham was a go-between.

•VERSE 8 In the south they had their king for 52 years, but now back to the north, there's chaos. They're going through kings like they're going out of style.

•VERSES 9-10 Earlier, when Jehu destroyed Jezebel and the worship of Baal, the Lord promised to give him four generations to sit upon the throne. It was the longest dynasty in the nation of Israel.

With the death of Jeroboam, the dynasty of Jehu ends. This was the fulfillment of the word of the Lord from Elisha to Jehu.

•VERSE 19 This is the first mention of Assyria beginning to rise in power. The King Pul took the title of Tiglath-Pileser, and from history we have learned that they are one and the same.

•VERSE 32 Now it goes back again to the southern kingdom of Judah.

CHAPTER 16:
AHAZ KING OF JUDAH

•VERSE 2 Ahaz was one of the exceptions, as far as Judah is concerned. He was a wicked king.

•VERSE 3 That was about the worst thing you could say about a man, because the kings of Israel were exceedingly sinful, wicked kings.

Both the worship of Baal and the worship of Molech involved the sacrifice of children.

•VERSE 5 Second Chronicles 28:5-8.

•VERSES 7-8 He made himself a vassal to the king of Assyria. He's calling upon him for help to deliver him from this confederacy of the Syrians and the Israelites, the northern kingdom.

•VERSES 10-11 When Ahaz saw the altar of the Assyrians, it fascinated him. Thus, he ordered Urijah the priest to make an altar that was similar.

•VERSE 14 When Urijah set the altar in the courtyard, Ahaz ordered that they move the brazen altar Solomon had made over to the north side—nothing between the altar and the entrance into the temple.

•VERSE 17 He set the great brass laver on the ground and desecrated the temple of God by fashioning an altar after the pagan temples in Damascus.

CHAPTER 17:
ISRAEL TAKEN CAPTIVE

•VERSE 4 Hoshea took the money for tribute to Assyria and sent it to the king of Egypt to hire mercenaries to fight against Assyria.

•VERSE 6 This is the end of the northern kingdom. It lasted for about 250 years.

•VERSE 7 The word "sinned" means missed the mark. They worshiped other gods, misinterpreting their history. They failed to realize that it was God who made them strong.

HEBREW KEY WORD

chata = to sin, to miss the mark (17:7).

•VERSE 15 The word "vanity" is emptiness. Following after vanity, you become empty.

•VERSE 19 Ahaz the king was doing evil in the sight of the Lord, leading Judah down the same path as Israel.

•**VERSES 23-24** In 721 BC, Israel fell to Assyria. The Assyrians had a practice of taking the people out of their land and relocating them to other places—scattering them—to demoralize the people and keep them from rebelling.

The Assyrians then took other nations that they had conquered and brought those people into the area of Samaria, the land of Israel.

CHAPTER 18:
ASSYRIA COMES AGAINST KING HEZEKIAH

•**VERSE 1** Inasmuch as the northern kingdom has been destroyed, the rest of 2 Kings deals with Judah.

•**VERSE 4** They were worshiping the brazen serpent from Numbers 21:6-9.

•**VERSE 14** He offered to surrender unto Sennacherib. The king of Assyria laid upon Hezekiah a tribute of 300 talents of silver and 30 talents of gold.

•**VERSE 17** These are titles of men. The Tartan in Assyria was the commander in chief. The Rabsaris was the chief of the eunuchs.

The Rabshakeh was the chief of staff—the low man on the totem pole—however, he was the spokesman because he spoke Hebrew.

•**VERSES 20-21** Hezekiah had summoned for help from Egypt, even though Isaiah said he shouldn't. He sent for help from the pharaoh, which never came.

•**VERSE 22** That shows how little the people understood Jehovah God. He thought that all these high places and pagan altars throughout the land were built unto Jehovah.

•**VERSE 25** He's saying that Jehovah told him to destroy the place; he's blaspheming God and threatening the people.

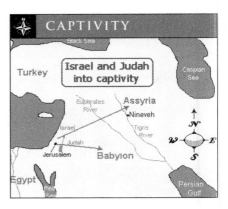

CHAPTER 19:
GOD DELIVERS JERUSALEM

•**VERSE 2** Isaiah was an influential prophet at the time of King Hezekiah.

•**VERSE 8** Shalmaneser heard some rumors that the king of Ethiopia was coming out to fight, that he was coming to Hezekiah's aid.

•**VERSE 14** He laid the whole thing out before the Lord—that's the best place to bring your problems.

•**VERSE 29** God has heard the threats; He's heard the blasphemy. The people have been shut up and there was a famine. God's sign is they'll eat what grows wildly. But the following year they'll plant again and dwell in peace.

•**VERSE 35** The reaction of the people living in Jerusalem is found in Isaiah 33:14.

CHAPTER 20:
HEZEKIAH'S ILLNESS AND RECOVERY

•**VERSE 2** At this point he's only 39 years old, and he hasn't had a son as an heir to the throne yet. Hezekiah prayed about everything. That's what made him such a successful king.

•**VERSE 3** Isaiah chapter 38 gives his prayer more completely.

•**VERSE 12** Babylon was only a little province. Assyria was too strong for any single nation to overthrow, and he was looking for an alliance with Hezekiah.

•**VERSE 17** Here is the first prophetic indication that Babylon would be the conqueror of Judah.

•**VERSE 20** He made a tunnel from the spring of Gihon to the pool of Siloam that they might have a fresh water supply when they were anticipating the attack from the Assyrians.

CHAPTER 21:
MANASSEH KING OF JUDAH

•**VERSE 1** Manasseh was the son of Hezekiah, conceived after Hezekiah's life was extended. Had Hezekiah died at that point, Manasseh would never have been born.

•**VERSES 2-7** Because of Manasseh's leading the people into such depths of sin, they could never recover. What would have happened to the nation had Hezekiah not insisted God heal him? There is a permissive will of God versus the direct will of God, where God permits me to do it, but it's not His direct will for my life.

CHAPTER 22:
JOSIAH REFURBISHES THE TEMPLE

•**VERSE 1** Here is when Jeremiah began his prophecies. Because the king said he was born again, this became a popular movement, but it wasn't a genuine movement within their hearts.

•**VERSES 3-8** During the reign of Manasseh, the temple was in a state of disrepair, but it had also been desecrated. Josiah began cleaning up and rebuilding the temple, and came across the copy of the Law of God, which had been lost for a long time. They didn't even know the Law of God.

•**VERSE 11** Josiah heard the law and he tore his clothes. He wept before God, showing a real repentance.

CHAPTER 23:
JOSIAH'S REFORMS

•**VERSE 16** First Kings 13:2.

•**VERSE 36** Jeremiah prophesied during the reign of Jehoiakim.

CHAPTER 24:
FIRST CAPTIVES TAKEN TO BABYLON

•**VERSE 2** When the weakness of the nation was displayed, all the nations attacked. The same kind of thing had happened to Israel.

•**VERSE 6** Jehoiachin is also known as Jeconiah, or in some places as Coniah.

•**VERSE 14** This is where you might read the book of Daniel, for Daniel was one of the 10,000 princes that was taken in this first captivity back to Babylon.

CHAPTER 25:
JERUSALEM DEVASTATED

•**VERSE 1** Nebuchadnezzar made his second invasion upon Jerusalem.

•**VERSE 2** Jeremiah 38:17-18.

•**VERSE 7** In Ezekiel 12:13, he is prophesying against the rebellious house, against King Zedekiah. This was fulfilled when Nebuchadnezzar put out the eyes of Zedekiah and carried him away as a captive.

•**VERSE 10** This time the city was completely devastated.

•**VERSE 26** They knew that after this act of treason against Babylon, it was going to be tough, and they all fled for safety to Egypt.

1. As Elijah's incredible ministry was ending, what did Elisha ask God? (2 Kings 2:9-12).

_____

_____

_____

2. Elisha truly had a heart for the Lord. According to 2 Kings 8:11-12, what reaction did he have when God revealed the atrocities that Hazael would commit? What reaction do you have toward the evil you see today?

_____

_____

_____

3. Second Kings 17:7-23 details the reasons why the northern kingdom of Israel fell to the Assyrians. In your own words, describe why they were taken captive.

_____

_____

_____

4. According to 2 Kings 18:1-7, who was one of Judah's best kings, and why? Who was one of their worst kings and why, according to 2 Kings 21:1-9?

_____

_____

_____

5. Our greatest strength and defense is always the Lord. What did King Hezekiah do when he received the letter from Rabshakeh, king of Assyria, threatening them and blaspheming the Lord? (2 Kings 19:14-15).

_____

_____

_____

THE BOOK OF
FIRST CHRONICLES

AUTHOR OF THE BOOK:
Ezra

PERIOD OF WRITING:
During the Babylonian captivity, and shortly thereafter, in the 5th century BC.

TYPE OF BOOK:
Historical

INTRODUCTION:
First and Second Chronicles are a repetition of the history of the southern kingdom of Judah, covering the same historical period as the books of Samuel and Kings combined.

First Chronicles tells the history from a mere spiritual perspective, with the emphasis on Judah and the messianic line of Christ.

These books helped the children of Israel, who were then returning from captivity, become aware of their connection with the past, and of the continuity of God's promises and programs. It is also the story of God preserving His people and keeping His promises.

CHAPTER 1:
ADAM THROUGH ESAU

•**VERSE 1** God promised to Abraham that through his seed the Messiah would come. To prove that Jesus was indeed the promised Messiah, it is necessary to have the genealogy from Adam to Abraham.

The Lord gave Jacob the prophecy that there would not depart from Judah a Lawgiver until Shiloh (the Messiah) came, and thus, the indication that the Messiah would come from the tribe of Judah.

Later, it was promised to David that there would never cease one sitting upon the throne from David's seed—David rightly interpreted the Messiah would come through David's family.

The Messiah had to be a descendant of Abraham, He had to be of the tribe of Judah, and He had to be of the family of David (Isaiah 11:1).

The names are listed to show the accuracy of God's Word. In Luke, chapter 3, we find the lineage of Mary traced back through the line, and many of the same genealogies listed here are repeated in Luke.

•**VERSE** 5 The descendants of Japheth are actually the Europeans and the Russians. Gomer and Magog were descendants of Japheth.

•**VERSE** 8 The descendants of Ham are those who went south from Israel into the African continent.

•**VERSE** 17 The descendants of Shem are the children of Israel and those toward the east.

•**VERSE** 19 "The earth is divided" could be a reference to the tower of Babel when the people were separated and had the confusion of tongues.

Or it could be a reference to some great cataclysmic event in which the continents were divided.

•**VERSES** 32-33 The sons that Abraham had after Sarah's death, through Keturah, or a concubine in later years.

•**VERSES** 35-54 The sons of Esau, the Edomites.

CHAPTER 2:
THE DESCENDANTS OF JUDAH

•**VERSES** 1-2 The 12 sons of Jacob.

•**VERSES** 3-12 Because the Messiah was to come out of Judah, we find the descendants from Judah to Jesse. He was to be a root out of the stem of Jesse.

•**VERSE** 7 Achar is also known as Achan; he took spoil from Jericho when that city belonged to the Lord. Achan was stoned to death because of this sin.

•**VERSES** 13-15 The sons of Jesse are listed. And from Jesse we focus on David, who was his seventh son.

•**VERSE** 16 David had a mighty general named Joab who gave him problems. Joab and his brother Abishai were actually David's nephews, the sons of David's sister.

•**VERSE** 18 This is another family in the tribe of Judah, the family of Caleb, the son of Hezron from verse 5.

CHAPTER 3:
THE DESCENDANTS OF DAVID

•**VERSES** 10-16 It lists a direct line of David's descendants to Zedekiah, the last king who was reigning when they went into captivity to Babylon at the end of the dynasty of David.

CHAPTER 4:
THE PRAYER OF JABEZ

•**VERSE** 1 This is another line of Judah by Caleb through Hur.

•**VERSE** 9 The word "Jabez" means sorrow.

•**VERSE** 10 He was outstanding because he was a man of prayer. God wants to bless us. He doesn't bless us because we're good, but because He's so good.

We seem to want to define our borders, draw our close circle, and to exclude others. We need to see beyond the narrow walls of denominationalism.

CHAPTER 5:
THE DESCENDANTS OF REUBEN

•**VERSE** 2 Even though the birthright was Joseph's, the leadership was to come from Judah, and ultimately from Judah to Jesus Christ.

•**VERSE** 9 They went over to what is present-day Iraq.

•**VERSES** 25-26 The tribes that settled on the east bank of the Jordan River were the first to fall. The reason was their worship of other gods.

CHAPTER 6:
LEVI, THE PRIESTLY TRIBE

•**VERSES** 2-15 Moses and Aaron both came from the family of Kohath in the tribe of Levi. Then from Aaron, his son Eleazar, following that line to the captivity of Nebuchadnezzar, taking them away to Babylon.

•VERSES 31-32 When the ark came back from the Philistines and was placed in the tabernacle, David hired priests to worship the Lord in song.

•VERSE 48 Another portion of the tribe of Levi, the descendants of Merari, were appointed to serve in the tabernacle as janitors to keep the physical aspects of repair.

CHAPTER 7:
THE DESCENDANTS OF EPHRAIM

•VERSE 27 Nun was the father of Jehoshua, who later was called Joshua by Moses. He took over after Moses died.

HEBREW KEY WORD

Jehoshua = Jehovah is salvation. This is the Hebrew equivalent of the Greek name Jesus (7:27).

CHAPTER 8:
THE DESCENDANTS OF BENJAMIN

•VERSE 33 The family of Kish, from which Saul was born: the first king over Israel.

CHAPTER 9:
PRIESTLY DUTIES IN JERUSALEM

•VERSE 27 It was their duty to protect it from vandals, and then every morning to set the instruments for worship.

•VERSE 33 They were free from other labors in order that day and night they could praise and worship the Lord.

•VERSE 35 The family of Saul through Jonathan and his descendants.

CHAPTER 10:
SAUL'S DEATH

•VERSE 11 Jabesh-gilead was across the Jordan River, ten miles away.

CHAPTER 11:
DAVID AND HIS MIGHTY MEN

•VERSE 9 The secret behind David's greatness: the Lord of hosts was with him.

•VERSE 11 Nothing is spoken in Kings of Jashobeam, and yet, he was a pretty powerful guy.

•VERSE 19 He poured the water on the ground, feeling unworthy to drink it. He poured it out to the Lord.

•VERSE 25 Benaiah became David's chief bodyguard.

CHAPTER 12:
MEN GATHER UNTO DAVID

•VERSES 1-7 These are the men gathered to him from the tribe of Benjamin, Saul's tribe. The Benjamites were known for their toughness.

•VERSE 8 Having moved on from Ziklag to the area of Adullam, came the men from the tribe of Gad.

•VERSE 15 Gad was over on the other side of the Jordan River. It was the month of March, which is flood time, and the Jordan was flooding. But they swam across the river to join David.

•VERSE 17 If they had come to hurt David by betrayal, notice rather than retaliation, he commits them to God. God is his defense.

•VERSE 19 The third group that came to help David were men from Manasseh.

•VERSE 21 The rovers were men that had kidnapped David's wives and children while David and his men had gone with the Philistines to fight against Israel and King Saul.

•VERSE 33 One of the weaknesses is a person who is double-minded or has double allegiance.

•VERSE 37 There were 339,600 men that joined David, plus 1,221 captains. It started out with about 600 men.

CHAPTER 13:
DAVID ATTEMPTS TO MOVE THE ARK

•VERSES 1-3 David's first activity as king was to bring the ark of the covenant to Jerusalem to acknowledge Jehovah in the life of the nation.

•VERSE 7 David inquired of the captains and leaders. He should have inquired of the Lord through the priests. He copied the methods of the Philistines rather than seeking God.

•VERSE 11 He called the name of the place Perez-Uzza. "Perez" means breaking forth, or a breach. God made a breach against Uzza.

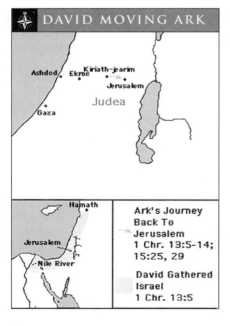

Ark's Journey Back To Jerusalem 1 Chr. 13:5-14; 15:25, 29

David Gathered Israel 1 Chr. 13:5

CHAPTER 14:
DAVID DEFEATS THE PHILISTINES

•VERSE 3 Deuteronomy 17 commands not to multiply wives. David was guilty.

•VERSE 11 "Baal-perazim" means the breach against Baal.

•VERSES 14-15 David was wise to seek counsel of the Lord, even though he faced the same enemy. Though the circumstances may be similar, God might have different methods than the last time.

CHAPTER 15:
THE ARK BROUGHT TO JERUSALEM

•VERSE 3 It had been three months since the last attempt to bring the ark of the covenant back. During this time, David erected a tent for it in Jerusalem, and searched the Scriptures to learn.

CHAPTER 16:
ESTABLISHING CONTINUAL WORSHIP

•VERSE 4 Then David ordered a choir so the people would remember the glorious works of God. Some of the psalms are for remembrance.

That word "record" is the title of two psalms: Psalm 38 and 70.

•VERSE 7 This is a psalm that defines the priests' duties as they were before the ark of the covenant.

As children of God in this dispensation, standing before the Lord, we should put this into daily practice.

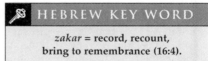

HEBREW KEY WORD

zakar = record, recount, bring to remembrance (16:4).

CHAPTER 17:
GOD'S PROMISE TO DAVID

•VERSE 11 Referring to Solomon, David's son that was to be raised up to sit upon the throne after David.

•VERSES 12-14 Now the prophecy exceeds Solomon to David's seed, even to Jesus Christ.

•**VERSE** 16 It was David's desire to build the temple, but he couldn't. David reflects on what God has done for him—asking so little in return.

CHAPTER 18:
DAVID'S CONQUESTS

•**VERSE 1** Gath was the most important city of the Philistines, right in the middle of the country.

•**VERSES 7-8** David gathered gold, brass, and silver to be used in building the house of the Lord. He couldn't build it, yet God allowed him to gather the materials for it.

CHAPTER 19:
BATTLE AGAINST THE AMMONITES

•**VERSE 13** A good rule to follow is to do your best and commit the rest. Do your part, and God does His part.

CHAPTER 20:
CAPTURING THE CITY OF RABBAH

•**VERSE 1** The Ammonites disgraced David's men sent to comfort the king at the death of his father, and it perpetrated the war. The Ammonites and Syrians were defeated by Joab, yet, the city of Rabbah was not taken.

•**VERSE 3** There is a discrepancy that Joab went against the Ammonites, fought and defeated the city of Rabbah, and David stayed in Jerusalem. But David then returned with the crown upon his head to Jerusalem.

Second Samuel chapter 11 gives insight. Joab had taken the city and sent a message to David to lead the army in the actual capture of the city.

It appears David cut them up with axes and swords. Actually, the Hebrew text is David put them to work with these things. He made slaves out of the people, rather than cutting them up.

CHAPTER 21:
DAVID TAKES A CENSUS

•**VERSES 1-2** David's desire to number Israel was a sin of pride, that he might know how great an army he had.

God records the sins of David—a man He used in a mighty way. God wants to use you in spite of the fact that you have failed, and in spite of the fact that you're far from perfect.

•**VERSE 14** David numbered the army to boast, but God cut it down to size.

•**VERSE 17** Sin has an effect on innocent people. No man lives to himself. Others are always affected by what you do, and sometimes in a very great way.

•**VERSE 24** God doesn't want our castoffs. He doesn't measure our gifts in monetary value, but rather what it costs us personally to give to God.

•**VERSE 25** In 2 Samuel 24:24, David gave 50 shekels of gold, but here it says 600 shekels. Two different Hebrew words are used. This word is "maqom," meaning the whole area around. He paid 50 shekels for the threshingfloor, and 600 for the whole field "around the place." He bought it to build the temple.

CHAPTER 22:
PLACE FOR THE HOUSE OF THE LORD

•**VERSE 1** God ordered this place for the altar to be built. They had been sacrificing only in Gibeon at the tabernacle. God is signifying this is where the house of the Lord is to be built. Solomon was to build the temple on Mount Moriah, the parcel of ground that David had purchased from Ornan.

It was also here at Mount Moriah that Abraham brought Isaac to offer him as a sacrifice unto the Lord. About 1,000 years after David, Jesus was led to the top of Mount Moriah, called Golgotha, and was crucified.

God chose this holy mount as a place of sacrifice, directed Abraham, and Abraham prophesied over it.

Here God stopped the angel above the threshingfloor, and David recognized that this was the place God had chosen for the temple.

The prophecy was then completely fulfilled when Jesus made the sacrifice for sin, and God offered His only begotten Son for our sins on this mount of sacrifice.

CHAPTER 23:
DUTIES OF THE LEVITES

•**VERSE 6** David organized how the Levites were to serve in the temple, and then return to their various villages.

CHAPTER 24:
THE DIVISIONS OF THE SONS OF AARON

•**VERSE 7** There were 24 courses, and they would serve two weeks each.

•**VERSE 10** In Luke 1:5-9 it says that Zacharias was of the course of Abia. "Abi" is the Greek for Abijah.

The program David inaugurated was still being followed 1,000 years later. Zacharias, the father of John the Baptist, descended from Abijah. They drew lots as to what part of the priesthood they would fulfill. It happened that Zacharias' lot was to offer the incense before the Lord.

CHAPTER 25:
THE MUSICIANS

•**VERSE 1** They were commissioned to prophesy—not foretelling, but forthtelling the works of God.

•**VERSE 6** There was continual worship and praise offered to God by the singers and various instrumentalists.

CHAPTER 26:
THE GATE KEEPERS

They guarded the outer court, which was the court of the Gentiles, but they could not come past a certain line. There were signs warning Gentiles not to enter, with a threat of death.

They also guarded the inner court and the gates that led into the temple.

CHAPTER 27:
ARMY DIVISIONS

•**VERSE 1** There were 12 captains; one for each month.

•**VERSE 34** When Absalom rebelled against David, Ahithophel had gone over to Absalom and then committed suicide.

CHAPTER 28:
DAVID'S PLANS FOR THE TEMPLE

•**VERSE 8** David's desire is to pass on the prosperity, the blessing, and the glory of a kingdom that is governed by God. He knew that the secret of success was their relationship with God.

•**VERSE 19** David had been inspired by God in drawing the plans for this new temple. Even as Moses was directed in the building of the tabernacle, David was directed by the Spirit of God.

CHAPTER 29:
GIVING

•**VERSE 4** A talent is thought to be 70 pounds. Multiply that by 3,000 talents, multiplied by 16 ounces, and then multiply it by the price per ounce for gold, and you'll find that David's contribution in gold was huge.

•**VERSE 29** These three men were prophets who wrote books. We have the books of Samuel, but we do not have the book of Nathan or the book of Gad. They are lost books.

STUDY QUESTIONS FOR FIRST CHRONICLES

1. David was surrounded by many mighty men as is listed in 1 Chronicles chapter 11. But what was the real secret of his success according to 1 Chronicles 11:9?

_____

_____

_____

2. Our sin affects others around us. How did David's sin of numbering the fighting men of Israel affect others? (1 Chronicles 21:7-14).

_____

_____

_____

3. David's psalms are a great source of inspiration to worship the Lord. List seven exhortations found in David's psalm of thanks in 1 Chronicles 16:8-36.

_____

_____

_____

4. Nothing is hidden from the Lord; He knows our thoughts before we think them. What advice did David give to Solomon in 1 Chronicles 28:9?

_____

_____

_____

5. Second Corinthians 9:7 gives an exhortation for gift-giving. In 1 Chronicles 29:6-9, how did the people give gifts toward the temple, and what was their reaction after giving?

_____

_____

_____

THE BOOK OF
SECOND CHRONICLES

AUTHOR OF THE BOOK:
Ezra

PERIOD OF WRITING:
During the Babylonian captivity, and shortly thereafter, in the 5th century BC.

TYPE OF BOOK:
Historical

INTRODUCTION:
This is a continuation of the chronicles of the kings of Judah. It does not really deal with the kings of Israel, but concentrates on the southern kingdom. Second Chronicles begins with the reign of Solomon and covers the remaining history of the kings of Judah and the messianic line of Christ.

Second Chronicles pertains to the lives of the kings of Judah and the decline of the kingdom. It was crucial for a people who were starting over to have a historical perspective on what made the kings of Judah succeed or fail and how obedience to God affects the well-being of a nation.

CHAPTER 1:
SOLOMON RECEIVES WISDOM

•**VERSES 3-4** There were two tabernacles at this time: David's tent in Jerusalem for the ark of the covenant; and the real worship center of the nation that was still at Gibeon where the tabernacle, modeled after the tabernacle in the wilderness, existed.

•**VERSE 7** God delights in giving good things to His children (Ephesians 3:20).

•**VERSES 9-10** Solomon, realizing his shortcomings, is asking the Lord to give him the capacity to fulfill the obligations as king over Israel—acknowledging his weakness.

•**VERSES 16-17** Solomon began this horse trading with Egypt early in his career, planting seeds of destruction in his kingdom (Deuteronomy 17:16).

Horses were a decisive weapon in battle, and a chariot was a fearsome weapon of war. God didn't want them placing their trust in horses.

CHAPTER 2:
HIRAM'S MATERIALS FOR THE TEMPLE

•**VERSE 3** Huram is also called Hiram.

•**VERSE 6** He had the proper concept of God—that God is not localized but omnipresent (Psalm 139:7-10).

•VERSE 10 A bath is about eight gallons.

•VERSE 16 They floated them down the Mediterranean Sea from Tyre to the only port in Israel, Joppa, 60 miles away. Then from Joppa they carried them overland to Jerusalem.

CHAPTER 3:
BUILDING THE TEMPLE

•VERSE 1 The place of worship and sacrifice for the nation of Israel was moved from Gibeon to Jerusalem. And the temple was built on Mount Moriah, the same mount that God showed to Abraham, with the prophecy, "The Lord will provide Himself a sacrifice. In the mount of the Lord it shall be seen."

•VERSE 3 The building was 90 feet by 30 feet.

•VERSE 8 A talent was 70 pounds.

•VERSE 15 About 50 feet tall.

•VERSE 17 "Jachin" in Hebrew is whom God strengthens. "Boaz" means strength and stability. The Lord is the one who strengthens and gives stability.

CHAPTER 4:
FURNISHINGS FOR THE TEMPLE

•VERSE 1 He made an altar of brass that was 30 feet long and wide, and 15 feet high. The temple built by Solomon was much larger than the tabernacle built by Moses—three times the size.

•VERSE 2 This was a huge brass bath for the priests to bathe in. It was seven and a half feet deep, 15 feet across, and the width was six to eight inches thick.

•VERSE 5 It held about 24,000 gallons of water.

CHAPTER 5:
GOD'S GLORY FILLS THE TEMPLE

•VERSE 3 This was the Feast of Trumpets.

•VERSE 10 Since the ark was taken by the Philistines and passed around, only the tables of stone were inside.

•VERSE 13 As the sound of the trumpets and the voices blended as one voice in praise and thanksgiving unto God, the cloud of God's glory came down and filled the temple.

HEBREW KEY WORD

halal = praise, celebrate (5:13).

CHAPTER 6:
SOLOMON'S PRAYER OF DEDICATION

•VERSE 1 Solomon preached a sermon to the people on the faithfulness of God. The very fact that the temple is here, built and completed, testifies to the faithfulness of God's promise.

•VERSE 30 Only God truly knows what's in the heart of men. We are guilty of misjudging people's motives.

•VERSE 36 Romans 3:10, 23.

CHAPTER 7:
GOD'S WARNING TO SOLOMON

•VERSES 17-20 The Lord is warning Solomon about forsaking Him. In the Scriptures, God warns people of the very thing that later becomes their stumbling block. He doesn't warn us needlessly. God knows our nature and characteristics, and He knows what will happen if we do certain things.

CHAPTER 8:
SOLOMON'S ACCOMPLISHMENTS

•VERSE 1 He spent seven years building the house of the Lord and 13 years building his own palace.

•VERSE 11 He should have known that's not the wife he should have had.

CHAPTER 9:
SOLOMON'S WEALTH

•VERSE 10 The algum is the red sandal-wood used in making instruments.

•VERSE 13 Six, from a symbolic standpoint in the Bible, is the number of man and man's imperfection. Seven is the number of completeness.

•VERSE 20 The house of the forest of Lebanon was his palace, made out of the cedars of Lebanon.

CHAPTER 10:
ISRAEL DIVIDED

•VERSE 8 He sought counsel of the old and the young men, but it said nothing of him seeking counsel of the Lord.

•VERSE 15 When Solomon was still king and Jeroboam was a rising star in the northern portion of the kingdom, a prophet by the name of Ahijah took hold of Jeroboam's coat and ripped it into 12 pieces. He said to Jeroboam that God would make him ruler over ten of the tribes. For David's sake, He was going to reserve two tribes that would be ruled by David's seed—Benjamin and Judah.

•VERSE 16 The ten northern tribes rebelled against Rehoboam and made Jeroboam the king, leaving him with the tribe of Benjamin, Judah, plus the tribe of Levi.

•VERSE 19 The northern ten tribes will now be referred to as Israel, and the two southern tribes will be referred to as Judah.

CHAPTER 11:
REHOBOAM FORTIFIES JUDAH

•VERSES 5-12 Rehoboam set about the task of fortifying the southern kingdom. Basically, these cities he fortified were south where Edom, Moab, or the Egyptians might attack.

•VERSES 13-16 The division of the nation brought those from the north—especially the Levites, who remained true to God. They moved into Judah.

•VERSE 15 King Jeroboam, rather than obeying the word of the prophet Ahijah, led them immediately into idolatry.

CHAPTER 12:
SHISHAK INVADES JERUSALEM

•VERSE 2 The reason for this invasion was that they had turned against the Lord.

•VERSE 5 This is the same prophet Shemaiah which had earlier told them not to go to war against Jeroboam in the northern kingdom.

•VERSES 6-7 In spite of the warnings and examples, they would forsake the Lord. God would forsake them; they would be oppressed and go into captivity to their enemies.

In the time of oppression under their enemies, they would seek the Lord. God would be merciful and deliver them, and then they would serve the Lord. In time, they would forsake the Lord again, and the cycle was repeated.

•VERSE 10 Brass is symbolic of judgment. Looking at the brass shields became a visible reminder of their consequences of forsaking God.

CHAPTER 13:
ABIJAH KING OF JUDAH

•VERSE 2 Michaiah was the granddaughter of Absalom, sometimes called Maachah.

•VERSE 13 While Abijah is making this speech, Jeroboam orders half his troops to get behind them to cut them off. He's outnumbered them two to one.

CHAPTER 14:
ASA KING OF JUDAH

•VERSE 8 They totaled 580,000 men.

•VERSE 9 A thousand thousand is a million men.

•VERSE 11 Recognizing that God does not need a big army. No matter what your problem may be, God is able to handle it.

CALVARY DISTINCTIVE

"O LORD, thou art our God; let not man prevail against thee" (2 Chronicles 14:11).

This passage of Scripture has meant very much to me through the years. I'm going to go out in Your name. Don't let them prevail against You.

CHAPTER 15:
AZARIAH WARNS ASA

•VERSE 2 This is God's eternal truth: the Lord will be with you as long as you'll be with Him. And if you seek Him, you will find Him. But if you forsake Him, He will forsake you.

Beware when God warns you of anything, no matter how strong you think you are in a particular area, because God doesn't waste words with you. If God is warning you about a particular thing, there's a reason.

HEBREW KEY WORD

darash = seek, inquire, to follow (15:2).

•VERSE 9 The people of the northern kingdom were seeing God's hand and blessing upon the southern kingdom, so a great number of them moved to the kingdom honoring God.

•VERSES 10-11 The Feast of Pentecost.

•VERSE 13 You cannot legislate righteousness. If there were laws that could make men righteous, then Jesus would not have had to die. But yet, it's admirable; their zeal for the Lord was at such a high pitch.

•VERSE 16 She was the grandmother, actually. They don't have the term grandchild or grandparent. Maachah was the daughter of Absalom's son Uriah.

CHAPTER 16:
ASA TRUSTS IN MAN

•VERSE 1 King Baasha built this fortified city on the main trade route to stop all supplies coming into Israel from the north.

•VERSE 2 For 25 years he rested in God. But now he had become rich and strong. He took money from the house of the Lord and sent it to Benhadad the king of Syria so that he began to attack Israel from the north.

There is always a danger of prosperity and success, and developing military might—trusting in the arm of the flesh rather than trusting in the Lord.

•**VERSE 9** God wants to use your life. God is looking for people that He can funnel His resources through to reach this world around us.

⚜ CALVARY DISTINCTIVE

"For the eyes of the LORD run to and fro throughout the whole earth, to show Himself strong in the behalf of them whose heart is perfect toward Him" (2 Chronicles 16:9).

God has a work that He desires to do, and God is simply looking for people who are in harmony with what He desires in order that He might show Himself strong on their behalf.

•**VERSE 10** The truth oftentimes creates anger and resentment.

•**VERSE 12** Had he sought the Lord, the Lord would have healed his diseased feet, but he began relying upon man.

CHAPTER 17:
JEHOSHAPHAT KING OF JUDAH

•**VERSE 5** Matthew 6:33.

•**VERSES 7-9** He sent out evangelistic teams to the cities of Judah to teach the ways and the Law of God.

CHAPTER 18:
JEHOSHAPHAT JOINS WITH AHAB

•**VERSE 1** Ahab was the most wicked of all the kings of the northern tribes.

•**VERSE 16** The king was going to fall in the battle.

CHAPTER 19:
JEHOSHAPHAT IS REBUKED BY JEHU

•**VERSE 2** The Bible warns against developing unequal yokes with unbelievers, and the king is severely rebuked for this (2 Corinthians 6:14-1).

•**VERSE 4** Jehoshaphat, unlike his father, accepted the rebuke of the prophet. He reinforced the people's commitment unto Jehovah.

CHAPTER 20:
GOD DELIVERS JEHOSHAPHAT

•**VERSE 6** God raises up wicked leaders of the earth for purposes of judgment (Ephesians 6:12).

•**VERSE 17** The consciousness of the presence of God is one of the greatest factors to dispel fear.

•**VERSE 21** What a strange army it must have looked like, with men singing praises unto God.

You have the victory before the battle even starts. Rejoice and praise God before you see the accomplished work of God.

•**VERSE 26** The "Valley of Berachah" means the valley of blessing.

•**VERSE 35** Ahaziah was the son of Ahab, an extremely wicked person; but Jehoshaphat had some strange drawing toward the kings of Israel.

CHAPTER 21:
JEHORAM KING OF JUDAH

•**VERSE 6** Jehoshaphat sought an affinity with the kings, arranging the marriage of his oldest son and the daughter of wicked Ahab and Jezebel. She had a wicked influence upon her husband Jehoram, son of Jehoshaphat, as did Jezebel upon Ahab.

•**VERSES 16-17** The kingdom deteriorated quickly.

The Edomites revolted, the people of Libnah revolted, and now the Philistines and the Arabians come in and take everything.

•VERSE 19 When the king would die, they would light bonfires, gathering around to mourn over the loss of the king—but not for this fellow.

•VERSE 20 He was only 45 years old at the time of his death.

CHAPTER 22:
AHAZIAH KING OF JUDAH

•VERSE 1 He's actually known by three different names: Azariah, Ahaziah, and Jehoahaz.

•VERSE 2 The 42 is a copyist error somewhere along the line. In 2 Kings 8:26 it says that he was 22 years old.

•VERSE 8 God promised He was going to cut off the seed of Ahab from ruling in Israel.

•VERSE 10 When her son was killed, Athaliah took over reigning Judah, and immediately killed all the other sons so there wouldn't be another heir apparent to the throne.

CHAPTER 23:
JOASH CROWNED KING OF JUDAH

•VERSE 1 Joash was the only son that escaped the sword of Athaliah. When he was seven years old, Jehoiada the priest called together the captains of Judah and the chief men.

•VERSE 11 They began to rejoice that God had placed a descendant of David upon the throne again.

•VERSES 16-17 In reality, Joash was a little puppet as a king, as long as Jehoiada the priest was alive. Jehoiada raised him from a child and influenced a spiritual revival. They executed Athaliah and all the other priests of Baal.

CHAPTER 24:
THE FALL OF JOASH

•VERSE 4 During the spiritual decline under Ahaziah and Athaliah, the temple went into a state of disrepair. When they built the temple to Baal, they sacked the temple built by Solomon, taking stones and doors, and used them for Baal. Now Joash sees the temple of God and repairs it.

•VERSE 10 Second Corinthians 9:7.

•VERSES 12-14 The temple was restored and there was an outward spiritual movement.

•VERSE 17 Joash evidently was a weak man and easily influenced. As long as Jehoiada was alive and exercising spiritual influence over him, he did well. As soon as Jehoiada died, the princes of Judah showed obeisance to Joash, and requested to worship Ashtoreth and idols.

•VERSE 22 Zechariah was the son of the priest, and probably grew up with Joash, but Joash turned against God.

•VERSE 23 These princes that asked to re-institute the worship of the Asherim were killed by the Syrians. The host of the Syrians executed God's judgment against Judah for their evil.

•VERSE 25 Joash had every opportunity to be a great king, influenced by Jehoiada the priest to re-establish temple worship. But at the death of Jehoiada, Joash's old nature returned, and thus he is not even buried in a place of honor.

CHAPTER 25:
AMAZIAH KING OF JUDAH

•VERSES 6-7 Amaziah hired 100,000 men of Israel to fight against the Edomites. This man of God said, "Why are you trusting in the Israelites for help? Trust in the Lord. Send them home."

•**VERSES 18-19** Be satisfied with the victory you had over the Edomites and don't go looking for trouble.

•**VERSE 23** When you fall into temptation, your defenses are destroyed. The next time you face that same temptation, you won't have the same amount of strength to resist.

CHAPTER 26:
UZZIAH KING OF JUDAH

•**VERSE 2** Eloth is present-day Eliot, a coastal city in the area of the gulf. His father Amaziah had conquered the Edomites.

•**VERSE 5** This isn't the prophet Zechariah who wrote the book of Zechariah, who comes on the scene after the Babylonian captivity. This is the only place in Scripture he's mentioned.

•**VERSE 16** This was exclusively the priest's duty. As the king, he could not intrude into the temple to offer incense.

•**VERSE 20** According to the law, a leper wasn't to come into the temple.

CHAPTER 27:
JOTHAM KING OF JUDAH

•**VERSE 2** Though he did that which was right, he was not a strong leader, and thus under his reign corruption began to break out among the people.

•**VERSE 3** Ophel was the hill that goes down from the area of the Temple Mount into the Kidron Valley and the Tyropoean Valley on the other side; the original area of the City of David.

•**VERSE 9** He died at the age of 41.

CHAPTER 28:
AHAZ KING OF JUDAH

•**VERSE 1** During his reign the kingdom sinks to its lowest, spiritually, beginning the final downward trend.

•**VERSES 9-13** Under the law of Moses, the children of Israel were not to take other Israelites as slaves.

•**VERSE 15** This is the shameful way in which they brought the captives back, naked and without shoes.

•**VERSE 23** Rather than turning to God, he went deeper into the abomination.

CHAPTER 29:
HEZEKIAH BECOMES KING OF JUDAH

•**VERSE 3** The first thing that Hezekiah does is re-establish the worship of Jehovah.

•**VERSES 21-24** The first offering needed was the sin offering, in order to establish fellowship with God.

•**VERSE 27** The next offering they made unto the Lord were the burnt offerings. The burnt offerings were for consecrating your life to the Lord.

•**VERSE 31** The worship of God must always arise out of a free heart. You cannot force people to worship God.

•**VERSE 35** Last of all was the peace offering, entering into peace with God, sitting down to eat together in fellowship.

CHAPTER 30:
PASSOVER REINSTITUTED BY HEZEKIAH

•**VERSES 1-3** In the law of Moses, those that were not ready or prepared in the first month were able to observe the Passover in the second month.

•**VERSE 5** They're going to include the invitation to the northern kingdom.

•**VERSES 7-9** The Assyrians had taken the northern kingdom captive and only a remnant of people were left. Hezekiah sent this letter to unite the people from the northern kingdom to worship the Lord—a beautiful attempt on the part of Hezekiah.

•**VERSES** 17-20 For the Passover it was necessary to go through a purification rite, shaving their heads and bathing to be sanctified and cleansed from the defilement of the Gentile world.

They didn't have time to go through the purification rite.

Hezekiah prayed the Lord would have mercy on them. The Lord spoke and said He would receive them without the rituals, and for them to observe the Passover. This was a turning point for the people and turning them back to God.

CHAPTER 31:
HEZEKIAH'S REFORMS

•**VERSES** 1-2 They cleansed the land from the remnants of their idolatry.

CHAPTER 32:
HEZEKIAH'S VICTORY OVER SENNACHERIB

•**VERSES** 3-4 This is referring to the conduit that Hezekiah built from the spring of Gihon to the pool of Siloam. The "stopping up" is the covering of the spring from the outside, and the water then flowed through this tunnel through the rock, and emptied out in the pool of Siloam.

During the siege, not only would the Assyrians be kept from the water, but they would have a sufficient supply of fresh water to maintain themselves during the siege.

•**VERSE** 8 As a child of God you shouldn't fear the enemy (1 John 4:4).

•**VERSE** 9 Messengers came to Hezekiah with threatening letters saying surrender or be destroyed. These letters were blasphemous against the Lord.

•**VERSE** 11 He didn't know that Hezekiah diverted the spring into the city.

•**VERSE** 14 The whole idea was to destroy faith and inspire fear. And Satan uses the same guise today. He plants fear in your heart to destroy your faith in God and seeks to focus your attention on your circumstances. Hezekiah was focusing the people's eyes on God.

•**VERSE** 21 The word of the Lord came to Hezekiah through Isaiah to rest in God. The Assyrians fled back to Assyria, including King Sennacherib, who went into the temple of his god where his two sons killed him. They saw the delivering power of God.

•**VERSE** 31 The king of Babylon sent emissaries to Hezekiah congratulating him for his deathbed recovery.

Hezekiah became prideful, showing off his treasure to these Babylonian emissaries (Proverbs 16:18).

CHAPTER 33:
MANASSEH KING OF JUDAH

•**VERSE** 1 He had the longest reign of any king.

•**VERSES** 11-13 Manasseh had a conversion experience. He was taken captive by the Assyrian king, who dragged him through thorns and brought him to Babylon. There he began to call out to God.

From that time on, Manasseh was a changed man. He brought about spiritual reforms, but he was not able to undo the folly of his earlier years.

•**VERSE** 22 Manasseh didn't get rid of them all.

CHAPTER 34:
JOSIAH KING OF JUDAH

•**VERSE** 3 He was eight when he began to reign. By the time he was 16, he sought the Lord. By the time he was 20, he purged the land of false images.

•**VERSE 19** He realized that these are the curses God said that He would bring upon the land because of their sin and iniquity.

•**VERSE 33** The temple was reopened and they began to worship again. The king's commitment was with all of his heart, with all of his soul. He made it a law that the people would serve the Lord—but the people weren't wholly committed.

CHAPTER 35:
THE LIFE AND DEATH OF JOSIAH

•**VERSE 1** Josiah instituted a Passover superseding that of his great grandfather Hezekiah.

•**VERSE 3** The ark was taken out when Manasseh profaned the temple. Now the ark of the covenant is returned back to its place.

•**VERSE 21** We don't know what Josiah's motivations were because the Bible doesn't tell us. Josiah had been a faithful servant and an instrument that God used for the salvation of the nation for 31 years. It could be that he was incensed and insulted that a pagan king would try to instruct him about the things of God.

•**VERSE 23** The course of history is changed by the hardheadedness of this king. How important that our lives be governed by God. Josiah would not listen. It was not until he was wounded that he surrendered. It's better that we submit to God before we are crippled.

•**VERSE 25** This is not the lamentation of Jeremiah over Jerusalem because of the destruction by the Babylonians.

CHAPTER 36:
THE FALL OF JERUSALEM

•**VERSE 1** Though Josiah was a good king in the sight of the Lord, three of his sons were all bad.

It is interesting that a good, godly man could have three ungodly sons. God has no grandchildren. It is incumbent upon parents to pass on to children the knowledge and understanding of God.

•**VERSES 2-3** It was Pharaoh Necho that killed their father Josiah in the battle of Megiddo.

Pharaoh Necho came to Jerusalem when Josiah's son only had a chance to reign for three months and captured him, took him to Egypt, and placed a tribute upon Judah for 100 talents of silver and a talent of gold.

•**VERSE 6** The Assyrians had been conquered by Babylon, leaving two major powers, Babylon and Egypt.

Jerusalem was between Babylon and Egypt, and whenever there was an excursion against either one, they had to pass through the land. Now under the reign of Jehoiakim, Babylon comes with their troops, conquers the city, and takes away captives.

•**VERSE 13** He swore before God to be faithful and to be a servant to Nebuchadnezzar.

•**VERSE 16** Genesis 6:3.

•**VERSE 21** Israel had existed for 490 years in the land God had given to them, but they didn't obey the commandments of God.

When God brought them into captivity He said, "Because you have not obeyed the Sabbath law for 490 years, but have planted the land year after year, I will allow the land to lie desolate for 70 years because 70 Sabbaths were missed by the land."

•**VERSE 22** This is 70 years later.

•**VERSES 22-23** These last two verses are the same as the first three verses in the book of Ezra.

STUDY QUESTIONS FOR SECOND CHRONICLES

1. Second Chronicles 1:14-17 states that Solomon began to accumulate horses and chariots. What is God's warning in Deuteronomy 17:16? Why do you think God warned against this practice of horse trading?

_____

_____

_____

2. What was the reason for Egypt's invasion upon Jerusalem in 2 Chronicles 12:1-2? What was the Lord's response when the people humbled themselves in verses 6-7?

_____

_____

_____

3. Jehoshaphat joined himself in battle with Ahab, the most wicked of all kings. What did God say about this in 2 Chronicles 19:2? How does 2 Corinthians 6:14-15 support this Scripture?

_____

_____

_____

4. Compare 2 Chronicles 31:20-21 and 2 Chronicles 32:25-26. List your findings about King Hezekiah.

_____

_____

_____

5. While cleaning out the temple, the book of the law was found and read to Josiah. What was his response when he heard the words of the law? (2 Chronicles 34:14-21).

_____

_____

_____

THE BOOK OF
EZRA

AUTHOR OF THE BOOK:
Ezra

PERIOD OF WRITING:
Some time in the 5th century BC.

TYPE OF BOOK:
Historical

THEME:
Encouraging others to obey God's Word.

INTRODUCTION:
The book of Ezra is the first of the post-captivity books. It pertains to an important part of the history of the nation of Israel—their release from captivity.

At the time that Cyrus gave the decree to build the temple, Ezra wasn't even alive. It is not until chapter 7 that Ezra comes into the story.

The first six chapters deal with the repatriation of Israel after the Babylonian captivity. Chapters 7 through 10 summarize Ezra's involvement as he encouraged the people to complete the restoration of the temple and a spiritual reformation.

Ezra wasn't just interested in finishing God's temple, he cared about the spiritual condition of the people. He knew their rejection of God's law caused them to be led away captive; and now as God was giving them another chance, he didn't want them to make the same mistakes.

CHAPTER 1:
THE PROCLAMATION OF CYRUS

•**VERSE 1** The Lord had predicted through the prophet Jeremiah that they would be in Babylonian captivity for 70 years in order to give the land the rest it didn't have during the 490 years that they were in the land (Leviticus 25:1-7; Jeremiah 25:11-13).

God also promised that He would bring them back after the 70 years (Jeremiah 29:10-14).

•**VERSE 2** Isaiah prophesied concerning Cyrus by name about 150 years before he was born (Isaiah 44:24, 28).

•**VERSE 3** Persia conquered the Babylonian Empire which conquered the Assyrian Empire, which conquered the northern kingdom.

Cyrus ruled all kingdoms of the earth, so his decree extended to the northern and southern kingdoms. Those who returned from captivity were people from all of the tribes of Israel. There weren't ten "lost" tribes of Israel.

CHAPTER 2:
UNDOCUMENTED PRIESTS REMOVED

•**VERSES 61-62** They could not accurately trace their family history to the tribe of Levi.

•**VERSE 63** They were kept out until they could find a priest with the Urim and Thummim to inquire of the Lord if these men belonged to the priesthood.

CHAPTER 3:
SACRIFICES RESUMED

•**VERSE 1** The seventh month is a month of religious celebrations, observing Yom Kippur and the Feast of Tabernacles.

•**VERSE 2** Zerubbabel was Jehoiachin's grandson and would have been the king had they followed the monarchy, but he didn't assume the position. He was the political leader, as Jeshua the priest was the spiritual leader of the people who returned.

•**VERSE 3** There was a lot of hostility from the people around them, and they were living in fear. They began to seek God's protection by offering sacrifices both morning and evening.

•**VERSE 5** Giving to God was always mentioned as a freewill offering. There should never be any pressure.

🗝 HEBREW KEY WORD

nedabah = freewill offering, offered willingly (3:5).

•**VERSE 6** They set up the altar to offer the sacrifices in the court of the temple, but they hadn't yet begun the rebuilding of the temple.

•**VERSE 7** They went to Tyre and Zidon for cedar timbers for rebuilding the temple, just as Solomon had done for building the first temple.

•**VERSE 12** The old men wept because the temple was pitiful in comparison to the splendor of Solomon's temple. The younger fellows were excited to have a temple again.

CHAPTER 4:
REBUILDING HINDERED BY OPPOSITION

•**VERSES 1-3** The Samaritans were the people Assyria placed in the northern kingdom after it was conquered and the Israelis were scattered.

They were taught to worship the Lord, but they also worshiped their own gods (2 Kings 17:24-33).

God became a part of their worship, but it wasn't a true worship of Jehovah, nor were they true descendants of Abraham or Israel.

The Samaritans wanted to help rebuild the temple because they also worshiped God—but their worship was mixed with idols.

So Zerubbabel, Jeshua, and the chief men didn't want their help. As a result, a tremendous animosity developed between the Samaritans and the Jews, even till the time of Christ.

•**VERSES 4-5** Their heart wasn't in serving God or in helping them. When their help was rejected, they sought to hinder the building of the temple.

•**VERSE 7** Artaxerxes was Smerdis of secular history.

•**VERSE 24** They fixed up their houses very nicely, but they forgot about the house of God and left it desolate.

Artaxerxes only reigned for ten months. He was then deposed and Darius became the king over Persia. In the second year of Darius there was a change of decree, and so the work only ceased for a little over a year.

CHAPTER 5:
OPPONENTS WRITE A LETTER TO DARIUS

•**VERSES 3-4** They discouraged them by intimidation to cause them to quit.

•**VERSE 7** Darius loved Daniel, who sat with him and had long conversations about God and the power of God.

•**VERSE 14** Sheshbazzar was known as Zerubbabel.

CHAPTER 6:
DARIUS' DECREE

•**VERSE 8** They were trying to stop them, but instead were ordered to give part of the taxes to help them. Many times God takes the evil intentions of man and turns them around for good.

•**VERSE 15** It was finished in the month of March, just in time for the Passover. The rebuilding of the temple took about 20 years.

CHAPTER 7:
EZRA RETURNS TO JERUSALEM

•**VERSE 1** There was a time gap of 57 years between the end of chapter 6 and the beginning of chapter 7.

Artaxerxes had given Ezra permission for 1,754 men to return with their wives, children, and their belongings.

This was now the second return to Jerusalem approximately 80 years after the first group.

Ezra had favor with the king and was granted permission to go back to teach and instruct the people in the ways of the Law of God.

•**VERSES 8-9** It was a four-month journey across a barren wilderness area from Babylon to Jerusalem.

•**VERSE 10** Ezra was preparing his heart, first to seek the Law of God, and then to do it (Luke 6:46; Romans 2:13; James 1:22).

•**VERSE 13** The king offered a free choice to either return with Ezra to Jerusalem or not. God also gives man a free choice to serve Him or not.

•**VERSE 15** God doesn't live in Jerusalem, but the temple was built there.

•**VERSE 26** He gave a lot of authority to Ezra: the authority of government, and the authority to impose the Law of God upon the people with the penalty of death, banishment, imprisonment, or the confiscation of their goods.

CHAPTER 8:
PEOPLE RETURNING WITH EZRA

•**VERSE 1** Chapter 7 is a synopsis of their four-month journey to Jerusalem.

Only 1,754 men returned with Ezra.

Most of the Jews were farmers up until captivity; afterward, they became wealthy businessmen and didn't want to return to the hardships of living in Israel and rebuild everything.

•**VERSES 2-14** The wives and children are not numbered.

•**VERSES 17-19** Since they didn't have ministering Levite priests among them, they wanted to take priests to minister.

•**VERSE 20** The Nethinims were the servants and janitors in the temple.

•**VERSE 22** On this route there were marauding gangs who preyed upon caravans that came through. Ezra was concerned because they were bringing a great amount of gold, silver, and vessels, which amounted to millions of dollars. Bragging about God, he was now ashamed to ask the soldiers for protection.

•**VERSE 36** There is a spiritual analogy drawn to this story. As we make our journey through the enemy's land to the Promised Land, we are sustained, protected, and strengthened by the hand of God.

One day, by the grace of God, we're going to arrive safely home in that heavenly kingdom, where we shall live and dwell with our Lord.

CHAPTER 9:
EZRA'S PRAYER OVER MIXED MARRIAGES

•**VERSES 1-2** God forbade interracial marriages only for the Jews. They were to be a separate people unto God because God was preserving the holy seed for the coming of His Son. There was also the danger that they would begin to worship the gods of the Canaanites and the Perizzites and the other inhabitants of the land.

•**VERSE 3** They had been in captivity for 70 years because of their idolatry and disobedience to God. Now after 80 years, they're back in their old idolatry. It's more than Ezra can believe. He's astonished.

•**VERSE 6** He didn't use the word "sin." "Sin" is missing the mark and it's usually not deliberate or willful. But "trespass" is a deliberate, willful violation of the Law of God. An "iniquity" is the sum of the sins and trespasses.

CHAPTER 10:
THE OFFENDERS CONFESS AND REPENT

•**VERSE 9** The ninth month corresponds to December—a lot of rain and very cold. They were trembling, partially because of the severity of the issue, and partially because they were soaked in the rain.

•**VERSE 11** Confession is the first step toward a renewed relationship.

Secondly, the question is not whether it is right or wrong. The question is does this please God? That should be the standard for what to allow and do.

And the final step: to separate themselves from the world (2 Corinthians 6:17-18).

They had the determination to confess, to please God, and to separate themselves, averting the judgment of God. God is gracious and merciful.

HEBREW KEY WORD

todah = confession (10:11).

•**VERSE 18** Even the sons of Jeshua, the high priest, were guilty of this sin.

•**VERSES 18-43** These are the infamous names of the violators. Their names were recorded so that throughout history their sin might be exposed as open shame for their trespass.

STUDY QUESTIONS FOR EZRA

1. What was the proclamation of Cyrus in Ezra 1:2-4? How was this a fulfillment of the prophecy in Jeremiah 29:10?

_____

_____

_____

2. Why did the returned exiles refuse help in rebuilding the temple? (Ezra 4:1-3).

_____

_____

_____

3. Many times God takes the evil intentions of man and turns them into good. What was King Darius' decree to those who attempted to stop the rebuilding? (Ezra 6:7-11).

_____

_____

_____

4. What does Ezra 7:10 say about Ezra? What can you do to prepare your heart today?

_____

_____

_____

5. After Ezra prayed for the people's sin, what three things did he tell them to do in Ezra 10:11?

_____

_____

_____

THE BOOK OF
NEHEMIAH

AUTHOR OF THE BOOK:
Ezra

PERIOD OF WRITING:
Some time in the 5th century BC.

TYPE OF BOOK:
Historical

THEME:
Accomplishing the work of the Lord.

INTRODUCTION:
The books of Ezra and Nehemiah are one book in the Hebrew Bible and should be seen as a unit. The first chapter of Nehemiah actually takes place about nine years after the close of the book of Ezra in 457 BC. The book of Nehemiah picks up 90 years after Cyrus gave the commandment to return to Israel and rebuild the temple in 536 BC. It's been 160 years since the beginning of the Babylonian captivity.

While the children of Israel were in captivity, the Babylonian Empire was conquered by the Persians, who allowed the Israelites to return to Jerusalem to rebuild the temple.

Fourteen years after Ezra had returned, Nehemiah heard a discouraging report from Jerusalem. The building project was getting bogged down, morale was low, and the people were being victimized by their surrounding neighbors.

Nehemiah was a patriot interested in the restoration of the people to Israel and what was happening there in Jerusalem—even though he had never been there. And yet, within his heart he identifies with Jerusalem and with the temple.

CHAPTER 1:
THE PRAYER OF NEHEMIAH

•**VERSES 1-2** Fourteen years after Ezra returned to Jerusalem, Nehemiah's brother told Nehemiah his impressions of what was happening.

The twentieth year is the twentieth year reign of Artaxerxes, stepson of Esther.

•**VERSE 3** They were afflicted and reproached because the city was a rubble.

•**VERSE 4** Being a true patriot, hearing of the saddened condition of Jerusalem, he wept and mourned.

Nehemiah was a man of prayer, always offering up prayers unto God.

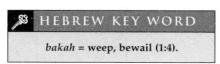

HEBREW KEY WORD

bakah = weep, bewail (1:4).

•**VERSE 5** The word "terrible" means awesome.

•**VERSES 5-9** God had warned them that He would forsake them if they would forsake the Lord, and that if the people would turn to Him, He would restore them to the land. Nehemiah was reminding God of the promises that He had made unto the people.

CHAPTER 2:
NEHEMIAH GOES TO JERUSALEM

•**VERSE 1** The story began the month of December and moved through Nisan, which would be the month of March.

•**VERSE 2** It insulted the king to be sad in his presence. Some of the Persian kings put their servants to death for this reason because they were supposed to be happy to serve the king. But Artaxerxes (also known as Longimanus) was easygoing according to secular history.

•**VERSE 8** The date the king gave to Nehemiah to restore and rebuild Jerusalem is one of the most important dates in history (Daniel 9:24-25). The commandment was given to Nehemiah on the fourteenth of March 445 BC.

The date of the coming of the Messiah can be ascertained from this date, which is when Jesus came in His triumphant entry into the city of Jerusalem on April 6, 32 AD. (Babylonian years are 360-day years.)

The prophecy of Daniel was accurate regarding the very day Jesus would come, also cut off—crucified without receiving the kingdom, and the Jews dispersed (Daniel 9:26).

•**VERSE 11** It was a long journey on horseback, so he rested for three days.

•**VERSE 14** They had gotten to a place where the rubble was so thick that they couldn't go any further.

•**VERSE 19** The first attempt from the opposition was through scorn—no one likes to be scorned or mocked.

CHAPTER 3:
BUILDERS OF THE WALL

•**VERSE 1** Nehemiah's plan for rebuilding the wall involved the people working together—each family group taking a certain section of the wall and working on it. So the whole wall went up at one time. They didn't start at one place and gradually work around.

CHAPTER 4:
OPPOSITION TO REBUILDING THE WALL

•**VERSES 1-3** Ridicule and mockery are tools that the enemy often uses to discourage the work of God. But Nehemiah met the challenge with prayer.

•**VERSE 6** The wall was built halfway to the height that they were planning to build it.

•**VERSE 8** Unable to stop the work through ridicule, they decided on a direct assault against the people.

•**VERSE 9** Again, Nehemiah answered this through prayer. Prayer does not preclude activity, it precedes activity. It is never an excuse to do nothing. We need a combination of prayer and wise precautionary measures—prayer and prudence.

HEBREW KEY WORDS

palal = pray, make supplication.
mishmar = watch, guard (4:9).

•VERSE 10 Satan sought to oppose from inside—more subtle and dangerous because we become more vulnerable.

•VERSE 12 Ten times they warned Nehemiah that they were getting ready for a surprise attack.

•VERSE 14 The cause for fear is getting our eyes upon the enemy and his threats. The cure is to keep our eyes on the Lord (Psalm 23:4).

•VERSES 16-23 Daniel 9:25.

CHAPTER 5:
THE RICH OPPRESS THE POOR

•VERSES 1-5 The priests and rulers took advantage of the people's plight. The rich took advantage of the poor.

•VERSE 14 Nehemiah had brothers with him, Hanani being one. They provided for themselves. They didn't live off the people by exacting taxes upon them in order that they might live a luxurious lifestyle.

CHAPTER 6:
THE WALL IS COMPLETED

•VERSE 2 They wanted to draw him out of the city to murder him.

•VERSE 5 An open letter in that Asian culture was an insult. It would be like sending it to the newspaper and you read it in the newspaper. It's an endeavor to put the person down.

•VERSE 9 The purpose was to put fear in his heart to weaken him. So he prayed.

•VERSES 11-13 Nehemiah was not a Levite and wasn't allowed in the tem-

ple reserved for the priests. The criteria to judge prophecy is the Word of God. God would never command us to do something contrary to His Word.

•VERSE 15 In spite of the obstacles both from without and within, the wall of Jerusalem was rebuilt in the record time of 52 days. It was many years before the city was completely rebuilt, but now they had protection from their enemies.

CHRONOLOGY OF RESTORATION

536 BC	49,000 RETURNED FROM BABYLON TO JERUSALEM.
536 BC	IN THE 7TH MONTH THEY BUILT THE ALTAR AND OFFERED SACRIFICES.
535 BC	THE WORK OF THE TEMPLE BEGAN AND CEASED.
520 BC	THE WORK BEGAN AGAIN BY HAGGAI AND ZECHARIAH.
516 BC	THE TEMPLE WAS COMPLETED.
478 BC	ESTHER BECAME QUEEN.
457 BC	EZRA WENT FROM BABYLON TO JERUSALEM.
444 BC	NEHEMIAH REBUILT THE WALL.

CHAPTER 7:
REGISTRY OF THOSE WHO RETURNED

•VERSE 5 A list of the registry of the people who returned when Cyrus had allowed some 49,000 to return is the same register that is in Ezra 2.

CHAPTER 8:
EZRA READS THE LAW TO THE PEOPLE

•VERSE 1 The water gate was probably the gate on the southeast corner of the city near the pool of Siloam.

•**VERSE 3** For about six hours he read the first five books, from Genesis to Deuteronomy.

•**VERSE 9** "Tirshatha" means governor.

•**VERSE 10** The work of God's Spirit causes changes in one's life. As they were convicted for their sins and began to weep over them, it was a good indication that God was working and there were going to be changes.

•**VERSE 11** It is a misconception that God wants to lay heavy burdens on us, making us grind through life. It is God's will that our life be filled with joy (John 16:24; 1 Peter 1:8).

•**VERSE 13** All men and women plus children, from perhaps junior high school on, stood for the reading and explanation of the Law of God. On the second day, the rulers gathered that they might be taught the Law of God.

•**VERSE 14** The purpose of the Feast of Tabernacles was to remind how God had preserved their fathers through the 40 years in the wilderness. Living in the booths gave a taste of the inconveniences their fathers experienced.

•**VERSE 18** The feast lasted for seven days, and the eighth day was a Sabbath day, a very solemn day.

The Feast of Tabernacles; they poured water from pitchers onto the temple pavement as a reminder of the water that came out of the rock (John 7:37).

Paul tells us Jesus was that rock from which the water came (1 Corinthians 10:4).

When they were filled with the Spirit, it would be like a river of water gushing forth from their lives (John 7:37-38).

CHAPTER 9:
CONFESSION OF SINS

•**VERSE 1** Sackcloth was a form of penance. It was itchy, miserable, and self-afflicting, even as fasting is a type of self affliction and denial of the flesh. They also put dirt on themselves as a sign of mourning.

•**VERSE 6** They are defining God since there were many gods worshiped by the people, such as Baal, Molech, and Mammon.

•**VERSE 7** They're rehearsing their history, which they have been reading and listening to from the first five books from morning till noon.

•**VERSES 16-17** God was faithful even when they were not.

CHAPTER 10:
THE RENEWED COVENANT

•**VERSE 1** These words were sealed and signed, starting with Nehemiah, the governor.

•**VERSES 2-8** Names of the priests who signed it.

•**VERSES 9-13** Names of the Levites who signed it.

•**VERSES 14-27** Names of the chiefs of the people who signed it.

•**VERSES 32-33** They imposed a temple tax upon themselves so that the sacrifices and the ministry within the temple could continue.

CHAPTER 11:
JERUSALEM'S POPULATION INCREASED

•**VERSES 1-2** It was a sacrifice to live within Jerusalem since there were nicer houses and farmland in the country. There were only about 50,000 people, and about 5,000 would dwell in Jerusalem.

•**VERSES 20-36** The names of the families that were to dwell in the other cities round about.

CHAPTER 12:
DEDICATION OF THE WALL

•**VERSE 1** Names of the priests and Levites that were serving at the time.

•**VERSE 43** A tremendous day of dedicating the wall and worshiping God. The shout, the joy, and the singing were so glorious, they were heard from a long distance.

CHAPTER 13:
OTHER REFORMS

•**VERSES 1-3** As they read the Law of God, they discovered that a Moabite or an Ammonite could not come into the house of God forever because of the treatment they gave to the Israelites during their exodus from Egypt to the Promised Land. So they separated all the mixed multitude from them.

•**VERSE 4** Tobiah was the one who had worked so hard to hinder the work of the rebuilding of the wall and was an enemy to Nehemiah. Yet here he was allied with one of the priests, Eliashib.

•**VERSE 6** After 12 years in Jerusalem rebuilding the walls, setting things up, and governing, Nehemiah returned to the palace in Shushan, to the king of Persia, and gave the king reports.

•**VERSE 9** He put the room back to its original intent and purpose.

•**VERSE 10** They already failed to keep the covenant they had made in chapter 10. Since they are not supporting the temple, the Levites had to return to their fields and work again.

•**VERSE 28** Sanballat was the other guy who had given Nehemiah a bad time. Eliashib the high priest was tied in marriage to both Tobiah and Sanballat, these two enemies of Nehemiah.

STUDY QUESTIONS FOR NEHEMIAH

1. What was significant about the commandment of King Artaxerxes to Nehemiah to rebuild Jerusalem? (Nehemiah 2:8; Daniel 9:24-26).

_____

_____

_____

2. The enemy will try to hinder the work of God. What were some of the ways the enemy tried to discourage Nehemiah from rebuilding the wall? (Nehemiah 4:1-3, 8, 10).

_____

_____

_____

3. After reading the Law of the Lord, the people confessed their sins. What confession did they make in Nehemiah 9:33?

_____

_____

_____

4. Strong leadership is important because people have a tendency to fall away from the Lord without it. According to Nehemiah 13:4-7, what did the high priest Eliashib do while Nehemiah was back in Persia?

_____

_____

_____

5. What promise was made in Nehemiah 10:32? After the promise was broken, what did Nehemiah do? (Nehemiah 13:11-13).

_____

_____

_____

THE BOOK OF
ESTHER

AUTHOR OF THE BOOK:
Unknown, but a likely candidate would be Mordecai.

PERIOD OF WRITING:
Middle of the 5th century BC.

TYPE OF BOOK:
Historical

THEME:
God's preservation of His people.

INTRODUCTION:
If the books of the Bible were placed in a chronological order, the book of Esther would come before the book of Nehemiah. The book of Esther fits halfway between the rebuilding of the temple and the rebuilding of the city of Jerusalem.

The book of Esther covers a period of 12 years, giving the historic setting for the Feast of Purim. The Feast of Purim is celebrated by the Jews to the present day, in the twelfth month of the Jewish calendar, equivalent to the month of March.

In the story of Esther, although it doesn't mention the word God, His overruling providence is seen throughout the entire book. The Jews hold this as one of the most important books in the Bible as a beautiful story of God's preservation of His people.

We see God working far in advance, setting people in specific places in order to save the Jews from this attempted extermination.

CHAPTER 1:
AHASUERUS DEPOSES QUEEN VASHTI

•**VERSE 1** Ahasuerus is the Xerxes of secular history, also called Artaxerxes.

•**VERSE 11** In that culture, it wasn't proper for a woman to be in public without her veil. The king was asking the queen to display her beauty without her veil for all to see.

•**VERSE 12** Women were actually considered only one step above slaves. They had very few rights. When Vashti refused the king's commandment, it was something unheard of.

CHAPTER 2:
ESTHER BECOMES QUEEN

•VERSE 1 Between chapters 1 and 2 there is a lapse of about four years time.

•VERSES 5-6 Mordecai was not personally carried away captive, because that would mean he was about 120 years old at this point. But he was of the tribe of Benjamin, of the family of Kish, which was carried away.

•VERSES 21-23 Esther's cousin Mordecai spoiled the plan to assassinate the king. The incident was recorded but Mordecai was not rewarded. That's all a part of God's plan.

God sets His people in His places, sometimes years in advance. Often when we are in the midst of a situation that we don't understand, we are prone to complain against the Lord.

CHAPTER 3:
HAMAN'S PLOT

•VERSE 1 "Agagite" is a term for the Amalekites' king, descendants of Amalek, the grandson of Esau. God ordered King Saul to destroy the Amalekites, but he left King Agag alive. For this sin he was deposed in God's eyes from being the king over Israel.

God has ordered that our flesh be put to death (Romans 6:6; 8:13).

•VERSE 2 The Jews literally followed the Law of God, not bowing down and reverencing any graven image or likeness. Mordecai carried that one step further—he didn't bow to any man.

•VERSE 5 Had Saul been obedient to God, Haman wouldn't have existed, and his edict and attempt to destroy God's people wouldn't have happened.

•VERSE 7 Esther has been queen for five years, but the purpose of God has not yet been revealed. God already had the chief characters in position.

•VERSE 9 He was planning to kill the Jews and rob all their goods, offering a bribe of millions of dollars.

CHAPTER 4:
MORDECAI INFORMS ESTHER

•VERSE 1 Sackcloth with ashes was the sign of extreme mourning.

•VERSE 14 Mordecai had tremendous faith and confidence in the purposes of God to be fulfilled. Though Esther may fail, God will not fail. The Jewish race shall be preserved. God has made promises and predictions for them that must be fulfilled, and Mordecai expressed tremendous faith in the purposes of God, knowing that they're going to be fulfilled, even if man fails.

CHAPTER 5:
ESTHER'S BANQUET AND HAMAN'S PRIDE

•VERSE 9 He was so happy and joyful until he saw Mordecai, and suddenly everything turned sour. It's amazing how quickly our emotions can fluctuate from extreme happiness to anger.

•VERSE 13 May God help us not to lose our joy because of some irritant.

•VERSE 14 Fifty cubits is 75 feet high.

CHAPTER 6:
TABLES TURNED ON HAMAN

•VERSE 10 God turns things designed to hurt or harm into good.

CHAPTER 7:
HAMAN HANGED ON HIS OWN GALLOWS

•VERSE 3 She had not yet revealed to the king that she was a Jewess. It could be that she was reluctant, because she didn't know how he was going to react. If she was frightened, it is interesting how the Lord exalted Mordecai. It no doubt gave her courage.

•**VERSE** 8 Covering his face was a Persian custom, indicating he didn't deserve to see the light of day. It signified his impending death.

CHAPTER 8:
THE KING'S NEW DECREE

•**VERSE** 7 It was a law of the Medes and Persians once the king had made and sealed a decree, it couldn't be changed.

However, he let Mordecai make another decree that on the thirteenth of March the Jews would be able to defend themselves from those who would seek to kill them.

•**VERSE** 11 They were given permission to destroy and kill anyone who came against them.

CHAPTER 9:
THE FEAST OF PURIM INSTITUTED

•**VERSE** 13 A practice of the Persians. After they had killed their enemies, they were placed on poles as a warning and a threat to anyone who thought to rebel against the king.

•**VERSES 20-26** Here is when the Feast of Purim was instituted. It actually means "a feast of lots," because Haman had determined by casting lots which day the Jews would be destroyed.

To the present day, on the thirteenth day of March on the Jewish calendar they have a day of fasting, but then on the fourteenth day in the villages, and on the fifteenth day in the city of Jerusalem, they celebrate the Feast of Purim.

It's an official Jewish holiday, a memorial of Esther's successful intercession and of God's preservation of His people; turning evil intended against them into good, turning their sorrow into joy.

In the present times, the children dress in costumes. The girls dress in beautiful Esther costumes, and some of the bad boys dress in Haman's villain clothes, and others dress as Mordecai. They have a special cookie that they bake for this particular time of year called the Hamantasch or Haman's ears.

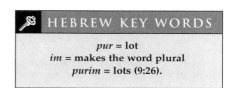

HEBREW KEY WORDS

pur = lot
im = **makes the word plural**
purim = **lots (9:26).**

CHAPTER 10:
MORDECAI'S GREATNESS

•**VERSE** 3 Mordecai exercised authority in a God-given way to bring wealth to the people. He was seeking the welfare of the people, not his own welfare.

When Esther's husband Ahasuerus died, his son, also called Ahasuerus in the Scriptures, became the next king.

He was the one who gave Nehemiah the decree to restore and rebuild Jerusalem, the decree from which the beginning date of the prophecy of the coming of the Messiah is calculated— 483 years after that date the Messiah would come. This is, no doubt, because of the influence that Mordecai and Esther had.

STUDY QUESTIONS FOR ESTHER

1. The Jews celebrate the Feast of Purim to the present day. What is the meaning of this feast?

_____

_____

_____

2. We can easily become discouraged during difficult times in our lives. What encouragement can we find in the book of Esther?

_____

_____

_____

3. Throughout this story we see how much Haman hated Mordecai. Why was Haman so irritated by him according to Esther 3:2? What was Mordecai's reasoning for his behavior?

_____

_____

_____

4. It was in Haman's heart to destroy not only Mordecai, but the entire Jewish nation. What is interesting about Haman's nationality? (Esther 3:1).

_____

_____

_____

5. In Esther 4:14 Mordecai shows tremendous faith and confidence in the purposes of God to be fulfilled. What was his thought-provoking question to Esther at the end of that verse?

_____

_____

_____

THE BOOK OF
JOB

AUTHOR OF THE BOOK:
Unknown

PERIOD OF WRITING:
Unknown; but it is believed to have taken place during the time of the patriarchs, before the exodus.

TYPE OF BOOK:
Poetical

THEME:
Human suffering and God's faithfulness to restore what Satan has stolen.

INTRODUCTION:
The book of Job begins the books of poetry in the Bible: Job, Psalms, Proverbs, Ecclesiastes, and Song of Solomon. The books do not fit a chronological order. Although the book of Job follows the book of Esther, Job probably lived during the book of Genesis, being a contemporary of Abraham. Job is believed by many to be the oldest book in the Bible.

Hebrew poetry does not rhyme or have a rhythm to it, but gives parallel thoughts or contrasting thoughts. The beauty of this poetry is the repetition of a thought with a slight change or addition.

Job was reduced to the bare essence of existence. Everything important was stripped away from Job: his possessions, family, friends, and his health. When you have lost everything, day-to-day worries lose their meaning. When everything is stripped away, what are the things that are expressed? What are the cries? And thus, Job becomes a godly example as we listen to his cries.

CHAPTER 1:
JOB'S FIRST TEST

•**VERSE 1** The word "perfect" in the Hebrew means a total man, a mature man. Today we'd probably say that he is a man who's got it together.

🔑 HEBREW KEY WORD

tam = **perfect, complete, upright (1:1).**

•**VERSE 6** "Sons of God" is a common name for the angels. After Satan's fall, he still had access to the throne of God.

The Bible says he's the accuser of the brethren before God day and night (Revelation 12:10).

•**VERSE 8** The word "considered" is a military term, referring to a general who studied a city before attacking, to develop his strategy to destroy it.

•**VERSE 10** God puts a hedge around His children (Psalm 91:11-12). Satan can only do what God allows him—no more. Don't fear, because God limits his powers.

•**VERSE 22** Many people charge God foolishly—maybe not cursing God, but saying, "I don't think God cares or loves me." Because of our circumstances, we are prone to make foolish charges against God, but Job didn't do that. He passed the first test.

THE LAND OF UZ

CHAPTER 2:
JOB'S SECOND TEST

•**VERSES 4-5** After Satan's first philosophy of Job was proven false, Satan developed a second one. Satan has a cunning understanding of human nature, as the psychologists tell us that one of man's strongest, most basic instincts is self-preservation.

•**VERSE 6** God places restrictions and limitations on what Satan can do. If the Lord controls Satan, then why doesn't God bottle him up and ship him out of the universe?

In order to receive meaningful love, there has to be a free will involved. God gave us the capacity of choice, but He allowed the opportunity of an alternate choice. And thus, Satan was allowed to rebel against God.

CHAPTER 3:
JOB'S LAMENTATION

•**VERSE 1** He didn't curse God, but cursed the day he was born.

•**VERSES 3-6** The repetition of darkness, blackness, darkness is Hebrew poetry—repetition with amplification.

•**VERSE 17** Job's words are not God's inspired truths. You shouldn't take Job's statements in his misery and develop biblical doctrine. Many have developed false teachings, such as the doctrine of soul sleep, from these statements of Job.

Job didn't understand what was going on behind the scenes (Job 38:2, 17).

Therefore, if you want to develop doctrine concerning what transpires when a person dies, you can't use Job's words; you had better go by the words of Jesus.

•**VERSE 25** There are blessed, misguided saints as ignorant as Zophar, Bildad, and Eliphaz who say Job lacked faith when he made this confession. God isn't listening for your negative comment and then acting upon your words. You don't control God.

CHAPTER 4:
ELIPHAZ SPEAKS

•**VERSE 7** This isn't logical to what Eliphaz is saying. Many innocent men have perished. In fact, the most innocent of all men was crucified.

•**VERSES 12-18** These men come off as super-spiritual.

•**VERSE 19** Second Corinthians 4:7.

CHAPTER 5:
ELIPHAZ CONTINUES

•**VERSE 5** The Sabeans and the Chaldeans had stolen everything Job had.

•**VERSE 17** Solomon was familiar with Job (Proverbs 3:11; Hebrews 12:5).

•**VERSE 19** This is a method of their poetry.

CHAPTER 6:
JOB RESPONDS TO ELIPHAZ

•**VERSE 5** When an ox is making noise, it's because he wants food. Once they have food, they're too busy eating to complain. Therefore, a man doesn't cry out unless there's a problem.

•**VERSE 14** This is in rebuke to Eliphaz and his speech.

•**VERSES 15-17** They are fair-weather friends. When things get hot, you'll never find them.

CHAPTER 7:
JOB FEELS HOPELESS

•**VERSE 2** He's referring to the shadow going over the sundial. The servant waits for that because he has rest in the evening and gets paid for his work.

•**VERSE 17** In the consciousness of the greatness of God, he became aware of the insignificance of himself.

CHAPTER 8:
BILDAD ACCUSES JOB OF HYPOCRISY

•**VERSE 3** Bildad correctly asserts that God doesn't pervert justice. But Satan challenges our minds as we try to understand life. Satan makes the subtle suggestion that God isn't being fair.

•**VERSES 11-12** The rush is the Egyptian papyrus growing on the banks of the Nile River. During the flood time, pools would form and the rushes would grow. But as soon as the pools dried, the rushes withered.

So he's saying, "Look, you grew up. You were green. You looked good, but now you're withered. You're cut down because you lack the true experience and relationship with God."

The flag is another form of river grass.

CHAPTER 9:
NO MEDIATOR BETWEEN GOD AND MAN

•**VERSE 2** In the Hebrew it is literally, "How can a man plead his cause to justify himself?"

•**VERSE 4** If you're fighting with God, you're fighting a losing battle—if you win, then you've really lost (Isaiah 45:9).

•**VERSE 25** A post is a messenger.

•**VERSE 33** The dilemma that Job sees is the greatness of God, and yet, Job himself is nothing. The gulf or the gap between them is too great.

The only solution that Job could see was for an arbiter, a daysman: one who could stand between man and God, who could touch them both. That's exactly what Jesus Christ is (1 Timothy 2:5). Jesus is the answer to the cry of Job for a daysman. Though man could never build a bridge to God, God in His mercy built the bridge to man.

CHAPTER 10:
JOB'S COMPLAINT TO GOD

•**VERSES 6-7** Job's friends kept insinuating that he is wicked, a hypocrite, and that somehow he's covering his sin. But Job is protesting his innocence here before the Lord.

•VERSES 14-15 As he's pouring out his soul, he's confused. He cannot understand why he was afflicted when he had sought to serve the Lord.

CHAPTER 11:
ZOPHAR REBUKES JOB

•VERSE 4 Job did not say his doctrine was pure. He did declare that he didn't know what he had done wrong that would justify this calamity that he's experienced.

•VERSE 6 None of us have experienced half of what we deserve. David, in writing of the mercies of God, said, "As high as the heavens are above the earth, so high is Thy mercy toward us. For You have not rewarded us according to our iniquity." God has shown His grace toward us.

•VERSE 7 The answer is no. Man, through an intellectual quest, cannot find out God or understand God completely. It's important to have foundational truths. In spite of what happens, God loves me, and God is wiser and can see much more than I can. My life is in His hand, and He is working in me according to His love and wisdom (Isaiah 55:8-9).

CHAPTER 12:
JOB'S RESPONSE: GOD IS SOVEREIGN

•VERSE 6 Job points out the fallacy of their arguments which are predicated upon the assumption that if you are righteous, you're going to be blessed of God; and the plague that he's experiencing is the proof of his sinfulness. If that were true, why do robbers prosper?

•VERSE 10 Daniel 5:23; Acts 17:28. We are dependent upon God for our every breath. And yet, with that very breath, how many times we've cursed God.

•VERSES 11-25 Job speaks of God's sovereignty over creation—God rules.

CHAPTER 13:
JOB MAINTAINS HIS INNOCENCE

•VERSE 5 Better to keep your mouth shut and let people think you're a fool than to open it and remove all doubts.

•VERSE 7 People speaking in the name of God, and speaking for God when God hasn't spoken (James 3:1).

•VERSES 15-16 This is a depth of faith. Job had it worse than any man, and yet, in this place, he says, "Even though He slays me, I'm going to serve Him." That's the kind of trust that we need.

•VERSE 18 Job maintained his innocence—infuriating his friends. It's completely opposed to their doctrine that a righteous man would suffer.

CHAPTER 14:
JOB'S VIEW OF LIFE AND DEATH

•VERSES 1-2 The shortness of life (James 4:14).

•VERSE 3 Job is speaking to God now.

•VERSE 12 Remember Job is not speaking divinely-inspired truths; therefore, his words cannot be taken as doctrine. Job is expressing his own ideas of what death is, not God's truth about death.

•VERSE 14 If a man dies, does he go on living? Yes, he goes on living in a new form, a new body, in the presence of God (John 11:25-26).

CHAPTER 15:
ELIPHAZ' SECOND SPEECH

The three friends have spoken. No one was able to convince anybody of anything.

•VERSE 10 Job went against the common philosophy developed through the years by these old men.

•VERSE 12 He's asking Job, "What sin are you closing your eyes to?"

•VERSE 13 This is a false accusation.

Job didn't turn his spirit against God, curse God, or charge God foolishly. He said he didn't understand God.

• **VERSE 18** These are the traditions that are passed down from fathers to sons.

• **VERSE 34** He is accusing Job of being a hypocrite, receiving bribery; and these things are happening because of his own iniquity.

CHAPTER 16:
JOB'S SECOND RESPONSE TO ELIPHAZ

• **VERSES 9-11** Job becomes a type of Christ. These very things are spoken in the Psalms of what should happen to the Messiah.

If these things in Job's life were a sign of wickedness and sin, then how is it that God allowed His own Son to go through similar experiences?

• **VERSE 19** Many times we are accused when we're not guilty. But my witness is in heaven; God knows the truth and knows what's in my heart.

• **VERSE 21** Why didn't they pray and intercede for Job instead of heaping abuse upon him?

CHAPTER 17:
JOB IN TOTAL DESPAIR

• **VERSE 6** The name "Job" became synonymous with a man who was suffering for his wickedness. Today the name "Job" is a byword for a man of extreme patience.

CHAPTER 18:
BILDAD ACCUSES JOB OF WICKEDNESS

• **VERSES 5-21** Bildad is intimating that Job is a wicked man and doesn't know God. That's why he's been caught in the snare, and that's why his children were all destroyed. Heavy charges against Job.

CHAPTER 19:
JOB'S FAITH IN THE MIDST OF DESPAIR

• **VERSE 6** Bildad had said, "The wicked get trapped in their own nets." Job continues to maintain that, "It's God who has overthrown me. I have been caught in His net." That's the thing that upsets them so much is that he is blaming God for the calamities.

• **VERSES 13-19** Everyone had turned against Job, even his own servants. He pleaded, and yet they ignored him.

• **VERSES 25-27** Out of the midst of the darkest despair, this cry of glorious victory: "I don't understand anything, but I know this: My Redeemer lives." Triumphant words of faith.

Probably one of the most triumphant declarations of faith in all of the Old Testament.

CHAPTER 20:
THE TRIUMPH OF THE WICKED IS SHORT

• **VERSE 19** These are suggestions of Job's wickedness.

• **VERSE 29** They kept insisting Job was wicked, hypocritical, and his problems stemmed from being sinful. The reason God allowed this to be pressed over from several different directions is to show the folly of human wisdom and understanding trying to reason the ways of God. There are still people today who hold to this philosophy.

CHAPTER 21:
JOB: THE WICKED DO PROSPER

• **VERSES 7-13** Job put down their whole philosophy by pointing out basic facts. In Psalm 73 the psalmist observed much the same thing concerning the wicked—that wicked people oftentimes prosper. This is the heart of the problem of Job. Why do the righteous suffer, and why do the wicked prosper?

CHAPTER 22:
ELIPHAZ: JUST GET RIGHT WITH GOD

•**VERSES 2-4** There is a note of truth in what Eliphaz is saying, that there's nothing that I can do to bring gain to God. Yet, the truth is that God has called and ordained that I should be His disciple, bring forth fruit, and be rewarded accordingly.

•**VERSES 5-9** These are accusations made against Job, assumptions without proof. Job doesn't answer them now, but in a couple of chapters he will answer these accusations.

CHAPTER 23:
JOB: HOW CAN I FIND GOD?

•**VERSE 9** He's seeking to find God in a material form. You will never discover God in material forms. God is a Spirit (John 4:24).

•**VERSE 10** He's having difficulties understanding his problems, but underneath his faith is rooted (1 Peter 1:7; 4:12). Peter speaks of God's refining process whereby impurities are removed.

•**VERSE 12** How much value do you put on the Word of God? The spirit is lusting against the flesh, the flesh against the spirit; these two are contrary. I see to it that my natural man is fed regularly and fed well. There is only one thing that feeds the spiritual man, and that is the Word of God.

CHAPTER 24:
JOB: GOD SEES THE WICKED

•**VERSE 2** The landmarks were piles of stones at the corners of their properties marking the borders. Unscrupulous people would sneak out in the night and move the piles of stones away from their neighbor's property, thus claiming more land for themselves.

CHAPTER 25:
BILDAD: GOD IS SUPERIOR

•**VERSE 1** Bildad has had it. He doesn't have much more to say to Job. In fact, all of the guys are phasing out at this point. They can't argue much against Job's logic. He has proved his case.

CHAPTER 26:
JOB'S RESPONSE TO BILDAD

•**VERSE 5** A more literal translation would be, "Dead tremble from under the waters." "Under the waters" is thought to be a reference to sheol, the place of the departed spirits of man. "And even those in sheol tremble and the inhabitants thereof."

•**VERSE 7** Job is one of the oldest books in the Bible, and yet Job declares that God hangs the earth upon nothing. Not until the thirteenth century did this become an acknowledgment of science.

The early men of science thought that the earth was on the back of a turtle, or that Hercules was holding it up.

CHAPTER 27:
JOB: LIFE AND DEATH FOR THE WICKED

•**VERSES 5-6** He is maintaining he's innocent—not that he is sinless.

This position that Job has taken—no condemnation because of deeds that he has done—is the position that is ours in Christ Jesus (Romans 8:1, 34). Many Christians have a sensitive nature, and Satan plays upon that and makes them feel guilty. The Lord doesn't want you to feel guilty. If you're His child, you're forgiven, pardoned, and cleansed.

•**VERSE 8** Matthew 16:26.

•**VERSES 14-23** The end result of the wicked life is destruction; it's misery. He may seem prosperous for a time, but he's going to be destroyed.

CHAPTER 28:
JOB: WHERE IS WISDOM FOUND?

• **VERSE 23** Wisdom and understanding are God's (Psalm 111:10; Colossians 2:3).

• **VERSE 28** Wisdom is the most precious treasure you could have. Where is it found? The fear of the Lord—that is wisdom. To depart from evil—that is understanding.

CHAPTER 29:
JOB'S FORMER GLORY

• **VERSE 7** The gates of the city were the places of judgment, and Job was one of the judges. It was a place of distinction and honor that he once had. He longs for those days.

• **VERSES 12-17** Job answered the false accusations against him, and declared the life that he had. It is confirmed by God, as God said, "He's a perfect man, loving good and hating evil."

CHAPTER 30:
JOB'S PRESENT CONDITION

• **VERSES 1-9** Job is describing the lowest category of people: nomadic outcasts living outside the realms of society. They were half savage. These people were as low as you can get, and now they look down on Job.

CHAPTER 31:
JOB MAINTAINS HIS INTEGRITY

• **VERSE 1** Job had determined that he was not going to look upon a woman to lust after her (Matthew 5:28).

• **VERSE 9** That is, if he waited in the back until his neighbor left, and then went for an adulterous affair with his wife.

• **VERSE 10** Grinding was one of the lowliest tasks; grinding the wheat or the olives, using the millstone.

• **VERSES 13-15** Job is saying he had not lorded over his servants, that he had looked upon them as equals.

• **VERSE 40** This is Job's final declaration of his innocence before his friends.

CHAPTER 32:
ELIHU SPEAKS UP

• **VERSES 1-3** Elihu was a young kid who listened to this debate. When they didn't respond to Job, he got mad and decided he could respond. He spends several chapters telling his understanding, but it's an introduction to a great speech that is never spoken.

Elihu became angry with Job because he sought to justify himself rather than to justify God. He was also angry with Job's friends for condemning him without pinning anything on him.

• **VERSE 14** Elihu suggested God does not always punish, but will use calamity as a reproof to turn man back to the right path. The judgments of God are corrective rather than punitive (Hebrews 12:6).

Oftentimes God uses suffering in a corrective way to turn us back to Him. This is the argument that Elihu will follow.

CHAPTER 33:
ELIHU CLAIMS TO SPEAK FOR GOD

• **VERSE 6** He's going a little far saying that he is standing there in God's stead.

• **VERSES 9-11** He's presuming to quote Job, but he doesn't quote Job exactly.

• **VERSE 14** God speaks in various ways, but our hearts need to be open to hear the voice of God. He can speak to us in dreams, visions, or angels; through His Word, or through a friend. You can't limit the ways by which God speaks to a man.

•**VERSES 26-30** God oftentimes uses chastisement to turn us away from the pit (Hebrews 12:5-6). If you can cheat and get by with it, then I would be worried. If you're a child of God, He's going to save you from the pit.

CHAPTER 34:
ELIHU: GOD IS JUST

•**VERSE 9** Psalm 37:4.

•**VERSE 12** Abraham said, "Shall not the Lord of the earth be just?" Elihu made the same claim, which is correct. God will not pervert judgment.

•**VERSE 19** These are characteristics of man in giving deference to the rich, but not so with God.

CHAPTER 35:
ELIHU REBUKES JOB

•**VERSES 2-3** Job didn't actually say that, but he's concluding what Job said.

•**VERSE 6** Our sins don't affect God—except God loves you, so your self-destructive path hurts Him.

•**VERSE 7** This is a good question to consider: What can I possibly give to God? He wants my love, trust, and my obedience. That's all.

CHAPTER 36:
ELIHU: HOW GOD DEALS WITH MAN

•**VERSES 1-4** He is assuming at this point to actually be speaking for God.

•**VERSE 11** Physical prosperity is not a sign of righteousness or purity (Philippians 4:11).

•**VERSES 27-33** Evidently as Elihu is talking, a storm moves in. He starts to weave into his speech the rain, the thunder, and lightning, drawing from the weather.

CHAPTER 37:
ELIHU: GOD IN THE WEATHER

•**VERSES 1-2** Referring here, in a figurative way, to the thunder, as though God was speaking through it.

CHAPTER 38:
GOD SPEAKS TO JOB

•**VERSE 4** God spoke to Job about the creation of the earth, pointing out that man talks with great pompousness of the origins of the universe of which he knows absolutely nothing.

•**VERSE 7** The word "star" refers to the angels (Revelation 13).

The "sons of God" refer to angels. In the first chapter of Job the sons of God were presenting themselves to God, and Satan also came with them.

•**VERSES 8-11** There is sufficient water in the oceans that if the mountains were removed, the entire surface of the earth would be covered with 6,000 feet of water.

•**VERSE 22** Under a microscope you'll see perfect geometric designs, and no two snowflakes alike. Talk about a God of variety.

•**VERSE 24** God is challenging Job about the dividing of light thousands of years before we even discovered the spectroscopes.

•**VERSE 31** The Pleiades is a winter constellation, a little cluster of stars that looks like a dipper, but it is the Pleiades or the Seven Sisters.

•**VERSE 32** Arcturus is known as the runaway star, larger than our sun.

•**VERSE 36** Where did you get your knowledge? Who gave you DNA and created memory cells? (Psalm 139:14).

•**VERSES 39-41** God indicated that not only is He the Creator, but He oversees His creation and is close to it.

CHAPTER 39:
GOD QUESTIONS JOB ABOUT NATURE

•**VERSES 9-10** The crib being the stall where they keep the corn. "Unicorn" is a translation of the Hebrew word *reym*, and probably a reference to an extinct wild ox. It was extremely large and fierce, and they were totally unsuccessful in trying to capture one.

 HEBREW KEY WORD

reym = a wild bull (39:9).

CHAPTER 40:
JOB HAS NO ANSWER FOR GOD

•**VERSE 2** Many times we instruct God in our prayer time. We take the power out of God's hands and put it in our hands. That's dangerous.

•**VERSE 8** Look out for this one—the practice of blaming God for what I have done.

•**VERSES 15-24** A description of some animal that is presently extinct.

CHAPTER 41:
GOD: POWER IN NATURE

•**VERSE 1** No one knows for sure what the leviathan is. Some think it is a crocodile, a dragon, or a hippopotamus with a hefty hide.

•**VERSE 32** When he goes through the deep, it leaves this white wake behind him.

•**VERSE 34** A description of Satan.

CHAPTER 42:
JOB CONFESSES

•**VERSE 3** That was God's question when He first came on the scene: "Who is this one who is hiding counsel without knowledge?" Job says, "I am the one, Lord. I am guilty."

•**VERSE 5** It's a glorious day when God is moved from our heads to our hearts, from a knowledge to an experience.

The Scriptures are suddenly opened as I am born again by the Spirit and come into the spiritual dimension. And in the discovery of God, there comes the resultant discovery of self.

•**VERSE 6** Seeing God gives insight about myself. I can see myself as God sees me—a sinful, hopeless wretch, deceiving and justifying myself (Daniel 10:8; Luke 5:8; Isaiah 6:5).

•**VERSES 7-8** God doesn't like you saying false things about Him, or speaking things that He has not said.

•**VERSE 10** The glorious thing about the ministry is that in ministering to others, you're always ministered to yourself.

•**VERSE 14** "Jemima" means a dove. "Kezia" is a spice. "Kerenhappuch" means a horn of paint.

•**VERSE 16** It is estimated Job was 70 years old when the calamity came. So God gave him twice as many years to enjoy the double blessings that came to him.

So Job lived to be 210 years old. If Job was a contemporary to Abraham, as is thought, that age is not unusual. Abraham lived to be 180 years old.

STUDY QUESTIONS FOR JOB

1. Job chapter 1 and Revelation 12:10 state that Satan is the accuser of the brethren. Why shouldn't we fear that statement? (Job 1:10; 2:6).

_____

_____

_____

2. Job could not plead his case before God because the gap between the finite and the infinite was too great. How has God bridged that gap for us? (Job 9:33).

_____

_____

_____

3. We seem to think we are in complete control of our lives and sometimes try to control God. How dependent upon God are we according to Job 12:10?

_____

_____

_____

4. Job 23:12 testifies to Job treasuring the Word of God above his daily intake of food. How much value do you place on the Word of God?

_____

_____

_____

5. According to Job 42:7-8, how did God feel about the counsel of Job's friends?

_____

_____

_____

THE BOOK OF
PSALMS

AUTHOR OF THE BOOK:
A variety of authors, including David, who wrote almost half of them. Some of the psalms were written by Asaph, Moses, Solomon, the sons of Korah, Heman, Ethan, and Hezekiah.

PERIOD OF WRITING:
They were written over hundreds of years, probably during the time of Ezra.

TYPE OF BOOK:
Poetical

THEME:
Praise to God.

INTRODUCTION:
A psalm is a hymn of praise to God. The book of Psalms was originally the hymn book for Israel. The psalms are a classic example of Hebrew poetry, which, unlike English poetry made of rhyme and rhythm, consists of parallel or contrasting ideas. Many of the psalms are known as acrostics because each verse begins with a succeeding letter of the Hebrew alphabet (for example, Psalm 119).

David, who authored many of the psalms, was considered a prophet, since many of the psalms contain prophecies about the Messiah. These predictions were direct references to Jesus Christ.

The collection of 150 psalms is divided into five smaller books: Psalms 1-41; 42-72; 73-89; 90-106; and 107-150. We aren't sure of the purpose of these divisions; perhaps it had something to do with the order of worship in the temple.

Many have seen a correlation between the content of these five books of psalms with the five books of the Pentateuch.

FIRST BOOK OF PSALMS
CHAPTER 1:
THE RIGHTEOUS AND THE UNGODLY

•VERSE 1 "Blessed" in Hebrew means "Oh, how happy!"

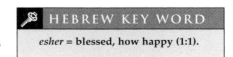

HEBREW KEY WORD

esher = **blessed, how happy (1:1).**

•**VERSE 3** This is the result of verse 2. We should bring forth fruit (John 15:8), and it should be lasting (John 15:16).

•**VERSES 4-6** Here is the contrast to verse 3. The wicked will perish.

CHAPTER 2:
THE KINGDOM AGE: A MESSIANIC PSALM

•**VERSES 2-3** His "anointed" is His Messiah. Man is rebelling against God and against Jesus Christ.

•**VERSES 4-5** God judges the Christ-rejecting world.

•**VERSES 6-7** The Father is speaking to His Son, Jesus.

•**VERSE 8** God is promising the kingdom to Jesus.

•**VERSE 9** During the kingdom age, judgment will be enforced on those who survived the great tribulation.

•**VERSE 10** The church will judge the earth and its kings.

CHAPTER 3:
THE LORD HELPS HIS PEOPLE

A psalm of David when fleeing from Absalom.

•**VERSE 5** David was able to sleep even while being pursued because of his confidence in the Lord.

•**VERSE 8** The psalm ends with a note of victory.

CHAPTER 4:
SAFETY OF THE FAITHFUL

This psalm mentions the use of a Neginoth, a stringed instrument, to accompany the verses.

•**VERSE 1** This psalm is a prayer of the evening.

•**VERSES 6-7** David's gladness will be greater than those who are against God when they are in the time of harvest.

CHAPTER 5:
PRAYER FOR GUIDANCE

Also accompanied by a Neginoth.

•**VERSE 6** "Bloody" is an old English term referring to a dirty or evil man.

•**VERSE 7** The contrast to verse 6.

•**VERSES 10-11** A contrast between the curses of the wicked and the blessings of the righteous.

•**VERSE 11** God wants our daily walk to be joyful.

CHAPTER 6:
PRAYER FOR DISTRESS

•**VERSE 1** David attributed human characteristics of anger and discipline to God.

•**VERSE 5** David expressed his own thoughts of death. Jesus' account in Luke 16:19-31 says death isn't oblivion.

CHAPTER 7:
PRAYER FOR DELIVERANCE

"Shiggaion" means loud crying. The text concerns Cush the Benjamite.

•**VERSE 1** David had many enemies.

•**VERSE 9** Our motives will be judged by God, who judges our hearts.

•**VERSE 13** God has planned the method of destruction of the wicked.

CHAPTER 8:
PRAISE THE LORD IN CREATION

"Gittith" means wine press, which gives the idea of a harvest of judgment.

•**VERSE 1** The first "LORD" in capitals is a translation of the Hebrew name for God, *YAHWEH*. This comes from the verb "to be" and means "I am who I am." The name describes God's relationship to you, for God desires to become to you whatever you need.

The second "Lord" means master and is a title indicating our relationship to Him (Philippians 2:6-10).

HEBREW KEY WORDS

YAHWEH = LORD, the Becoming One, self-existent.
Adonai = lord, master (8:1).

•**VERSE 2** God has revealed Himself in simple terms so that even children can understand.

•**VERSE 4** David began with God as the focal point and put man into his proper perspective.

"The son of man" is God coming down to visit man.

•**VERSE 5** Man isn't the product of random chance. He was created in God's image and is the highest order of God's creation, surpassed only by the angels, God's ministering spirits.

•**VERSE 6** "Dominion" implies watching over and taking care of the earth. "Thou hast put all things under His feet" refers to Jesus Christ, who was also made a little lower than the angels so that He could die for us.

•**VERSE 8** "The paths of the sea" are the sea currents.

CHAPTER 9:
PRAYER FOR RIGHTEOUSNESS

"Muthlabben" means the death of the son and could refer to the death of Bathsheba's first son.

•**VERSE 16** "Higgaion" means meditate on that.

CHAPTER 10:
PRAYER FOR VICTORY OVER EVIL

•**VERSES 2-11** These verses describe the wicked man in his deeds and his claim that God has forgotten them.

People mistake God's patience for blindness because He hasn't already destroyed them.

CHAPTER 11:
THE LORD'S RIGHTEOUSNESS

•**VERSE 1** The righteous man has no need to flee because his trust is in the Lord.

CHAPTER 12:
GOD'S CONSTANCY

•**VERSE 5** David said that the Lord will prevail over the wicked.

CHAPTER 13:
PRAYER FOR MY HEART

•**VERSES 5-6** You've heard prayer changes things. Our mistake is we think that it can change God. The purposes of God are not changed by my prayers, but prayer changes my own heart.

CHAPTER 14:
TRIUMPH OVER UNGODLINESS

•**VERSES 1-3** God's appraisal of the human race: none are righteous or seek after Him (Romans 3:10).

CHAPTER 15:
DWELLING WITH THE LORD

•**VERSES 1-2** David asked a question and then answered it.

•**VERSE 4** A truly honorable person will acknowledge his error even though it brings his own hurt. God honors a man who keeps his word.

CHAPTER 16:
HOPE OF THE FAITHFUL

A michtam is a meditation or a prayer. Several psalms have this form.

•**VERSE 2** "My goodness extendeth not to Thee" is a poor translation and would better read, "I have no goodness but Thee."

•**VERSE 4** David described those who worship other gods. "The drinking of blood" was exactly what God meant. He was referring to pagan sacrifices.

•**VERSE 7** "My reins" means my mind. Many times God speaks to His people in the night.

•**VERSES 8-10** David prophesied of Him who was to come, "the Holy One," Jesus Christ. Peter quoted this verse on the day of Pentecost in Acts 2:25-27.

•**VERSE 11** This is a description of the exalted place of Jesus Christ at the right hand of God.

CHAPTER 17:
PRAYER OF CONFIDENCE

Another prayer of David in which he pleaded his own cause.

•**VERSE 1** It's important that we don't pray with deceitful lips. God can't help us unless we're totally honest with Him.

•**VERSE 14** The wicked have their portion in this life but God is interested in our eternal welfare (Psalm 73). My portion is coming in the life to come with Jesus Christ in His kingdom.

•**VERSE 15** Second Corinthians 3:18.

CHAPTER 18:
GOD, THE SOVEREIGN SAVIOR

This psalm was written when David escaped from Saul and lived in Ziklag among the heathen. He was safe as he wrote these words.

•**VERSE 2** God is my defense.

•**VERSE 6** "His temple" refers to God's temple in heaven.

•**VERSE 10** A cherub is an angelic being.

•**VERSE 43** David went down to Ziklag in the area of the Philistines. He was the leader of the city of Ziklag. "The people that served" refers to David but it also predicts Jesus Christ and the manner in which the gospel would reach the Gentiles.

CHAPTER 19:
REVELATION OF THE LORD

This is a beautiful psalm speaking of God and nature.

•**VERSES 1-3** God speaks to men everywhere through nature. He has spoken to us personally so that we may know His love and plan for salvation.

•**VERSES 7-8** God has given us His laws, covenants, and commandments.

CHAPTER 20:
THE ASSURANCE OF GOD

Throughout this psalm "LORD" refers to *YAHWEH* or *JEHOVAH.*

•**VERSE 8** We stand firm because we trust in the name of the Lord.

CHAPTER 21:
JOY IN THE SALVATION OF THE LORD

•**VERSE 2** "Selah" indicates the beginning of a new thought. It signifies a break or rest.

•**VERSE 5** God is gracious with the king who delights in the Lord.

CHAPTER 22:
SUFFERING AND PRAISE OF THE MESSIAH

This prophetic psalm stands out more than the other messianic psalms. Written by David, it gives a graphic description of the death of Jesus Christ by crucifixion.

At the time it was written, stoning was the form of capital punishment.

One thousand years later, the Romans introduced death by crucifixion.

•**VERSE 1** This verse was quoted by Jesus on the cross. He was forsaken by God for a moment so that we would not be forsaken by God eternally.

•**VERSE 2** Darkness covered the land when Jesus was crucified. He was separated from God because a holy God could not be in fellowship with sin. "Fellowship" means oneness.

•**VERSE 6** Isaiah 53.

•**VERSE 8** The high priests mocked Jesus when He was on the cross.

•**VERSE 10** Life begins before birth. There is a great deal of awareness by the fetus.

•**VERSE 14** Here is another description of the cross. When Jesus' side was pierced, blood and water came out of the wound. In hanging on the cross, the muscles fatigued and the joints fell out of place.

•**VERSE 18** The Roman soldiers cast lots for Jesus' robe (vesture) because it was too good to be divided. Jesus' death was perfectly planned before the foundation of the earth.

•**VERSE 21** On the temple altar were horns. When a person was desperate, he held onto the horns.

•**VERSE 24** God heard Jesus when He cried.

•**VERSE 27** Salvation for the Gentiles is predicted.

•**VERSE 29** The resurrection is prophesied. God has given Jesus the kingdom and everyone will bow before Him (Philippians 2:10).

CHAPTER 23:
THE LORD IS MY SHEPHERD

David sees three aspects of God: shepherd, guide, and banquet host.

•**VERSE 1** We shall not lack provision.

•**VERSE 2** We shall not lack refreshment.

•**VERSE 3** We shall not lack strength.

•**VERSE 4** One day we will see the valley of the shadow of death, but will fear no evil. Death holds no fear for the child of God (1 Corinthians 15:54-57).

•**VERSE 5** God is seen as a banquet host, caring for us in overflowing love.

•**VERSE 6** God prepares a place for us.

CHAPTER 24:
THE KING OF GLORY

•**VERSES 3-4** Only one with a pure heart can be in the presence of the Lord.

CHAPTER 25:
A PLEA FOR FORGIVENESS

•**VERSE 10** All of God's paths are merciful when we keep His covenant and His testimonies.

•**VERSE 14** God's secret is Christ in you, the hope of glory (Colossians 1:27).

CHAPTER 26:
PRAYER FOR REDEMPTION

•**VERSES 1-2** Examine me and judge me, O Lord.

•**VERSE 9** "Bloody" here is murderous.

CHAPTER 27:
DECLARATION OF FAITH

•**VERSE 5** We don't need to prepare a shelter for ourselves for the tribulation period.

•**VERSE 6** We no longer give sacrifices of animals or bread, but we do give the sacrifice of praise.

CHAPTER 28:
REJOICE IN ANSWERED PRAYER

•**VERSE 2** At times David lifted up his hands to God.

CHAPTER 29:
PRAISE GOD FOR HIS HOLINESS

•**VERSE 3** This is Jewish poetry showing the use of repetition.

CHAPTER 30:
THE BLESSING OF ANSWERED PRAYER

When we read a psalm like this, we should do what the psalmist exhorts. This experience can be a great blessing. We should follow the psalm rather than just read it.

CHAPTER 31:
THE LORD IS A FORTRESS

This psalm is divided into three sections. In the first section, verses 1-8, David expresses a mixture of trust and suffering. In the second section, verses 9-18, the trial is overcome. In the last section, there is the triumph that comes from trusting the Lord.

•**VERSE 3** When David spoke of God as a rock, he was speaking of Him as a place of defense. Knowing our own weaknesses, we ought to make our home in the rock. Jesus then becomes our rock and fortress.

•**VERSE 5** Jesus cried this on the cross (Luke 23:46).

•**VERSE 24** After triumph of trusting in God, we will encourage others to receive God's work in their lives.

CHAPTER 32:
THE JOY OF FORGIVENESS

This was written after David's sin with Bathsheba, when Nathan the prophet revealed the sin to David (2 Samuel 12).

Psalm 51 is also a penitential psalm, written during David's repentance.

•**VERSE 1** A sin isn't always willful. The word "sin" means to miss the mark. The mark is perfection, and all of us have missed it.

A transgression is a willful missing of the mark, deliberate disobedience.

•**VERSE 2** God doesn't keep a blacklist of our failures and sins (Romans 8:1).

•**VERSE 3** "When I kept my silence," that is, when I was trying to hide my sin and wouldn't confess it. Guilt must be released and relieved.

•**VERSE 5** The Hebrew language implies an immediate process. The moment I confess the transgressions in my heart, even before the words come out of my mouth, God has already forgiven me (1 John 1:9).

•**VERSE 9** Don't be stubborn when God speaks to you, otherwise He'll have to use harsh methods to guide you. God doesn't delight in painful processes, but wants to guide you with His eye.

CHAPTER 33:
THE SOVEREIGNTY OF THE LORD

•**VERSE 1** "Comely" means beautiful.

•**VERSE 2** The psaltery is an instrument of ten strings. David was an inventor of many instruments and a musician.

•**VERSES 6-9** How great is the power of God's Word! He spoke and it was done.

•**VERSE 12** Blessed is the nation that puts God at its center. Our nation at one time had a strong foundation in God.

•**VERSES 13-14** God is watching you.

CHAPTER 34:
THE JOY OF TRUSTING GOD

When David was fleeing from Saul, he was taken before King Achish in the land of the Philistines. David acted like a madman so that he would be released and could escape from them. Once he was safe, he wrote this psalm.

• **VERSE 4** Proverbs 29:25.

• **VERSE 7** Hebrews 1:14.

• **VERSES 15-17** Isaiah 59.

• **VERSE 20** This is a prophecy concerning the death of Jesus Christ. To hasten the deaths of Jesus and the two robbers, the Roman soldiers wanted to break their legs. Since Jesus was already dead, they didn't break His bones. This qualified Him as the sacrificial Lamb, without spot or blemish.

CHAPTER 35:
THE LORD IS OUR AVENGER

• **VERSE 11** This is a prophecy relating to the trial of Jesus Christ.

• **VERSE 21** "Aha, aha" was an evil and contemptuous expression.

CHAPTER 36:
WICKEDNESS AND GOD'S PERFECTIONS

• **VERSES 1-5** David spoke of his enemies and other wicked men. Then in verse 5, he turned to God's mercy, faithfulness, and righteousness.

CHAPTER 37:
THE HERITAGE OF THE RIGHTEOUS

• **VERSES 3-4** God is in control. We needn't fret or be envious of evildoers, for they'll be cut off. So put your trust in God, and delight yourself in the Lord through praise.

• **VERSE 7** One of the greatest blessings of the Christian is to rest in the Lord.

• **VERSE 11** Matthew 5:5.

• **VERSE 25** If you're a child of God, you'll never beg for food.

CHAPTER 38:
PRAYER IN TIME OF CHASTENING

David, through some unknown sin, became very sick. This psalm was occasioned by that sin.

CHAPTER 39:
PRAYER FOR WISDOM AND FORGIVENESS

Jeduthun was one of David's musicians.

• **VERSE 4** Life is short. God help me to number my days.

• **VERSE 5** Man is ignorant in the things he knows best.

CHAPTER 40:
PERSEVERANCE IN TRIALS

• **VERSE 6** What is most important to God is to offer Him your life. "Mine ears hast Thou opened" refers to becoming a bondslave or servant by choice to the Lord. The bondslave had his ear pierced as a sign of voluntary commitment.

• **VERSES 6-7** These two verses are prophecies of Jesus. "The volume of the book," the Old Testament, was written about Him.

• **VERSE 16** "The Lord be magnified" is a phrase we should use continually.

CHAPTER 41:
GODLY BLESSING AND SUFFERING

• **VERSE 1** This psalm begins with a beatitude. God is constantly exhorting us to help the poor.

• **VERSE 9** This is a prophecy about Jesus Christ and His betrayal by Judas Iscariot (John 13:18).

• **VERSE 13** The first book of psalms, like each of the five books, ends in a benediction.

SECOND BOOK OF PSALMS
CHAPTER 42:
YEARNING FOR GOD

• **VERSE 1** Matthew 5:6.

• **VERSE 2** John 7:37-38.

CHAPTER 43:
PRAYER IN TIME OF TROUBLE

This is similar to Psalm 42. Some believe that both were originally one psalm, as found in some manuscripts.

CHAPTER 44:
REDEMPTION REMEMBERED

• **VERSE 9** In contrast, David began to complain. God hasn't promised to keep us from problems, but He has promised to be with us in every trial (1 Peter 4:12; 1 Corinthians 10:13).

• **VERSE 26** The psalm ends with a cry to God for help. We assume that God took care of David's problem.

CHAPTER 45:
THE MESSIAH AND HIS BRIDE

A messianic psalm that portrays the beautiful mystery of Christ and His bride, the church (Revelation 19).

• **VERSE 6** The book of Hebrews acknowledges that this verse was written concerning Jesus Christ, showing His superiority over angels.

• **VERSE 9** The "queen" is the church.

• **VERSE 11** It is an intimate relationship between Christ and the church.

CHAPTER 46:
GOD IS OUR REFUGE

• **VERSES 4-5** The people in the Old Testament looked forward to the city of God (Ezekiel 47:1; Revelation 22).

• **VERSE 6** This speaks of the tribulation period before the kingdom age.

• **VERSE 7** A reference to the God of the vast angelic host might seem remote and impersonal. So the psalmist lowers the scope to the God of Jacob. This is my level, because Jacob wasn't a very honorable man. If He can be Jacob's God, He can be my God.

• **VERSE 8** The "desolations" are the results of the tribulation period. I believe that part of the kingdom age will include the rebuilding of the earth.

• **VERSE 9** No more wars or weapons of battle. What a glorious anticipation we have of the kingdom age (Isaiah 2:4).

CHAPTER 47:
GOD IS THE RULER OF THE EARTH

This psalm is sung seven times before blowing the trumpet to announce the beginning of the Jewish new year. It also looks at the dawn of the kingdom age, when Jesus establishes His kingdom over all the earth.

CHAPTER 48:
THE GLORY OF GOD IN ZION

• **VERSE 2** Here is the kingdom age and "the Great King." Jesus Christ and His throne will be on the north side of Mount Zion that slopes down into Jerusalem.

CHAPTER 49:
THE FOOLISH

• **VERSES 6-8** You cannot buy salvation (1 Peter 1:18).

• **VERSES 14-15** The wealthy will be consumed at death, but God will redeem my soul.

• **VERSE 20** The man who isn't born again is living in a body-conscious state like a beast. An animal only thinks about food or procreation.

CHAPTER 50:
GOD, THE RIGHTEOUS JUDGE

•**VERSE 1** The Hebrew begins *El Elohiym, Jehovah,* which means God (singular), God (a plural of majesty), and Jehovah. *El* is translated mighty, so we have here "mighty God."

•**VERSE 3** When our Lord returns, He'll once again break into history. This event will occur in the climax of man's rebellion against God.

•**VERSES 9-13** Our gifts should be given with a heart of love (2 Corinthians 9:7).

•**VERSE 14** Usually I vow when I am in trouble. God says that I should keep my vows.

•**VERSE 16** God asks the wicked why they should come into the kingdom since they hated His instruction and didn't want anything to do with Him.

•**VERSE 18** "Adulterers" also refers to spiritual adulterers, the followers of other gods.

•**VERSE 21** Because God didn't judge immediately, the wicked thought that He approved of their actions. God will never condone wickedness.

•**VERSE 23** "Conversation" is old English meaning manner of living.

HEBREW KEY WORD

El Elohiym = mighty God (50:1).

CHAPTER 51:
PRAYER OF REPENTANCE

David was called "a man after God's own heart," not because he was sinless, but because his heart was always open to God. In this psalm, God dealt with David in his sin.

•**VERSE 1** David cried for mercy. Mercy isn't getting what you deserve. Justice is getting what you deserve.

•**VERSE 3** You cannot hide your guilt from yourself. There is no forgiveness in justifying your actions (1 John 1:9).

•**VERSE 4** Sin is an act against the holy nature of God. We need to be conscious that God is with us (Acts 17:28).

•**VERSE 7** The hyssop bush was used to sprinkle the blood of the sacrifices. Becoming "whiter than snow" reflects David's concept of total forgiveness.

•**VERSE 14** "Bloodguiltiness" probably refers to the blood of Uriah, since David was responsible for his murder.

•**VERSE 17** God desires that we be broken over our sin.

CHAPTER 52:
THE PEACE OF THE GODLY

This psalm was directed against Doeg. David was upset with Doeg because he told Saul that David was hiding at Ahimelech's house. Saul had Ahimelech killed for helping David.

CHAPTER 53:
THE RESTORATION OF ISRAEL

This psalm is similar to Psalm 14.

•**VERSE 1** According to God, an atheist is a fool (Romans 1:21-22).

•**VERSES 2-3** Romans 3.

•**VERSE 6** This is a prayer for the future of Israel.

CHAPTER 54:
DELIVERANCE FROM ADVERSARIES

This psalm was directed to the Ziphites. They told Saul that David was hiding in the wilderness of Ziph.

•**VERSE 3** "Strangers" are the Ziphites.

CHAPTER 55:
TRUST IN GOD

This psalm was evidently written when David was fleeing from Absalom.

•**VERSES 12-14** This refers to Ahithophel, David's close friend and counselor. He revolted against David and counseled Absalom to destroy David.

CHAPTER 56:
PRAYER FOR RELIEF

A psalm that David wrote when he heard a mourning dove.

•**VERSE 8** The Bible teaches that God keeps a book of remembrances.

•**VERSE 9** God is for us! This is so important to remember (Romans 8:31).

CHAPTER 57:
PRAYER FOR SAFETY

A prayer of David when he fled from Saul and hid in a cave.

•**VERSE 6** Saul fell in a trap that he had set for David.

CHAPTER 58:
JUST JUDGMENT OF THE WICKED

Because of the Christian ethic that we learned from Jesus in the New Testament, we have difficulty understanding David's ethics. We're asked to forgive our enemies. God says, "Vengeance is Mine." So we must never take personal vengeance upon anyone who has wronged us (Psalm 37).

CHAPTER 59:
ASSURED JUDGMENT OF THE WICKED

This psalm was written after David fled from his enemies. He was lowered into a basket and escaped.

God is David's defense, and He'll be our defense as long as we allow Him.

If we try to defend ourselves, God will let us be our own inadequate defense.

CHAPTER 60:
PRAYER FOR RESTORED FAVOR

•**VERSES 5-12** These verses are identical to Psalm 108:6-13.

•**VERSE 11** Rather than looking to man, we should look to God for help.

CHAPTER 61:
ASSURANCE OF GOD'S PROTECTION

David wrote this psalm when he was in exile during his son Absalom's rebellion. David capitulated to Absalom rather than fighting against him.

•**VERSE 1** The word "cry" in Hebrew is loud wailing.

•**VERSE 2** "From the end of the world" is as far as a man can go. When I get to the end of the road, what do I do? David said, "Lead me to the rock that is higher than I." A rock is a symbol of strength and shelter.

For many, this psalm reflects the time of tragedy, when God has begun to take control and work in a person's life.

HEBREW KEY WORD

rinnah = cry, loud wailing (61:1).

CHAPTER 62:
WAIT FOR THE SALVATION OF GOD

•**VERSES 2, 6** David's faith increased between these two verses. This is true in our own prayers. Our faith increases as we pray because our attitude is changed through prayer.

•**VERSE 10** We shouldn't be seeking wealth for its own sake (1 Timothy 6:9; Matthew 6:24).

CHAPTER 63:
JOY IN FELLOWSHIP WITH GOD

This psalm was written when David was in the wilderness of Judah, east of Jerusalem, fleeing from Saul.

•**VERSES 1-2** David uses the barrenness of the desert to describe his own soul.

•**VERSE 4** At times we're so formal in praising the Lord. The Jews are uninhibited in prayers and worship.

CHAPTER 64:
OPPRESSION BY THE WICKED

•**VERSE 1** Preserve me from fear.

•**VERSE 3** David imagines his enemies speaking against him.

CHAPTER 65:
PRAISE TO GOD FOR HIS PROVIDENCE

This psalm looks forward to the kingdom age.

•**VERSE 2** Philippians 2:10.

CHAPTER 66:
PRAISE TO GOD FOR HIS WORKS

•**VERSE 4** Romans 14:11.

•**VERSE 6** The "sea" refers to the Red Sea (Exodus 14:21).

•**VERSES 10-12** God took us through the fire and water to purify us (John 15). After God works in you, He works through you to touch others.

•**VERSE 18** Isaiah 59.

CHAPTER 67:
PRAYER FOR GOD'S HELP

•**VERSE 2** The desire for God to be revealed is the motive behind David's request in verse 1.

•**VERSE 4** Matthew 24; Jude 14-15.

•**VERSE 6** The earth and the plants will respond to the praises to the Lord.

CHAPTER 68:
GOD'S GOODNESS TO ISRAEL

•**VERSE 4** *JAH* is short for Yahweh or Jehovah, "I am."

•**VERSE 18** This prophecy about Jesus Christ was quoted by Paul in Ephesians 4:8.

The "gifts" refer to the gifts in the church.

CHAPTER 69:
A MESSIANIC PSALM

•**VERSE 7** For God's sake, Jesus bore reproach.

•**VERSE 8** Jesus' brothers didn't believe in Him.

•**VERSE 9** We remember the account in John 2:14-17 of the terrible things done in the temple in the name of God.

•**VERSE 20** Jesus brought forth blood and water when His side was pierced, indicating that He died of a ruptured heart.

Jesus looked to His disciples, the "comforters," but they fell asleep while He was praying (Luke 22:45).

•**VERSE 21** Matthew 27:34; Mark 15:23; John 19:29.

•**VERSE 25** Peter quotes this verse about Judas in Acts 1:20.

CHAPTER 70:
PRAYER FOR RELIEF

•**VERSE 4** God's people should proclaim their love of salvation and say, "Let God be magnified!"

CHAPTER 71:
THE ROCK OF SALVATION

This is the psalm of an elderly man probably written by David in old age.

•**VERSE 3** The name of Jehovah is a strong tower (Proverbs 18:10). When faced by danger we should run to the Lord for safety.

•**VERSE 9** This indicates David's age.

•**VERSE 20** Here David declared his confidence in the resurrection.

The Bible teaches that the grave (sheol or hades) is more than a sepulcher where the body is laid. It's a place in the heart of the earth where the spirit of man goes after death. It's divided by a gulf into two sections (Luke 16:22-24).

CHAPTER 72:
THE MESSIAH'S REIGN

This psalm is entitled "A Psalm for Solomon." It goes beyond Solomon to prophesy about the Son promised to David, Jesus Christ, in the kingdom age upon the throne of David.

•**VERSE 1** When Jesus Christ comes again, the first order of business will be to judge the earth.

•**VERSE 11** We will be the kings (Romans 14:11; Revelation 1:7).

•**VERSE 20** Ends in a doxology.

THIRD BOOK OF PSALMS

Now begins a series of psalms ascribed to Asaph, the chief musician appointed by David. "Asaph" may be his name or his title as the chief musician. If it's a title, then these psalms may have been written by various chief musicians.

Some of these psalms go beyond Solomon's reign (10th century BC) and after the fall of the nation Israel (6th century BC).

CHAPTER 73:
TRUST IN GOD

•**VERSE 1** This psalm begins with an affirmation of a foundational truth concerning God: He is good to those who are pure in heart.

•**VERSES 2-3** Envy occurs when I get my eyes off God and onto people. The psalmist declares, "I almost went under because I was envious."

•**VERSE 11** The wicked deny the existence of God.

•**VERSE 17** Second Corinthians 4:18; Romans 8:18.

•**VERSE 22** I was as an animal without reasoning capacities.

CHAPTER 74:
PLEA FOR RELIEF

Here the psalmist talks about the desolation of Israel and God's apparent quietness in the face of their trouble.

•**VERSE 6** During the desolation, the carved works in the sanctuary were destroyed.

CHAPTER 75:
THANKSGIVING FOR GOD'S JUDGMENT

•**VERSES 1-2** The psalmist gave thanks to God for who He is and what He has done.

•**VERSE 3** God answered the psalmist, as he does in several psalms.

> **CALVARY DISTINCTIVE**
>
> **"For promotion comes neither from the east, west, north or south" (Psalm 75:6).**
>
> **Many pastors spend their time and energy trying to promote a church or themselves. But true promotion comes from the Lord.**

•**VERSE 7** Here we're presented with the folly of man's endeavors to promote the program of God.

•**VERSE 8** This cup full of foaming wine is God's cup of wrath (Revelation 14).

CHAPTER 76:
MAJESTY OF GOD IN JUDGMENT

• **VERSE** 1 Judah was the southern kingdom. Israel was the northern kingdom.

• **VERSE** 2 "Salem" is Jerusalem.

CHAPTER 77:
GOD'S REDEMPTIVE WORKS

The first part of this psalm is centered around "I."

• **VERSES** 7-9 When my attention is on myself, I lose the consciousness of God and become separated from Him.

• **VERSE** 12 The psalmist changed and put his emphasis on God. Prayer changes my heart and my attitude. When I get my eyes off myself and focus on God, He can work in my life.

CHAPTER 78:
GOD'S KINDNESS TO REBELLIOUS ISRAEL

This psalm recounts the history of God's people. It's a reminder to the coming generations of the works of the Lord. We too are obligated to keep our eye on God who is continually doing great works. We mustn't let these works turn into a mere memorial.

• **VERSE** 39 The "wind" is the breath of life. It passes away and will not return. This Scripture refutes reincarnation.

• **VERSE** 41 One way in which we lack belief is by denying the Holy Spirit.

• **VERSE** 49 The "evil angels" were the destroying angels who struck down the firstborn of the Egyptians.

• **VERSE** 60 The tabernacle was originally in Shiloh, the land given to the tribe of Ephraim.

• **VERSE** 67 When God chose a leader, He refused to take him from the tribe of Joseph or Ephraim.

CHAPTER 79:
A PRAYER FOR ISRAEL

This psalm discusses the invasion of Israel and asks God to take vengeance upon those who brought destruction on the nation.

CHAPTER 80:
PRAYER FOR ISRAEL'S RESTORATION

• **VERSE** 1 In the book of Revelation, John describes the throne of God and the four cherubim around the throne.

• **VERSE** 8 The "vine of Egypt" is the nation of Israel.

• **VERSE** 9 The people of God filled the land of Israel.

• **VERSE** 18 "Quicken us" means make us alive.

CHAPTER 81:
APPEAL FOR ISRAEL'S REPENTANCE

This psalm was read for the Feast of Trumpets. The instruments were sounded in the holy month, the seventh month on the Jewish calendar.

• **VERSE** 1 Here we have a proclamation for the feast day.

• **VERSE** 7 God is speaking. He recounts to the Israelites some of their wilderness experiences. At the waters of Meribah is where the people strived with Moses and God.

🔑 HEBREW KEY WORD

meribah = **strife (81:7).**

• **VERSE** 9 The psalmist declared the first commandment. Our worship should be given completely to God.

• **VERSE** 12 Romans 1:24; Genesis 6:3.

• **VERSE** 13 God is lamenting over His people.

CHAPTER 82:
PLEA FOR JUSTICE

This psalm is directed to the judges. It is solemn because the psalmist was unhappy with man's judgments.

•**VERSE 1** The Hebrew word for "gods" is also translated judges because a judge has authority over a person's destiny. God will judge the judges.

•**VERSE 2** "The persons of the wicked" refer to the unrighteous rich and the prominent.

•**VERSE 6** Here again "gods" means judges (Exodus 22:28). Jesus also quoted this in John 10:34. A god in this sense is anyone or anything having power over our lives.

•**VERSE 8** The only righteous judgment will be executed when God judges the earth.

CHAPTER 83:
PRAYER FOR ISRAEL'S DELIVERANCE

This psalm asks for deliverance from the calamities on Israel. The psalmist was addressing God.

•**VERSE 1** God's silence is a hard thing for people to accept.

•**VERSES 2-12** Judges 4-7.

•**VERSE 18** The psalmist asked the Lord to act so that men might know He is over all things, and thus respect Him.

CHAPTER 84:
DWELLING IN THE HOUSE OF THE LORD

•**VERSE 2** Matthew 5:6.

•**VERSE 4** "Blessed" means happy.

•**VERSE 6** "The Valley of Baca" relates to dry places.

•**VERSE 10** Better the lowest place in the house of God than the highest place in the house of Baal.

CHAPTER 85:
PRAYER FOR FAVOR

•**VERSES 1-2** The psalm declares God's favor with His people bringing them out of captivity and forgiving them.

•**VERSES 5-8** Although the psalm began with the restoration of the land and people, full spiritual renewal hadn't taken place. The psalmist was asking for revival.

CHAPTER 86:
PRAYER FOR MERCY

Nearly every verse here is taken from other psalms. This shows David's knowledge of the psalms. In verses 5, 10, and 15, he states the different aspects of God's character.

•**VERSE 5** God is good and ready to forgive. He is plenteous in mercy.

•**VERSES 8-9** "Lord" here is master.

•**VERSE 11** "LORD" here is Jehovah.

All of us experience a heart divided between the desires of our flesh and our desires for God.

•**VERSE 16** The psalmist responded to God's character and made his request. It's important to know God's character and nature. That gives us the confidence to seek Him.

CHAPTER 87:
THE GLORY OF THE CITY OF GOD

This psalm extols Zion, which is the city of Jerusalem.

•**VERSES 5-7** The Lord is the source and giver of life.

CHAPTER 88:
PRAYER FOR HELP

This is a sad and somber psalm.

CHAPTER 89:
REMEMBERING THE COVENANT

•**VERSE 7** "Feared" is revered. We can learn much about reverence toward God from the Jews. We need to be highly conscious of His greatness.

•**VERSE 22** To "not exact upon him" meant that he wouldn't be paying tribute to his enemies.

•**VERSE 24** The horn is a symbol of strength.

•**VERSE 27** This verse refers to Solomon, the son of David, and also to the seed of David, Jesus Christ.

•**VERSES 35-37** Here is a prophecy of Jesus Christ.

•**VERSE 52** This benediction closes the third book of psalms.

FOURTH BOOK OF PSALMS
CHAPTER 90:
A PSALM OF MOSES

•**VERSE 2** Moses declares the eternal nature of God.

•**VERSE 4** Second Peter 3:8.

•**VERSE 10** God chose us outside the frame of linear time (Ephesians 1:4).

CHAPTER 91:
ABIDING IN GOD'S PRESENCE

This psalm tells us that the righteous man dwells with God.

•**VERSE 3** Bird-trapping was an art at that time. The "snare of the fowler" refers to the traps. In a spiritual sense, Satan has laid traps for us, but God will deliver us.

•**VERSE 4** Ephesians 6:13-17.

•**VERSES 5-10** Because the Lord is your habitation, or place of dwelling, no evil or plague will come near you.

•**VERSE 8** Don't harden your heart (Hebrews 3:8-12).

•**VERSE 11** Satan quoted this Scripture when tempting Jesus, but Jesus said, "Thou shalt not tempt the Lord thy God." In other words, don't test the Scriptures, don't jeopardize yourself to prove that the Scriptures work.

There is a vast heavenly host of angels with different rankings. The Scriptures don't specify when angels were created, but they serve the Lord.

CHAPTER 92:
THE SABBATH DAY

•**VERSE 2** To start and end the day, praise His name.

•**VERSE 7** It's foolish to envy the wicked, since they'll be destroyed.

CHAPTER 93:
THE ETERNAL REIGN OF GOD

The Lord reigns and His statutes stand firm.

CHAPTER 94:
GOD IS OUR REFUGE

The psalmist was troubled because of the oppression of the wicked. He acknowledged that God is a God of vengeance who will avenge and uphold the righteous.

CHAPTER 95:
A CALL TO WORSHIP

This psalm encourages us to sing unto the Lord and to praise Him.

•**VERSES 7-11** We have the example of the Israelites and should draw spiritual analogies from their experiences.

Coming into the Promised Land is symbolic to coming into spiritual rest. God takes the bitter experiences of my life and makes them sweet, as He did with the bitter waters at Marah.

CHAPTER 96:
GOD COMING IN JUDGMENT

This psalm encourages us to praise and worship the Lord declaring the glory of God and the wonders of His work.

•VERSE 13 The psalmist anticipated the Lord's coming day of judgment. This psalm parallels Psalm 98.

CHAPTER 97:
A SONG OF PRAISE

•VERSE 5 A reference to Mount Sinai.

•VERSE 10 If you love God, then hate evil. Because of the gross iniquity on the earth today, we have developed a tolerance for evil.

CHAPTER 98:
SONG FOR SALVATION AND JUDGMENT

•VERSE 9 We can trust that God will judge righteously—something we don't find in our courts of law today.

CHAPTER 99:
PRAISE FOR GOD'S HOLINESS

•VERSE 1 The cherubim are an angelic class described in Ezekiel 1 and 10, and Revelation 4. Satan is one of the fallen cherubim.

•VERSE 8 Their "inventions" were the golden calf and other idols. Yet God forgave them.

CHAPTER 100:
A SONG OF FAITHFULNESS

•VERSE 2 Loss of joy often occurs because a person has been pushed into something that God hasn't directed.

•VERSE 3 Our very breath depends upon God (Daniel 5:23).

•VERSE 5 Praise the Lord for His goodness, mercy, and truth.

CHAPTER 101:
PROMISED FAITHFULNESS

A psalm of David.

•VERSE 1 Though David said that he'll sing of God's mercy in this psalm, he seemed to speak only of judgment. David wanted judgment for his enemies but mercy for himself.

•VERSE 2 "Perfect" here refers to complete.

CHAPTER 102:
THE LORD'S ETERNAL LOVE

•VERSE 12 A contrast between mortal man and sovereign God.

•VERSE 14 The people of Israel take pleasure in Jerusalem, a city made of stone and dust.

•VERSE 15 This refers to God's set time to favor the nation of Israel (Ezekiel 38:23; 39:27-29).

•VERSE 18 The psalmist was writing for a generation to come. These words are for our own generation. Daniel also wrote for another generation.

•VERSES 25-26 Matthew 24:35. The psalmist also recognized the first and second laws of thermodynamics here.

CHAPTER 103:
A SONG OF PRAISE

A favorite psalm at Thanksgiving time.

•VERSE 1 This was David's commandment to himself.

•VERSE 4 "Redeemeth thy life from destruction" is to save you from hell. There are more positive aspects to the Christian life than negative.

•VERSE 8 The Old Testament God isn't a God of wrath, but of mercy. He is slow to anger.

•VERSES 20-22 David called on angels and all God's works to praise the Lord.

CHAPTER 104:
A SONG FOR HIS CREATION

•**VERSE** 6 The psalmist here spoke about the flood in Noah's time.

•**VERSE** 9 God has set the oceans' boundaries to never cover the earth.

•**VERSE** 18 "Conies" are small animals similar in appearance to rabbits.

•**VERSE** 26 Some think that the leviathan is the whale.

CHAPTER 105:
THE ETERNAL FAITHFULNESS OF GOD

In verses 9-45 David reviews Jewish history, emphasizing how God has preserved the people.

•**VERSES** 9-10 Israel's right to possess its land is an everlasting covenant.

•**VERSE** 39 The cloud was a covering for shade and a fog to hide the Israelites from the Egyptians.

CHAPTER 106:
JOY IN FORGIVENESS

Another review of the Jewish history, with emphasis on the people. We saw how faithful God is; now we see how unfaithful man is.

•**VERSE** 15 "Their request" was to satisfy their stomachs. God granted their request, but it brought leanness to their souls (1 Timothy 6:9).

•**VERSE** 32 Moses, who disobeyed God, couldn't go into the Promised Land. He was God's example of the importance of obedience.

•**VERSE** 35 The people of God were to destroy the heathen, but they followed the pagan practices.

•**VERSES** 37-38 Behind all idol worship lies Satan worship.

•**VERSE** 48 The "amen" brings us to the end of the fourth book of psalms.

FIFTH BOOK OF PSALMS
CHAPTER 107:
THANKSGIVING TO THE LORD

This psalm begins with an exhortation to give thanks to the Lord because of His goodness and His mercy.

•**VERSE** 9 The soul is the consciousness of man. Every man has an awareness that life must be more than what he has experienced. Man's soul longs after spiritual fulfillment.

•**VERSES** 10-11 David described those bound in afflictions because of their rebellion against the words of God.

•**VERSE** 22 In the Old Testament there were different kinds of sacrifices. Besides the sacrifices for sin, there were peace offerings for communion with God; and the burnt offerings of consecration signifying a person's commitment to God.

Jesus made our sacrifice for sin once and for all. The New Testament exhorts us to make sacrifices of praise and a commitment of ourselves by yielding to Him.

CHAPTER 108:
ASSURANCE OF GOD'S VICTORY

•**VERSE** 2 The psalmist called for praise with instruments.

•**VERSE** 12 Vain is the help of man. God is our only true help.

CHAPTER 109:
DAVID SPOKE AGAINST HIS ENEMIES

•**VERSE** 4 We should pray rather than lash out. Satan's trick is to draw me into a physical conflict. The big gun in spiritual warfare is prayer, for prayer isn't restricted to time, space, or material. Jesus defeated the spiritual forces of Satan and darkness at the cross (Colossians 2:15).

•**VERSES 5-20** David wanted to avenge himself against his enemies. David's words are far from Jesus' teachings on forgiveness in the New Testament.

•**VERSE 8** Acts 1:20.

•**VERSE 21** David prayed for himself.

CHAPTER 110:
FULFILLMENT IN JESUS CHRIST

This is a messianic psalm with its fulfillment in Jesus Christ.

•**VERSE 1** In Hebrew this reads "Yahweh said unto my Lord." Jesus is sitting at the right hand of the Father in glory. God will judge the earth and bring all into subjection under Christ.

•**VERSE 4** A priest of the most high God, Melchizedek (also known as the king of peace), came to Abraham. Abraham gave him one-tenth of all his goods. Melchizedek was greater than Abraham because he received tithes from him.

The high priest acted as a mediator between man and God because the people couldn't approach a holy and righteous God.

Jesus Christ is of the order of Melchizedek, which precedes and is superior to the priesthood of Levi because the father of Levi and Abraham paid tithes to Melchizedek.

CHAPTER 111:
PRAISE TO GOD

This psalm is an acrostic since each verse begins with a succeeding letter of the Hebrew alphabet.

•**VERSE 1** The psalm begins "Hallelujah!"

•**VERSE 10** "Fear" means reverence. The reverence of the Lord is the beginning of wisdom.

CHAPTER 112:
THE BLESSING OF RIGHTEOUSNESS

•**VERSE 1** "Hallelujah!" Happy is the man who reveres the Lord.

•**VERSE 2** Man's children are "his seed."

•**VERSE 4** Jesus rises as a light in the darkness.

•**VERSE 7** We're living in days of evil tidings, but the man who trusts the Lord will not fear the day of evil. The psalmist was saying, "Come what may, the Lord is with me."

•**VERSE 10** The wicked are contrasted with this righteous man. A contrast or repetition is true Hebrew poetry.

CHAPTER 113:
THE MAJESTY OF GOD

Psalms 113-118 are called the Hallelujah or Praise Psalms. These traditional psalms are sung on the Jewish feast days. No doubt Jesus sang these psalms with His disciples. Psalm 113 begins and ends with "Hallelujah!"

CHAPTER 114:
THE DELIVERANCE OF ISRAEL

This psalm recalls the deliverance of the children of Israel from the bondage of Egypt.

CHAPTER 115:
TRUSTWORTHINESS OF GOD

•**VERSE 8** Man has an innate desire to worship, making his own gods. His gods are like himself. Thus, he's actually worshiping himself, yet his gods are much less than he is. They have eyes but do not see, feet but do not walk.

To worship the infinite, true, and living God is to become more like Him each day (2 Corinthians 3:18; 1 John 3:2).

•**VERSE 16** The heavens belong to God. God gave the earth to man, but man gave the earth to Satan.

•**VERSE 17** The psalmist spoke of physical death.

CHAPTER 116:
PRAISE FOR THE REDEEMED

The gratitude of the redeemed is stated here.

CHAPTER 117:
LET ALL PEOPLE PRAISE THE LORD

This is the shortest psalm. It celebrates the universal reign of Jesus Christ who will come to rule over the earth.

CHAPTER 118:
PRAISE GOD FOR EVERLASTING MERCY

Jesus probably sang this psalm with His disciples on the night of the Passover Feast.

•**VERSES 19-20** This may be related to Jesus' triumphant entry into Jerusalem through the East Gate. Psalm 24:7-9 also refers to the gates.

•**VERSE 22** This is prophetic. The "stone" is Jesus Christ Himself (Matthew 21:42-44; Acts 4:11). The "builders" were the Jews who rejected Jesus Christ. They refused the gospel, so it was then given to the Gentiles.

•**VERSE 24** This refers to Jesus' triumphant entry into Jerusalem when His disciples cried "Hosanna, O Lord," which means, "Save now, O Lord."

•**VERSE 26** As the disciples sang this psalm with Jesus, they were actually singing a prophecy that had been fulfilled a few days earlier when the "stone" was rejected.

CHAPTER 119:
MEDITATE ON GOD'S WORD

In this psalm, each section—indeed, almost each verse—is independent. It's an acrostic psalm where each group of eight verses begins with the same letter. This psalm is dedicated to God's Word. Each verse exalts the Scriptures.

•**VERSE 11** God wants you to hide His Word in your heart.

•**VERSE 18** This is a prayer to say before reading the Scriptures so your spiritual eyes might be opened.

•**VERSE 24** Look to the Word of God for guidance and counseling.

•**VERSE 41** Romans 10:17.

•**VERSES 71-72** It's good to be afflicted, for God's Word in our lives is better than all the riches in the world.

•**VERSE 89** Nothing is more permanent than the Word of God (Matthew 24:35). It's wrong to challenge or change the Word of God.

•**VERSE 91** "They" refers to the earth and heavens, which continue as God has ordained from the beginning.

•**VERSES 99-100** I'm wiser than the ancients because I have God's Word. God's Word is true knowledge.

•**VERSE 105** God's Word is life's guide.

•**VERSE 130** The entrance of God's Word gives light to those in darkness.

•**VERSE 136** This reflects the psalmist's grief for those who break God's law.

CHAPTERS 120-134:

This group of psalms has the heading "Psalms of Degrees," literally "Songs of Ascents."

These are marching psalms sung by Israel as they came to worship in Jerusalem. These psalms were sung in holy anticipation of communal worship.

CHAPTER 120:
PLEA FOR RELIEF

•VERSES 5-7 The psalmist has come from Mesech and Kedar where the people hate God and oppose those who worship Him. The world we live in also opposes those who worship God.

CHAPTER 121:
HELP FOR THOSE WHO SEEK HIM

•VERSE 1 "From whence cometh my help" is a question. The hills cannot help you.

CHAPTER 122:
THE HOUSE OF THE LORD

•VERSE 3 "Compact together" is gathering together in a group.

CHAPTER 123:
PRAYER FOR RELIEF FROM CONTEMPT

•VERSE 2 A servant constantly watched his master's hand because the master gave signals with it. Similarly, we're to keep our eyes fixed on the Lord.

•VERSE 3 People are contemptuous to Christians. But we fix our eyes on the Lord, not on those who trouble us.

CHAPTER 124:
THE LORD DEFENDS HIS PEOPLE

•VERSE 1 Second Corinthians 1:10.

•VERSE 8 There's great power in the name of Jesus (John 16:23-24).

CHAPTER 125:
THE LORD IS OUR STRENGTH

•VERSE 1 Zion will abide forever, but when Jesus returns and puts His foot on the Mount of Olives, it'll split down the middle. This event will also form a new underground river.

CHAPTER 126:
THE JOY OF ZION

•VERSE 1 The Lord freed Zion from her captivity.

•VERSES 5-6 This is also true about the ministry. Our attitude in ministry is vitally important. God has taken His glorious treasure, the "seed," and put it in earthen pots, us. God wants us to pour forth His love to the needy world around us so they're captivated by Him, not by us.

CHAPTER 127:
LABORING WITH THE LORD

•VERSE 1 Unless the Lord builds His church, our labor is in vain. Using gimmicks and programs to promote the church is futile.

•VERSE 2 It's worthless to spend the night worrying.

•VERSE 3 Children are a blessing from God.

☪ CALVARY DISTINCTIVE

"Except the LORD build the house, they labor in vain that build it" (Psalm 127:1).

Another distinctive characteristic of Calvary Chapel is our relaxed, casual style. We simply trust in the work of the Holy Spirit, and of Jesus Christ, who is building His church.

CHAPTER 128:
FEAR THE LORD

This psalm deals with the family.

CHAPTER 129:
SONG OF VICTORY

•VERSE 1 Israel to this day is afflicted by others, but she stands up to them.

CHAPTER 130:
WAITING FOR REDEMPTION

• **VERSE 3** If the Lord were to list man's iniquities, we'd all be guilty.

• **VERSE 7** We can receive mercy and plenteous redemption from Him.

CHAPTER 131:
TRUST IN THE LORD

• **VERSE 1** The psalmist declares, "Lord, I'm a simple man."

• **VERSE 3** Hope is in the Lord.

CHAPTER 132:
THE ETERNAL DWELLING OF GOD

• **VERSES 1-5** David wanted to build a beautiful temple for God. David wouldn't rest until it was built.

• **VERSE 11** God promised David that one from his lineage would sit upon the throne forever (Isaiah 9:6-7). Mary, a direct descendant of David, gave birth to Jesus.

• **VERSE 12** Jesus promised that the church would sit upon His throne too.

• **VERSES 17-18** "Mine anointed" is the Messiah.

CHAPTER 133:
UNITY

This psalm pictures the beauty of brethren dwelling in a family-like unity.

CHAPTER 134:
BLESS THE LORD

• **VERSES 1-3** First you bless the Lord, then you receive His blessings.

CHAPTER 135:
PRAISE TO GOD

This psalm begins and ends with "Hallelujah!" It's an exhortation to praise God.

• **VERSE 4** "Peculiar people" in old English means that we're God's possession (1 Peter 2:9).

• **VERSE 6** I have no right to challenge or resist God. I was made for His pleasure and find true fulfillment when I please Him.

• **VERSES 15-18** Men worship gods like themselves instead of the true and living God.

CHAPTER 136:
THANKSGIVING TO GOD

Throughout this psalm, we have the phrase "For His mercy endureth forever." The purpose of the repetition was to impress truth upon the hearts of the people. In all situations, God's mercy endures forever.

• **VERSE 5** Here the psalmist exhorts us to praise God for His creative acts.

• **VERSE 10** The psalmist commands praise and thanksgiving to God for His blessings upon Israel.

CHAPTER 137:
LONGING FOR ZION

This is a psalm of captivity written long after David's time by one of the Jewish captives in Babylon.

• **VERSE 3** The Babylonians made their captives sing songs from their homeland. As captives, the Jews found it difficult to sing because they were so distraught.

• **VERSE 7** The Edomites would always join others who wanted to attack Israel.

•**VERSES 8-9** These expressions of judgment are the psalmist's own feelings. He wants God's justice to fall on the wicked, but God would rather show mercy by forgiving repentant men. God has great sorrow when He must judge (Matthew 5:43-44).

CHAPTER 138:
THE LORD'S GOODNESS

•**VERSES 1-2** In all the earth there is no name like the name of God. The Jews held His name in such high esteem that they wouldn't even pronounce it.

•**VERSE 4** The Word of God is magnified even more than His name (Luke 16:17).

CHAPTER 139:
GOD'S PERFECT KNOWLEDGE

•**VERSE 1** David realizes that God knows him completely.

•**VERSE 6** "Such knowledge" refers to self-knowledge. Few people know the true motives behind their actions. God looks at our motives.

•**VERSE 23** The man who prays, "Search me, O God, and know my heart," recognizes that he doesn't know himself.

•**VERSE 24** God will destroy the wicked, so David asked God to purge anything in him that was displeasing.

The work of the Holy Spirit in our lives not only reveals Christ to us, but also reveals ourselves to us, including those areas unpleasing to God.

CHAPTER 140:
PRAYER FOR DELIVERANCE

•**VERSE 5** The word "gins" means traps.

CHAPTER 141:
PRAYER FOR SAFEKEEPING

•**VERSE 2** Incense in the tabernacle and later in the temple symbolized sweet prayers of the saints rising up to God and His response of love and joy.

•**VERSE 3** God help control my tongue.

•**VERSE 5** The wounds of the righteous are kindness.

CHAPTER 142:
A PLEA FOR RELIEF

A psalm of David when he was hiding from Saul in the cave of Adullam. Typical of David, this psalm begins with mourning and ends with an uplifting tone.

CHAPTER 143:
A PRAYER FOR GUIDANCE

•**VERSE 2** David cried, "God, I don't want justice, I want mercy!"

•**VERSE 6** David was a man after God's own heart because he was thirsty for God (Matthew 5:6).

•**VERSES 9-11** David's prayer: "Deliver me, teach me, lead me, quicken me."

CHAPTER 144:
A SONG TO THE LORD

•**VERSE 3** In comparison to the vastness of the universe, what is man? Yet God is mindful of me (Matthew 10:29-31).

•**VERSE 4** Though life is so short, I'm extremely important to God.

CHAPTER 145:
A SONG OF GOD'S LOVE

•**VERSE 8** The grace and compassion of the Lord revealed in the Old Testament.

•**VERSE 14** God will hold me when I fall (Romans 14:4).

CHAPTERS 146-150:
These final hymns are the Hallel psalms. They begin and end with "Hallelujah."

CHAPTER 146:
GOD'S GLORIOUS WORKS

A psalm of praise declaring God's glorious works.

•**VERSE 8** A reference to the kingdom age.

CHAPTER 147:
PRAISE TO GOD

•**VERSE 1** Praise is desirable and beautiful.

•**VERSE 4** There are as many stars as grains of sand. God calls each star by its name.

•**VERSE 6** The meek are exalted.

CHAPTER 148:
PRAISE TO GOD FOR HIS CREATION

This is a psalm of praise from nature.

CHAPTER 149:
PRAISE TO GOD FOR HIS SALVATION

Praising the Lord with song, dance, and on the timbrel and harp. Praise shouldn't draw attention to us but to God.

CHAPTER 150:
LET ALL THINGS PRAISE GOD

An exhortation to praise the Lord!

STUDY QUESTIONS FOR PSALMS

1. In Psalm 1 we see the contrast between the godly and the ungodly man. What four things do you find in verses 1 and 2 that would make a righteous man blessed or happy?

_____

_____

_____

2. Psalm 16:8-10 is one example of David's prophetic psalms. What was David prophesying here? (Acts 2:25-27; 13:35-37).

_____

_____

_____

3. In Psalm 32 David speaks about the importance of God's forgiveness. How does he describe hiding his sin? What happened once he confessed? (1 John 1:9).

_____

_____

_____

4. Asaph shares his frustration in seeing the wicked prosper in Psalm 73. Although he came to the wrong conclusion initially, what changed in verse 17? Why is this important? (2 Corinthians 4:18; Romans 8:18).

_____

_____

_____

5. There are many reasons to give thanks to the Lord. List five findings in Psalm 136.

_____

_____

_____

THE BOOK OF
PROVERBS

AUTHOR OF THE BOOK:
The sayings in this book were either written or collected by Solomon.

PERIOD OF WRITING:
During Solomon's adulthood after becoming king, around 1000 BC.

TYPE OF BOOK:
Poetical

THEME:
Wisdom and instruction.

INTRODUCTION:
When Solomon ascended to the throne, God said to him, "Ask of Me whatever you would like." Solomon said, "Lord, grant to me wisdom, that I might rule over these, Your people." The Lord was pleased with Solomon's request, and He said, "Because you did not ask for money or fame, but for wisdom, I will not only give you wisdom; but I will also give you riches and fame." Thus, Solomon became a very wise man.

Solomon was a very prolific writer. He wrote 1,005 songs. He wrote 3,000 proverbs—short little sayings that incorporate a lot of wisdom. He wrote books on biology, zoology, and many different fields. People came from all over the world to sit and to hear his wisdom, as he expounded on plants, animals, and things of this nature.

CHAPTER 1:
DON'T REJECT WISDOM

•**VERSE 1** The first seven verses are a preface to the book.

•**VERSES 2-5** The purpose of proverbs is to know wisdom, to receive instruction.

For the most part, they are put in such a picturesque way they can fasten themselves upon your memory.

•**VERSE 7** This word "beginning" in Hebrew means the head or the sum total.

In Proverbs 9:10, the word translated beginning is a different word in Hebrew and means the first steps of wisdom. So the fear of the Lord is the first step, but it is also the total.

> ⚜ HEBREW KEY WORD
>
> *reshiyth* = **beginning, the head or the sum total (1:7).**

217

•VERSE 8 "My son" is not literally Solomon's son, of which he had many, but as a teacher addressing his pupils.

•VERSE 20 He personifies wisdom and lets wisdom speak directly.

•VERSES 31-32 Calamity will ultimately come to those who reject wisdom, which is to hate evil.

CHAPTER 2:
PURSUE WISDOM

•VERSES 2-5 A true search for knowledge, understanding, and wisdom will lead you to God, and then you'll understand the fear of the Lord.

•VERSE 7 The buckler was part of the armament that protected the body.

•VERSE 12 The word "froward" means perverse.

CHAPTER 3:
BENEFITS OF WISDOM

•VERSES 1-2 To keep the commandment in your heart will grant you length of days, long life, and peace.

•VERSES 5-6 "How can I know the will of God?" is a question so often asked. Three steps: (1) Trust in the Lord with all your heart; (2) Lean not to your own understanding; (3) In all your ways acknowledge Him. The result? He shall direct your path.

•VERSES 9-10 There are basic laws of nature such as magnetism and gravity. There's a cause and effect. By the same token God has established basic spiritual laws concerning giving, and though we cannot understand exactly how it works, it does.

"Honor the Lord with the firstfruits of your increase." God challenges you to test this law (Malachi 3:8, 10; Matthew 7:2; 2 Corinthians 9:6).

•VERSE 10 "Presses" would be the winepresses.

•VERSES 11-12 If you're a child of God, He's not going to let you get by with evil.

•VERSE 18 Things that we count as important—pleasantness, peace, life, happiness—come to those who have gained wisdom and understanding.

•VERSE 27 If you have the capacity to do good and fail to do it, that's as much a sin as an overt, sinful act (James 4:17).

CHAPTER 4:
WISDOM IS THE PRINCIPAL THING

•VERSE 3 Solomon is speaking of his father David and mother Bathsheba.

•VERSE 7 There are people who are knowledgeable but they're fools. If there is to be a choice made between wisdom and knowledge, it's better to choose wisdom.

•VERSE 23 It is not what goes into a man's mouth that defiles him, but what comes out (Matthew 12:34; 15:11).

CHAPTER 5:
WARNING AGAINST ADULTERY

•VERSES 3-8 This is a prostitute or an adulterous woman.

•VERSE 11 When you have contracted some venereal disease.

•VERSE 15 Enjoy a marital relationship with your own wife.

•VERSE 21 God is watching you. You can't do anything in secret.

CHAPTER 6:
WARNINGS AGAINST FOOLISHNESS

•VERSES 1-5 Someone once said the best way to lose a friend is to loan him money.

•VERSES 6-11 An exhortation against laziness.

•**VERSE** 16 I should seek to hate the things that God hates and avoid doing them.

•**VERSE** 17 Proverbs 16:18.

•**VERSE** 19 God hates division that so often comes within the body of the church (Psalm 133:1; Romans 16:17).

•**VERSE** 23 The purpose of the commandments is not to restrain or restrict, but to give life.

•**VERSE** 25 Jesus said, "If any man looks upon a woman and lusts after her in his heart, he's already committed adultery" (Matthew 5:28). It's the inner attitude of a man that is so important.

•**VERSE** 26 They can destroy everything valuable in your life; your relationship with your wife, the admiration of your children, and your position.

CHAPTER 7:
BEWARE OF THE ADULTERESS

•**VERSE** 14 After a woman's menstruation, she was to bring the peace offering to become ceremonially clean for sexual relationships. Here this woman is showing a strange paradox of obedience to the law, and yet disobedience to God.

•**VERSE** 18 Outside of marriage this is an expression of lust, not love.

•**VERSES** 22-23 The disobedience to this command of God costs you dearly.

CHAPTER 8:
THE CRY OF WISDOM

•**VERSE** 1 Solomon personifies wisdom, and because of this chapter, some have even likened wisdom unto Jesus Christ (Colossians 2:3).

•**VERSE** 10 Prefer wisdom to wealth; wisdom is more important than riches.

•**VERSE** 13 You cannot fear the Lord and embrace evil.

CHAPTER 9:
WISDOM'S INVITATION

•**VERSES** 4-6 Wisdom invites everybody to come and partake of her.

•**VERSE** 7 If you reprove a scorner, he's going to turn right around and mock you. He's not going to receive it.

•**VERSE** 10 The difference between wisdom and knowledge: knowledge will give facts; wisdom will give the correct action in lieu of these facts.

•**VERSE** 13 Solomon evidently knew a lot about women. He had 700 wives and 300 concubines.

CHAPTER 10:
RIGHTEOUSNESS

•**VERSE** 1 Beginning in chapter 10 we have individual proverbs, contrasting the wise with the foolish, or the wicked with the righteous. Each is separate and complete and unrelated to the next.

•**VERSE** 2 If you have gained by wickedness, then you're apt to lose by wickedness.

•**VERSE** 12 If you're filled with hatred, it's going to stir up strife. But if you're a loving person, they'll overlook your faults (1 Peter 4:8).

•**VERSE** 19 The more you talk, the greater the possibility you will sin.

CHAPTER 11:
COUNSEL

•**VERSE** 1 Merchandising was done with balanced scales, but some would have two sets of weights: one to buy and the other to sell. This was known as a false balance. If you're in business, God wants you to be upstanding and to deal fairly and honestly with people.

•**VERSE** 2 There's no way that a person can come into a real relationship with God and still be proud.

•**VERSE 4** When God's day of judgment comes, riches will be of absolutely no value.

•**VERSE 7** Those who do not believe in Jesus Christ have no hope (1 Peter 1:3).

•**VERSE 22** The ornament of gold is beautiful, but out of place in a swine's snout. A fair woman is beautiful, but out of place if she lacks discretion.

•**VERSE 24** This is a spiritual law, you increase by giving (Mark 4:24; Luke 6:38; 2 Corinthians 9:6).

CHAPTER 12:
KINDNESS AND WICKEDNESS

•**VERSE 3** Wickedness might prosper awhile, but it will catch up with you. You can't be established by wickedness. You're building on a foundation of sand; when the storm comes it's going to crumble.

•**VERSE 4** Proverbs 31 is a description of the virtuous woman.

•**VERSE 10** Kindness to animals is a sign of a righteous man.

•**VERSE 18** Words can be devastating. God help us not to have a sharp tongue.

•**VERSE 28** This is death from a scriptural standpoint. In the way of righteousness, there is no separation from God (John 11:26).

CHAPTER 13:
PRIDE AND STRIFE

•**VERSE 7** True riches are not measured in material things but have a standard in spirituality.

•**VERSE 10** When contention arises, behind it is someone's pride. It's important to come to the cross and reckon our old man to be dead—the only way to get rid of pride.

CHAPTER 14:
PATHS

•**VERSE 4** Don't brag because your corn crib is so clean. It could be that you have no oxen.

•**VERSE 12** Matthew 7:13-14; John 14:6.

•**VERSE 14** Backsliding begins in the heart.

•**VERSE 31** God is interested in the welfare of the poor.

•**VERSE 34** You can go back in history, and find this is always true: a nation that follows after righteousness is exalted. A nation that opens the door to sin will be destroyed.

CHAPTER 15:
WORDS

•**VERSE 1** The best way to end a fight is to give a soft answer. A soft answer can mellow out a situation. Grievous words only stir it up.

•**VERSE 3** There's nothing in the world that will change your actions more than the awareness that you're in the presence of God wherever you are. The eyes of the Lord are everywhere. More than that, He knows our thoughts.

•**VERSE 8** God isn't interested in the sacrifices the wicked might offer. It's like they're trying to buy God off; buy forgiveness or favor with God. If a sacrifice is to appease your conscience, it's an abomination to God.

•**VERSE 33** Matthew 23:12; James 4:10.

CHAPTER 16:
MORE OR LESS

•**VERSE 1** Many times the work of God is unconscious to us; we're not even aware of it (Philippians 2:13).

•**VERSE 2** God will forgive, no matter what you've done. It isn't by your justification; it's by your confession.

•**VERSE 4** Revelation 4:11.

•**VERSE 6** You cannot walk in fellowship with God and have a desire or love for evil (1 John 1:6).

•**VERSE 8** You're better off to be the poorest saint in heaven than the richest man in hell (Psalm 37:16).

•**VERSE 12** Those in leadership have a greater responsibility before God.

•**VERSE 28** A whisperer is a gossiper.

•**VERSE 31** A hoary head is gray hair. Old people should be sweet and kind. If they are ungodly, it's out of place.

•**VERSE 32** It takes more power to rule your own spirit than to conquer a city.

•**VERSE 33** Casting lots to get guidance or direction was like flipping a coin. Real direction comes from God.

CHAPTER 17:
A MERRY HEART

•**VERSE 1** The house full of sacrifices refers to a house full of meat.

•**VERSE 2** A lot of times the natural children brought heartache, and the wise servant within the house was a greater blessing.

•**VERSE 3** Fires were used to take out the impurities. God puts us through the fire to burn out the impurities in our hearts, to remove things that are destructive (1 Peter 1:7).

The Bible speaks about God testing our works by fire (1 Corinthians 3:13). The testing of our works is not what we have done, but the motive behind what was done (Matthew 6:1-2).

•**VERSE 5** James 2:5.

•**VERSE 9** "Love covers a multitude of sins" (1 Peter 4:8).

•**VERSE 22** Scientists are learning what a healthy thing it is to be happy.

CHAPTER 18:
A MAN'S ANSWER

•**VERSE 1** A man who fulfills his own passions and separates himself to a lustful life is far from real wisdom.

•**VERSE 9** If you are careless in your work, you are wasting things. You have to do it over again, and you've wasted the time and the material.

•**VERSE 10** Strong towers were built on the walls of the city as places of defense. In times of danger, the people would run into them.

Today we get to the place where we are weary and in despair because of the forces and the powers that we are facing. We can run into the strong tower, the name Jehovah.

•**VERSE 14** Suffering develops a depth of character. If you have a strong spirit, it will sustain you to overcome physical weakness.

•**VERSE 15** The greatest knowledge that we can attain is knowledge of God.

•**VERSE 16** Giving gifts opens doors.

•**VERSE 17** There are two sides to every story. The wise person will listen to both sides before making judgment.

•**VERSE 19** Once someone is offended, he's harder to be won than a strong city.

•**VERSE 24** The greatest way to get friends is to be friendly.

CHAPTER 19:
A FOOLISH SON

•**VERSE 2** The person who hurries into a situation will make a mistake.

•**VERSE 3** If you become perverse in your ways and practices, your heart will turn against God.

•**VERSE 5** God hates lying lips, and he that speaks lies shall not escape.

•**VERSE 17** If you have pity on the poor and give to them, God will repay you.

•**VERSE 18** While children are still being formed in character, it's important to discipline and let them know their limitations.

•**VERSE 19** If a person can't control his temper, he'll get in trouble. If you help him, you'll have to do it again.

CHAPTER 20:
INTEGRITY

•**VERSE 6** Your children are looking at you as a role model.

•**VERSE 9** The answer is no one. Only the blood of Jesus will cleanse you.

•**VERSE 17** You may enjoy the things you've gained by deceit, but in the end it's like a mouthful of gravel.

•**VERSE 22** Simply give it to the Lord (Romans 12:19).

•**VERSE 25** If you make a vow to God, don't modify it; keep it.

CHAPTER 21:
THE RICH AND THE POOR

•**VERSE 3** First Samuel 15:22.

•**VERSE 5** Those that are looking for a get-rich-quick scheme—they will leave you broke.

•**VERSE 23** The Bible talks about the tongue being an unruly member, and how much better it is to keep your mouth shut.

•**VERSE 25** He has so much to say about the slothful man, the lazy person. You desire; you want, but you're too lazy to work. The desire of the lazy person eats him up. It kills him.

•**VERSE 31** The horse was like the tank and the advantage in a battle. What are you trusting in for safety? Better to trust in the Lord than to take it in your own hands.

CHAPTER 22:
SPIRITUAL RICHES

•**VERSE 1** A good reputation of being honest is very important.

•**VERSE 4** When the Bible talks about riches, it's spiritual riches.

•**VERSE 7** Keep from borrowing if you possibly can.

•**VERSE 10** Galatians 5:9.

•**VERSE 13** Benjamin Franklin said, "The man who's good at making excuses is seldom good for anything else."

•**VERSE 15** Solomon, no doubt, observed his father David's mistake of being a poor disciplinarian. As a result, his sons rebelled against him.

•**VERSE 17** At this point, the proverbs change. The proverbs more or less have been isolated. Now the proverbs will take two or more verses to expand on a particular thought.

•**VERSE 28** Unfortunately, men have sought to remove the landmarks or the foundational truths of God, questioning God's Word, questioning the deity of Jesus Christ. And when men remove these landmarks, confusion results.

CHAPTER 23:
FATHERLY EXHORTATIONS

•**VERSES 1-3** These proverbs refer to fatherly exhortations to a son. Part of the training of the son was teaching etiquette more than spiritual things.

•**VERSES 4-5** Psalm 62:10.

•**VERSE 6** Referring to an evil person.

•**VERSE 9** If you try to rationalize with a fool, you're wasting your time.

•**VERSES 10-11** Don't take advantage of the defenseless—God watches over the fatherless and the poor.

•**VERSE 35** The tragic effects of alcoholism described quite graphically.

CHAPTER 24:
A WISE HOMEMAKER

•VERSE 1 A man is known by the company he keeps.

•VERSES 11-12 If you fail to help someone when you have the capacity to do it, God knows.

•VERSE 16 Everybody stumbles and falls and God knows that we're not perfect. But don't just lie there; get up.

•VERSES 19-20 Psalm 37:1-2.

•VERSE 29 Don't return evil for evil, let God take care of it (Romans 12:19).

•VERSES 30-34 The Bible continually encourages us toward hard work, and against slothfulness or laziness.

CHAPTER 25:
FURTHER WISE SAYINGS OF SOLOMON

•VERSE 1 These proverbs were gathered by King Hezekiah about 300 years after the death of Solomon, and were added to the book of Proverbs by Hezekiah's scribes.

During Hezekiah's reign, it was a period of national revival. As is true in all spiritual revivals, there was a renewed interest in the Word of God.

•VERSES 6-7 Luke 14:8-11.

•VERSES 9-10 It is better to settle issues in quiet. If a wrong has been committed, go to that person; don't reveal it to everybody.

•VERSES 21-22 Heaping coals of fire on the head refers to an activity of kindness (Matthew 5:44).

•VERSE 23 If someone is backbiting, give them a dirty look. It'll stop them.

CHAPTER 26:
THE FOOL

•VERSE 1 The biblical definition of a fool is a man who has said in his heart,

"There is no God." Snow in summer and rain in harvest are out of place; thus, honor is out of place for a fool.

•VERSE 2 The swallow's flight pattern is quite erratic. So if a person tries to curse you without a cause, don't worry about it.

•VERSE 4 Don't engage in an argument with a fool. It's a waste of time.

•VERSE 5 If you answer a fool, answer him according to the folly that he has declared, putting down the statement he has made; lest he thinks he's wise.

•VERSE 9 A drunkard with something in his hand could be a very dangerous person because he's not responsible for his actions. So too, a parable in the mouth of a fool can be dangerous.

•VERSE 21 One of the best ways to light coals is to set them beside the burning coals.

•VERSE 23 The silver dross was a leaden substance that they would put over clay pots to give them a glaze, a shininess. It looks like it's valuable, but it's nothing but a clay pot that's covered.

•VERSE 26 There is no real secret sin. God will reveal it. If you try to cover your hatred by deceit, it will be known (Luke 12:3).

•VERSE 27 Your sins will come back to you.

CHAPTER 27:
TODAY AND TOMORROW

•VERSE 1 No one knows tomorrow. It's all in God's hands. You don't even know if you're going to be here (James 4:13-15).

•VERSE 2 If you praise yourself, it's called bragging.

•VERSE 10 Assuming your brother is far away, it's better to go to a neighbor for help than to go across the country.

•**VERSE 14** That is, the guy that's still sleeping. I don't want any blessings at five in the morning.

•**VERSE 17** How great it is to sit down with a friend and share ideas back and forth. You sharpen each other.

•**VERSE 19** This is like looking into a clear pool of water and seeing your reflection.

•**VERSE 20** One of the characteristics of the flesh is the insatiable appetite for sinful desires.

•**VERSES 23-27** Be diligent in taking care of your welfare.

CHAPTER 28:
GOD'S MERCY

•**VERSE 2** When a nation has deteriorated morally and spiritually, anarchy almost takes over. When you have a good ruler who is diligent, fair, and honest, he usually rules over a long period.

•**VERSE 5** First Corinthians 2:14-15.

•**VERSE 9** Psalm 66:18; Isaiah 59:1-2.

•**VERSE 13** Just confess and forsake your sins. God will be merciful to you (1 John 1:8-9).

•**VERSE 22** If you're looking for a get-rich scheme, you're going to end up poor.

•**VERSE 26** Walk in the wisdom of the Lord, seeking the guidance and the counsel of God (Jeremiah 17:9).

CHAPTER 29:
FLATTERY

•**VERSE 1** This applies mainly to the sinner, as God gives His mercy and grace, and a person hardens his heart to the wooing of the Holy Spirit; there finally comes a day when God says, "It's enough."

•**VERSE 5** The purpose of flattery is to trip you up or to soften you up.

•**VERSE 9** There's nothing you can do for a fool. Rage at him, or laugh at him; it doesn't make any difference.

•**VERSE 11** A wise man will wait before he makes his decision or his judgment.

•**VERSE 13** God is the judge of the earth. We all stand before Him no matter what our position is.

•**VERSE 18** This "vision" is the word of the Lord.

•**VERSE 25** A lot of people buy in to peer pressure, which is nothing more than the fear of man.

•**VERSE 27** If you're truly a righteous person, then those that do wickedly are an abomination to you, but you in turn are an abomination to them.

CHAPTER 30:
THE WORDS OF AGUR

•**VERSE 1** Now we have a collection of proverbs that are ascribed to Agur Ben Jakeh. It is called a prophecy, and thus there is the acknowledgment that this is inspired of God, speaking through the inspiration of the Holy Spirit.

•**VERSE 2** He begins by confessing his own sin and nothingness. He isn't making any claims for himself.

•**VERSE 4** Not man. He's talking about God.

•**VERSE 5** These things come from God; it's a prophecy. And every word of God is pure.

•**VERSE 6** Men so often purportedly speak for God when indeed God hasn't spoken (Revelation 22:18-19).

•**VERSE 7** This is the prayer of Agur unto God.

•**VERSE 17** When a person was hanged, the ravens would usually come and pluck out their eyes.

•**VERSE 25** From the ant we learn the wisdom of preparing for the future.

•**VERSE 26** The conie, the little hyrax, teaches wisdom in recognizing our own weakness and feebleness and to take shelter in that which is stronger.

He makes his home in the rocks. We recognize our own weakness and hide ourselves in that rock, Jesus Christ.

•**VERSE 27** The locust shows wisdom in his cooperative efforts. By himself, the locust can do no harm. As he goes forth in bands, he can be devastating.

Oh, that the church would learn the cooperative endeavors for the kingdom of God.

•**VERSE 28** It is translated spider, but in the Hebrew it is a lizard or a gecko. Each toe of the gecko has a little pad that has several thousand tiny hooks. The gecko can climb right up a pane of glass holding on. So they do invade houses, mansions, and kings' palaces.

God has given to us exceeding rich and precious promises that we need to hold on to because one day we're going to dwell in the King's palace.

HEBREW KEY WORD

semamiyth = a lizard or a gecko (30:28).

CHAPTER 31:
THE VIRTUOUS WOMAN

•**VERSE 1** These are the words of King Lemuel's mother—the advice of a godly mother to her prince son. There are those who think that Lemuel is indeed Solomon, and that these are the words of Bathsheba unto Solomon.

This is declared to be a prophecy, thus inspired of God.

•**VERSE 4** Wine was forbidden for a man who was an overseer in the church (1 Timothy 3:1, 4).

Here we are told that wine is not for kings—anyone in the ruling capacity. Why? Because God doesn't want anything to cloud your judgment. He wants your mind to be perfectly clear.

•**VERSE 8** Speak up for the underdogs and the oppressed.

•**VERSE 10** In verse 3 she warns him about strange women. Now she tells him the kind of a woman he should look for, yet how hard she is to find.

•**VERSE 11** She's trustworthy.

•**VERSES 13-14** She shops for bargains and gets the best buys from the various markets.

•**VERSE 15** She looks over the affairs of the family.

•**VERSE 16** She's very industrious.

•**VERSE 17** She's a strong woman.

•**VERSE 30** There's nothing more beautiful in all the world than a woman who is righteous and loves God. That's true beauty.

•**VERSES 23, 31** The gates were an important place of a city, for the gates were the place of judgment. When anyone had any kind of business transaction or legal business, they would always come into the gates of the city. The men who sat in the gates were renowned men and the people would come to them for judgments.

STUDY QUESTIONS FOR PROVERBS

1. What is the purpose of a proverb? (Proverbs 1:2-4).

_____

_____

_____

2. We should diligently seek to avoid doing those things that God hates. What are the seven things that are an abomination to the Lord? (Proverbs 6:16-19).

_____

_____

_____

3. Proverbs 14:12 says, "There is a way which seemeth right unto a man; but the end thereof are the ways of death." What does Jesus say is the right path that leads to life in Matthew 7:13-14 and John 14:6?

_____

_____

_____

4. Solomon has much to say about the fool. What is the biblical definition of a fool? (Proverbs 26:1). What are some characteristics of a fool? (Proverbs 10:23; 14:16-17; 28:26; 29:11).

_____

_____

_____

5. Proverbs 31 states the value of a virtuous woman is far above rubies. What are characteristics of a virtuous woman found in verses 10-31?

_____

_____

_____

THE BOOK OF
ECCLESIASTES

AUTHOR OF THE BOOK:
Solomon

PERIOD OF WRITING:
When Solomon was an elderly man.

TYPE OF BOOK:
Poetical

THEME:
The meaninglessness of Solomon's life.

INTRODUCTION:
The book of Ecclesiastes deals with the natural man searching for meaning in life. The word *Jehovah* is not used in this book. He did refer to God, the *Elohiym*, but not to Jehovah God in the sense that a person can know God. Solomon referred to God as a worldly man speaks: as a force, a power, a title—the *Elohiym*.

First Kings chapter 11 gives a background for the observations that Solomon made in Ecclesiastes: "King Solomon loved many strange women, together with the daughter of Pharaoh, women of the Moabites, Ammonites, Edomites, Zidonians, and Hittites; and of the nations concerning which the LORD had said to the children of Israel, You shall not go into them, neither shall they come in unto you: for surely they will turn away your heart after their gods: Solomon clave unto these in love"—and his wives turned away his heart from God.

In reflecting on his disobedience to God, Solomon wrote this book. So at the end of Solomon's life, he looked back at all he had done and realized that the only fruitfulness and meaning in life comes from being in an obedient relationship with God. That is wisdom.

CHAPTER 1:
EVERYTHING IS EMPTY

•**VERSE 1** The word "preacher" might be better translated the debater, or one who is searching, the searcher. The book of Ecclesiastes is indeed a search.

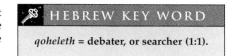

HEBREW KEY WORD

qoheleth = debater, or searcher (1:1).

• VERSE 2 He began with the conclusion of his search. After searching through everything, this is his conclusion of life.

The word "vanity" literally means that which vanishes. It is emptiness. It is similar to trying to grab hold of a breath; there is nothing there.

A person who lives only to satisfy his body needs, denying the spiritual aspect of his nature, is going to end up ultimately with this feeling of emptiness and frustration.

HEBREW KEY WORD

hebel = vanity, that which vanishes; nothing, emptiness (1:2).

• VERSE 3 The phrase "under the sun" will be repeated through the book. It refers to life apart from the consciousness of God and the pursuit of your own selfish ambitions.

• VERSE 4 Solomon spoke of the cycles of life.

"But the earth abideth forever" is not literal. The Hebrew text does not translate this to mean the earth is eternal. Some people use this verse to try to prove that the earth is going to abide forever. But the Bible says that the earth will dissolve with a fervent heat; it will pass away.

• VERSE 11 Even as the past is forgotten, so the present will be forgotten.

• VERSE 14 "Vexation of spirit" could be translated frustration.

• VERSE 15 The Greek philosophers concluded that redemption of man was impossible. But John the Baptist declared of the ministry of Jesus, "All flesh shall see the salvation of God" (Luke 3:6).

There are so many things lacking in a person's life that you cannot number them.

CHAPTER 2:
UNSATISFYING PLEASURES

• VERSES 1-7 As you follow Solomon's search, it was in the lust of his flesh, the lust of his eyes, and the pride of life. He concluded that these things are empty (1 John 2:16).

• VERSE 10 Whatever he desired, he had. Very few men can say that. We think we'll be happy if we have certain things. He had everything, but he was not satisfied.

• VERSE 11 You will never find satisfaction living apart from God.

• VERSES 13-16 With all his wisdom, he couldn't prolong his life. Death is the great equalizer.

• VERSES 18-19 Solomon's worries were not unfounded. His son Rehoboam no sooner got on the throne and then angered the tribes of the north. They had a revolution and he lost the kingdom. The glory that Solomon had built up was blown.

CHAPTER 3:
A TIME FOR EVERYTHING

• VERSES 1-8 The Hebrew meaning is the monotony of life.

• VERSE 11 The "world" in the Hebrew refers to eternity or the ages. Some men deny the consciousness of the eternal. But God has placed eternity in the heart of every man—a desire to seek after more than a part of this monotonous routine of life.

HEBREW KEY WORD

olam = eternity, vanishing point (3:11).

• VERSE 12 God uses trials to develop character and to develop His plan in us.

•VERSE 13 If I labor only for myself, the fruit of that labor can be very empty. But if I labor for the kingdom of God, the fruit of my labor is glorious.

•VERSE 14 The work of God is eternal. You can't add to or take away from the work of God. The work of God is complete (Philippians 1:6).

•VERSE 15 God is outside of our time dimension. He lives in the eternal (2 Peter 3:8).

•VERSES 18-19 You're in the same category as an animal, possessing a mind and living in a body. It's not until you are born again that your spirit is made alive, lifting you from the animal kingdom to the divine kingdom. Thus, once a person is born of the spirit, he begins to relate to God rather than to the animal kingdom (John 3:3).

CHAPTER 4:
OPPRESSION

•VERSE 2 "You're better off dead than alive" is a conclusion of the natural man.

•VERSE 8 Man has to keep laboring. No matter how rich, he's never satisfied.

•VERSE 16 It seems that life goes on. There are multitudes before you and after you.

CHAPTER 5:
ATTITUDE TOWARD GOD

•VERSE 1 When you go into the house of God, listen. Be more ready to hear.

•VERSES 2-4 Usually when a person makes a vow to God, he is seeking to drive a bargain with God. So he is warning us not to be hasty in making vows or promises.

•VERSE 8 God sees. There is a higher judgment than they, and they will one day stand before the judge of all the earth.

•VERSE 9 God has made the fields to bring forth food; the profit of the earth is for everyone.

•VERSE 10 If to be rich is your goal in life, you'll never have a place of satisfaction. You'll never have enough riches, and you'll always be after more.

•VERSES 18-19 God has given you the power to eat; take your portion and rejoice in your labor.

How different this is than what Jesus said concerning our riches. He said, "Lay up for yourself treasures in heaven" (Matthew 6:19-20).

•VERSE 20 How tragic is the man who lives only for the temporal material things: how empty is his life that comes to the end of the road. On the other hand, how full and rich is that life that is lived for Christ; the beginning of the eternal inheritance for the saints of God in Christ (2 Corinthians 4:18).

CHAPTER 6:
GOD KNOWS BEST

•VERSE 3 A child stillborn is better off than a man who has a hundred kids but his soul isn't filled with good.

•VERSE 7 We labor to satisfy our desire for things, yet the appetite can never be satisfied (John 4:13).

•VERSE 10 "Woe unto him who strives with his Maker" (Isaiah 45:9).

•VERSE 12 Sometimes we contend with God because He doesn't give us everything we want. But God knows what's best for us.

CHAPTER 7:
A SERIES OF PROVERBS

•VERSES 1-4 Because he was seeking life apart from God, he experienced the emptiness of it, and thus, he became a bitter old man.

•**VERSE 6** In the Hebrew there is a play on words, unlike English. The word is "seer" for thorn and pot. If we would put it into English, you'd probably say, "The crackling of nettles under the kettles."

The crackling of the thorns is having a fire using kindling and small twigs; the fire comes quickly and is hot, but it goes out quickly too.

•**VERSE 7** A gift of bribery destroys your true judgment.

•**VERSE 9** Don't be quick-tempered.

•**VERSE 10** We always refer to the "good old days," and he's against that because every age has its advantages and opportunities.

•**VERSE 13** This is speaking about the sovereignty of God.

•**VERSE 14** God brings joy into your life and God brings adversity. They work together in creating what you are.

•**VERSE 15** There are times when the righteous are cut off early and the wicked live for a long time.

•**VERSE 16** Do not be overly righteous.

•**VERSE 18** The main thing is to have a fear of God or reverence for God.

•**VERSE 20** Romans 3:10, 23.

•**VERSE 21** Don't be an eavesdropper— you might hear someone curse you.

•**VERSE 29** Man schemes and devises. God made us upright, but we turn to scheming and devising to accomplish our own purposes.

CHAPTER 8:
OBEY THE KING

•**VERSE 2** He is exhorting to keep the commandment, especially in regard to taking these oaths before the Lord.

•**VERSES 3-4** The sovereignty of the king also speaks to the sovereignty of God (Romans 9:20).

•**VERSES 6-7** Moving ahead of God without waiting upon Him, we don't know what the future holds, and thus we can make grave mistakes.

•**VERSE 8** When the time comes for you to die, you don't have any power over your spirit to retain it or to cause it to remain.

•**VERSE 11** People misinterpret the nature of God. Because God is patient and hasn't speedily executed judgment against evil, people assume that God has withdrawn Himself, or that Jesus isn't coming again, and they give their lives over to evil.

•**VERSE 13** In the end, God's judgment will come.

•**VERSES 16-17** You can't understand the ways of God. He is pleased when you just trust Him though you don't understand.

CHAPTER 9:
EVERYONE DIES

•**VERSE 2** The rain falls on the just and on the unjust.

•**VERSE 3** No matter how well you live or how poorly you live, there is one event common to us all—we all die. You have eternal life, though one day physically, your spirit will leave your body (John 11:26).

•**VERSE 5** Solomon is expressing thoughts that are not biblical. Paul said, "There is laid up for me a crown of righteousness to all that love His appearing" (2 Timothy 4:7-8). There is a reward to those who live for God.

•**VERSE 10** Solomon's mistake is he lived for himself, for his own pleasures. If you live for God, your life will be very satisfying (Colossians 3:17).

•**VERSE 11** He concluded it doesn't matter how fast, strong, or wise you are; it's all a matter of blind chance. There is no purpose in life.

But the Bible says that nothing happens to me by accident. It is appointed by God and is intended for my good (Romans 8:28).

•VERSE 12 It's true, we don't know what time we might be taken.

CHAPTER 10:
A LITTLE FOLLY

•VERSE 1 A little bit of folly can take a man of great reputation and bring him down very quickly.

•VERSE 2 A wise man's heart will lead him to right actions; whereas a fool's heart will lead him to wrong activities.

•VERSE 4 It's so easy to bring an end to a dispute by saying, "Maybe you're right."

•VERSE 8 They used to have these rock walls between their vineyards, and snakes used to nest inside. So in taking down a rock wall you were very apt to be bitten by a snake.

•VERSE 10 Rather than using all your strength with a dull axe, take a little effort to sharpen it.

•VERSE 20 This is where they got the phrase, "A little bird told me." Solomon is saying to be careful of what you are saying, even in secret. It's amazing how your words can get out and be exposed.

CHAPTER 11:
BREAD UPON THE WATERS

•VERSES 1-2 You don't know what the future holds, so be generous with what you have. You'll find that it will come back to you in the future.

•VERSE 4 You can't let problems stop you from doing what is necessary.

•VERSE 8 You might live a lot of years, but you're going to be dead longer than you're alive.

CHAPTER 12:
THE CONCLUSION—FEAR GOD

•VERSE 1 Most conversions are made during the teenage years.

•VERSE 2 A graphic description of the aged person.

•VERSE 3 The grinders are the teeth. The windows are a reference to the eyes, the windows of your body, and you begin to go blind.

•VERSE 6 The wheel was the thing that they would use to put the rope down to pull the water out of the cistern. A picturesque speech concerning death.

•VERSE 11 The goad was a stick with a nail at the end of it. They used it while they were plowing with the oxen. If an ox was getting lazy, they would use the goad to get him moving again.

•VERSE 13 This is why you exist. This is the purpose for life. God created you that you might fellowship with Him and stand in reverence and in awe of God. In the worship of God and in the awe of His greatness of heart is to fear God and keep His commandments.

•VERSE 14 Someday you are going to stand before the eternal God, and all of the things that you have done will be brought before God, whether good or evil—unless you are a child of God and the evil is erased (Romans 8:1).

STUDY QUESTIONS FOR ECCLESIASTES

1. Solomon is reflecting upon everything he has done and searching for the meaning of life. What is his initial conclusion of this search in Ecclesiastes 1:2?

_____

_____

_____

2. According to Ecclesiastes 2:10-11, what kind of fulfillment did Solomon experience from total self-indulgence?

_____

_____

_____

3. Solomon was incredibly wealthy. What were his thoughts in regard to riches in Ecclesiastes 5:10, 15?

_____

_____

_____

4. Everyone in life experiences good things as well as bad. Read Ecclesiastes 7:14 and Job 1:21. What do you learn from these verses?

_____

_____

_____

5. After all of his searching, what is Solomon's final conclusion in Ecclesiastes 12:13-14?

_____

_____

_____

THE
SONG OF SOLOMON

AUTHOR OF THE BOOK:
Solomon

PERIOD OF WRITING:
It was written when Solomon was a young man.

TYPE OF BOOK:
Poetical

THEME:
The loving relationship between Christ and His church.

INTRODUCTION:
There are many possible interpretations of the Song of Solomon. There are some who see it purely as a sensuous love song between Solomon and one of his wives, or as a biblical marriage manual. Others see it as a song depicting the relationship between God and the nation of Israel, as in the prophecy of Hosea. Still others see it as the story of the relationship between Christ and His church.

We look at it as a spiritual allegory that represents the loving relationship between Christ and His church—Solomon becoming a type of Christ, and the Shulamite woman becoming a type of the church in their expression of their love for each other.

Jesus desires to have a loving relationship with you. As Paul was praying for the Ephesian church, he prayed that they might know the length, the breadth, the depth, and the height of the love of Christ, which he said, "passes knowledge." The love of Christ for you is so great, so intense, so deep, and so rich you'll never know the full depth of His love.

CHAPTER 1:
THE BEGINNING OF THE SONG OF SONGS

•**VERSE 1** By the title it indicates that Solomon felt that this was the finest of the 1,005 songs that he wrote.

•**VERSES 2-3** The bride begins, and she speaks of her longing for him.

•**VERSE 5** Now she speaks of herself. The word black in Hebrew is dark-skinned.

HEBREW KEY WORD

shachor = **black, dark-skinned, or suntanned (1:5).**

233

•**VERSES 9-11** The king's response to her is loving. The Lord gives His love to you, establishing your life and enriching your life with His fullness.

•**VERSE 12** The bride responds.

•**VERSE 14** Camphire is a very sweet and beautiful plant that grows to about six feet tall. In the springtime, it fills the whole area with fragrance.

•**VERSE 15** The king answers.

•**VERSES 16-17** She responds that she's actually a girl of the outdoors. "The bed is green" refers to the grassy hillsides. The grassy hillside under the fir and the cedar tree is the setting for this beautiful love story.

CHAPTER 2:
THE INVITATION

•**VERSE 1** There are divisions as to who is speaking in verse 1. Some believe this is the groom speaking and others believe it is still the bride speaking.

The lily of the valleys is thought to be the anemone that covers the fields and hillsides in the springtime in Israel—beautiful red, blue, and white flowers.

•**VERSE 2** This is the groom speaking. She is the lily among thorns. Growing in the thorny areas, she stands out. In the midst of the world that is filled with such ugliness, Jesus sees His church whom He loves.

•**VERSE 3** The bride responds. Most of the trees in the woods do not bear fruit. If you find an apple tree in the midst of the forest, it's great because the apple tree provides sustenance and quenches thirst. So Jesus to us is the one who provides our sustenance; He quenches that thirst within our spirit.

•**VERSE 5** We would say lovesick.

•**VERSES 10-13** In a spiritual allegory, we see this as the return of Jesus Christ. He is inviting the bride to arise and come away into the glorious future that God has for the church (Matthew 25:34). We see this as the invitation of the groom to the bride.

•**VERSE 14** He is our Rock, and our lives are hid there in the cleft of the rock: that place of refuge and strength that we find in Jesus Christ.

HEBREW KEY WORD

sela = rock, stronghold (2:14).

CHAPTER 3:
THE ARRIVAL OF THE GROOM

•**VERSE 7** This is a magnificent couch or bed with tapestries that they would carry. Sixty men were carrying this chariot without wheels.

In ancient weddings, the bride-to-be would wait with the virgins who were the bride's attendants. She wouldn't know exactly when the groom was coming. It was always an intriguing mystery. The guys would be carrying the bed, and the groom would be sitting in it, and they would come and stand before the house. The bride would come out and enter into his bedchamber. There would be rejoicing and celebration at the marriage of the bride and groom.

CHAPTER 4:
THE BRIDE'S BEAUTY

•**VERSE 1** Solomon speaks to her describing how he sees her beauty.

The goats were black and they grazed on the hillsides in Israel. The mountain can be covered with these black goats, looking like flowing hair down the mountainside. So he is describing her beautiful flowing black hair.

•**VERSES 3-5** He is totally enraptured by her beauty in which he sees her.

•**VERSE 6** Most commentators see this as the bride's response, embarrassed by this lavish flattery.

•**VERSE 7** He's telling her she's perfect. That's how Christ sees you, without spot, without blemish. He sees you in that perfected state that God has for you. We see ourselves in our present state of development, not the finished work.

•**VERSE 16** In the spiritual realm, the church is the bride of Christ.

Inviting the wind to come and take the beauty of Christ so that the influence of the church might spread throughout the world.

CHAPTER 5:
THE BRIDEGROOM'S BEAUTY

•**VERSE 1** The bridegroom replies.

•**VERSE 2** The bride speaks about a dream and yet it seems to be real. She's sleeping yet her heart is awake. She hears this voice calling for her to open.

I think there are times when the Lord calls us into fellowship. He's longing for that close intimacy.

•**VERSE 4** When you are touched to the deepest part of your emotional being, you'll feel it down in your stomach region. You won't feel it in your heart or in your head. There's this feeling down deep—in the deepest area of the emotions of man.

•**VERSE 6** The Lord has called us for this intimacy, this communion, this close fellowship with Him, but we are slow to respond. But then when your heart is moved and you come, it seems like the Lord has withdrawn Himself.

What a feeling of emptiness when we lose the consciousness of His presence, and feel an absence of His nearness.

•**VERSE 8** She turns to the young maidens and says she's lovesick.

•**VERSES 10-16** She takes this opportunity to share what he is to her. God gives us many opportunities to share what Jesus is to us. I am sure that the daughters of Jerusalem didn't fully understand her love toward him.

Many times we find it difficult to relate to people what Jesus means to us, yet we seek to relate the beauty and the glory of our Lord Jesus Christ.

CHAPTER 6:
WHO IS THE BRIDE?

•**VERSE 1** They were impressed by her witness. They want to seek him with her.

•**VERSE 4** Jerusalem was called the perfection of beauty.

•**VERSES 8-9** This historically gives the time Solomon met this woman that became the favorite among them all. At this time Solomon's harem was limited. There were only 60 queens and 80 concubines, virgins without number, but that increased later as we know. Yet among them all, there was one who stood out, even as the church stands out to the Lord. His love for His church exceeds that of everything else.

•**VERSE 10** The church is living in the anticipation of the new day that is going to dawn for man. Not only to the world, but a new day can dawn in your life. God's work is a new beginning; letting you start all over again (2 Corinthians 5:17).

The moon's light is the reflected light of the sun. And so the church's light is a reflected light. It is the light of Jesus Christ (John 8:12).

The more the world gets between you and the Lord, the less the Son reflects.

The church should be a terror to the evil within the world. We should be as terrible, as frightening to the evil as an army with banners.

CHAPTER 7:
SWEET LOVE

•**VERSE 1** These are the daughters of Jerusalem that are expressing the beauty of the bride. Evidently she is dancing, because the word "feet" can also be translated steps.

HEBREW KEY WORD

paamah = feet, or steps (7:1).

•**VERSE 10** Many people have been destroyed by flattery. But rather than accepting flattery, her heart is so enraptured with the groom that she casts aside these words of flattery.

The main thing that stands out more than anything else is that, "I am my beloved's and he desires me."

•**VERSES 11-12** She has been brought into Jerusalem, into all of the glory of the palace. She has seen the world with all of its glitter. Her desire is to return to the country with him, back to the simple life and the simple things.

•**VERSE 13** She speaks of the fresh fruit and the dried fruit. Dried fruit is old, but it seems to be sweeter, because the starches have been transformed into sugars.

Love should become sweeter with time. As you are growing together in love, your love should be sweeter, richer, and more pleasant as the years go by. Yet, there needs to be a freshness to romance. Sometimes there is a freshness at the beginning, but as the years go by, we don't give the same attention. The Lord notices that.

CHAPTER 8:
MAKE HASTE

•**VERSE 1** The bride desires to have a bond that could not be broken.

•**VERSE 5** They return back to the simplicity, the little village where she was born.

It would seem that this apple tree had a significance in their relationship. It was probably where they first met.

•**VERSE 6** She is asking to set the seal. The seal was the signet ring. It was the mark of ownership. Set your mark of ownership upon me, upon my heart.

Paul the apostle declares that God has placed His seal upon us—the Holy Spirit.

God has given to us the Holy Spirit as a deposit by which God places upon us His mark of ownership until He redeems the purchased possession (Ephesians 1:13-14).

•**VERSE 10** She declares her joy in finding favor in the eyes of the one she loves.

•**VERSE 11** As a footnote here, Solomon was to receive a thousand pieces of silver for the lease of each of the fields.

•**VERSE 13** Her desire is to hear his voice. Give me a sensitive ear that I might hear the voice of my Lord when He speaks to me.

•**VERSE 14** This takes us to the book of Revelation when Jesus said unto John, "Behold, I come quickly." And John responded, "Even so, come quickly, Lord Jesus" (Revelation 22:20).

STUDY QUESTIONS FOR SONG OF SOLOMON

1. What is the spiritual allegory of the Song of Solomon?

2. In chapter 2, verse 2, Solomon describes his bride as a lily among the thorns. What does this signify?

3. Solomon uses many similes to describe his bride's beauty. What are the seven comparisons he makes in Song of Solomon 4:1-5?

4. What is the bride describing in Song of Solomon 5:10-16? How does this relate to our relationship with Jesus?

5. Read Song of Solomon 8:14 and Revelation 22:20. What plea do you hear in both Scriptures?

THE BOOK OF
ISAIAH

AUTHOR OF THE BOOK:
Isaiah

PERIOD OF WRITING:
8th century BC.

TYPE OF BOOK:
Prophetic

INTRODUCTION:
The book was written by Isaiah, the son of Amoz. Amoz, according to rabbinic tradition, was the brother of Amaziah, king of Judah, the father of Uzziah. This would then mean that King Uzziah was a first cousin of Isaiah, placing Isaiah as a part of the royal family of Israel.

Isaiah prophesied during the days of Uzziah, Jotham, Ahaz, and Hezekiah, who were kings of Judah. While Isaiah was prophesying in the southern kingdom, the northern kingdom fell to Assyria. He warned of the destruction and devastation that would come to Israel because of their rejection of God, but Isaiah also foretold of the restoration that would follow.

The book of Isaiah is a marvelous book of prophecy. Of course, it is the longest book of prophecy in the Bible; and it would seem that, more than any other of the Old Testament prophets, God gave to Isaiah a clearer vision of the redemptive work of Jesus Christ . He writes much concerning the Messiah who is to come.

CHAPTER 1:
CALL TO REPENTANCE

•**VERSE 1** Second Chronicles 26-32 gives historical background of Isaiah's prophecies.

•**VERSE 2** God gives His indictment against Judah. His own children have rebelled against Him.

•**VERSE 4** The nation is sinful and backslidden from God.

•**VERSES 7-9** As a result of their sin, the nation and land have suffered.

•**VERSE 10** They are likened to Sodom and Gomorrah.

•**VERSES 11-15** The attitude of the heart is more important than outward religious exercises (Psalm 51:17).

God wearies of the religious form if our heart isn't in it. God declares He will not listen to their prayers because of iniquity (Psalm 66:18; Isaiah 59:1-3).

•**VERSES 16-17** God was concerned that they seek an honest judgment.

•**VERSE 18** God calls Israel to repent. The Lord wants to reason with them. He does not want us to experience a non-reasoned religious experience, but He becomes our reason and our base.

Prophecy is one of His ways of providing us with evidence of who He is so we have a basis for faith.

Even though the sins have permeated the very fiber of our being, God freely offers His grace.

HEBREW KEY WORD

yakach = reason, dispute, convince (1:18).

•**VERSES 21-23** Jerusalem became a harlot spiritually and had a corrupt judicial system.

•**VERSES 24-29** God will restore the city unto Himself and the people will repent of their cultic past.

CHAPTER 2:
THE COMING KINGDOM

•**VERSES 2-3** In the kingdom age Jesus will establish His throne on Mount Zion, and we will also be taught by Him (Revelation 1:6; 3:21; 5:9-10).

•**VERSES 6-8** An apt description of humanism today. Man worships the creature rather than the Creator.

•**VERSES 9-21** The Lord will bring down the proud and shake the earth (Revelation 6:12-17; Hebrews 12:26).

CHAPTER 3:
DISINTEGRATION OF JERUSALEM

•**VERSES 1-4** God is speaking of a present situation rather than future.

•**VERSES 16-26** They did not take God into consideration in their daily lives. God describes His judgment for their iniquity and materialistic lifestyle.

CHAPTER 4:
VISION OF THE COMING KINGDOM

•**VERSES 2-6** Speaking of Jesus' righteous reign upon the earth in the future (Zechariah 3:8).

CHAPTER 5:
ISRAEL AND THE SIX WOES

The Lord likens Judah or Israel unto a vineyard.

•**VERSES 1-7** God was looking for good fruit to come from Israel, as He had provided for it. Jesus wants us to bear fruit (John 15:1-10; Galatians 5:22).

He will forsake Judah, as it did not bear fruit.

•**VERSE 20** Men that stood for righteousness were ridiculed while the perverse were built up.

•**VERSE 21** Woe unto them that judge by their own standards and not God's.

•**VERSES 22-23** Woe to all the judges and men in the government who are alcoholics.

CHAPTER 6:
ISAIAH'S COMMISSION

•**VERSE 1** At Uzziah's death the people were led to the Lord and recognized that He is on the throne; previously they had been trusting in a man.

•**VERSES 2-3** Description of the throne of God and His holiness (Revelation 4, 5; Ezekiel 1, 10).

•**VERSE 5** Truly seeing God in His holiness humbles us and helps us see ourselves and our condition in a true light (Matthew 5:3-4).

•**VERSES 6-7** Matthew 3:2; 1 John 1:9.

•**VERSES 8-13** Isaiah's commission is described. After God touched his life, he became an available instrument.

The nation of Israel will appear to be dead, but God promises to bring the people back from captivity.

CHAPTER 7:
THE SIGN OF THE VIRGIN'S SON

•**VERSES 1-9** God promises Judah will not be ruined by the confederacy of Rezin and Pekah.

Isaiah contains two-fold prophecies that have an immediate and distant fulfillment.

•**VERSES 13-14** Isaiah wrote of things he did not understand, but he was inspired by the Holy Spirit. The Holy Spirit interprets this to be the prophecy fulfilled through the virgin birth of Jesus Christ (Matthew 1:23).

•**VERSES 17-20** God will raise up another kingdom, Assyria, to invade and destroy Syria.

CHAPTER 8:
OVERTHROW AND REMNANT

Continued description of Assyrian invasion.

•**VERSES 7-8** Likens Assyria to a flood.

•**VERSES 11-13** Matthew 10:28.

•**VERSES 14-15** Prophecy concerning Jesus Christ (1 Corinthians 1:23).

•**VERSE 19** People were looking to the dead for guidance rather than looking to the living God.

CHAPTER 9:
THE DIVINE CHILD AND GOD'S JUDGMENT

•**VERSE 2** Prophecy describing the present-day position.

•**VERSES 6-7** Prophecy of Jesus Christ's birth and ministry.

The disciples were confused regarding Jesus' death. They knew this prophecy, but felt His reign and kingdom on earth would be set up immediately (Matthew 16:21-23).

•**VERSES 8-12** Despite the enemy's attack, the people's hearts are hard toward God.

•**VERSE 16** Description of spiritual "hype" in today's world (Matthew 15:14).

•**VERSE 17** God's hand is outstretched in judgment, but Israel still doesn't accept it.

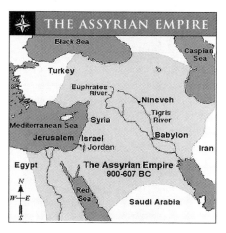

CHAPTER 10:
DEFEAT OF ASSYRIA

•**VERSES 1-3** God will deal with the false leaders. Second Peter 2 describes how to recognize a false prophet.

•**VERSES 5-11** God used Assyria as His instrument of judgment to destroy Samaria. The Assyrians, in turn, were judged. They became proud and didn't recognize that God used them.

•VERSES 12-14 The Assyrians believed their idols were more powerful than the Lord. He punishes them for their pride.

•VERSE 15 The instrument by itself can do nothing. We cannot take credit for anything God has wrought.

•VERSE 20 The future when God preserves the remnant during the great tribulation. These Jews will turn to the Lord in revival and not the Antichrist.

•VERSES 28-34 The gathering of nations for the battle of Armageddon.

CHAPTER 11:
DAVIDIC KINGDOM SET UP BY CHRIST

Speaking of the time after the battle of Armageddon.

•VERSE 1 Picture of the nations being leveled as a forest; the "stem" arising is Jesus Christ. Prophecy regarding Jesus Christ coming from David's line.

•VERSES 2-4 Refers to the second coming of Jesus Christ to judge the earth (Matthew 25).

•VERSES 6-9 The earth and animal kingdom will no longer suffer from man's rebellion against God.

•VERSE 10 This is what the disciples had expected Jesus to do immediately, and the reason why they were confused at His death.

•VERSE 11 God will gather Israel together a second time when Jesus Christ comes again.

•VERSE 12 The "elect" is not the church but the outcasts of Judah (Matthew 24:31).

CHAPTER 12:
THANKSGIVING IN THE KINGDOM

•VERSE 1 The declaration of Israel: Jesus is the true Messiah (Zechariah 12:10; Revelation 1:7).

•VERSE 2 "God" here means Joshua or Jesus. "Jehovah is salvation" is the literal meaning of the name "Jesus."

•VERSE 3 John 4:10, 14; 7:37-38; Revelation 21:6.

•VERSES 4-5 In that day they will exalt and praise God's name. Contains near and distant prophetic fulfillment.

CHAPTER 13:
PROPHECY OF LAST DAYS

Punishment will be visited upon the nations, and Israel shall pass through the great tribulation (Revelation 17 and 18: ecclesiastical Babylon and commercial Babylon).

•VERSES 1-4 Prophecy regarding Babylon in end times. Worldwide wars are one of the signs of Jesus' second coming.

•VERSES 5-10 Description of the great tribulation period (Matthew 24). This punishment is against the iniquity of the evil world, not the church (Romans 2:5-10; 1 Thessalonians 5:9).

HEBREW KEY WORD

paqad = punish, judgment (13:11).

•VERSE 13 Isaiah 2:9-21. The shaking of the earth could be one of the ways God restores it to its original state.

•VERSE 14 The Babylonian invasion (near prophetic fulfillment).

•VERSES 17-19 Isaiah predicts the Medes' destruction of the Babylonian Kingdom before the Medes even became a strong nation.

CHAPTER 14:
CHRIST'S KINGDOM ON EARTH

•VERSES 1-8 At the end of the age, Israel will be restored and exalted.

•**VERSES 12-14** Lucifer's five "I will's"—the beginning of sin and rebellion in the universe, as he opposed God's will (Ezekiel 28:12-14).

God will conform us back to our original state, making us again into the image of Jesus Christ by the Holy Spirit.

CHAPTER 15:
GOD'S JUDGMENT AGAINST MOAB

•**VERSE 2** A song of great mourning.

Moab today is Jordan.

CHAPTER 16:
MOAB REFUSES SANCTUARY

Background: Assyria has been rising as a strong, powerful military force. Isaiah is speaking to the nations that will be in battle with the Assyrians.

•**VERSES 1-4** Prophetically, God has one more seven-year cycle to fulfill in the history of the nation of Israel. The 69 seven-year cycles were fulfilled from the time of the commandment to restore and rebuild Jerusalem to the coming of Jesus Christ: March 14, 445 BC to April 6, 32 AD, Jesus' entry into Jerusalem (Daniel 9:24-26).

Far fulfillment of prophecy unfolds at the point of Israel's fleeing, as Jesus said in Matthew 24:15-16. According to Jesus, when the Antichrist demands to be worshiped as God, then flee Jerusalem (Revelation 12:14).

•**VERSE 5** The outcome: Jesus comes and sits on the throne and judges righteously—1,290 days from the day the Antichrist comes and declares he is God (Daniel 12:11).

•**VERSES 6-12** Immediate condition of Moab is pride. Their vineyards are to be destroyed by conquering armies.

•**VERSES 13-14** Within three years Assyria conquered Moab.

CHAPTER 17:
DAMASCUS AND HER ALLIES FALL

•**VERSES 1-7** All the inhabitants are destroyed by Assyria, but those who remain turn to God.

•**VERSES 8-11** Because the Israelites had forgotten God and gone after false idols, God allowed Assyria to be used as His tool to punish them.

•**VERSES 12-14** Foreshadow of God's judgment against Assyria.

CHAPTER 18:
WOE TO ETHIOPIA

•**VERSES 1-2** Ethiopia had come to Jerusalem to make a confederacy against Assyria. God did not want this confederacy.

•**VERSES 3-7** Isaiah is saying that God will cut down Assyria. There is no need to have a confederacy.

CHAPTER 19:
EGYPT'S DECLINE AND COLLAPSE

•**VERSES 1-5** Civil war in Egypt.

•**VERSES 6-11** Prediction of Aswan Dam and the ecological disasters created by the damming of the Nile River.

•**VERSES 21-22** Egypt will become a religious center for worship of the Lord.

•**VERSES 24-25** Egypt, Assyria (Iraq), and Israel will be joined together in harmony in the day of the Lord.

CHAPTER 20:
CONQUEST OF EGYPT AND ETHIOPIA

•**VERSES 1-6** Assyria conquers and leads their captives away in shame. This is why Isaiah told Israel not to look to a confederacy to stand against the Assyrians, but to look to the Lord.

CHAPTER 21:
THE MEDES' INVASION

• **VERSES 1-2** Prediction of Medes and Elam (Persia) destroying Babylon.

• **VERSES 3-4** Isaiah's physical reaction to the vision.

• **VERSES 4-10** The invasion and fall of Babylon (Revelation 14:8).

• **VERSES 13-17** Saudi Arabia will take the side of Israel when Russia begins to invade (Ezekiel 38:13). Immediate prediction: within one year Arabia was conquered by Sargon in 716 BC.

CHAPTER 22:
THE BURDEN OF THE VALLEY OF VISION

• **VERSES 1-4** Isaiah sees the destruction of Jerusalem.

• **VERSES 5-10** Jerusalem's preparations against the invasion of Assyria.

• **VERSE 11** The Jews have tried to fortify themselves, but have not looked to God for their protection.

• **VERSES 15-21** Shebna and Eliakim were two men of state in Israel. Eliakim is "God's choice" and Shebna is "moved on." Shebna is a type of Antichrist, and he will come and be hailed, then he will be destroyed and the true Messiah will come. Eliakim is a type of Jesus Christ.

• **VERSES 22-23** Revelation 3.

CHAPTER 23:
THE FALL OF TYRE

• **VERSES 1-16** Tyre is laid waste by the Chaldeans (Ezekiel 26-28).

• **VERSES 17-18** The Lord will use Tyre again to supply the kingdom of the Lord (Psalm 45:12).

CHAPTER 24:
PURGING BEFORE SECOND COMING

• **VERSE 1** This could mean a polar-axis flip of the earth.

• **VERSES 2-6** The great tribulation period will affect all people. Very few shall come out of it alive.

• **VERSE 17** The "pit" the Antichrist shall come out of (Revelation 11:7; Luke 21:34-35).

• **VERSES 19-20** The earth will be devastated by earthquakes. Present-day physicists who believe in a polar-axis shift also say the earth will wobble as a top and flip on its axis.

• **VERSE 21** The "high ones" refers to the angelic hosts of evil.

• **VERSE 22** Satan will be shut up for a period and released, but ultimately cast into the outer darkness forever (Revelation 20:7-10).

CHAPTER 25:
TRIUMPHS OF THE KINGDOM AGE

• **VERSES 1-4** God is praised by Isaiah for being our refuge and strength (Luke 21:36).

• **VERSE 8** Jesus has "swallowed up" death (1 Corinthians 15:54-55).

CHAPTER 26:
RESTORED AND CONVERTED ISRAEL

• **VERSES 3-4** In order to have the peace of God, we must receive Jesus Christ. To know the peace of God we need to keep our eyes on Him and not on our trials (John 14:27; Philippians 4:7).

• **VERSES 5-9** Before the kingdom age God will bring down the unrighteous.

• **VERSES 12-18** Israel speaking to the Lord. When they were in prosperity they turned away from God, but in their adversity they repented and turned back to Him.

•**VERSE 19** Prediction of the resurrection of Jesus Christ. Those born before Jesus' time did not enter heaven but into Abraham's bosom (Luke 16:22-31). When Jesus died He descended there to set them free (Matthew 12:40; 27:52-53; Acts 2:24-35).

Our bodies will be changed (John 11:25-26; 1 Corinthians 15:52-54; 2 Corinthians 5:1-8).

•**VERSES 20-21** Refers to the last three and a half years of the great tribulation when God's wrath is poured upon the earth for sin. But God hides His people (Revelation 4:1).

CHAPTER 27:
DELIVERANCE OF ISRAEL

•**VERSE 1** "That day" refers to the great tribulation period upon the earth. "Leviathan" is Satan.

•**VERSE 6** Prophecy stating how God will again bless the nation of Israel and make them His vineyard. Already this prophecy is being fulfilled, as Israel is the third largest fruit exporting nation in the world, even though it is smaller than the state of California.

•**VERSES 12-13** After the barren period God regathers His people back into the land.

CHAPTER 28:
WOE TO EPHRAIM

•**VERSES 1-3** The northern kingdom of Israel was filled with pride and folly. The people did not seek God even in the midst of adversity.

•**VERSE 7** Their heavy drinking has caused their judgment to err.

•**VERSES 11-12** Paul interprets this Scripture referring to speaking in tongues (1 Corinthians 14:2, 21). Tongues are a restful experience for those who exercise the gift.

 CALVARY DISTINCTIVE

"But the word of the LORD was unto them precept upon precept, line upon line; here a little, and there a little" (Isaiah 28:13).

It's so important to take the people through the Word, line upon line, precept by precept. When we do, we are delivering to them the whole counsel of God.

CHAPTER 29:
DISCIPLINE AND BLESSING

•**VERSES 1-10** Spiritual blindness and lethargy had overcome the people.

•**VERSE 16** Analogy of man as clay in God the Potter's hands.

CHAPTER 30:
WARNINGS TO TURN TO GOD, NOT MAN

•**VERSES 1-2** The Israelites in their stupidity turn to man (Egypt), not to God, for their help. There is no real substance to Egypt.

•**VERSE 7** God asks His people not to worry, but to be still and trust in Him.

•**VERSES 16-19** Those who fled to Egypt were destroyed, but those who stayed at Jerusalem were safe.

•**VERSE 26** The sun possibly going into a supernova (Revelation 16:8-9).

•**VERSE 33** Tophet is the place of the burning fire, the final place of the wicked. The New Testament Greek word for this is *gehenna* (Mark 9:44, 46).

 HEBREW KEY WORD

Tophet = place of the burning fire (30:33).

CHAPTER 31:
THE LORD WILL DEFEND

Background: Impending invasion of Assyria and pressure on Israel to ally with Egypt.

• **VERSE 1** Woe to those who are seeking help from man as their first resort.

• **VERSE 5** Dual fulfillment: In 1917 the Turks held Jerusalem. It was preserved from destruction when the British reconnaissance planes flew over and frightened the Turks, who fled without battle.

• **VERSES 8-9** The Assyrians will be destroyed, not by man, but by the Lord (2 Kings 19:35). Angels are given charge over us for protection (Psalm 34:7; 91:11-12).

CHAPTER 32:
CHRIST, THE COMING RIGHTEOUS KING

• **VERSES 1-4** There will be restoration of man physically.

• **VERSES 6-7** The liberal theology will be seen in a true light, as it has not fed those who were hungry for God.

• **VERSES 9-11** Defiled womanhood represents a defiled nation. Women are often used to portray the moral condition of a nation.

• **VERSES 14-16** Signs of the last days: Israel's budding and God's Spirit being poured out (Joel 2:28-32; Acts 2:14-18).

• **VERSE 17** Righteous living guarantees a quietness and assurance that one has done the right thing.

CHAPTER 33:
JERUSALEM DELIVERED

• **VERSES 10-13** God punishes the Assyrians.

• **VERSE 14** The fire of God (Hebrews 12:29). For the Christian, it's a refining process (James 1:2).

CHAPTER 34:
ARMAGEDDON IN THE DAY OF THE LORD

• **VERSES 1-4** Descriptions of the earth during Armageddon. There will be much meteorite activity.

• **VERSES 5-16** Isaiah encourages turning to God's Word when these events happen, realizing God foreknew it.

CHAPTER 35:
KINGDOM BLESSINGS FOR ISRAEL

• **VERSES 1-6** In the kingdom age both the earth and man will be restored to God's original intent.

CHAPTER 36:
RABSHAKEH'S THREATS

• **VERSES 1-7** Rabshakeh shows his ignorance in two areas: the worship of the Lord by Israel, and the counsel God had given Israel not to trust in Egypt but in God. Isaiah was encouraging Israel to trust in Him.

• **VERSES 9-10** Rabshakeh ridicules them and blasphemes God by indicating the Lord directed him against Israel.

• **VERSE 22** After hearing Rabshakeh's threats, men tore their clothes, as was the custom when one was distressed.

CHAPTER 37:
GOD'S PROMISED DELIVERANCE

• **VERSE 1** Sackcloth was used to "afflict" oneself in a sense of mourning.

• **VERSES 6-7** God's answer to Sennacherib's threats.

• **VERSES 14-20** Hezekiah immediately brings his problem to the Lord. He gives the facts to God, asking the Lord to glorify Himself.

• **VERSES 36-38** The Lord fulfills His promise. Sennacherib and the Assyrians are slain.

CHAPTER 38:
HEZEKIAH'S HEALING

•**VERSE 1** Isaiah was referring to Hezekiah setting his relationship with the Lord in order.

•**VERSES 2-8** As proof to Hezekiah of His promise, the Lord changes the degrees of the sun. God is not held to the laws of the universe that He has set.

•**VERSES 9-20** It would appear that there is a "direct" will of God and a "permissive" will.

Because Hezekiah had begged to live, two years later he had a son, Manasseh, who led Judah downward. When we insist on our own way over the Lord's, it is never the best way, and the result is negative.

CHAPTER 39:
BABYLONIAN CAPTIVITY OF JUDAH

•**VERSES 1-8** Another evil, out of the prolonging of Hezekiah's life: the king of Babylon approaches Hezekiah and learns of Judah's defenses.

CHAPTER 40:
JOYFUL PROSPECT AND REPROOF

This chapter begins a new theme in Isaiah.

•**VERSES 1-2** Here we see God's forgiveness and reconciliation.

•**VERSES 3-5** The declaration of the coming of the Messiah and His return (Mark 1:3).

•**VERSES 6-8** Weakness and frailty of man contrasted with the power of God. The Lord's Word is eternal.

•**VERSES 10-11** Reference to Jesus Christ (John 10:11).

•**VERSES 13-14** Trying to instruct or inform God only indicates our lack of a true comprehension of His omniscience.

•**VERSE 15** Merchants, to show their honesty, blew dust off a scale before weighing the merchandise. This is the dust these nations are likened to.

•**VERSES 20-22** God is so awesome and great that there is no figure man can create that accurately represents Him.

The Bible teaches us that the earth is round (Job 26:7).

•**VERSES 29-30** His strength is perfected in our weakness (2 Corinthians 12:9; Hebrews 11:34).

CHAPTER 41:
PREDICTION OF CYRUS' REIGN

•**VERSES 1-4** The Lord raised up Cyrus.

•**VERSES 8-10** Promises for Israel and the church. God has not cast them away (Romans 11:25-27).

•**VERSE 11** Many things done in the name of Christianity have misrepresented God. The outcome has been bitterness toward the church.

•**VERSES 15-20** Prediction of the tremendous agricultural success Israel enjoys today.

•**VERSES 21-24** God challenges the people in the area of prophecy to see if their false idols can accurately tell of things to come.

CHAPTER 42:
CHRIST, SERVANT OF JEHOVAH

•**VERSE 1** Prediction of Jesus Christ and His gospel coming to the Gentiles.

•**VERSES 2-4** Hebrews 2:8-9; Colossians 3:1.

•**VERSE 8** We must take care that we do not seek to serve God to bring glory to ourselves.

•**VERSE 14** God has been patient with the earth for a long time.

•**VERSES 15-16** The Lord will make the earth waste during the tribulation period, but then He will begin His restoring work.

•**VERSES 19-20** Mark 8:18; John 1:11.

•**VERSES 21-25** The Jews were driven out of the land because of their rejection of the Messiah, yet they did not realize that this was the reason.

CHAPTER 43:
ISRAEL TO BE REDEEMED AND RESTORED

•**VERSES 5-6** God predicts the regathering of the Jewish people to Israel.

•**VERSES 10-11** God is declaring that there is no other God but Himself, and no other gods to come.

•**VERSES 22-28** Israel had not been keeping the covenant with God by sacrifice and offerings, and experienced desolation.

CHAPTER 44:
THE PROMISE OF THE SPIRIT

•**VERSES 3-5** The Lord foretells of a revival among the young.

•**VERSE 6** The Father and the Son.

•**VERSES 16-17** The lack of logic and inconsistency of man in trying to create his own god.

•**VERSE 18** They have rebelled so much against God that He allows their eyes to be shut (John 12:39-40).

•**VERSE 19** Romans 1:25.

CHAPTER 45:
PROOF OF GOD'S SOVEREIGNTY

•**VERSE 1** Daniel 5:6.

•**VERSES 2-4** The Lord predicts Cyrus' invasion 190 years before the event takes place. Cyrus gave the decree for the rebuilding of Jerusalem after Israel's Babylonian captivity.

•**VERSE 7** Hebrew word translated "evil" here means sorrow, wretchedness, calamity, adversity, or affliction.

HEBREW KEY WORD

raah = **evil, sorrow, wretchedness, calamity, adversity, or affliction (45:7).**

•**VERSE 9** To strive with God is the height of folly; fighting Him is fighting your own good (Jeremiah 29:32). We are as clay in God's hands and can only discover the potter's plan as we yield ourselves to Him.

•**VERSE 13** God formed Cyrus for the purpose of setting the people of Israel free to rebuild Jerusalem.

•**VERSE 17** God will never cast off Israel, but has promised to keep them.

•**VERSE 18** This is also used as a proof-text for the "gap" theory of creation.

•**VERSES 20-23** God has revealed and declared Himself in the Bible. We can make our own picture of God, but the truth is shown in His Word.

CHAPTER 46:
POWER OF GOD AND POWERLESS IDOLS

•**VERSES 1-2** Their false gods became a burden even to the beasts that had to carry them.

•**VERSES 3-4** Rather than having to be carried and supported by man, the true and living God carries them Himself.

•**VERSES 6-7** They worship gods that can't help them. People today may not acknowledge the true and living God, yet they worship their own idols of power, intellect, wealth, pleasure, etc.

•**VERSES 12-13** God promises His righteousness will be placed in Zion.

CHAPTER 47:
JUDGMENT UPON BABYLON

•**VERSE 3** He will not meet Babylon as a man but as God in judgment.

•**VERSES 4-10** God speaks against Babylon for her horrible treatment of God's people (Matthew 25:41-45).

•**VERSES 7-8** The Babylonians thought they would reign forever. Isaiah predicts their destruction in Daniel 5:17-31.

•**VERSES 14-15** All the wise men and astrologers will not even be able to save themselves, much less anyone else.

CHAPTER 48:
ISRAEL REMINDED OF GOD'S PROMISES

•**VERSE 1** The name "Israel" means governed by God. They call themselves after God, but do not live by Him.

•**VERSES 8-9** God knew they would be hard-headed, but because of His mercy He did not cut them off.

•**VERSE 10** Affliction would be their refining process.

•**VERSES 16-18** Speaking in regard to Jesus Christ (John 8:58).

•**VERSES 21-22** If they had obeyed His command, they would have had peace.

CHAPTER 49:
ISRAEL'S COMING REDEEMER

•**VERSES 1-7** Jesus Christ (Revelation 2:16; 19:15; Psalm 22:9-10).

•**VERSE 5** The purpose of Jesus Christ was to bring Israel back to God.

•**VERSE 6** Jesus, rejected by the Jews, became a light to the Gentiles.

•**VERSE 7** The gospel will permeate many nations.

•**VERSE 10** Revelation 7:16.

•**VERSE 25** If one fights against Israel, he fights against the Lord.

CHAPTER 50:
THE HUMILIATION OF THE HOLY ONE

•**VERSE 1** The nation was "put away" from God by their sins. They turned from Him. God did not sell them; they sold themselves.

•**VERSES 4-6** This is a prophecy regarding Jesus Christ. Jesus willingly submitted Himself to the Father's will. A willing servant is a bondslave.

•**VERSE 6** Jesus was scourged by the Roman government. Spitting was a sign of ultimate disdain and disgust (Matthew 27:26, 30).

•**VERSE 11** Description of a pagan ritual that Israel practiced with fire. The Lord promises that those who took part in it shall "lie down in sorrow."

CHAPTER 51:
GOD'S REMNANT EXHORTED

•**VERSE 1** Matthew 5:6.

•**VERSES 4-5** The Lord will come and reign in righteousness.

•**VERSE 6** Matthew 24:35.

•**VERSE 12** Why fear man? He will die like everyone else (Matthew 10:28; Proverbs 29:25).

•**VERSES 22-23** The day of their trouble will be over and there will be a glorious reuniting of God and His people. The Lord will judge those who have afflicted Israel. The reason for the severity of Israel's judgment is that they failed the responsibility God had given them (Luke 12:48).

CHAPTER 52:
JERUSALEM IN THE KINGDOM AGE

•**VERSE 3** Man would not be redeemed with money.

•**VERSE 6** When Jesus came to His own they did not recognize Him, but a time is coming when they will.

•VERSE 11 Separation from the world to God (Romans 12:1-2; 1 John 2:15).

•VERSES 13-15 Description of Jesus Christ (John 12:32).

CHAPTER 53:
VICARIOUS SACRIFICE OF CHRIST

•VERSE 2 We will not be attracted to Jesus by His physical beauty. It is the love and spiritual beauty we will be attracted to (Revelation 1:7; 5:4-6).

•VERSE 5 The Jews should not be held responsible for Jesus' death as has been the church's pattern historically. We are all equally responsible.

•VERSE 6 God forsook His Son when our sin was placed upon Him (Matthew 27:46).

•VERSE 7 Matthew 26:62-63.

•VERSE 8 Daniel 9:26.

•VERSE 9 Matthew 27:57-60.

•VERSES 10-11 Christ became the sin offering for us according to God's will because He loved us. Jesus was satisfied seeing us in fellowship with God. Through Jesus we are justified.

•VERSE 12 To reject Jesus after seeing His fulfillment is to sin against the truth (Matthew 27:38; Luke 23:34).

CHAPTER 54:
ISRAEL RESTORED AS JEHOVAH'S WIFE

•VERSES 1-2 The Lord will enlarge the nation as He receives them again and places His blessings on them.

•VERSE 4 Israel as an adulterous wife had forsaken the Lord.

•VERSES 7-8 The great mercies of God.

•VERSE 17 Our righteousness is not of ourselves nor comes by our works but by God's grace alone.

CHAPTER 55:
SALVATION THROUGH GOD'S GRACE

•VERSE 1 God detests commercialism and those who exploit or profit from the poor. In the kingdom age God will bless the earth to provide abundantly for everyone.

•VERSE 3 Christ will come and sit upon the throne of David.

•VERSE 8 The difference between our thoughts and ways and God's is that He knows the end from the beginning. Therefore, He does not have to wonder if what He has done is right.

•VERSE 9 Man's folly is he becomes angry with God because God has done something that doesn't agree with him. If we insist on our own way we are exalting our knowledge above God's, making us supreme over God (Psalm 37:5).

•VERSES 10-11 God uses a common thing to illustrate His Word. As rain waters the earth to spark life, so our lives by His Word are brought to life (2 Timothy 3:15-16). The Word comes to our spirit and brings all of God's potential into our lives.

The first effect of the Word is what it does for us personally. The second effect is what it does through us for others (Psalm 126:6).

•VERSES 12-13 As you come into harmony with God, you come into harmony with nature and see things as you have never seen them before.

CHAPTER 56:
REWARDS FOR OBEDIENCE TO GOD

•VERSE 1 The time of the Lord is always very close for each one of us. Knowing we only have one short life, we need to remember that the only lasting things will be those we have done for Jesus Christ (1 Corinthians 3:12-15).

•**VERSE 2** God wants us to live an honest life. A man who does is blessed by God.

"Sabbath" is a covenant God set up with the nation of Israel. The Gentile church was not required to keep it, yet it would benefit us all to have one day of rest each week for health (Exodus 31:16; Acts 21:25; Romans 14:5).

•**VERSES 4-5** First Corinthians 7:32-34.

•**VERSE 7** God wanted those who followed after Him to have access to Him at the temple, even though they weren't Jews (Mark 11:17).

CHAPTER 57:
FALSE LEADERS REBUKED

•**VERSE 1** May be a description of what happens at the rapture of the church.

•**VERSE 3** Addressing those who had been involved in pagan religions. These people were to be joined to God likened unto a husband-wife relationship. Their adultery was they didn't devote themselves totally to the Lord.

•**VERSE 5** In their worship of Baal, the people would offer their children as sacrifices to him.

•**VERSE 13** The Lord contrasts the difference between trusting in Him and in a false god.

•**VERSES 15-19** Even though they had forsaken God, He still promises His restoration.

•**VERSES 20-21** There is constant turmoil for the man who has set his heart against God.

CHAPTER 58:
HYPOCRITICAL RELIGION

•**VERSES 1-2** The contrast was that outwardly they sought the Lord, but inwardly they still worshiped their idols.

•**VERSES 3-5** They weren't fasting to seek God, but to prove a point. Their fast was outward, not inward (Matthew 6:16).

•**VERSES 6-8** When they fast as God wants, they should take their substance and give it to someone else.

CHAPTER 59:
SINS

•**VERSES 1-2** Answers to prayer are hindered by our sin. Our sin separates us from the Lord (Psalm 66:18).

•**VERSES 11-15** Describing the perversity of man.

•**VERSE 17** Ephesians 6:13-17.

•**VERSE 19** There is no man to help, but the Spirit of the Lord is our defense.

•**VERSES 20-21** Romans 11:17-26.

CHAPTER 60:
THE DELIVERER OUT OF ZION

•**VERSES 1-13** The glorious events that will come to Israel when the Messiah returns.

The Jews had difficulty in recognizing Jesus because of the suffering in His life. The Jews had spiritualized the Scriptures that had foretold the suffering that the Messiah would endure (Matthew 16:16-23).

•**VERSE 18** Many people will be coming to worship the Lord in great annual celebrations.

•**VERSES 21-22** The Lord declares His glorious restoration will be taking place in His time.

CHAPTER 61:
CHRIST'S TWO ADVENTS IN ONE VIEW

•**VERSES 1-2** Prophecy of Jesus and His ministry.

Jesus quoted this as a description of Himself (Matthew 11:4-5; Isaiah 26:19). The "day of vengeance" still has yet to take place during the great tribulation.

The "wrath" is not for the church. The Christian's tribulation is from Satan and a part of living in this world.

The wrath that the non-Christian will go through is from God (1 Thessalonians 5:9; John 16:33; Hebrews 10:30).

•VERSE 6 The word "minister" means servant (Matthew 20:27).

CHAPTER 62:
DIVINE UNREST UNTIL ISRAEL RESTORED

•VERSE 1 God will not rest until it is accomplished.

•VERSE 4 The people have felt forsaken, especially those who were part of the Holocaust.

•VERSE 5 God relates to Israel as in a marital relationship.

In the New Testament, Christ and the church are likened this way as well (Ephesians 5:22-32).

•VERSES 8-9 Outsiders who invade the land will no longer be able to take advantage of the profit from the work the Jews have done for it.

CHAPTER 63:
DAY OF VENGEANCE

•VERSES 1-4 The Lord will be spreading the fierceness of His anger upon the earth (Revelation 14:10; 19:11-16).

•VERSES 4-6 God's coming judgment upon the earth.

•VERSE 9 Our persecutions are actually faced and suffered by Jesus Christ.

CHAPTER 64:
THE REMNANT'S PRAYER

•VERSES 1-4 Prayer requesting God manifest Himself as He had in the past.

Our problem is that we don't wait on God but feel that we must help Him to carry out His work (1 Corinthians 2:9-16; Ephesians 1:17-19).

•VERSE 8 Whatever the Potter decides for us is best. As we yield to Him, we know what His desires are for us.

CHAPTER 65:
ANSWER OF JEHOVAH TO ISRAEL

•VERSES 1-5 God declares how He stretched out His hands to the Gentiles (Romans 10:21).

•VERSES 8-9 God will bring a faithful remnant, His elect, back to the land. This follows along with God's promise to never forsake them.

•VERSE 15 The new name for the servants of God is "Christians" (Acts 11:26).

•VERSE 17 To "create" here means to create something out of nothing. This takes place beyond the millennial age (2 Peter 3:10-13).

Since the material universe will be destroyed, we will not recall the horrible period of history when man rebelled against God (Matthew 6:19-21). We should not be living for the physical but the spiritual.

•VERSES 18-19 In the millennial age, the earth will be restored as in the pre-flood condition, when men lived extremely long periods of time.

Those who are in their new bodies will not be subject to death, but will reign with Christ enforcing righteousness.

There will be people who will have lived through the tribulation to the second coming of Christ, and they will be subject to death.

•**VERSE 25** The earth, man, and animals will all be in harmony with God.

CHAPTER 66:
BLESSINGS OF THE UNIVERSAL KINGDOM

•**VERSE 1** We can give nothing to God that does not already belong to Him.

God does not require a place built by man to dwell in, for He dwells in the heavens.

•**VERSES 22-23** In the new heavens and earth, all will be in harmony with the Lord. Those who did not accept Him will have another destiny.

•**VERSE 24** God's wrath or judgment is eternal. Before the great white throne judgment of God, hades will give up their dead.

This verse speaks of the second death. *Gehenna*, the place of eternal punishment, was originally meant for Satan and his angels, but those who follow him in this life will be placed there also (Mark 9:44, 46).

STUDY QUESTIONS FOR ISAIAH

1. Isaiah's vision of God's throne and His holiness is described in chapter 6. What was his reaction and his response to seeing God's holiness in verses 5-7?

_____

_____

_____

2. God warns Judah against making an alliance with Egypt in Isaiah chapter 30. Why didn't He want them aligning with them? (Isaiah 30:1-3, 15; Proverbs 3:5-6).

_____

_____

_____

3. What did King Hezekiah do when he received the blasphemous, threatening letter from the enemy according to Isaiah 37:14-20? What ultimately happened in Isaiah 37:36-37?

_____

_____

_____

4. Isaiah 53 gives a detailed description of the suffering servant. Compare verses 3-9 with Matthew 26:63; 27:46; 57-60. What do you see?

_____

_____

_____

5. Many times we don't understand what God is doing. What is God's explanation in Isaiah 55:8-9?

_____

_____

_____

THE BOOK OF
JEREMIAH

AUTHOR OF THE BOOK:
The prophet Jeremiah.

PERIOD OF WRITING:
Around the time of the fall of Jerusalem to the Babylonians in 586 BC.

TYPE OF BOOK:
Prophetic

THEME:
The death of a nation.

INTRODUCTION:
About sixty years after Isaiah died, God called Jeremiah to what must have been one of the most difficult calls of any man. He was called by God to prophesy to a nation that was dying. The people did not respond to the message resulting in 40 years of what you might say was fruitless ministry. They continued in their evil paths until they were destroyed.

As we see Jeremiah, "the weeping prophet," mourning the judgment of the nation, we see the heart of God for His rebellious people. God continued His witness to them until they were carried away captive to Babylon.

But Jeremiah's ministry wasn't to be successful as far as bringing these people back to a spiritual relationship with God. There was no recovery at this point and he had to sadly watch these people as they disregarded his warnings and as they went on into captivity.

CHAPTER 1:
JEREMIAH'S CALL AND COMMISSION

•**VERSES 1-3** Jeremiah was the son of Hilkiah, a priest in Anathoth in the land of Benjamin.

The word of the Lord came to him in the thirteenth year of the reign of King Josiah, who reinstituted spiritual reform and worship in the temple. The reform was only superficial in the hearts of the people, so God sent Jeremiah to tell the people, "Trust not in lying vanities" (Jeremiah 7:4). After King Josiah's death, Jeremiah was persecuted, accused of treason, and imprisoned.

•**VERSES 4-5** Jeremiah was set apart by God and ordained to be a prophet before he was born. This is an answer to the claims of the abortionists today. God's purposes for our lives are established from the beginning of time.

We must discover and come into harmony with His plan. Our destiny is already determined (Ephesians 2:10; Galatians 1:15).

•**VERSES 6-7** Jeremiah, somewhere between the ages of 17 and 25 years, thought he was too young to be called of God.

The Lord commands Jeremiah to speak for Him. Jeremiah is aware of his inabilities, as so often we are when called of God (Exodus 4:10; Judges 6:15; 1 Samuel 9:17-21).

God isn't looking for people of ability but of availability. God calls men to work in the power of His Spirit, not in their own strength (Zechariah 4:6).

☖ CALVARY DISTINCTIVE

"Ah, Lord GOD! behold, I cannot speak: for I am a child" (Jeremiah 1:6).

Calvary Chapel is not the first time that God has used society's cast-offs to do a wonderful work. But it's interesting that once God begins to use us, we start looking for reasons why God would use us. We try to become perfected in the flesh.

•**VERSES 8-10** God commands Jeremiah to "fear not" and then tells him of his calling and ministry.

Corruption must be eliminated before a new work begins.

•**VERSE 11** "I see a rod of an awakening tree." The Hebrew for "almond tree" is awakening tree, because it's the first tree to awaken in the spring.

•**VERSE 12** God will "watch over" His word to perform it.

•**VERSES 13-15** This is a reference to Babylon and their coming invasion against Israel.

•**VERSE 16** God pronounces judgment on their wickedness.

Through archaeological findings in the old City of David and dating back to the time of Jeremiah, multitudes of idols have been discovered confirming the word of the prophet Jeremiah.

•**VERSES 17-19** Jeremiah is called to a difficult work. He faced Israel alone, knowing the people would fight against him. God laid out a ministry for Paul the apostle, telling him what he would "suffer for His name's sake" (Acts 9:3-16). Christians should recognize that they may be called to suffer for Christ (John 15:20; Matthew 16:24). The Lord promises to be our defense.

CHAPTER 2:
FIRST MESSAGE TO BACKSLIDDEN JUDAH

•**VERSES 1-2** God is calling to His people in the same way Jesus did to the church in Ephesus (Revelation 2:1-5).

•**VERSE 10** Chittim is called Cypress. It is considered to be the door to that whole part of the world. Kedar was the gateway to the east.

•**VERSE 11** Nations continue to serve their gods, yet God's people had turned away from the one true God.

•**VERSE 13** Water is often used as a symbol of life because it's so essential for existence. The Lord speaks to us spiritually when He says, "I am the water of life" (John 4:14; 6:35; 7:37; Revelation 22:17).

Because of the lack of water, the people depended on cisterns for their supply. Run-off water was gathered but often stagnated. How often we stagnate spiritually, and broken cisterns leave us empty and thirsty.

•**VERSE 18** Assyria was soon to fall to the Babylonians. Thus an alliance would be useless.

•**VERSE 20** The "high hill" and the "green tree" are places of worship.

•**VERSE 21** The "strange vine" is figuratively described in Isaiah 5.

•**VERSE 22** "Nitre," a residue found on the bottom of lakes, was often used for making soap.

•**VERSE 23** "Dromedary" is a camel.

•**VERSE 24** The figure of the wild donkey is one of a female in heat. She sniffs the wind trying to find a male donkey. She doesn't care what donkey she finds. God uses this illustration as a type of Israel, who had turned away from God to worship almost anything.

"In her occasion" means in the time of her season. "In her month" means in her heat.

•**VERSE 27** "Stock" is a piece of wood carved into an idol.

•**VERSE 28** Each of the cities had their own local pagan deities. God vows to turn a deaf ear to man if he persisted in sin and disobedience (Matthew 7:22-23; Jeremiah 7:15-16; 11:14).

CHAPTER 3:
THE POLLUTED LAND

•**VERSES 1-5** This is the end of the first message to backslidden Judah. God shows His great patience and long-suffering toward Judah in a plea for her return to Him.

•**VERSE 6** This is the beginning of the second message to backslidden Judah.

•**VERSE 8** Judah didn't learn her lesson. She continued in her sin even as she watched the northern kingdom being carried away by Assyria.

•**VERSES 10-15** Judah's responsibility to God is greater than Israel's, because she saw consequences of Israel's sin.

•**VERSE 16** This is a reference to the kingdom age and the new covenant (Hebrews 8:8; 10:16; Matthew 26:28).

•**VERSES 20-25** Here we see confession of sin.

CHAPTER 4:
SECOND MESSAGE TO JUDAH

•**VERSES 1-4** God called Israel by His promise (Romans 2:28-29).

•**VERSE 22** Romans 16:19.

•**VERSE 23** Genesis 1:2; Isaiah 24:1; Isaiah 45:18. "The earth was without form and void" can be translated, "The earth became wasted and desolate."

•**VERSE 31** "Bewailed" means wailed.

CHAPTER 5:
THE SECOND MESSAGE CONTINUES

•**VERSES 1-31** The sins of Judah and her perversity are seen throughout the entire chapter.

•**VERSE 22** "Bound" means boundary.

•**VERSE 24** "Fear" means reverence.

•**VERSE 30** "Wonderful" means amazement in the sense that it causes amazement. It's an appalling thing.

•**VERSE 31** The people loved corrupt leadership. As we read of the death of Israel, we're reminded of what is happening in our own nation.

CHAPTER 6:
JEREMIAH WARNS THE PEOPLE

•**VERSES 1-6** Jeremiah warns the tribe of Benjamin of the impending doom.

•**VERSE 7** This describes the symptoms of a dying nation. We can compare this Scripture with our own country today.

•**VERSE 30** "Reprobate silver" means refuse silver.

CHAPTER 7:
JEREMIAH CALLS FOR REPENTANCE

•**VERSE 4** Jeremiah rebuked the people. God isn't interested in our "religious" activities, but in our personal, living relationship with Him.

•**VERSE 12** Shiloh was the first location of the temple.

•**VERSE 16** God is speaking to Jeremiah (Genesis 6:3; John 12:38).

•**VERSE 27** Though Jeremiah's ministry wasn't to be successful, God blessed him for his faithfulness and obedience. God's rewards are given according to our response to Him, not according to man's response to us.

•**VERSES 30-31** Altars to their idols were built in the temple of God. Tophet was known as the "Valley of Slaughter." *Gehenna* is the Hebrew word for Hinnom. It means "place of fire" (Matthew 25:41).

CHAPTER 8:
JEREMIAH MOURNS STATE OF THE JEWS

•**VERSE 3** The last of the Jews to hold out against the Roman government were in Masada. This Scripture fulfills that prophecy.

•**VERSE 4** Suicide is denoted here. God's grace is shown that He will return.

•**VERSE 16** The Babylonian army was moving down from Dan.

•**VERSE 20** The day of salvation will soon be over (Romans 13:12).

CHAPTER 9:
DISOBEDIENCE BRINGS GOD'S JUDGMENT

•**VERSE 1** Jeremiah is called the weeping prophet.

•**VERSE 11** "Heaps" mean heaps of destruction.

•**VERSES 17-22** An appeal for trust in God.

•**VERSES 23-24** Knowledge of God is man's glory.

•**VERSES 25-26** Romans 2:28-29.

CHAPTER 10:
GOD AND THE IDOLS

•**VERSES 3-9** Some see these verses as a reference to the custom of decorating fir trees on December 25 and cutting down fir trees to be carved into decorated idols.

The custom of decorating the fir tree on December 25 antedates Christianity by several thousand years.

•**VERSE 8** "Stock" means little idol.

CHAPTER 11:
MESSAGE OF THE BROKEN COVENANT

•**VERSE 4** Emphasis is placed on obedience to the commission (1 Corinthians 7:19; James 1:22; 4:17).

•**VERSES 10-11** Matthew 7:22-23; Jeremiah 7:15-16; 11:14

•**VERSES 22-23** God promises to bring judgment to those who would seek to kill Jeremiah.

CHAPTER 12:
JEREMIAH'S COMPLAINT

•**VERSE 1** Job 12:6; 21:7; Psalm 37:1, 35

•**VERSE 7** This is in reference to the house of Israel.

•**VERSES 14-17** Jeremiah makes it known that Israel will be taken out of the land for 70 years (Jeremiah 25).

CHAPTER 13:
THE SIGN OF THE LINEN GIRDLE

•**VERSES 1-11** The nation which was once beautifully bound to God turns away from Him and is now repulsive to look upon.

•**VERSE 12** The lesson from the filled bottles is a message of prosperity.

•**VERSE 17** Again we have an illustration of the weeping prophet.

•**VERSE 23** We cannot change our own nature. It is only accomplished by the power of the Spirit of God (John 3:3).

CHAPTER 14:
THE MESSAGE ON THE DROUGHT

•**VERSE 22** "Can any of these pagan gods cause it to rain?" is another translation for "Are there any among the vanities?"

CHAPTER 15:
THE MESSAGE ON THE DROUGHT

•**VERSE 1** Because of their dedication to intercessory prayer, Moses and Samuel were used as examples. They had an ear turned toward God. We have power with God when we have an ear turned toward the voice of the Lord (1 Samuel 3:4-9; Exodus 3:4).

•**VERSE 4** Manasseh was the wicked son of Hezekiah who introduced these pagan gods to the people.

•**VERSE 9** To have "given up the ghost" is to have died.

•**VERSES 10-14** A true prophet is often unpopular.

•**VERSES 15-18** Jeremiah laments (Matthew 5:11-12).

•**VERSES 19-21** The Lord gives His assurance to Jeremiah.

•**VERSE 20** "Brasen" means brass.

•**VERSE 21** "Terrible" means awesome.

CHAPTER 16:
THE SIGN OF THE UNMARRIED PROPHET

•**VERSES 1-2** Jeremiah is commanded by God not to marry and have children. This was a sign to the people that difficult days were coming.

•**VERSE 6** At the death of a family member, mourning Jewish males wouldn't shave for 30 days. When the hair was finally cut, it was sacrificed to the Lord.

•**VERSE 8** Feasting was a form of entertainment and celebration for them. They were to stop these customs as a sign of the devastation to come.

•**VERSES 11-12** The Jews would speak of "their fathers" from generation to generation. Stephen spoke of the evil "their fathers" had committed, and Jesus spoke of "their fathers" as the Jews sought to kill Him for telling the truth (John 8:40-56).

•**VERSE 19** Jeremiah cries out to the Lord in what sounds like a psalm. Prophecy of the Gentiles (Romans 11:11, 25; 15:12, 27).

•**VERSE 21** "The LORD" is Jehovah.

CHAPTER 17:
THE SIN OF JUDAH

•**VERSE 5** God promises a curse upon those who would trust in an alliance with Egypt. The people thought that Egypt would deliver them from the Babylonian invasion.

•**VERSES 9-10** Our hearts are deceitfully wicked. "Trying our reins" could mean trying our motivations. Only by abiding in God can we obtain righteousness (Psalm 139:1, 23-24; 1 Corinthians 3:12-13; Matthew 6:5).

•**VERSE 12** "The place of our sanctuary" is God's glorious high throne.

•**VERSES 19-27** This is the message in the gates concerning the Sabbath.

CHAPTER 18:
THE SIGN OF THE POTTER'S HOUSE

•**VERSES 1-6** Romans 9:20-21.

Israel is like clay in God's hands. He'll work a new work in them.

•**VERSES 7-9** Jeremiah 1:10.

•**VERSES 21-23** Jeremiah is willing to see the people destroyed. He doesn't want to pray for them any more.

CHAPTER 19:
THE SIGN OF THE BROKEN FLASK

•**VERSE 2** Jeremiah 7:31.

•**VERSE 5** Idols of Baal made of iron and stone are at the Museum of Natural History in Israel. The hands on the idols are always pointing upward. In the Valley of Hinnom the people placed these idols in the fire until they were red-hot. Then they would sacrifice their small children to Baal in the same fire as they danced and worshiped the idols.

CHAPTER 20:
JEREMIAH IS IMPRISONED

•**VERSE 1** "Pashur" means prosperity.

•**VERSE 3** "Magor-missabib" means terror all around.

•**VERSE 9** Jeremiah was ready to give up his ministry, but God's word was burning in his heart and he couldn't deny his call.

•**VERSES 14-18** Jeremiah lapses into discouragement. The enemy will try to rob us of our joy. We must keep our eyes on the Lord and His grace toward us.

CHAPTER 21:
THE MESSAGE TO KING ZEDEKIAH

•**VERSE 1** Pashur is sent to Jeremiah by Zedekiah.

•**VERSES 3-10** The destruction of Jerusalem is foretold by Jeremiah.

•**VERSE 8** Genesis 2:17; Romans 8:13; John 3:36.

•**VERSES 11-14** The third part of the message to the King of Judah.

CHAPTER 22:
THE MESSAGE TO ZEDEKIAH

•**VERSE 1** Jeremiah takes his message to the house of Judah. He prophesies against the kings of Judah.

•**VERSE 5** Hebrews 6:13, 17.

•**VERSE 6** Gilead and Lebanon are both beautiful, plush, green countries.

•**VERSE 9** They have forsaken the covenant of the Lord (Hebrews 8:7-10; 9:11-15, 22; Matthew 26:28).

•**VERSE 10** The term "goeth away" means dead.

•**VERSE 11** Shallum (Jehoiakim) was taken captive in Egypt and died.

•**VERSE 28** Coniah reigned for three months.

•**VERSE 30** The end of Zedekiah's reign and dynasty.

CHAPTER 23:
FUTURE RESTORATION OF ISRAEL

•**VERSES 1-40** The chapter is a warning against faithless shepherds.

•**VERSE 5** The righteous "Branch" is Jeshua, another name for Jesus.

•**VERSE 6** The Lord our Righteousness in the Hebrew is *Jehovah-tsidkenu*. This name refers to Jesus Christ (Philippians 3:9).

 HEBREW KEY WORD

Jehovah-tsidkenu = **The Lord our righteousness (23:6).**

•**VERSES 7-8** Referring to the future restoration of the Jews, and when God's kingdom on earth will be fulfilled.

•**VERSES 16-17** Even today we have false teachers lying to the people. They say, "There is no evil. All is good. Be at peace."

•**VERSES 23-24** God is near us (Acts 17:28; Psalm 139:8).

•**VERSES 28-29** "Chaff" could represent supernatural experiences. They do not promote growth. Wheat could be likened to the Word of God producing deep spiritual growth.

•**VERSES 33-40** Matthew 11:30.

CHAPTER 24:
THE LESSONS FROM THE FIGS

•**VERSE 1** During the first captivity Nebuchadnezzar captured the young princes, Daniel, Shadrach, Meshach, and Abednego. This message came after the first captivity had taken place.

•**VERSES 5-6** Daniel, Shadrach, Meshach, and Abednego represent the good figs. They are rescued from destruction because they have been taken captive.

CHAPTER 25:
PROPHECY OF THE CAPTIVITY

•**VERSE 3** Jeremiah had been prophesying for approximately 23 years. He was probably around 40 years of age.

•**VERSES 11-14** Jeremiah predicts that the Babylonian captivity will last for 70 years. Jeremiah's prophecies guided the life of Daniel (Daniel 9:2). Disobedience caused the captivity of the people—a lesson on the importance of obedience to God's Word.

•**VERSES 15-38** The time of the great tribulation (Revelation 14:9-20).

•**VERSE 26** Sheshach is another name for Babylon.

•**VERSE 31** God is a just God. He will care for the righteous and rescue them from evil (Genesis 18:26-33; 19:22; Matthew 5:13; 2 Peter 2:7-9).

The church will not go through the great tribulation (Revelation 6-18).

Q JEREMIAH TIMELINE	
639 BC	JOSIAH BECAME KING IN JUDAH AT 8 YEARS OF AGE.
626 BC	JEREMIAH CALLED TO BECOME A PROPHET .
621 BC	BOOK OF THE LAW FOUND. JOSIAH INITIATED GREAT REFORMATION.
612 BC OR 607 BC	NINEVEH DESTROYED BY BABYLON.
606 BC	JUDAH SUBDUED BY BABYLON. FIRST CAPTIVITY TAKEN.
605 BC	BABYLON CRUSHED EGYPT.
597 BC	NEBUCHADNEZZAR TOOK JERUSALEM. JEHOIAKIM DIED. JEHOIACHIN AND THEN ZEDEKIAH BECAME KING IN JUDAH. SECOND CAPTIVITY TAKEN.
593 BC	ZEDEKIAH VISITS BABYLON.
588 BC	BABYLON BEGAN TWO-YEAR SIEGE OF JERUSALEM.
586 BC	JERUSALEM BURNED. ZEDEKIAH KILLED (TEMPORARY END OF DAVID'S KINGDOM). THIRD CAPTIVITY TAKEN.

CHAPTER 26:
JEREMIAH IN KING ZEDEKIAH'S COURT

•**VERSE 3** The root word for repent is "sigh," as a sigh of relief. God is not wanting to punish them, not willing that any should perish (Ezekiel 33:11; 2 Peter 3:9).

This "evil" purpose spoken of by God is His allowing the king of Babylon to come and destroy them (1 Samuel 15:29; Malachi 3:6; Isaiah 45:5-7).

•**VERSE 6** Shiloh was where the tabernacle was placed. It has now become desolate.

CHAPTER 27:
THE LESSONS OF THE YOKES

•**VERSE 2** "Yoke" is a sign of servitude. The yokes attracted attention and sparked questions from the people. This gave Jeremiah the opportunity to speak the word of God to them.

•**VERSE 6** At this time the Babylonian world power had risen to world dominance (Daniel 5:20-22; 3:1, 4-6).

•**VERSE 7** Belshazzar was Nebuchadnezzar's grandson. During the time of Belshazzar's reign the kingdom of Babylon fell to the Medo-Persians.

•**VERSE 12** The sign of yokes continues. Habakkuk, prophesying at the same time as Jeremiah, was perplexed at God's methods of punishment (Habakkuk 1:5, 2:3-4, 14, 20).

The conditions that existed in Israel when Jeremiah was warning of God's judgment to come exist in America today (Luke 12:47-48; James 4:17).

CHAPTER 28:
THE FALSE PROPHECY OF HANANIAH

•**VERSE 10** Hananiah breaks Jeremiah's yoke.

•**VERSES 15-17** Jeremiah predicts Hananiah's death.

CHAPTER 29:
JEREMIAH'S LETTER TO THE JEWS

•**VERSE 1** Daniel was a chief prince. Jeremiah's letter came to him while he was in captivity (Daniel 9:1-2).

•**VERSE 7** "Seek the peace" means don't rebel (Daniel 9:1-3).

•**VERSE 11** "To give you an expected end" could be translated "to bring you to a good end."

•**VERSE 12** Daniel 9:3.

•**VERSES 21-22** A reference to Jeremiah 24:8-10. An example of punishment in the fiery furnace (Daniel 3:6).

•**VERSES 23-32** Shemaiah and all of his seed shall be wiped out. He instigated rebellion against the Lord.

CHAPTER 30:
PROPHECY OF THE GREAT TRIBULATION

The writings of Jeremiah are not written in consecutive order. Chapters 30-36 are written on the future events of Israel as a nation, especially in the "last days."

•**VERSES 2-3** This is a reference to the regathering of Israel.

•**VERSE 6** Description of the anguish shown in the men of Israel.

•**VERSES 7-9** "Breaking the yoke" means breaking the yoke of the Antichrist's oppression. "Jacob's trouble" is the great tribulation.

•**VERSE 10** Jesus will gather His elect from the four corners of the earth. Israel will acknowledge Him as Lord (Matthew 24:31; Mark 13:27).

•**VERSES 11-17** Israel will be restored (Malachi 4:6).

•**VERSE 18** This prophecy has been fulfilled.

•**VERSES 19-20** It's important to maintain a pro-Israel position as a nation (Matthew 25:33-46).

•**VERSE 23** God has made these promises to Israel, not to the church (Revelation 6:9-17). "For God hath not appointed us to wrath. . ." (1 Thessalonians 5:9a). Revelation 22:17, 20.

CHAPTER 31:
ISRAEL IN THE LAST DAYS

•VERSE 5 This refers to the West Bank of Israel.

•VERSE 6 A reference to Christ's coming, establishing His kingdom, and sitting on His throne in Zion.

•VERSE 9 "Firstborn": pre-eminence or prominence.

•VERSE 15 Matthew 2:18.

•VERSE 20 God's mercy to Ephraim.

•VERSE 23 Judah is to be restored.

•VERSE 28 Jeremiah 1:10.

•VERSE 31 The new covenant. The old covenant was established on man's faithfulness to obey the law. The new covenant is established on God's faithfulness (Hebrews 8:8-12).

•VERSE 33 God gives us a new nature (John 3:3; Hebrews 10:16-18).

•VERSE 34 Matthew 26:28.

CHAPTER 32:
THE FIELD IN HANAMEEL

•VERSE 9 Jeremiah buys a field at Anathoth. This was a sign of Jeremiah's faith in God, for the field was occupied by the Babylonian armies.

•VERSE 15 A sign of the coming restoration.

•VERSES 16-25 Jeremiah's prayer.

•VERSE 24 "Mounts" refer to machines.

•VERSES 26-27 God's answer to Jeremiah.

•VERSE 37 "I will gather them out" is a future prophecy of the gathering of Israel.

CHAPTER 33:
RETURN PROMISED TO THE CAPTIVES

•VERSE 3 Jeremiah is admonished to continue to call unto the Lord.

•VERSES 10-13 Judah will be revived.

•VERSE 15 The "Branch" is Jesus Christ (Jeremiah 27:5).

•VERSE 16 "The Lord our righteousness" (Jeremiah 23:6).

•VERSE 18 "Meat offering" is literally meal offering. This is an offering of consecration, an offering of fellowship (Hebrews 7:27).

CHAPTER 34:
THE MESSAGE TO ZEDEKIAH

•VERSES 1-7 This is Jeremiah's warning to Zedekiah.

•VERSE 8 The broken covenant concerning servants.

•VERSE 16 "Subjection" here refers to slavery.

CHAPTER 35:
THE OBEDIENCE OF THE RECHABITES

This prophecy dates back to the reign of Jehoiakim, in the time of Josiah, before Zedekiah was king.

•VERSES 14-19 The Rechabites were obeying the laws of their ancestors, and yet God was speaking to Judah.

CHAPTER 36:
JEREMIAH IN THE DAYS OF JEHOIAKIM

•VERSE 3 The purpose for giving the word of God is to give opportunity for repentance (Ezekiel 33:11).

•VERSES 6-9 A "fast" is usually a time to seek the Lord.

•VERSE 23-32 King Jehudi destroyed the scroll. The destroyed scroll was rewritten by Baruch.

The law was written to warn the people of the judgments to come and lead them to repentance.

CHAPTER 37:
JEREMIAH'S IMPRISONMENT

•**VERSE 1** Zedekiah was king under the order of Nebuchadnezzar.

•**VERSE 2** Zedekiah and the people refused to hear the word of God.

•**VERSES 16-21** Jeremiah transferred to the court of the guard.

CHAPTER 38:
JEREMIAH'S IMPRISONMENT CONTINUED

•**VERSES 1-6** Jeremiah was put in a dungeon for doing the will of God (1 Peter 3:13-17).

•**VERSES 7-13** Jeremiah was rescued from the dungeon.

•**VERSE 14** Zedekiah seeks advice from Jeremiah, though he doesn't heed it.

•**VERSE 20** Jeremiah pleads with Zedekiah to obey the Lord's word.

CHAPTER 39:
THE FALL OF JERUSALEM

•**VERSES 1-2** The siege was 16 months.

•**VERSES 4-5** Zedekiah tried to escape but failed. The plains of Jericho were approximately 18 miles from Jerusalem.

•**VERSE 7** Prophecy fulfilled: "Thou shalt not see Babylon."

•**VERSES 11-14** Nebuchadnezzar cares for Jeremiah.

•**VERSES 15-18** God's promise of deliverance to Ebed-melech.

CHAPTER 40:
JEREMIAH'S PROPHECY TO THE REMNANT

•**VERSES 1-12** Jeremiah lives with Gedaliah.

•**VERSES 13-16** Ishmael's conspiracy (Revelation 2:11, 29, 3:6, 13, 22).

CHAPTER 41:
JEREMIAH'S PROPHECY CONTINUES

•**VERSE 1** In the seventh month the people would gather to worship. They celebrated the Feast of Tabernacles and the Feast of Trumpets.

•**VERSE 2** Ishmael murders Gedaliah. The military Jews come against him.

•**VERSE 5** Shaving beards, rending clothing, and cutting themselves were pagan customs of worship (1 Kings 18:26-28).

•**VERSE 12** Second Samuel 2:13.

•**VERSE 17** Chimham is near Bethlehem.

CHAPTER 42:
JEREMIAH WARNS THE REMNANT

•**VERSE 7** Jeremiah waits ten days for the word of the Lord. Many times God's delayed answer to prayer is to bring about the harmony of His perfect will (1 Samuel 10-28).

•**VERSES 15-16** God warns them of the destruction coming to Egypt.

CHAPTER 43:
JEREMIAH WARNS OF JUDGMENT

•**VERSES 1-7** Jeremiah was taken by force to Tahpanhes in Egypt. Egypt represents a type of sin—the sin of trusting in the flesh.

•**VERSES 8-13** Nebuchadnezzar is to conquer Egypt. The very stones that Jeremiah buried have been found. This is a witness to the truth of God's Word. Nebuchadnezzar set his throne above the stones that Jeremiah buried.

CHAPTER 44:
THE MESSAGE TO THE JEWS IN EGYPT

•**VERSE 1** Jeremiah's final message to the nation.

•**VERSES 2-5** The desolation took place because they had forsaken God to worship other gods.

•**VERSE 17** The worship of Mary stems from this tradition (Jeremiah 7:18).

•**VERSES 21-22** Again Jeremiah sets them straight. It is forsaking God and turning after other gods that brought the judgment against them.

•**VERSE 26** God can swear by no greater than Himself.

•**VERSE 28** In the midst of apostasy, God always has His faithful remnant.

•**VERSE 30** History tells us that Nebuchadnezzar conquered Egypt. God's Word is faithful!

CHAPTER 45:
MESSAGE TO BARUCH

•**VERSE 1** Baruch was a friend and scribe of Jeremiah. He wrote the words of Jeremiah in a scroll.

•**VERSE 2** A personal message to Baruch from the Lord.

•**VERSE 3** Jehoiakim wanted to destroy Baruch because he had read the scroll (Jeremiah 36:10).

•**VERSE 5** Do not seek great things (Matthew 16:26).

CHAPTER 46:
PROPHECIES AGAINST GENTILE NATIONS

•**VERSE 1** About the Gentiles: Jeremiah 46:1-26; 46-51. About Egypt: Jeremiah 46:27-28.

•**VERSE 2** The battle of Carchemish is where Pharaoh defeated Babylon.

•**VERSE 11** Gilead is known as the place of medicine.

•**VERSE 13** This is the second part of the prophecy: the coming invasion of Egypt.

•**VERSE 20** "Out of the north" means from Babylon.

CHAPTER 47:
PROPHECIES AGAINST THE PHILISTINES

•**VERSE 1** "Philistine" comes from the word "Palestine." The Philistines are utterly destroyed.

CHAPTER 48:
PROPHECIES AGAINST MOAB

•**VERSE 1** Destruction coming on Moab.

•**VERSE 7** They were trusting in their works and riches.

•**VERSE 11** The reason for their fall: "Moab hath been at ease from his youth."

•**VERSE 13** Chemosh was the Moabites' god.

•**VERSES 21-34** The cities of Moab are named.

•**VERSE 37** The signs of mourning.

CHAPTER 49:
PROPHECIES AGAINST AMMONITES

•**VERSE 1** The cities that belonged to the tribes of God were now inhabited by the Ammonites.

•**VERSE 2** Rabbah is the ancient name for Ammon in Jordan.

•**VERSE 3** Israel will have their land returned to them.

•**VERSE 7** Edom is an area south of Moab. Teman is a city in Edom.

•**VERSE 8** Dedan is Saudi Arabia. Dedan will not be an enemy to Israel in the major conflict of the last days (Ezekiel 38:10-23).

•**VERSE 13** Hebrews 6:13.

•**VERSE 16** This is Petra, the Rock City.

•**VERSE 23** Damascus was the capital of Syria. She had already fallen to Nebuchadnezzar at this time.

•**VERSE 27** Ben-Hadad is a title for the leaders of Syria.

•**VERSE 28** A prophecy against Kedar and the kingdoms of Hazor.

•**VERSE 39** A prophecy against Elam. Elam today includes the area of Iraq and Iran.

CHAPTER 50:
PROPHECY AGAINST BABYLON & CHALDEA

•**VERSE 1** This prophecy was given 65 years before the fall of Babylon. There is a twofold fulfillment: the destruction of Babylon as prophesied, and the future destruction of spiritual Babylon (Revelation 17-18; Daniel 2:31-35).

Israel was the ten tribes of the northern kingdom, and Judah was the two tribes of the southern kingdom.

•**VERSE 5** They had forsaken the covenant. This was the reason for their exile.

•**VERSE 6** God still recognizes them as His people. God places the blame on the false shepherds.

•**VERSE 15** Romans 12:19.

•**VERSE 19** This refers to the northern kingdom of Israel.

•**VERSE 20** Romans 4:6; 2 Corinthians 5:19; Psalm 32:2.

•**VERSE 29** Daniel 5:27.

CHAPTER 51:
PROPHECY AGAINST BABYLON

•**VERSE 6** The destruction of commercial Babylon (Revelation 18).

•**VERSE 8** The merchants howl and wail over the loss of the commercial system.

•**VERSE 11** Jeremiah by the word of the Holy Spirit names the Medes as the conquering nation. Cyrus destroyed Babylon.

•**VERSE 15** Psalm 104:2.

•**VERSE 17** Who is man to contend with God? (1 Corinthians 1:19-20; Job 40:2).

•**VERSE 19** God has created all things. God has formed all things.

•**VERSE 31** A "post" is a man who carried the message.

•**VERSE 39** Belshazzar was slain in the midst of this drunken party.

•**VERSE 47** Revelation 18:4.

•**VERSE 51** The temple, the holy place, is being profaned.

•**VERSE 58** The walls of Babylon were 80 feet thick.

•**VERSE 63** Revelation 18:21.

CHAPTER 52:
THE OVERTHROW & CAPTIVITY OF JUDAH

•**VERSES 1-3** The reign of Zedekiah (Jeremiah 37; 2 Kings 25).

•**VERSES 4-11** The fall of Jerusalem. The Babylonian army was cruel in war. They starved the people in the cities, then moved in for the slaughter.

•**VERSES 12-30** The captivity of Judah.

STUDY QUESTIONS FOR JEREMIAH

1. Jeremiah 1 reveals God's call upon Jeremiah's life. What was it? (Jeremiah 1:5, 7, 10, 17).

2. Why was Jeremiah known as the "weeping prophet"? (Jeremiah 9:1).

3. Jeremiah 18 describes the potter and the clay. Who does he reference them to symbolize in verse 6? In Romans 9:20-21, how are we to be as clay in God's hands?

4. "Yoke" is a sign of servitude. In Jeremiah 27:11, what does the Lord declare? In the New Testament whose yoke are we to put on and why? (Matthew 11:28-30).

5. In Jeremiah 38:4, what was the reason they put Jeremiah in the dungeon? According to 1 Peter 3:13-17, how are we to respond when we suffer for righteousness' sake?

THE BOOK OF
LAMENTATIONS

AUTHOR OF THE BOOK:
The prophet Jeremiah.

PERIOD OF WRITING:
After the destruction of Jerusalem by the Babylonians in 586 BC.

TYPE OF BOOK:
Prophetic

THEME:
Grief over the destruction of Jerusalem.

INTRODUCTION:
The book of Lamentations is a funeral dirge over the desolation of Jerusalem. It is read each year in the synagogues as the Jews commemorate the destruction of Solomon's temple in 586 BC. Jeremiah wrote the Lamentations as he wept bitterly over the city he had desperately tried to save.

Jeremiah was a prophet whose heart was in tune with God. Here God found it necessary to inflict His people because of practices that would lead to spiritual death. He never punishes willingly.

It breaks the heart of the Father to have to bring pain to His children in order to teach them lessons that are important for them to know. Now that the nation had been judged and the city had been destroyed, Jeremiah became the reflection of the heart of God. As he looked over the rubble and the desolation, he wept until he could not shed any more tears. But he wept over what was necessary in order to preserve the nation itself.

CHAPTER 1:
THE DESOLATION OF JERUSALEM

•**VERSE 1** Jerusalem, once great among the nations, now sits in rubble.

There is a cave that is called Jeremiah's Grotto on the site of Golgotha. Tradition declares that Jeremiah sat in this grotto when he wrote the book of Lamentations. It is interesting that you have a tremendous view of the city of Jerusalem from that cave, for Golgotha is actually the top of Mount Moriah.

•**VERSE 2** Those in whom Jerusalem once trusted have become her enemies.

•**VERSE 5** Jerusalem's affliction was because of her many transgressions.

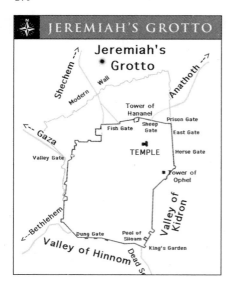

•**VERSE 8** The blame was placed upon Jerusalem for her calamities. It's unjust to blame God for our calamities.

•**VERSE 10** A stranger or a heathen was not allowed to enter the sanctuary and the Holy of Holies.

•**VERSE 11** The people had given all their money and treasures for bread.

•**VERSE 16** "For these things I weep." Thus, the "lamentations" of Jeremiah.

•**VERSE 18** We can always be certain of the righteousness of God in judgment (Revelation 16:5-7).

•**VERSE 19** The people died of starvation while searching for food.

CHAPTER 2:
JERUSALEM'S MISERY

•**VERSES 1-14** Jeremiah reflects on the awesome scene of the destruction of Jerusalem by the Babylonian army.

•**VERSE 15** Jerusalem's beauty had departed.

•**VERSE 17** God was faithful to His warnings.

•**VERSES 18-19** These verses are a call to intercessory prayer.

The people had not been desperate enough to seek God with their whole heart (James 5:16).

CHAPTER 3:
JEREMIAH SHARES ISRAEL'S AFFLICTION

•**VERSES 1-19** Jeremiah related his depth of despair and hopelessness over his calamities. Hopelessness always leads to depression.

•**VERSE 19** Jeremiah was at one of the lowest points of his life.

•**VERSE 20** There is a dramatic change as Jeremiah adjusts his thinking.

•**VERSE 21** We can think ourselves into hopelessness and despair, or by the renewing of our mind we can come into a whole new awareness of God to attain victory and hope (Ephesians 4:23; 2 Corinthians 10:5; Isaiah 26:3).

•**VERSES 22-23** The fact that I wake up each morning is proof of God's mercy, compassion, and faithfulness (1 Corinthians 13:8).

HEBREW KEY WORD

racham = compassion, pity, tender love (3:22).

•**VERSE 24** The Lord is all I need.

•**VERSE 30** This is a prophecy of Jesus Christ.

•**VERSE 32** The forsaking of the people by God will not last forever.

•**VERSE 33** It doesn't please God to have to afflict us. Any time we rebel against God we make it hard on ourselves. God will chasten us because He loves us and is faithful (Jonah 2:8; Hebrews 12:6).

HEBREW KEY WORD

oniy = affliction, misery (1:7).

• **VERSE 38** Evil and good don't proceed from God's mouth as they do from the mouth of man (James 1:18, 3:9-11).

• **VERSES 39-42** These verses are a call to self-judgment and confession.

• **VERSES 52-65** This is a description of Jeremiah's prison experience.

• **VERSE 66** In the New Testament Jesus teaches us to bless those who curse us (Matthew 5:44).

CHAPTER 4:
HORRORS OF THE SIEGE OF JERUSALEM

• **VERSE 3** The ostrich forsakes her eggs in the sand.

• **VERSES 21-22** Edom will also be recompensed.

CHAPTER 5:
A PITIFUL COMPLAINT OF ZION

• **VERSE 21** Turn your heart back to God (Revelation 2:4-5).

• **VERSE 22** The book closes with a sad note of rejection.

This black period of history could have been avoided if the people had only harkened to the voice of God. God was faithful, and that which He declared He would do, He did.

 HEBREW KEY WORD

maac = reject, refuse, despise (5:22).

STUDY QUESTIONS FOR LAMENTATIONS

1. In Lamentations 2:18-19 Jeremiah describes intercessory prayer. How are we called to pray according to 1 Thessalonians 5:17 and James 5:16?

2. In Lamentations 3:1-18 Jeremiah related his depth of despair and hopelessness. According to Proverbs 13:12 what happens to our heart when we are hopeless?

3. According to Lamentations 3:23, how new are the Lord's mercies toward us?

4. Lamentations 4 describes the horrors of the siege of Jerusalem. How is the city described in verse 1?

5. How could the people have avoided this black period of history? (Lamentations 5:21-22).

THE BOOK OF
EZEKIEL

AUTHOR OF THE BOOK:
The prophet Ezekiel.

PERIOD OF WRITING:
Ezekiel ministered from 593 to 571 BC.

TYPE OF BOOK:
Prophetic

THEME:
"They shall know that I am God."

INTRODUCTION:
As Judah was falling to the powers of Babylon, there were three separate sieges in which the Babylonians conquered Jerusalem and took many captives. In the first siege, Daniel the prophet was taken as a captive. In the second siege, Jehoiachin was taken captive, along with Ezekiel. There was a third siege in which Jerusalem was utterly destroyed, and they carried away the remaining people at that time.

Ezekiel became a prophet in Babylon at the same time that Daniel was a prophet. Daniel was in the capital, in the city of Babylon itself as a statesman in the Babylonian kingdom; whereas Ezekiel prophesied about 200 miles north of the city of Babylon, where the river Chebar flows into the Euphrates.

Ezekiel was prophesying to the captives, and when he began his prophecy Jerusalem was still standing. At this same time, Jeremiah was prophesying to the Jews who were still in Jerusalem. Their messages were the same: the judgments of God are coming upon His people because they have forsaken Him, and they have turned to other gods.

CHAPTER 1:
THE VISION OF THE FOUR CREATURES

•**VERSE 1** Ezekiel was probably 30 years old at this time. The fifth day of the fourth month is equivalent to the fifth day of July on our calendar.

•**VERSE 2** He was taken captive at the same time as Jehoiachin.

•**VERSE 4** The whirlwind is used as a symbol of the judgment of God. He saw God's judgment from the north.

•**VERSE 5** This is a spiritual vision, basically of heavenly scenes.

•**VERSES 6-10** The description of these four living creatures are paralleled to the four living creatures in Revelation 4. They're described again in chapter 10, and there he identifies these as cherubim—created intelligent beings of God that surround Him (Isaiah 6).

•**VERSE 10** Bible commentators see the four faces of Jesus as in the Gospels. In Matthew, Jesus is the Lion of the tribe of Judah. Mark pictures Jesus as the servant, or the ox used for plowing. Luke represents the human side of Jesus, thus, the face of a man. John brings out the divine power and majesty of Jesus, thus, the face of the eagle.

•**VERSE 16** Beryl would be green. They looked alike; they were identical.

•**VERSES 18-21** Many liken their view of the flying saucer to be parallel to Ezekiel's description of cherubim. Could it be possible that we are seeing fallen cherubim—even Satan? This is a suggestion; something to think about.

•**VERSE 22** "Terrible" in Hebrew is awesome. It was awesome crystal.

•**VERSES 26-28** This is his vision of God upon the throne (Daniel 7, 9, 10; Isaiah 6; Revelation 4). These give a pretty good composite of what the heavenly scene looks like.

John describes this rainbow in Revelation 4. A bow-like emerald, greenish in color, is around the throne of God. Ezekiel describes it here. John had the same reaction as did Ezekiel of falling on his face. Daniel was weak as a result of his vision.

CHAPTER 2:
EZEKIEL'S CALL

•**VERSES 3-4** He is now called by God to go to the children of Israel.

•**VERSE 5** God does not require success in Ezekiel's ministry. His responsibility is just to warn them.

•**VERSE 6** It was a practice afflicting a person by taking thorn bushes and raking them across his body.

•**VERSE 10** Man brings judgment upon himself because of his rebellion against the Law of God. God laments over this.

CHAPTER 3:
EZEKIEL'S COMMISSION

•**VERSE 1** The eating of the scroll is symbolic, meaning to absorb it. He was to devour it and then give it forth. That's what ministry is all about. You read and absorb the Word until it becomes a part of your very life, and then you give it out to others.

•**VERSE 3** Revelation 10:9-10.

•**VERSES 5-6** Had God sent Ezekiel to the heathen, they would have listened.

•**VERSE 7** God commands His word be given to Israel, though they have hardened their hearts to God's word.

•**VERSE 9** The same Hebrew word for "adamant" is translated diamond in another place.

•**VERSE 15** He now has the anointing of God for the ministry as the power of God's Spirit comes upon him. He is being equipped for ministry as he sits where they sit. He sits there for seven days in silence, in awe and astonished.

☩ CALVARY DISTINCTIVE

"I sat where they sat" (Ezekiel 3:15).

I believe that's a very good thing to try to do, at least in your own mind. Put yourself in the other man's shoes. See it from his side. I've found that the key to compassion is understanding.

•**VERSES 18-19** Notice he wasn't told to convince the wicked to turn. He was only told to declare to them the warning of God. That's all.

•**VERSE 26** His message to the people is going to be visual, as his tongue sticks to the top of his mouth. He's not able to talk, yet it's going to draw attention.

•**VERSE 27** This was to impress upon Ezekiel that he wasn't to blurt out his own ideas, but wait until God spoke.

CHAPTER 4:
SIEGE OF JERUSALEM SYMBOLIZED

•**VERSE 9** Bread was made of wheat for the rich, whereas the poor had barley bread. But mixing in all these other ingredients makes a very unpalatable bread. This represents Jerusalem under siege until the people are starving; making bread out of anything.

Ezekiel will eat this unpalatable bread for the 390 days that he is lying on his left side.

•**VERSE 10** About 12 ounces every day.

•**VERSE 11** Less than a quart of water a day.

•**VERSES 12-13** When a city is under siege, wood was one of the first things used up quickly. They would use dried cow dung as fuel for fire. Human excretion was unclean. Thus, it was not used as fuel for fire. Yet, because of the condition during the siege that was to come, God was saying to do this.

CHAPTER 5:
JERUSALEM'S DESTRUCTION

•**VERSE 2** This illustration foretold the nation's destiny. A third will die from pestilence and hunger. Then when the Babylonians breach into the city, a third of the people will be slain by the sword. The last third will be scattered through the world as slaves, or captives to the Babylonians.

•**VERSE 10** They'll cannibalize each other to survive their hunger.

•**VERSE 11** They built altars unto the other gods within the temple grounds; defiled under the reign of Manasseh.

•**VERSE 13** The fulfillment of the prophecy is the affirmation and the proof that God was the author of that prophecy.

•**VERSE 15** Those who do not learn from history are doomed to make the same mistakes. We should learn to follow the Lord, to serve the Lord, and not forsake Him. If you forsake Him, He will forsake you.

CHAPTER 6:
IMPENDING JUDGMENT UPON ISRAEL

•**VERSE 3** God is prophesying that these places of pagan worship were to be destroyed.

•**VERSE 5** A dead body was considered to be unclean. Thus, to scatter the bones on the altars spoke of the defilement of the altars that would take place.

•**VERSE 8** God will always have His faithful remnant; though driven from the land, they will be faithful to God.

•**VERSE 9** These people had a whorish heart. Rather than being faithful unto God, they began to commit spiritual adultery. Their hearts were not after God any more.

•**VERSE 14** Diblath was on the southeastern part of the Dead Sea, and beyond that there is nothing but the Arabian wilderness.

CHAPTER 7:
PUNISHMENT TO COME

•**VERSE 2** He's been prophesying to the mountains desolation. Now he's to prophesy to the land.

•**VERSES 5-9** Hebrew poetry involves repetition. It's a little repetitious to us, but in Hebrew it's very poetic and has a rhythm to it.

•**VERSES** 12-13 Those who were selling their property in Jerusalem knew that as they went into captivity they would not have the opportunity to buy it back.

•**VERSE 14** The blowing of the trumpet was summoning the people to battle. God said, "I'm not coming forth with you any more. You're going to be turned over to your enemies."

•**VERSE 19** Their gold and silver won't purchase anything, much less their salvation. It's been a stumbling block to them.

•**VERSE 22** The Holy of Holies will be polluted by their enemies.

CHAPTER 8:
ABOMINATIONS IN THE TEMPLE

•**VERSE 1** The prophecies of Ezekiel began in the fifth year of the captivity of King Jehoiachin. This is a year later.

•**VERSE 3** He was brought by the Spirit in a vision where he saw the temple.

•**VERSE 11** These were the elders of the house of Israel. Shaphan was the scribe that read to Josiah out of the law. He repented and ordered a mass repentance of the people. Shaphan was a faithful scribe, but his son was not.

•**VERSE 12** Hebrews 4:13; 2 Corinthians 10:5.

•**VERSE 14** Tammuz was a god of the Babylonians. This ancient Babylonian religion was Satan's counterfeit to God's redemptive program through Jesus Christ.

There was a woman named Semiramis, who bore a son named Tammuz. Supposedly Semiramis was a virgin, and thus Tammuz was born of a virgin. The mother and child were worshiped.

Semiramis was called the queen of heaven and was portrayed with a halo about her head.

According to legend, she had a daughter named Ashtart, and Tammuz was seduced by Ashtart, his sister, and she became his wife.

Tammuz was hunting and was killed by a boar. His spirit descended into Hades, and Ashtart was so grieved over his death she went into the netherworld to mourn. Through her weeping and intercession, he was released from the underworld and resurrected.

Thus, the earth began to spring forth with flowers. They worshiped the spring solstice, called Ashtart, or what we call Easter. Celebrating the resurrection of Tammuz, Satan's counterfeit.

This was the Babylonian religion and became part of Judah's religion. It was an abomination God detested.

Constantine, the Emperor of Rome, made Christianity a state religion. To get the support of the people, he incorporated into the church the pagan practices the Romans and Greeks took from the Babylonians. Rather than celebrating on December 25th the birth of Tammuz, they celebrated the birth of Jesus.

•**VERSES 16-17** They're in the inner court, but their backs are against the Holy of Holies. They were involved in sun worship right in the temple of God. They are snubbing God.

CHAPTER 9:
IDOLATERS KILLED, FAITHFUL SAVED

•**VERSES 1-2** God commanded angels to destroy the city. He looked north, symbolic as destruction was to come from Babylon.

The one clothed in linen is Jesus Christ, a theophany—a manifestation of Jesus Christ in the Old Testament.

•**VERSE 3** The glory of God is no longer in the Holy of Holies, and has moved to the threshold of the house of God.

•**VERSE 4** The inkhorn marked those who grieved the abominations. God kept them from the judgment to come (2 Peter 2:9). The word "mark" is not a word. It is the Hebrew letter *tav*, the last letter of the Hebrew alphabet. In ancient Hebrew, the *tav* was written in the form of a cross.

When judgment comes, I will be sheltered by the cross of Christ.

CHAPTER 10:
GOD'S GLORY DEPARTS FROM THE TEMPLE

•**VERSE 3** The cloud was the sign of God's presence with them.

•**VERSES 16-17** The wheels are controlled by the cherubim for propulsion.

CHAPTER 11:
THE PROMISE OF RESTORATION

•**VERSE 1** In chapter 8 he saw 25 men who were priests, now ruling council with the king.

•**VERSE 3** The iron cauldron was a protection from the fire.

•**VERSES 9-11** Riblah is in the border of Israel. They were brought to Nebuchadnezzar for judgment.

•**VERSE 17** The promise of God's rebirth of the nation. Isaiah, Jeremiah, and Hosea prophesied when God would bring them back and give them the land. That was not fulfilled in Ezra or in the time of Nehemiah.

This actually is a prophecy that refers to the last days' gathering and the re-establishing of the nation.

•**VERSE 23** He watches as the Spirit of God moves from the east gate of the temple to the Mount of Olives, east of Jerusalem.

It was on this same mountain that Jesus came in His entry to Jerusalem as the King, as the Messiah (Zechariah 9:9).

It was on this same mountain that Jesus ascended into glory. And it is upon this same mount that Jesus will return (Zechariah 14:4).

CHAPTER 12:
EZEKIEL DEMONSTRATES THE EXILE

•**VERSES 3-4** This is going to be a little illustrated message to catch their attention.

•**VERSES 10-13** Ezekiel prophesied about King Zedekiah escaping through a passage in the wall of Jerusalem. But he will get caught and have his eyes put out. He'll be brought to Babylon, blinded. This prophecy was completely and literally fulfilled.

•**VERSE 18** Drink a little; measure your swallows. Shake as you eat your bread like you're frightened.

•**VERSE 22** Second Peter 3:4.

VISIONS & PARABLES	
VISIONS	**SCRIPTURE**
FOUR CREATURES & DIVINE GLORY	CHAPTER 1
SCROLL	2:9
ABOMINATION IN THE TEMPLE	CHAPTER 8
SIX ANGELS	CHAPTER 9
THRONE OF GOD	CHAPTER 10
THE GLORY OF THE LORD DEPARTING	CHAPTER 10
TWENTY-FIVE WICKED PRINCES	11:1-3
VALLEY OF DRY BONES	CHAPTER 37
NEW TEMPLE	CHAPTERS 40 - 47
PARABLES / ILLUSTRATIONS	**SCRIPTURE**
CLAY TABLET	4:1
LYING ON HIS SIDES	4:4, 6
EZEKIEL'S BREAD	4:9
SHAVING HEAD AND BEARD	5:1
PACKING HIS THINGS	CHAPTER 12
USELESS VINE	CHAPTER 15
TWO EAGLES AND A VINE	CHAPTER 17
SWORD OF THE LORD	CHAPTER 21
TWO SISTERS	CHAPTER 23
BOILING POT	CHAPTER 24
EZEKIEL'S WIFE DIES	24:18

CHAPTER 13:
FALSE PROPHETS CONDEMNED

•**VERSES 2-3** God had not given these false prophets the message that they were bringing to the people. They were only pretending to hear from God.

•**VERSE 8** God is against them because they actually keep people away from God. They comfort people in their sin.

•**VERSE 9** Israel kept a record of all genealogies. They were the people of God, but their names will not be listed in God's Book of Life.

Untempered mortar is sand without any lime. It looks solid and strong, but the rain will wash it out.

•**VERSE 22** They comforted those dying in their wickedness, and because of the comfort they are not repenting.

CHAPTER 14:
JUDGMENT FOR IDOLATRY

•**VERSE 1** These men had come to Ezekiel the prophet that he might inquire of the Lord for them.

•**VERSE 3** Idolatry begins in the heart (Proverbs 4:23; Romans 10:9).

•**VERSE 9** God will allow them to be deceived. If you don't love the truth in your heart, God will turn you over to believe a lie.

•**VERSE 13** The purpose was to turn the people back to God. In Leviticus chapter 25, God goes through the series of calamities that can befall a nation.

•**VERSE 14** Daniel was alive at this time and one of Nebuchadnezzar's counselors. He had a reputation as a spiritual leader. He purposed in his heart not to defile himself with the king's meats that had been sacrificed to pagan idols.

•**VERSES 15-16** Every man must have his own personal relationship with God. God has no grandchildren.

CHAPTER 15:
THE USELESS VINE

•**VERSE 2** Isaiah 5; Psalm 80:8.

•**VERSES 4-5** A vine is good to bring forth fruit. The purpose of Israel was to bring forth fruit, a demonstration to the world of the blessings of people who make God their King and serve Him.

•**VERSE 6** Israel burned for failure to fulfill its purpose of bearing fruit. The city of Jerusalem was burned by the Babylonians (John 15).

CHAPTER 16:
UNFAITHFUL JERUSALEM

•**VERSE 3** "Thy father was an Amorite, thy mother an Hittite" referred to the nations that inhabited the land prior to the coming in of Abraham.

•**VERSES 7-8** God claimed them as His bride entering into that covenant relationship.

•**VERSES 16-19** They took God's blessings and used them on their own lusts and in the worship of these false gods.

•**VERSES 20-21** They followed the practice of the pagans of the land offering their own children as sacrifice.

•**VERSE 27** Even the heathens around became ashamed of what they did.

•**VERSE 50** Looking for things to fill their idle time, they indulged their flesh. This brought homosexuality and other sins upon the land.

•**VERSES 53-55** God is promising a future restoration of the nation of Israel and He will also restore many nations. Egypt will be restored and be a light unto God as well as Syria.

Babylon will be destroyed completely, but Samaria and Sodom will be restored.

CHAPTER 17:
PARABLE OF TWO EAGLES AND A VINE

•**VERSE** 3 This greatest eagle is Nebuchadnezzar, the king of Babylon, who conquered Israel. The highest branch of the cedar would be the house of David, the king of Israel, taken as a captive to Babylon.

•**VERSE** 7 The second eagle is Egypt that Israel turned toward for help.

•**VERSES** 8-10 This alliance with Egypt will not stand.

•**VERSE** 12 This rebellion was encouraged by the false prophets telling Zedekiah that the Lord would deliver the Babylonians unto them.

•**VERSE** 16 The prediction was that Zedekiah would die in Babylon and would not be successful in the rebellion. That's exactly what happened.

•**VERSES** 22-24 This is the promise of the Messiah. God would raise up the low tree, the tender branch, and make it a great tree for the world to find refuge under its branches. He's going to come again and set up God's kingdom upon the earth; it shall last, stand, flourish, and bring forth fruit.

CHAPTER 18:
GOD JUDGES INDIVIDUALS FAIRLY

•**VERSE** 1 Now Ezekiel speaks to those who have been taken to Babylon.

•**VERSE** 2 Jeremiah makes reference to this proverb also.

•**VERSE** 4 Every man is responsible to God for himself.

•**VERSE** 13 Your unrighteous son cannot be justified by the good you have done.

•**VERSE** 20 Those who are righteous will live because of their righteousness; those who are unrighteous will die because of their sins. Each man will be judged individually by God.

•**VERSE** 21 God's grace and mercy is shown if the wicked will turn.

•**VERSE** 23 God has done everything short of violating your free will to save you (2 Peter 3:9).

•**VERSE** 28 No matter what you may have done, if you will turn to God, there is forgiveness. There is cleansing and new life in Christ for you.

CHAPTER 19:
LAMENT FOR ISRAEL'S PRINCES

•**VERSE** 2 The lion figure is one of Jerusalem and of the tribe of Judah.

•**VERSE** 4 That is, trapped. They would catch lions by digging a pit.

This is a reference to King Jehoahaz. This lamentation is for the end of the Davidic Kingdom (2 Kings 23).

•**VERSES** 6-9 Jehoiachin became king over Judah at the death of Jehoiakim. The Syrians, along with the Moabites, Ammon, and the Chaldeans, came against him. The declaration of nations were set against him on every side, and he was taken in their pit. He was captured and taken to Babylon.

•**VERSE** 10 The vine was the symbol of the nation of Israel; a nation that God raised for the purpose of bringing His salvation to the world.

•**VERSE** 13 That is, in Babylon.

CHAPTER 20:
GOD REHEARSES ISRAEL'S HISTORY

•**VERSE** 1 This would be the seventh year of their captivity.

Though they had come to hear the Word of God, they did not have a heart ready to obey it. That puts a person in a position of greater condemnation. To hear the Word of God and not obey is worse than not hearing at all.

•VERSE 11 God gave the laws to Moses. If people obey them, they will be blessed, prosperous, and healthy.

•VERSE 26 The firstborn belonged to God. But they began to offer their first-borns unto the pagan gods.

•VERSE 28 They made places of worship for the pagan gods in the beautiful mountains of Jerusalem.

•VERSE 29 "Bamah" means high place.

•VERSES 34-36 God is not going to let them go. He's going to shake them up a bit, but He's not going to let them go.

•VERSE 41 That sweet savor is Jesus Christ. The sacrifice of Jesus was a sweet savor to God, whereby we are acceptable. God will reject you on the basis of your own righteousness.

•VERSE 43 There will be a national repentance. During the great tribulation there will be a great turning to Jesus Christ by the Jews. They'll recognize Jesus is the Messiah.

•VERSE 47 They were in the north, in Babylon. He was to face the south and make this prophecy against the forest—a fire that would not be quenched and consume the land.

CHAPTER 21:
PARABLE OF THE SWORD OF THE LORD

•VERSE 2 God had His prophets illustrate the message, to attract attention, getting the message across to people.

•VERSE 7 This is in contrast to what the false prophets were saying in Babylon.

•VERSE 10 "Furbished" is polished.

•VERSES 19-21 Nebuchadnezzar moved south with his forces, and came to a fork in the road. The road to the left led to Rabbah, the capital of the Ammonites. The one to the right led to Jerusalem. There he determined to go left or right.

•VERSE 22 It was determined that Jerusalem would be the victim.

•VERSE 24 God prophesied the people would fall to Babylon, in spite of the false prophets declaring otherwise.

•VERSE 25 This is speaking of Zedekiah, the last of the kings. Zedekiah continued in the ways of wickedness, imprisoning the prophet Jeremiah, and going on with politics, creating an alliance with Egypt.

•VERSE 27 That is, that descendant of David, the promised Messiah.

There has not been a king over Israel since the death of Zedekiah. When they returned from their captivity, they did not establish another monarchy.

When Jesus returns, He will establish the kingdom of God upon the earth

•VERSE 32 The Ammonite race passed from history. They no longer exist.

CHAPTER 22:
THE SINS OF ISRAEL

•VERSE 2 It used to be known as the holy city of God, but now it was known as the bloody city.

•VERSE 3 The people sacrificed their babies to their pagan god Molech.

•VERSE 4 Once feared as the people of God, now they are a reproach because they had turned from God and were worshiping idols.

•VERSE 8 There's no fear of God, taking that which should be holy and profaning it.

•VERSES 10-11 Incest and immorality were taking place in the land.

•VERSES 18-22 God will put them through the fire, like dross which is to be destroyed by the furnace.

•VERSE 25 The prophets were polluted. They lied to the people, joking about the things of God.

•**VERSE 27** All the priests and government were corrupt.

•**VERSE 30** God needs a man who will stand in the gap, through intercessory prayer, to forestall His judgment. But God said, "I found none."

CHAPTER 23:
THE ADULTEROUS SISTERS

•**VERSE 4** "Aholibah" is My tent is in her. That is, Jerusalem was the place God established for the people to worship and meet with Him. There were ten tribes in the northern kingdom, and two in the southern. So Ephraim was called the older sister, and Judah was called the younger sister.

HEBREW KEY WORDS

Aholah = her tent.
Aholibah = My tent is in her (23:4).

•**VERSE 5** The people became attracted to the Assyrians and to the worship of the Assyrians.

•**VERSE 11** When the southern kingdom observed the results of sin in the northern kingdom, it should have been an eye-opener to them.

•**VERSES 37-39** They worshiped Molech, the god of pleasure, resulting in lascivious worship involving sexual intercourse. This resulted in unwanted babies. They sacrificed these babies in the fire, then they would go to the temple to worship God.

CHAPTER 24:
PARABLE OF THE BOILING POT

•**VERSE 2** This was the day that the siege against Jerusalem started (Jeremiah 52:4; 2 Kings 25:1).

It would take two weeks or so by fast express to get word back and forth in those days from Babylon to Israel. Only by the knowledge of God could he have known these things.

•**VERSE 5** They used bones for fire when they were short of wood.

•**VERSE 7** When something was sacrificed, they poured the blood on the ground and covered it with dirt for hygiene. It was part of the law.

•**VERSES 8-11** There is a scum that forms as bones are boiled. When the water goes out and you've got the bones and the scum left, they smell horrible as they begin to burn.

•**VERSE 14** There are actions that bring natural, inevitable consequences. It's a natural consequence of the path that you've chosen. God gave us laws to protect us.

•**VERSES 17-18** He is not to do any signs of the traditional mourning for the dead when his wife died.

•**VERSE 23** He's telling them rather than mourning for the dead, you're to mourn for yourself and for your sins.

CHAPTER 25:
JUDGMENT ON SURROUNDING NATIONS

•**VERSE 3** It is important to notice how many times the Bible purports to be the Word of the Lord. The Bible refers to the Lord speaking 866 times.

It is displeasing to the Lord when you gloat over the misfortune of an enemy (Proverbs 24:17).

•**VERSE 4** The nation of the Ammonites was to be overrun by the Bedouin tribesmen from the east of Ammon.

•**VERSE 7** God's word was fulfilled. They've been destroyed. It is a nationality that no longer exists.

•**VERSE 11** The same Midianite tribal people that conquered Ammon will also conquer Moab.

•**VERSE 12** When the Babylonians conquered Jerusalem, the Edomites took advantage of Judah's weakened condition.

•**VERSE 15** The Philistines were perennial enemies of Israel.

CHAPTER 26:
PROPHECY OF JUDGMENT ON TYRE

•**VERSE 1** This would be the year 586 BC, the year in which Jerusalem was destroyed by Nebuchadnezzar.

•**VERSE 2** There was a commercial competition between Tyrus and Jerusalem. They gloated when Jerusalem fell because it wiped out their competition.

•**VERSES 7-11** One year after the prophecy was written, Nebuchadnezzar began his siege of Tyre. The common practice was to lay siege upon a city, cutting off all outside supplies. Because Tyrus was a port city on the seacoast, he was not able to totally cut off the supplies. The siege went on for 13 years.

By the time Nebuchadnezzar finally made the onslaught, there was only a small part of the population left, and no spoils.

•**VERSE 12** There is a change of pronoun here; "they" instead of "he." The prophecy was that many nations would come against Tyre.

•**VERSE 14** Alexander the Great utterly destroyed the island city of Tyre, utterly destroyed the walls, the houses.

He did this by building a causeway out to the island, using the rubble of the city destroyed by Nebuchadnezzar, and scraping the dust to cover the jetty.

This particular area was always thought to be a peninsula, but they discovered that it actually was the causeway that Alexander the Great had built. Thus we now can go over there and see the site of the ancient city of Tyrus.

•**VERSE 21** We can't tell exactly where the city was because it was so totally devastated and all you have is barren rock in the area where Tyre once existed. There is a modern city of Tyre near the site of the ancient city, which is a Palestinian stronghold in southern Lebanon.

CHAPTER 27:
A LAMENTATION FOR TYRE

•**VERSE 5** Senir is Mount Hermon.

•**VERSE 6** Bashan was famous for its oaks on the other side of the Jordan River.

•**VERSE 8** Zidon was a neighboring city to Tyre.

•**VERSE 14** Togarmah was the area of Armenia.

•**VERSE 15** This is not Dedan of Arabia, but this is Dedan that is further north.

•**VERSE 17** Minnith and Pannag were areas in Israel noted for wheat.

•**VERSE 18** Helbon was an area north of Beirut, where they grew grapes for a famous wine in those days.

•**VERSE 20** This is the Dedan of Arabia.

•**VERSE 24** Tyrus was a tremendous commercial center.

•**VERSE 31** The heathen shaved their heads at the death of a loved one. The people of Israel should not do that.

•**VERSES 32-36** Revelation 18:9-14.

CHAPTER 28:
PROPHECY AGAINST THE KING OF TYRE

•**VERSE 2** The prince of Tyrus becomes an interesting type of the Antichrist, declaring himself to be God and setting himself up as a god. This indeed will happen (2 Thessalonians 2).

•**VERSE 3** Daniel was a contemporary of Ezekiel and was living in Babylon.

When Nebuchadnezzar had his dream, it was Daniel that was able to interpret the dream. Nebuchadnezzar made him head over all of his counselors.

•**VERSES 9-10** Though he declared himself to be God, when the enemy comes over the wall, he'll die like a man.

•**VERSE 12** The description now is that of Satan, who was the one giving his power to the king of Tyre.

This biblical description of Satan is far different from an ugly monster. Sin doesn't come with a lot of ugliness on the front. The ugliness is the byproduct and the result of sin. On the surface it looks attractive. According to the description here, Satan was all of that.

•**VERSE 13** Satan was an angel, and is not at all in any way equal to or on a par with the eternal God.

•**VERSE 14** The fiery crystal sea that is before the throne of God.

•**VERSE 15** Isaiah 14:12-14 gives a little insight into this iniquity that was found in Satan.

•**VERSE 17** Isaiah 14:15.

•**VERSE 18** Satan will ultimately be cast into the lake that is burning with fire.

•**VERSES 25-26** God speaks now of the regathering of His people and Israel will be saved.

CHAPTER 29:
PROPHECY AGAINST EGYPT

•**VERSE 1** This is the time the siege of Jerusalem had begun by Nebuchadnezzar. They were hoping for help from the pharaoh of Egypt. It was on the promise of help that they were emboldened to rebel against Babylon.

•**VERSE 3** The Hebrew word for "dragon" can be translated crocodile.

•**VERSE 5** Prophecy that the Egyptians are going to be defeated and cast out into the fields.

•**VERSE 6** They were trusting in the pharaoh, but the pharaoh did not save them. It turned out that as he came, he was defeated by the Babylonians, and thus he was a broken staff to Judah.

•**VERSES 8-9** The indictment God had against the pharaoh was his bragging, his pride, and that he failed to help the people of God.

•**VERSE 11** Scripturally the number 40 is the number of judgment.

•**VERSES 14-15** Egypt will never rise to world dominance or world power.

•**VERSE 17** There is a 17-year gap between verses 16 and 17. By now the prophecies against Tyrus have been partially fulfilled.

•**VERSE 21** The horn is a symbol of power. God will again restore the power unto His people.

CHAPTER 30:
A LAMENTATION FOR EGYPT

•**VERSE 3** "The day of the Lord" in Scripture is often a reference to the day of God's judgment.

•**VERSE 20** This is a prophecy that came to him three months after the prophecy of chapter 29.

This is a prophecy that God gave to Ezekiel. Nebuchadnezzar defeated the Egyptian army, came back, finished the siege of Jerusalem, and destroyed it later in the same year.

CHAPTER 31:
EGYPT LIKENED TO ASSYRIA

•**VERSE 1** This would be the eleventh year of King Zedekiah (June 1, 586 BC).

•**VERSE 11** The mighty one of the heathen was Nebuchadnezzar of Babylon.

•**VERSE 14** God has brought them down to destruction.

CHAPTER 32:
A LAMENTATION FOR PHARAOH

•**VERSE 1** March 1, 584 BC. This is only a short time before the fall of Egypt to Babylon.

•**VERSE 2** Rather than using Assyria and the tree, He's using the lion and the crocodile, translated here "whale," but most commentators believe it's the crocodile of the Nile River.

•**VERSE 17** This one came 14 days later.

•**VERSES 21-22** Egypt is going to fall and go into hell where Asshur has already been slain.

CHAPTER 33:
THE WATCHMAN

•**VERSES 2-7** When a nation is expecting an invasion, they hire a man to be a watchman. If he doesn't warn them and they are taken, the Lord will hold the watchman responsible for the blood of the people. God is commissioning Ezekiel to speak His word to the captives, the people of God, in the land of Babylon.

•**VERSE 11** The Bible does not teach that God sends men to hell. They go there by their own choice (2 Peter 3:9).

•**VERSE 21** News finally arrived 18 months after the fall of Jerusalem.

•**VERSE 24** God is speaking to Ezekiel concerning the attitude of the people who were part of the remnant Nebuchadnezzar had left there.

•**VERSE 25** It was in the law they were not to eat anything that had not been bled, and yet these people were doing that. They were transgressing the Law of God.

•**VERSE 27** The judgment of God was going to come upon them because of their sin.

•**VERSE 30** These people talked against Ezekiel, yet when they came they sat there in front of him so that he could prophesy to them the word of the Lord.

•**VERSE 31** James 1:22.

•**VERSE 32** Usually the prophets in those days would play a harp. They were just going for entertainment.

CHAPTER 34:
THE SHEPHERDS AND THE SHEEP

•**VERSE 2** God blames the leadership for failing to provide for the common welfare of the people. The primary duty of the shepherd was to see that the people were taken care of and fed.

•**VERSE 4** They were lording over the flock of God. They had misused the position.

•**VERSE 10** God holds them personally responsible for the condition of the sheep.

CALVARY DISTINCTIVE

"I will require my flock at their hand" (Ezekiel 34:10).

I believe God will be far more lenient with me and my errors of grace than He will be if it is the other way around and I condemn someone that He has pardoned and forgiven.

•**VERSE 12** The Jews were scattered at the time of the writing. The remnant were fleeing down to Egypt, Syria, and Babylon, but God said He would bring them back.

•**VERSE 24** This is not a reference to King David being resurrected and becoming king again. It is a reference to that righteous Branch who shall come out of David, who is Jesus.

•**VERSE 25** This is yet future, the kingdom age.

CHAPTER 35:
PROPHECY AGAINST MOUNT SEIR

•**VERSE 2** Mount Seir is the area south of the Dead Sea and east of the valley. Petra is in that mountain area. The Edomites inhabited that area, and it was a powerful nation.

•**VERSE 5** The Edomites were descendants of Esau, who hated his brother Jacob, and that hatred was so deep-rooted that it lasted for centuries. The Edomites were perpetual enemies of Israel.

When Jerusalem fell to the Babylonian army and the people were fleeing, the Edomites rejoiced in the fact that Jerusalem had fallen, and they took advantage of it.

•**VERSE 14** That area will still be desolate the day Jesus returns. The whole earth will be rejoicing in the glorious kingdom of God, rejoicing in all of the abundance of blessings that God will bestow upon the earth.

CHAPTER 36:
PROPHECY TO MOUNTAINS OF ISRAEL

•**VERSE 1** This was the second time he prophesied to the mountains of Israel. The first time was in chapter 6, prophesying about the desolations because they had built the high places on the mountains and worshiped the idols and gods. That prophecy was fulfilled, and the mountains of Israel remained desolate for 19 centuries. This prophecy is about God's work in making the desolate mountains inhabited.

•**VERSE 5** Idumea was Edom, or Mount Seir, in the previous chapter.

•**VERSE 10** At the turn of the century, fewer than 100,000 Jews were in all of the land of Israel; today they number into the millions.

•**VERSE 20** It's a sad thing to bring shame on the name of the Lord.

The world is always ready to pick up on anything in order to blaspheme God. As David was faced with his sin with Bathsheba, the prophet said to him, "And you have given cause for the enemies of God to blaspheme."

•**VERSE 24** It is a miracle how the Jews were able to maintain a national identity for close to 2,000 years without having a homeland. It is unparalleled in history.

•**VERSE 25** This is still in the future, God's grace being restored upon Israel.

•**VERSES 33-34** That land laid there desolate for close to 2,000 years. Now in the last century the agricultural development is amazing.

CHAPTER 37:
VISION OF THE VALLEY OF DRY BONES

•**VERSE 5** In Hebrew, the word translated "breath" is *ruach*. It is also translated spirit and wind.

> **HEBREW KEY WORD**
>
> *ruach* = **breath, spirit, or wind (37:5).**

•**VERSE 6** This is one of those exciting places where God's Word comes alive, as you see the Jews and their return to Israel, the rebirth of the nation.

•**VERSE 9** The four winds represent the north, east, south, and west—all locations throughout the world.

•**VERSE 13** Resurrected from the dead.

•**VERSE 14** It has come to pass. The Hebrew language has even been revived.

•**VERSES 19-22** Ephraim was the major tribe of the northern kingdom. Judah was the southern kingdom. God has brought them back into the land, and there is one nation of Israel.

•**VERSE** 24 This goes into the future when Jesus Christ comes to sit upon the throne.

•**VERSE** 26 There's probably two more great conflicts; the one in chapter 38, and then the great battle of Armageddon, which will culminate in the return of Jesus Christ.

The battle of Armageddon will be the forces of the west under the Antichrist facing the forces of the east (China) in the Valley of Megiddo.

•**VERSE** 28 God has made a covenant with Israel that He is going to keep. God is yet to work among His people, the nation of Israel.

CHAPTER 38:
GOG'S INVASION OF ISRAEL

•**VERSE** 2 Gog is not a land or territory in this sense, but is the chief prince of Magog. Magog has been identified by the historians as the Scythians.

At the time when Ezekiel was writing, they were a very insignificant race of semi-wild people. They dwelt mainly in the area north of the Caucasus. Today that would be the southern provinces of the former Soviet Union.

•**VERSE** 5 He listed the nations that are involved in this war, but also significant are the nations that are not named, because of their past or recent history attempting to exterminate Israel.

Persia is Iran.

•**VERSE** 6 Gomer was in the area north of Turkey. Togarmah is the area of Turkey.

•**VERSE** 8 God is predicting that in the last days when Israel is gathered back into the land, there will come an invasion by these nations, combining themselves together in a massive invasion of the land of Israel.

The Hebrew word for "safely" literally means confidently. They may not be safe, but they're confident.

> **HEBREW KEY WORD**
>
> *betach* = safely; confidently, the feeling of security (38:8).

•**VERSE** 13 Sheba and Dedan are Saudi Arabia.

There is a difference of opinion among Bible commentators as to who Tarshish is. Some say Spain; some say England.

If it is England, then the young lions could possibly include the United States, as we were established as an English colony and then broke off.

•**VERSE** 15 Moscow is about due north of Jerusalem.

•**VERSE** 18 Many of the biblical battles describe God's divine intervention. He destroyed their enemies with hailstones, fire, and brimstone from heaven.

God is once again going to manifest Himself in this battle in a supernatural intervention.

•**VERSE** 21 There will be such confusion that these nations will fight each other.

CHAPTER 39:
PROPHECY AGAINST GOG

•**VERSE** 2 Five out of the six invading troops will be destroyed.

•**VERSE** 8 This defeat of their enemies will trigger the beginning of the last seven years. This is the day when God will restore His Spirit upon Israel.

•**VERSE** 11 They will be buried over in the area of Jordan, the Valley of Passengers. They will call it the Valley of Hamongog, meaning the Valley of the Multitude of Gog.

•**VERSE 15** The people don't touch the bones. They set up a flag near them so that the professionals can come and handle the bones .

Zechariah 14:12 tells us their flesh shall consume away while they stand on their feet. It sounds like death from severe radiation. Perhaps the people are afraid to touch the bones because of radiation. It could possibly indicate that nuclear devices will be involved in this war and in the destruction of Israel's enemies.

•**VERSE 22** This marks the day in which they again turn to God.

•**VERSES 23-25** Right now Israel is blind to Jesus Christ and to the truths of God, but that day will come when God will work again (Romans 11:25-26).

•**VERSE 27** This takes place at the destruction of the Russian army and is a reference back to 38:23.

•**VERSE 29** Daniel 9.

The seventieth seven will begin when God pours out His Spirit upon the nation of Israel.

The sequence of events:

(1) The northern army invading Israel.

(2) The church raptured.

(3) The invaders being destroyed.

(4) The eyes of Israel being opened.

(5) God pouring out His Spirit upon them, and simultaneously the arising of this man of sin out of the federation of ten European nations.

CHAPTER 40:
VISION OF THE TEMPLE MEASUREMENTS

•**VERSE 5** The temple that Ezekiel sees is the future temple during the millennial kingdom age. It could be the temple that John sees in Revelation is destroyed, and this is a completely new temple in the kingdom age.

According to the definition, the cubit he measured is a cubit plus a span. The cubit is the length from your elbow to your fingertips, about 18 inches, and the span is from your thumb to your fingertip. This cubit is about 24 inches.

•**VERSE 39** The offerings mentioned here during the millennial kingdom age will be memorials. They will put us in remembrance of the sacrifice Jesus made for us.

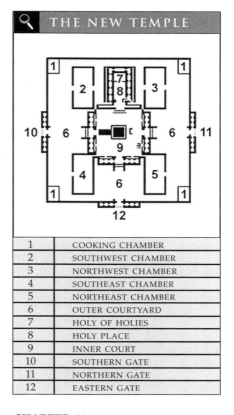

THE NEW TEMPLE

1	COOKING CHAMBER
2	SOUTHWEST CHAMBER
3	NORTHWEST CHAMBER
4	SOUTHEAST CHAMBER
5	NORTHEAST CHAMBER
6	OUTER COURTYARD
7	HOLY OF HOLIES
8	HOLY PLACE
9	INNER COURT
10	SOUTHERN GATE
11	NORTHERN GATE
12	EASTERN GATE

CHAPTER 41:
THE INNER TEMPLE

•**VERSES 2-4** The temple house was 40 by 80 feet, and was a fairly good size room in itself. The measurement of the most holy place was 30 by 30 feet.

CHAPTER 42:
THE TEMPLE CHAMBERS

•**VERSE 14** There are special robes for the priests when they are in this place and they're not to be worn outside.

•**VERSE 20** The word "reeds" in italics indicates it was inserted by translators, but they probably were wrong. It should read "cubits." A reed was about ten feet long, and that would make the place a mile square. Since the rest of the measurements of the temple are in cubits, it probably should read cubits.

CHAPTER 43:
GOD'S GLORY FILLS THE TEMPLE

•**VERSE 2** Earlier Ezekiel saw the glory of God leaving the temple. It settled at the gate toward the east and ascended, and God's glory was removed from Israel.

Here we find the glory of God returning to Israel. Even as the glory of God departed by the gate to the east, so the glory of God returns (Luke 21:27).

•**VERSE 18** The burnt offerings were the offerings of consecration.

•**VERSES 19-21** After making sin offerings for seven days, they are to offer burnt offerings unto the Lord.

•**VERSE 27** Peace offerings were communion, fellowshiping with God.

CHAPTER 44:
RULES FOR THE PRIESTS

•**VERSE 3** Chapter 44 introduces a leader who is known as the prince, who has a portion of the land given to him, and has a very prominent place in the leading of the people, especially in their worship.

•**VERSE 7** The church is raptured and the Lord then begins to deal directly with the nation Israel again. First, Israel will be deceived by the Antichrist.

Priests will be in collusion with the Antichrist. Many of them will be deceived and will worship him as the Messiah.

•**VERSE 18** The Lord doesn't want ministry to Him to be laborious, something that causes sweat. Perspiration is quite often the lack of inspiration (Matthew 11:30).

•**VERSE 21** God does not want service under any false stimulant. He doesn't want anybody to worship Him with a fuzzy mind.

•**VERSE 24** They were to give decisions concerning controversies that would arise among the people.

•**VERSE 25** They were not to be near any dead person, because it was unclean.

If Satan is bound in the abusso for this thousand-year kingdom age, how is it there will be death? It is important to know that the place of the church in this kingdom age is different from the place of Israel. These Israelites will not be in their glorified bodies, but still in their mortal bodies, subject unto death, and they are the ones who will die during the kingdom age.

•**VERSE 30** They didn't have their own fields of grain, or they didn't have to raise their own cattle or sheep because the Lord was their inheritance and their possession.

CHAPTER 45:
DIVISION OF THE LAND

•**VERSE 1** It should say "by allotment" because they're not going to be casting lots. They did that in Joshua's time, but now Ezekiel prophesies the portions of the land that are given to each tribe.

•**VERSE 2** This land is dedicated to the Lord. It is the place of His sanctuary.

•**VERSE 17** In the reestablishing of the temple worship, no high priest is mentioned but this prince who does these various offerings for the people.

•**VERSE 21** The Feast of the Passover is to be re-instituted.

CHAPTER 46:
THE PRINCE WORSHIPS THE LORD

•**VERSE 2** There is reason to believe that the prince is not Jesus Christ because he worships the Lord, offers sacrifices, and he also has sons that he will apportion a part of his land to.

•**VERSE 5** An ephah is about a bushel and three pints, and a hin of oil is about six quarts. They mix flour and oil and bake it as an offering unto the Lord.

•**VERSE 6** When the sin offerings are made in the kingdom age, they will be made as memorials, looking back and remembering what Jesus has done.

•**VERSE 12** It is a voluntary offering. God wants a meaningful relationship with you so He gives you a choice.

•**VERSE 13** This is a national commitment unto the Lord.

•**VERSE 16** The prince has a portion of the land allotted to him. If he gives it to his sons, it's theirs as an inheritance.

CHAPTER 47:
WATER FLOWS FROM THE TEMPLE

•**VERSES 3-5** This river comes from the throne of God and flows eastward (Zechariah 14; Revelation 22). It would seem that the temple and the city of Jerusalem is a replica of the New Jerusalem. In the New Jerusalem there is a river that proceeds from the throne of God. This one described seems to proceed from the Holy of Holies.

When Jesus comes again, He's going to set His foot on the Mount of Olives, splitting it in the middle.

This indicates a tremendous geological upheaval, probably opening up fissures of water.

•**VERSE 8** The water in the Dead Sea will be healed. Today there is no life in the Dead Sea. The water will be healed as this new river flows into it.

•**VERSE 12** Every month a different kind of fruit.

This is a model of the New Jerusalem (Revelation 22).

•**VERSE 13** Ephraim and Manasseh, the sons of Joseph, will have the portions.

•**VERSE 14** The lifting up of the hands indicates the taking of an oath.

•**VERSE 15** We don't know where these places are any more, but we do know that they start about 60 miles north of Damascus.

•**VERSE 16** Hamath is perhaps Hama today, the area about 60 miles north of Damascus.

•**VERSE 22** In other words, it won't be exclusively for Israel, but those who are there will share in the land.

CHAPTER 48:
TRIBE PLACEMENT IN THE LAND

•**VERSES 31-34** The city of Jerusalem is going to have twelve gates named after the tribes of the children of Israel. The three gates on the north will be named for Reuben, Judah, and Levi. On the east: Joseph, Benjamin, and Dan. On the south: Simeon, Issachar, and Zebulun. On the west: Gad, Asher, and Naphtali.

STUDY QUESTIONS FOR EZEKIEL

1. Ezekiel was called to go to the children of Israel. What did God tell Ezekiel in 2:6-7?

_____

_____

_____

2. God spoke to Ezekiel about false prophets in chapter 13. In 1 John 4:1-3, how can we know if someone is a false prophet?

_____

_____

_____

3. Ezekiel 26 is a prophecy against Tyre. In verse 12 the pronoun changes from "he," referring to Nebuchadnezzar, to "they." Why?

_____

_____

_____

4. In Ezekiel 34:10, God exhorts the shepherds of Israel who feed themselves. In contrast, what will the Good Shepherd do in verses 11-16?

_____

_____

_____

5. What do the dry bones in the valley represent in Ezekiel 37:21? Was the prophecy fulfilled?

_____

_____

_____

THE BOOK OF
DANIEL

AUTHOR OF THE BOOK:
Daniel

PERIOD OF WRITING:
Approximately 536 BC.

TYPE OF BOOK:
Prophetic

INTRODUCTION:
The prophecies in the book of Daniel are so detailed and accurate that scholars who don't believe in the Bible as the inspired Word of God have trouble accepting Daniel as the author of this book. All the evidence we need is the fact that Jesus ascribed the authorship to Daniel in Matthew 24:15. If Jesus said Daniel wrote Daniel, that is all the evidence I need.

The book of Daniel is not only one of the most exciting books of the Bible, but a very important book. The book of Revelation would be almost impossible to understand without the prophecies of Daniel. The book not only predicted the various kingdoms as they would unfold in history, but it predicted the coming of the Messiah to the very day.

When Daniel wrote about the Babylonian Kingdom, he wrote in the Aramaic language. When he wrote about the Hebrews, he wrote in Hebrew. He also used three Greek words that were the names for instruments. He was well-educated and used the Aramaic and Hebrew languages with ease.

CHAPTER 1:
DANIEL TAKEN CAPTIVE

•**VERSE 1** Nebuchadnezzar besieged Jerusalem at the end of the third year of Jehoiakim's reign. He took the city in the fourth year (606 BC).

•**VERSES 2-3** Isaiah 39:1-7.

•**VERSES 6-7** The names of the young Hebrew princes were changed to pagan Babylonian names.

"Daniel" means God is Judge, but his name was changed to "Belteshazzar," which means Bel's Prince.

"Hananiah" means beloved of the Lord, but his name was changed to "Shadrach," which means illumined by the sun.

"Mishael" means Who is as God? but his name was changed to "Meshach," which means Who is like Shach? a pagan god.

"Azariah" means the Lord is my help, but his name was changed to "Abednego," which means the servant of Nego, a pagan god.

•VERSE 8 Daniel was between 15 to 20 years of age, but he determined to live a life of purity unto God.

•VERSE 12 "Pulse" means vegetables. Daniel chose to drink water instead of wine.

•VERSES 17-20 If we're diligent in our study, God will bless us with special wisdom, recall, and understanding (John 14:26).

CHAPTER 2:
GOD REVEALS THE DREAM

•VERSE 2 The magicians practiced magical arts. The astrologers read men's fortunes in the stars. The sorcerers used witchcraft, enchantments, and contacted the spirit world.

•VERSES 10-11 Only God can know what was in the king's dream. When God revealed the dream to Daniel, God received the glory.

•VERSE 30 Daniel didn't try to strengthen his standing with the king by taking credit for the work of God in his life. When God exercises His grace in us, we should minimize our part and maximize His part (Romans 12:3).

•VERSE 36 Daniel spoke with authority because he knew God had shown him the dream.

•VERSES 38-41 Nebuchadnezzar held absolute rule while subsequent rulers were restricted by the laws of their empires.

(1) The golden head symbolized the autocratic rule of Nebuchadnezzar's Babylonian Empire.

(2) The breast and arms of silver symbolized the divided Medo-Persian Empire.

(3) The stomach and thighs of brass symbolized the Grecian Empire of Alexander the Great.

(4) The legs of iron symbolized the Roman Empire.

(5) The feet and toes of iron and clay symbolized the ten nations of the European Community.

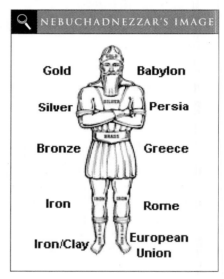

•VERSES 42-43 Since the days of the Roman Empire there hasn't been a world-governing empire.

The European Community will gain strength and recognition. It will rule the earth less than seven years.

•VERSE 45 Jesus is the stone that will put an end to the world governments.

CHAPTER 3:
THE FIERY FURNACE

The events in this chapter foreshadow the resistance of the Jews to the worship of the Antichrist during the coming great tribulation period.

(1) King Nebuchadnezzar is a symbol of the Antichrist.

(2) The fiery furnace represents the great tribulation.

(3) The three Hebrew men that God protected in the furnace represent the 144,000 Jews God will seal and protect during the tribulation.

(4) The golden image represents the image of the Antichrist that will be set up in the rebuilt Jewish temple.

(5) Daniel represents the church, which will not be around during the great tribulation.

• VERSE 1 The king made the image of gold in defiance of the prophecy that his kingdom would one day fall to the Medo-Persian Empire.

• VERSE 13 Revelation 12:13-17.

• VERSE 19 The great tribulation will be worse than any calamity the world has ever seen (Matthew 24:21).

• VERSE 25 The three Hebrew men knew that God would protect them. God will also deliver the 144,000 Jews from the Antichrist (Revelation 7-9).

• VERSE 30 Daniel wasn't mentioned at all in this chapter. He would have never bowed to the image, so we conclude that he wasn't there. In the same way, the church won't be here when the great tribulation comes upon the earth.

CHAPTER 4:
THE CONVERSION OF NEBUCHADNEZZAR

• VERSE 2 Nebuchadnezzar saw that God gave signs and wonders to testify of Himself to us.

• VERSE 13 The "watcher" was probably an angel. We're so concerned with the material world that we often forget how much the spirit world is involved in our lives (Ephesians 6:12; James 4:7).

• VERSE 22 King Nebuchadnezzar was the most powerful king of all world governments.

• VERSE 25 God wanted Nebuchadnezzar to realize that his kingdom and power were given to him by God.

• VERSES 34-37 At the end of seven terrible years, Nebuchadnezzar was converted and submitted himself to God. Some people will go through seven years of the great tribulation before they will submit to God.

CHAPTER 5:
THE FALL OF BABYLON

There was a gap of about 20 years between the preceding chapter and this one. King Nebuchadnezzar died and was replaced by a succession of men who were removed by their enemies.

His grandson Belshazzar was a co-ruler with another man when the events in this chapter took place.

Cyrus, the king of the Persians and nephew of Darius (king of the Medes), were besieging Babylon. Belshazzar felt safe within the city's walls because Babylon was extremely well-fortified to withstand many years of siege.

• VERSE 6 Isaiah 45:1.

• VERSE 10 This queen was probably the mother of Belshazzar.

• VERSES 11-13 Daniel was now about 88 years old. He apparently had been retired for some time and wasn't known in Belshazzar's court.

• VERSES 18-22 Daniel was a faithful prophet, for he preached to Belshazzar before he gave the interpretation of the writing on the wall. Since Belshazzar knew the story of Nebuchadnezzar's pride, insanity, and conversion, he was guilty of willful defiance of God.

• **VERSE 26** "Mene" is numbered (Psalm 90:12).

• **VERSE 27** "Tekel" means weighed.

• **VERSE 28** "Upharsin" is the plural form of *peres* which means divided. The plural form was used because Babylon was to be divided by the Medes and Persians.

• **VERSE 30** Darius diverted the river Euphrates when the soldiers of Babylon were drunk and had neglected to bolt the gates (Isaiah 44:28, 45; Jeremiah 50:38).

The fall of Babylon foreshadows the fall of the great commercial center also called Babylon in Revelation 18.

• **VERSE 31** "Threescore and two" is 62.

CHAPTER 6:
DANIEL IN THE LION'S DEN

• **VERSES 4-5** Daniel lived a faultless life in subjection to the authority of the king.

• **VERSE 6** "Assembled together" means came with haste and tumult.

• **VERSE 7** All world governments deified their leaders. In the final world government, the Antichrist will put to death those who don't bow down and worship his image (Revelation 13:15).

• **VERSE 10** Daniel obeyed the higher Law of God (Acts 5:28-29). Daniel prayed throughout the day and faced Jerusalem because of Solomon's prayer (2 Chronicles 6:34-39, 7:14).

• **VERSE 12** "Came near" means they came with haste and tumult.

• **VERSE 14** The king was bound by the law he had signed, unlike King Nebuchadnezzar who was able to change any law he wanted. The Medo-Persian rule was inferior to the rule of Nebuchadnezzar (Daniel 2:39).

• **VERSE 16** Apparently Daniel had made a strong impression on Darius.

• **VERSE 20** Jeremiah 32:27; Romans 4:20-21; Ephesians 3:20.

• **VERSE 22** Hebrews 1:13-14.

• **VERSE 23** Hebrews 11:33.

• **VERSE 28** Daniel symbolizes the 144,000 Jews protected from harm by God during the great tribulation.

CHAPTER 7:
A VISION OF WORLD GOVERNMENTS

Daniel moves out of a chronological sequence to begin the description of his visions.

These were the days when Daniel was retired from public service. Daniel in the Old Testament and the apostle John in the New Testament were given many great prophecies about the future. Both of them were close to 90 years old and were "greatly beloved" by God.

• **VERSE 2** The "sea" usually refers to the nations (Revelation 17:15).

• **VERSE 3** Nebuchadnezzar's dream was also about world governments, but it was from man's perspective. Daniel's dream was from the heavenly perspective (Revelation 13:1).

• **VERSE 4** The man's heart given to the beast is symbolic of the conversion of Nebuchadnezzar, the first world ruler.

• **VERSE 5** The three ribs refer to the three kingdoms that comprised the Medo-Persian Empire when it assimilated Babylon.

• **VERSE 6** The Grecian Empire built by Alexander the Great was divided into four parts, represented by the beast's four heads.

• **VERSE 7** The ten horns of this beast are the counterparts of the ten toes of the feet of iron and clay in Nebuchadnezzar's dream.

The last world government will be a partial revival of the ancient Roman

Empire (Matthew 24:29-34; Jeremiah 24; Hosea 9:10).

•VERSE 9 The "Ancient of Days" means days without beginning. The Ancient of Days is a title given to Jesus and to God the Father.

•VERSE 10 This isn't the great white throne judgment; it's Jesus judging the people who have survived the great tribulation (Matthew 25:31-46).

•VERSE 18 When we pray "Thy Kingdom come, Thy will be done in earth, as it is in heaven," we're praying for this kingdom (Revelation 1:6; 5:10).

•VERSES 19-20 We usually describe this person as Antichrist, though the Bible calls him the beast and the son of perdition. As Jesus is the Son of God, the Antichrist will be like the son of Satan. He'll do miracles and convince people to trust him (Revelation 13:2-8).

The "saints" in these verses are the Jews who have turned their hearts to God in the troubled times for Israel.

CALVARY DISTINCTIVE

"I beheld, and the same horn [the Antichrist] made war with the saints, and prevailed against them" (Daniel 7:21).

The fact that he makes war on the saints and prevails against them means that they are the Jewish saints, not the church. I do not believe that the church will see the Antichrist empowered upon the earth.

CHAPTER 8:
MEDO-PERSIAN AND GRECIAN EMPIRES

•VERSE 1 This vision came two years after the vision of chapter 7.

•VERSE 3 The ram with two horns is the Medo-Persian Empire. The empire is commonly known as the Persian Empire. The symbol on the coins of the Persian Empire was a ram.

•VERSE 5 The goat is the Grecian Empire. The notable horn is Alexander the Great. The symbol on the coins of the Grecian Empire was a goat.

•VERSE 7 "Choler" means anger.

•VERSE 8 Alexander the Great was only 32 years old when he died ("the great horn was broken"). After Alexander's death the Grecian Empire was divided by four of his generals.

•VERSE 9 This little horn was Antiochus Epiphanes from Syria. He foreshadows the Antichrist in 7:8-26, who will replace three of the ten horns.

•VERSE 10 "Even to" should be translated even against. The "hosts of heaven" are the Jewish people, and the "stars" are the priests and spiritual leaders (Revelation 1:20). Antiochus Epiphanes persecuted and killed thousands of pious Jews.

•VERSE 11 The "prince of the host" is the Lord. Antiochus Epiphanes stopped the daily sacrifices in the temple and defiled the sanctuary.

•VERSE 13 King Nebuchadnezzar described the spiritual beings as "watchers" and "holy ones." Daniel called the watchers "saints" and was able to hear their comments.

•VERSE 14 The sanctuary was cleansed by Judas Maccabaeus on December 25, 165 BC.

•VERSES 15-16 Gabriel took the form of a man to speak to Daniel about the visions. Perhaps Jesus told Gabriel to explain the vision to Daniel, for Gabriel is a messenger of God.

•VERSE 19 The "last end of the indignation" is the last part of the great tribulation. The Old Testament refers to the great tribulation as the "indignation" as it will be an outpouring of God's judgment on a wicked world.

Gabriel is showing Daniel the parallels between the vision and the Antichrist.

•**VERSE 21** Gabriel makes it very clear that the "great horn" on the goat is Alexander the Great, the first king of Greece.

•**VERSE 23** Now Gabriel moves ahead to the great tribulation and describes the Antichrist (beast). The earth is under Satan's control and dominion right now, but he'll hand over his power to the Antichrist (Matthew 4:8; Revelation 13:4).

•**VERSE 25** The Antichrist's "peace" will deceive people on the earth. When the Antichrist stands against Jesus, he'll be broken by Jesus' word.

•**VERSE 26** Gabriel affirms this vision is a true prophecy of future events.

CHAPTER 9:
DANIEL'S PRAYER

•**VERSE 1** The Chaldeans were the Babylonians.

•**VERSE 2** Daniel read the prophecies of Moses (Deuteronomy 28:25) and Jeremiah (Jeremiah 29:10-11). He knew that the captivity would last 70 years.

•**VERSE 3** Though Daniel was 90 years old, he had authority in the court of Darius.

Fasting, wearing uncomfortable sackcloth, and putting on ashes were ways the Jews afflicted themselves to show God they were sincere.

•**VERSE 12** God had given so much to the Jews as His chosen people that they were under a greater responsibility to obey Him than those who were more ignorant (Luke 12:48).

•**VERSE 14** Proverbs 28:13.

•**VERSE 21** The time of "evening" prayer was 3 p.m.

•**VERSE 24** "Weeks" here is actually sevens. Some of the six things prophesied have already happened, and others are in the future.

Jesus made an end of transgressions and sins, reconciling man to God when He sacrificed Himself on the cross.

The kingdom of everlasting righteousness hasn't yet come to power. All the visions and prophecies haven't yet been fulfilled; so the book cannot yet be closed and sealed. The "most Holy" has yet to be anointed.

The Old Testament prophets faithfully wrote as God directed them, though they couldn't reconcile the seeming diversities concerning the Messiah (Ephesians 3:3-5).

•**VERSE 25** The angel foretells of the commandment to restore and rebuild Jerusalem given by King Artaxerxes on March 14, 445 BC. The prophecy was based on a Babylonian 360-day a year calendar.

April 6, 32 AD was the day Jesus rode into Jerusalem (483 years [173,880 days] after March 14, 445 BC) (Psalm 118:22-26; Zechariah 9:9).

•**VERSE 26** The "prince" of Rome was Caesar Nero. He ordered his general, Titus, to destroy Jerusalem.

•**VERSE 27** The seventieth seven will begin when the Antichrist makes a covenant with Israel for a seven-year period (Isaiah 28:14-17).

There are several hints in the Bible that tie Caesar Nero to the Antichrist. It appears that the same demon that controlled Nero will enter the European leader who will arise from the ten nations. He will be the Antichrist (Revelation 17:8-11).

(Matthew 24:15-22; Romans 11:1).

This seven-year period will not start while God is still working in the church to bring forth a bride for Christ. Once the church is complete, God will take it up to heaven. Then He'll turn to Israel and make the Jews His special people once again.

After three and one-half years the Antichrist will put a stop to the daily sacrifices and prayers in the rebuilt temple. Jesus will come to earth with His church to establish His Kingdom and to fulfill the other prophecies concerning the Messiah that have not yet been fulfilled 1,290 days from this day (Matthew 24:15-22; 2 Thessalonians 2:4; Revelation 12:14).

CHAPTER 10:
SPIRITUAL BATTLES

•VERSE 4 Daniel was fasting during the Passover Feast.

The Hiddekel is the Tigris River.

•VERSES 5-6 Daniel's description of Jesus parallels the description by John in Revelation 1:12-16.

•VERSE 8 Daniel reacted to this vision the same way as many do when they see God (Isaiah 6:1-5; Luke 5:8).

•VERSE 12 From the first day Daniel began his fast, his prayers were heard by God and the angel was sent to him with God's message.

•VERSE 13 There's constant warfare in the spiritual world over the control of people's lives. Through prayer we're able to bind the works and power of the enemy and to battle for God's side (Ephesians 6:12; 1 Peter 1:12).

•VERSE 14 The prophecies the angel had for Daniel concerned Israel in the very distant future.

•VERSE 21 Michael is the prince of the people of Israel. He was the only one to stand up for Israel against the world powers.

CHAPTER 11:
PROPHECIES OF FUTURE KINGDOMS

•VERSE 1 The angel is speaking here. He helped establish Darius as king in the first year of his reign.

•VERSE 2 There were three other kings of Persia after Cyrus: Ahasuerus, Artaxerxes, and Darius. These were followed by a fourth, Xerxes.

•VERSE 3 The "mighty king" is Alexander the Great.

•VERSE 5 The "king of the south" was Ptolemy, the general who ruled Egypt. The "king of the north" was Seleucus, the general who took Syria. Israel was between the two kingdoms and suffered from the warfare between them.

•VERSES 7-8 Bernice's brother was now the Egyptian king. He invaded and defeated Syria to avenge his sister's death. He took the fortresses and plundered Syria of its gods, gold, and costly vessels.

•VERSE 16 The "glorious land" is Israel.

•VERSE 17 The Syrian king gave his daughter, Cleopatra, to the young Egyptian king. However, Cleopatra turned against Syria and stood with Egypt.

•VERSES 18-19 The Syrian king attacked Rome along the shores of Asia Minor. He was defeated and killed when he plundered a temple for tax money.

•VERSES 21-24 Antiochus Epiphanes was the next king of Syria. He won his throne by flattery. Antiochus hated the Jews, killing and enslaving thousands.

•VERSES 30-31 Antiochus was angry and frustrated by the Roman defense. He lashed out at Israel and on God's temple. His sacrifice of a pig on the holy altar was "the abomination which maketh desolate." Antiochus is a symbolic Antichrist.

•VERSE 32 Judas Maccabaeus and other young Jewish men were angered by the pollution of the temple. They took revenge on Syria.

•**VERSES** 33-35 This prophecy concerns the plight of the Jews and the sufferings they have endured. They will still be in great danger until the end of the great tribulation.

Even though the United States has been a close ally of Israel, lately it has been moving away from this position because of the dependence on Arab oil. When the U.S. finally abandons Israel, Russia will feel free to attack her without fear of retaliation.

•**VERSE 36** The king described here is the Antichrist (Isaiah 14:12-14; Matthew 4:8-10; 2 Thessalonians 2:4).

"Indignation" here refers to the great tribulation (Isaiah 26:19-21).

•**VERSE 37** This Scripture has led many people to believe that the Antichrist will be an apostate Jew. He may be homosexual.

The "desire of women" could refer to every Jewish woman's hope that she would bear the child who would bruise the serpent's head (Genesis 3:15).

Jesus was the child who fulfilled this prophecy with His atoning death on the cross. This verse could mean that the Antichrist will not regard God or Jesus.

•**VERSE 39** At this point the Jews who are close to God will flee to the Jordanian rock city of Petra. Sela is Petra (Isaiah 16:1-4; Matthew 24:15-21; Revelation 12:14-17).

•**VERSE 40** The "chariots" I believe to be tanks.

•**VERSE 41** Ammon is Jordan and Iraq.

•**VERSE 43** The Antichrist will be at the borders of Libya and Ethiopia. It will probably be a planned attempt to conquer the continent of Africa.

•**VERSE 44** The Antichrist's European federation of nations begins to move against Africa, passing through Israel and taking Egypt.

The Chinese will send their armies, along with the remnant of the Russian army, to battle his forces (Revelation 16:12). These armies will meet in the Valley of Megiddo for the great and final battle of Armageddon.

•**VERSE 45** Jesus will destroy the Antichrist with the words from His mouth (Jude 14-15; Colossians 3:4; Revelation 19:11-17).

Jesus wants us to understand the prophecies in Daniel (Matthew 24:15).

CHAPTER 12:
THE END OF THE VISION

•**VERSE 1** Michael is the angel who oversees Israel. Michael and his angels will fight Satan and his angels and will cast them out of heaven (Revelation 12:7-9). Satan will return to earth in fury, for he'll know that his days are numbered.

•**VERSE 2** This may be referring to the second resurrection (Ephesians 4:8-10; 1 Peter 3:18-20; Matthew 27:52-53; Isaiah 61:1; 2 Corinthians 5:1-8; Revelation 20:5-6).

Or referring to the resurrection of the nation Israel (Ezekiel 37:1-14).

•**VERSE 3** Psalm 111:10.

⚘ CALVARY DISTINCTIVE

"And they that be wise shall shine as the brightness of the firmament; and they that turn many to righteousness as the stars for ever and ever" (Daniel 12:3).

Do you want to shine as a star forever and ever, or do you want to be like a sky rocket with a sudden flash, coming on the scene dramatically, but with no staying power?

•**VERSE 4** The Holy Spirit has opened up our understanding of the book of Daniel in these last days because the information wasn't for earlier times.

God told John not to seal the book of Revelation and even promised a blessing to those who would read and understand it (Revelation 1:3; 22:10).

•**VERSES 5-6** Jesus was the "man" clothed in linen. The "men" were probably angels.

•**VERSE 7** A "time" is a year, "times" is two years, and "a half time" is half a year. This equals three and one-half years (Revelation 12:14).

•**VERSE 9** The book of Daniel was to be sealed until these end times we're living in today.

•**VERSE 11** The Bible doesn't reveal what will happen during the 30 days between the 1,260th and 1,290th day at the end of the great tribulation.

•**VERSE 12** In the 45 days between the 1,290th and 1,335th day, Jesus will judge all the nations of the earth.

Those who are spared until the 1,335th day will be allowed to enter into the glorious kingdom age with Jesus (Matthew 25:31-46).

STUDY QUESTIONS FOR DANIEL

1. Daniel and many others were captured and taken to Babylon. Although he was in an ungodly place, what did he determine in his heart? (Daniel 1:8).

_____

_____

_____

2. Even though they faced death, the three Hebrew men would not bow down and worship the image. What happened to them according to Daniel 3:27?

_____

_____

_____

3. Daniel had faithfully followed the laws of the government until it tried to regulate his relationship with God. What was his action in Daniel 6:10?

_____

_____

_____

4. Daniel prophesies in great detail regarding the coming of the Messiah. According to Daniel 9:25, when would the Messiah come? What would happen to Him? (Daniel 9:26).

_____

_____

_____

5. After the Antichrist sets up his throne in Jerusalem, the great tribulation will begin. What time will this be? (Daniel 12:1; Matthew 24:21).

_____

_____

_____

THE BOOK OF
HOSEA

AUTHOR OF THE BOOK:
Hosea

PERIOD OF WRITING:
During the 8th century BC, during the reign of Uzziah in Judah, and Jeroboam II in Israel.

TYPE OF BOOK:
Prophetic

THEME:
God reaching out to Israel and offering restoration, healing, and forgiveness.

INTRODUCTION:
The book of Hosea is the first of the Minor Prophets. They are called minor because they are generally shorter in length than the major prophetic books.

Hosea's ministry was concurrent with that of Isaiah. Hosea is prophesying to the northern kingdom of Israel, while Isaiah was prophesying to the southern kingdom of Judah.

The name Hosea means "savior." The story of Hosea was a tragic personal story. God called him to marry a prostitute. After they had several children, she left her family and sold herself into prostitution again. God called Hosea to buy her back out of her slavery to prostitution and to forgive her and love her.

There are important eternal principles set for us by the prophet Hosea. As he spoke to the nation of Israel, he speaks to every nation who has forsaken the Lord and has adopted other gods. What is true of a nation is true of an individual. If you forsake the Lord and worship other gods, you'll be brought to desolation. But, if you will return to the Lord, you can experience the blessings of God, the fruitfulness, the forgiveness, and the grace.

CHAPTER 1:
HOSEA'S WIFE AND CHILDREN

•**VERSE 1** Hosea prophesied to the northern kingdom of Israel at the same time Isaiah prophesied to Judah.

HEBREW KEY WORD

Hosea = **savior, deliverer (1:1).**

•VERSE 2 For Hosea to take a wife who was a prostitute is a similitude of the nation of Israel that was committing spiritual whoredom in God's eyes.

•VERSE 4 This is referencing when Jehu was the king of Israel. King Jeroboam (verse 1) was a descendant of Jehu, who became king of Israel by force and caused a bloody slaughter of the 70 sons of the wicked King Ahab.

Hosea named his own son Jezreel, the name of the place where they buried Ahab's sons, to remember this atrocious act of Jehu. This was a fulfillment of the prophecy.

•VERSE 6 "Ruhamah" means no mercy or no pity.

•VERSE 7 Second Kings 19:35.

•VERSE 9 The implication here is that his wife had been unfaithful and Loammi was not his son. It was as if God was saying to Israel, "I'm through. You're not My people, and I will not be your God."

•VERSE 11 This is the prophecy of the rebirth of Israel, which was fulfilled in 1948, as Israel became a nation where both the northern and southern kingdoms united.

CHAPTER 2:
PUNISHMENT AND RESTORATION

•VERSE 1 Removing the "Lo" in front of her name changes the meaning to "having obtained mercy."

•VERSE 5 She was devoted to the gods of materialism.

•VERSE 8 They failed to realize that the source of their blessings is God, resulting in misusing those blessings and using them against God. The children of Israel were taking the wine, oil, gold, and silver that God had given them and offered them as a sacrifice unto Baal.

•VERSE 9 God takes away the blessings which we abuse.

•VERSE 13 Baalim is the plural of Baal, the various gods that they were burning incense to.

•VERSE 16 God will again be a husband unto the nation of Israel.

•VERSE 18 This is equivalent to Isaiah's prophecy where they will beat their swords into plowshares, their spears into pruning hooks, and the lion will eat grass with the ox, and a little child shall lead them.

•VERSE 23 There is a seven-year period in which God is going to bring the return of the Spirit to Israel, and they will turn to God spiritually and begin to seek Him nationally.

CHAPTER 3:
THE REDEEMED WIFE

•VERSE 2 Gomer has become a cast-off of society and was placed on a slave auction. The normal price of a slave was 30 pieces of silver. Fifteen pieces of silver indicates how completely destitute she had become; probably sick and anemic through her wasted life; lost her beauty, and lost her desirability.

CHAPTER 4:
GOD'S INDICTMENT AGAINST ISRAEL

•VERSE 1 In the first three chapters God was speaking to them through similitudes. Now God is speaking directly to the nation.

•VERSE 5 The priesthood and the prophets were corrupt. It comes to the final stage when those who are supposed to be teaching people the knowledge of God are apostate.

•VERSE 6 The lack of the knowledge of God ultimately brings destruction.

•**VERSE 15** The people of Judah were warned not to come up to Gilgal, one of the religious worship centers of the northern kingdom.

Bethaven is the house of idols which was originally called Bethel, the house of God. There they put up the golden calf and invited people of the northern kingdom to worship.

•**VERSE 17** Genesis 6:3.

CHAPTER 5:
GOD'S JUDGMENT AGAINST ISRAEL

•**VERSE 1** The place they had established altars of idol worship was at Mizpah on Mount Tabor, the dome mountain in the Valley of Jezreel in West Jordan. It had become a snare to the people.

•**VERSES 3-4** Turning from God and worshiping these false gods is considered by God as whoredom.

•**VERSE 5** A prediction of the fall of both the northern kingdom of Israel and the southern kingdom of Judah. Judah lasted 100 years beyond Israel, but they both fell.

•**VERSE 10** When Assyria attacked Israel from the north, Judah looked at it as an opportunity to expand its borders. The Lord rebukes them for this attitude (Deuteronomy 27:17).

•**VERSE 15** The great tribulation, when they will be afflicted and will then seek the Lord. They will say, "Blessed is He who comes in the name of the Lord," and then Jesus will return to establish the kingdom of God.

CHAPTER 6:
ISRAEL'S RESPONSE

•**VERSE 3** A reference to the glorious blessings of the last days when God restores Israel.

•**VERSE 4** The heart of God is revealed. He does not punish willingly.

When the sun rises in the sky, the early morning clouds burn off. In the same way the goodness of Ephraim and Judah would burn off.

CHAPTER 7:
THE LORD'S RESPONSE

•**VERSE 1** Ephraim is the major tribe of the northern kingdom and Samaria is the capital.

•**VERSE 3** The government was encouraging the wickedness of the people by making laws that gave freedom for their wickedness.

•**VERSE 9** Ephraim was weak and powerless, but didn't know it. It is tragic when people are still going through the motions, but God has left and they're not aware of it.

•**VERSE 11** God likened Ephraim to a silly dove flying off to Assyria and then down to Egypt, looking for help from man rather than turning to God.

CHAPTER 8:
SOW THE WIND; REAP THE WHIRLWIND

•**VERSE 1** The trumpet was used to warn the people of danger or an invading army, much like an air raid.

•**VERSE 4** The nation came under the rule of corrupt men with corrupt ideals, doing things that were against the Law of God.

These false gods were the things that would ultimately destroy them. A sex-crazed society worshiping Ashtoreth and Molech, the god of pleasure, their strength was gone and they're going to be cut off.

•**VERSE 5** They set up the calf in Samaria and said, "This is the god that brought you out of Egypt."

•VERSE 7 Galatians 6:7. The swirling of the whirlwind scatters things all over. They were going to be scattered into the various parts of the world.

•VERSE 8 They're going to be outcasts living among the Gentiles, persecuted and hated.

•VERSE 13 No longer were their sacrifices acceptable. God isn't looking for sacrifice, but for obedience.

CHAPTER 9:
PUNISHMENT

•VERSE 3 He prophesied and predicted some being carried away to Assyria as captives while others fled to Egypt.

•VERSE 4 They would be scattered and unable to come into the house of the Lord.

•VERSE 6 They would die in these places. The once pleasant places would now be fields of nettles and weeds.

•VERSE 9 Judges 19.

•VERSE 13 Their children will be murdered by the Assyrians.

CHAPTER 10:
FAILURE TO PRODUCE FRUIT

•VERSE 1 Isaiah was prophesying at the same time as Hosea, and he also used the symbol of the vine in Isaiah chapter 5.

It is God's purpose for our lives that we bring forth fruit. In their failure to bring forth fruit unto righteousness, Israel failed in the purposes that God had ordained and established for them as a nation. As a result, Israel would soon be destroyed by their enemies, the Assyrians.

They only used their prosperity to build altars to false gods.

•VERSE 2 Psalm 86:11; Jeremiah 29:13.

•VERSE 4 Hemlock is a poisonous plant. The fields that were once fertile and blessed now grew poisonous plants.

•VERSE 5 "Bethaven" means house of wickedness or house of idols. It was formerly known as "Bethel," house of God. It was where the calf was set up as a national symbol of worship in the northern kingdom. Their place of worship would become desolate.

HEBREW KEY WORDS

Beth = house
Aven = wickedness
El = God
Bethel = house of God

•VERSE 8 According to the accounts in history, the Assyrians were so cruel to their captives that the city they surrounded would often commit mass suicide. The Assyrians would pull out the tongues of their captives, gouge out their eyes, and maim their bodies. Thus the cry of the people to the mountains to cover them.

•VERSE 9 Judges 19-20. God didn't totally destroy them. In His mercy He allowed a few to escape.

•VERSE 10 Hebrews 12:6.

•VERSE 14 Shalman is short for Shalmaneser, the king of Assyria. In the first invasion, they took the northern part of the kingdom as far south as Betharbel.

CHAPTER 11:
GOD'S LAMENT OVER ISRAEL

•VERSE 1 There was a beautiful love relationship with God and the children of Israel when He brought them out of the land of Egypt. The people were so excited about God and their worship of God.

Matthew quotes this as a prophecy concerning Jesus, "He called His Son out of Egypt" (Matthew 2:15).

•VERSE 2 God called them out of Egypt, but soon they were sacrificing unto Baalim, not God.

•VERSE 8 Admah and Zeboim were neighboring cities that were destroyed by the same fire and brimstone that destroyed Sodom and Gomorrah.

•VERSE 12 Ephraim and Israel were about to fall. Judah, under King Hezekiah, was still faithful. When Hezekiah died and his son Manasseh took over, Judah followed in the same steps of her treacherous sister Israel. The judgment upon Israel would come upon Judah also.

CHAPTER 12:
ISRAEL'S SIN

•VERSE 1 They tried to escape the destruction of God by making a covenant with the Assyrians, and by trying to buy mercenaries from Egypt by sending oil down to Egypt. They were playing both sides of the fence, but all of these devices failed.

•VERSES 3-4 How could a man wrestle with an angel of God and prevail? We know the story from Genesis 32, but Genesis doesn't give us the answer.

Jacob prevailed as he wept and made supplication. We prevail when we pray.

•VERSE 7 Referring to Ephraim.

•VERSE 9 During the Feast of Tabernacles they dwelled in booths and remembered God's provision through the wilderness.

•VERSE 11 They offer sacrifices but not unto God. It was a place of pagan worship.

•VERSE 13 A reference to Moses.

CHAPTER 13:
CONSEQUENCES OF SIN

•VERSE 1 God exalted the nation. When they turned from God and began to worship Baal, they brought destruction to the land.

•VERSE 2 They made little silver calves and wore them around their necks on a chain, and it was a good luck omen to kiss it.

•VERSE 6 Many people seek God in times of trouble, need, and poverty, but when riches increase they forget Him.

•VERSES 13-14 They've destroyed themselves by not turning to God. But the Lord never leaves us in the dark, dismal dungeon.

He now speaks of the future. God will bring them from the grave and redeem them from death. We have seen the reviving of the nation of Israel.

•VERSES 15-16 Horrible days were coming because they have taken the path that leads to destruction: their own self-willed ways.

CHAPTER 14:
REPENT AND BE BLESSED

•VERSE 1 God's plea with the people. His arms are always open and He is always ready to forgive.

•VERSE 3 The recognition that, "Our salvation cannot come from Assyria."

•VERSES 4-8 God is saying, "Just ask Me to forgive your iniquities, to be gracious to you, and I will love you." God is promising blessings if they'll only turn to Him.

STUDY QUESTIONS FOR HOSEA

1. Many times God spoke to the people through similitudes. How is Hosea 1:2 a similitude?

_____

_____

_____

2. After God rebuked Israel for her unfaithfulness, He once again promised future restoration. Read Hosea 2:18-19 and Isaiah 11:6-9. Describe what that time will be like.

_____

_____

_____

3. The judgment of God is always good. Once the people recognized the goodness of God's judgment, what did they say in Hosea 6:1?

_____

_____

_____

4. The children of God were continuing the rituals, but without repentance. What was written regarding this in Hosea 8:13?

_____

_____

_____

5. Many people only seek the Lord in times of trouble. According to Hosea 13:6, why did Israel forget God?

_____

_____

_____

THE BOOK OF
JOEL

AUTHOR OF THE BOOK:
Joel

PERIOD OF WRITING:
Sometime in the early 9th century BC.

TYPE OF BOOK:
Prophetic

THEME:
The coming judgment.

INTRODUCTION:
We have absolutely no background for Joel. All we know is that he was the son of Pethuel.

Joel was a prophet to Judah, the southern kingdom. He was probably familiar with Elijah, and no doubt was well-acquainted with Elisha, because the time of his prophecy corresponds to the time that Elisha was prophesying to Israel, the northern kingdom.

Most of the prophecies of Joel reference the day of the Lord, yet he began with local events. There was evidently a plague of locusts at this time, and Joel took from that and jumped into the prophecies of events that are yet future.

CHAPTER 1:
THE DESTRUCTION OF THE LOCUSTS

•**VERSE 3** In those days most of the history was passed by word of mouth.

•**VERSE 4** These are thought to represent the four stages of a locust's development.

•**VERSE 5** The locusts have moved through the vineyards. The first people that are going to suffer as the result of this locust plague will be those who drink wine.

🔑 HEBREW KEY WORDS

gazam = palmerworm; to gnaw off
arbeh = locust; many or multitude
yekeq = cankerworm; to lick off
chaciyl = caterpillar; to devour (1:4).

•**VERSES 6-7** The vine is used as a symbol of the nation of Israel, as is also the fig tree. The nation has been devastated; wasted by this plague of locusts.

•VERSE 9 The meal offering was fine flour which came from wheat. But the locusts devoured the wheat fields so there's nothing to offer unto the Lord. There also isn't any wine to bring an offering to the Lord from the vine, so the priests are to mourn.

•VERSE 15 Joel moves prophetically to the time when the land will be devastated through God's judgment.

Another time is coming in which the world is going to be made desolate with worldwide famine. The events of this day of the Lord are detailed in the book of Revelation.

•VERSES 17-20 The events of the great tribulation period, and these cataclysmic events that are going to come to pass upon the earth and destroy the food supplies and fresh water supplies.

CHAPTER 2:
PROMISED DELIVERANCE

Joel speaks of a future devastation that comes from armies invading the land. As he describes this invading army, it is interesting to notice the description of a nuclear warfare. These things were totally unknown and unheard of in his day, yet they are common in modern warfare.

•VERSE 2 Nations from the north are going to attack Israel (Ezekiel 38, 39). There will be an evil thought in the mind of the leader of Magog, which is the city and people of the north of the Caucasus Mountains, including those southern provinces, as well as Russia. They will align with Iran, Turkey, Libya, and Ethiopia; a tremendous army described in Ezekiel to invade the land of Israel.

•VERSES 4-5 It sounds almost like he is seeing tanks, but doesn't understand what they are.

•VERSE 12 Half-hearted repentance with God will not do (Jeremiah 29:13). Be serious with God; be desperate before the Lord.

•VERSES 15-17 The priests and ministers were to lead the people in this repentance, crying out to God, and seeking the mercies of God for the nation, preventing being conquered.

•VERSE 23 In the nation of Israel, the months of November and December produce former rains, great downpours causing the land to turn green.

Then in the early spring, they begin to get the latter rains that water the crops. They do a lot of dry farming in Israel. That is, during this interim time they plant, and then their irrigation is only by rain.

So, God is promising the former and the latter rains that the land might produce abundantly. Something that the land did not have for over 2,000 years but now are experiencing again.

•VERSE 25 This is a beautiful spiritual analogy. The very nature of sin is destructive. It destroys. It eats away at your life. But now the Lord is promising to restore the years that the locusts, the cankerworm, the caterpillar, and the palmerworm have eaten.

When you turn your life over to the Lord, He makes your whole life new. The Lord restores the things that you lost: the things that were destroyed in that time of sin.

•VERSE 28 The word "afterward" is the Hebrew word for latter or last. "It shall come to pass in the latter days, or the last days."

Here is the promise that the day is going to come when the Lord is going to pour out His Spirit upon all people. In the Old Testament, the Spirit of God was only upon individuals such as Samson, Saul, and David. But it wasn't a general outpouring of God's Spirit on the people. Here's the promise in Joel that in the last days God is going to pour out His Spirit upon all flesh.

In Acts chapter 2, Peter quoted this and declared that what they were seeing was what Joel had spoken about. But people have assumed that it was the complete fulfillment of the prophecy of Joel.

Not so; in fact, Peter didn't even say it was the fulfillment of the prophecy. You see, the fulfillment indicates a complete filling. It wasn't. It was the beginning of the outpouring of God's Spirit. But the real prophecy of Joel does not pertain to the day of Pentecost, but to the last days.

HEBREW KEY WORD

achar = afterward; latter or last (2:28).

•**VERSES 30-31** The Bible speaks of these wonders that will happen in the great tribulation: the wonders in the heaven, the sun darkened, the moon turning to blood. These are referenced by Jesus in Matthew 24 as a part of the period of the great tribulation.

CHAPTER 3:
JUDGMENT OF THE NATIONS

•**VERSES 1-4** When the Lord returns He is going to gather together the nations for judgment. As He separates people as a shepherd separates the sheep from the goats, it will be determined which of the people will be allowed to go into the glorious millennial kingdom age, and which will be cast out at that time (Matthew 25).

Many nations are going to come into severe judgment because of their ill treatment of the Jews. The blessing that God promised to Abraham still stands. "I will bless those that bless you, and curse those that curse you."

•**VERSES 9-12** The call for the people to be gathered, that they might be judged by God in this great battle of Armageddon.

•**VERSE 13** Revelation 14:15, parallel passage, as he speaks about the cup of the indignation overflowing, the wrath of God.

•**VERSE 14** The valley where they are to be judged.

•**VERSE 16** Revelation chapter 10 gives a very graphic description of the return of Jesus Christ, this mighty messenger of God, the angel, clothed with a rainbow, with a scroll in His right hand that is open.

So when Jesus comes again, there's going to be an earth-rending roar as the Lion of the tribe of Judah proclaims His absolute mastery and victory to reign over the earth. His foes subdued and defeated, He begins His glorious reign.

•**VERSE 18** This glorious day of the Lord is coming. He describes this kingdom age, the glory of the land, and this fountain coming out of the throne of God, described in Ezekiel. This river will come from the throne of God and flow down to the Dead Sea and heal the waters.

STUDY QUESTIONS FOR JOEL

1. As Joel begins his book, he tells of an event that has taken place in Israel. What has happened according to Joel 1:4, 6-7?

_____

_____

_____

2. Joel prophesies of a future event in Joel 1:15. What is this prophecy?

_____

_____

_____

3. After reading about a terrible battle that will take place, we find the Lord pleading with the people in Joel 2:12-13. Write it here.

_____

_____

_____

4. The Lord will provide deliverance in response to repentance. What is His promise in Joel 2:25? How can this apply to you?

_____

_____

_____

5. According to Joel 2:28, what will happen in the last days?

_____

_____

_____

THE BOOK OF
AMOS

AUTHOR OF THE BOOK:
Amos

PERIOD OF WRITING:
During the reign of Uzziah; approximately 800 BC.

TYPE OF BOOK:
Prophetic

THEME:
Warnings of the coming judgment and the promise of ultimate restoration.

INTRODUCTION:
Amos was a herdsman, and chapter 7 also tells us that he was a fruit picker. He picked the sycamore fruit, which was the fig. He was not a prophet—he was not the son of a prophet. He was not from a line of ministers. He was just a common person like all of us. And yet, while he was there watching his sheep, God spoke to him to go to the northern kingdom and prophesy against them. Although he was from Tekoa in the land of Judah, God called him to go to Israel to prophesy.

During the time of Jeroboam's reign, the northern kingdom of Israel came to its zenith of glory and power. But though they were very rich in the material things, they were very poor in spiritual things. So Amos comes to spiritually awaken them unto God.

CHAPTER 1:
JUDGMENT ON ISRAEL'S NEIGHBORS

•**VERSE 1** Tekoa is a little valley about six miles southwest of Bethlehem. Amos was a shepherd there.

Somewhere between the year 810 and 792 BC, there was a tremendous earthquake that devastated the whole area. According to Zechariah, the people fled from that area terrified.

Isaiah also made mention of this great earthquake.

•**VERSE 2** Hosea 11:10, Joel 3:16, and Revelation 10:3 all speak of this time when the Lord will roar. Many commentators believe that these prophecies of the Lord roaring as a lion from Zion is a prediction of that glorious day when the He comes to lay claim to the earth.

shaag = roar mightily (1:2).

•**VERSE 3** Amos doesn't actually name the three indictments. "For three transgressions, and for four" is a figure of speech that's declaring the cup of God's indignation is full and is going to overflow now in judgment.

Damascus was the capital of Syria.

They came with their iron chariots and destroyed Gilead.

•**VERSE 4** Second Kings 8:7-15 will give some background to this story.

•**VERSE 5** Kir was in Assyria. Just as God predicted, the Assyrians came, captured, and destroyed Syria. The prophecy was literally fulfilled when those of Damascus were taken back to Kir in Assyria as captives.

•**VERSE 6** He prophesied against the Philistines who were perennial enemies to Israel.

There were five major cities of the Philistines. Four of them come into view in this prophecy: Gaza, Ekron, Ashdod, and Ashkelon. In their conquering of the people of God, they turned the captives over or sold them to the Edomites.

•**VERSE 9** Tyrus (Tyre) was a coastal city and the headquarters of the ancient Phoenicians. It was a very wealthy, prosperous, and powerful kingdom. Their merchant ships ruled the Mediterranean.

Tyrus had been consistently a friend of Israel. David and Hiram had made a covenant together which was carried on by Solomon. Hiram the king of Tyre furnished the cedars for David's palace and later for the great temple of Solomon. But in time, Tyrus also turned against Israel.

•**VERSE 10** A partial fulfillment took place under Nebuchadnezzar, but it was completed by Alexander the Great. Ezekiel gives a complete prophecy against Tyrus describing in great detail the two sieges of Tyrus.

•**VERSE 11** The Edomites were descendants of Esau, the brother of Jacob, and thus God still looks at them as having a brotherly relationship. Yet the hatred Esau had for Jacob never ceased in the descendants. The Edomites were the perennial enemies of Israel and they attacked at every opportunity.

•**VERSE 12** Teman was the capital of Edom. Today it's barren wilderness. There are no major highways or even roads that go into the area, only a few primitive villages. It was once the area of a thriving civilization. God pronounced His judgment against Edom.

•**VERSE 14** Rabbah was the capital of Ammon at the time.

ISRAEL'S NEIGHBORS

CHAPTER 2:
JUDGMENT ON JUDAH AND ISRAEL

•VERSE 1 Ammon and Moab were adjacent to each other. The Moabites, having conquered the king of Edom, not only killed him but threw his body in lime and let it dissolve.

•VERSE 4 Amos was dealing with those nations around Israel. Because Judah was also a neighbor to Israel, he prophesied against Judah.

God speaks of the judgment that is coming against Moab, Ammon, Edom, Tyrus, Syria, and the Philistine countries. In each case He made mention of their moral sins that are a part of man's innate understanding and knowledge of good and evil, without mentioning the law.

God judges them apart from the law, but they that have the law will be judged by the law (Romans 2:12).

•VERSE 5 Nebuchadnezzar came and burned Jerusalem; the fire devoured the palaces, and the temple was destroyed.

•VERSE 9 The Amorites were rooted out of the land and wiped out completely by the power of God.

•VERSE 12 Nazarites were men who had committed their lives to God, vowing a complete consecration to God. Part of the Nazarite vow was not to drink wine, but here they were given wine to drink. Men who had been called to prophesy were told to stop.

•VERSES 14-15 Even a fast runner was unable to flee from the judgment that was coming. There would be no escaping from God's judgment.

HEBREW KEY WORD

nuwc = flee away, hide (2:16).

CHAPTER 3:
THE CHOSEN NATION GUILTY

•VERSE 2 God chose Israel out of all the nations in the world, that they might be God's instruments to receive revelation, and to declare the truth of God unto the world.

Special privileges come with special responsibilities. "To whom much is given, much is required" (Luke 12:48).

•VERSE 3 We cannot walk with God and be constantly pulling against Him, wanting to go our own way, or insisting that God comes our way.

•VERSE 6 The trumpet was blown when the enemy was coming, warning of an attack. The sound of trumpets strikes fear.

God allowed the evil of judgment to come.

•VERSE 8 Jeremiah determined that he wasn't going to prophesy any more in the name of the Lord when he was thrown in prison. But he said, "His word was like a fire in my bones, and I became weary of trying to hold it back, and I had to speak" (Jeremiah 20:9).

Paul said, "Woe is me if I preach not the gospel of our Lord Jesus Christ" (1 Corinthians 9:16).

Amos said, "The Lord has spoken, and who can withhold?" You've got to speak it.

•VERSES 9-10 The northern kingdom was in chaos—there was violence and robbery. God called their enemies to observe it.

•VERSE 12 If you were a shepherd and a lion took one of your sheep, you would have to pay for it unless there was proof that a lion had devoured it.

•VERSE 14 Bethel is where they had established the worship of the calf, so God is speaking out against those altars.

CHAPTER 4:
ISRAEL HAS NOT RETURNED TO GOD

• **VERSE 1** Bashan is the northern part of the Galilee region. It was excellent pastureland, and the cows were known for their sleekness and fatness.

• **VERSE 2** When the Assyrians captured Samaria, they were literally led away captive with fishhooks through their nostrils.

• **VERSE 4** Gilgal was three or four miles from Jordan, where the rite of circumcision took place for those coming into the land. It was considered a holy place, a place of consecration to God, but it had become a place of transgression against the Lord.

• **VERSE 5** Leaven was a type of sin and was never to be used in the offerings that were put upon the altar.

• **VERSE 6** God often uses judgments or chastisements in order to turn us from our path of destruction (Hebrews 12:6).

• **VERSE 12** They are not meeting God in friendly terms, but to face His judgment. His holiness demands a punishment for sin. We do not want to meet God without the faith and trust in Jesus Christ, whereby our sins have been forgiven and cleansed.

CHAPTER 5:
GOD CALLS ISRAEL TO REPENT

• **VERSE 2** Some people interpret this verse to mean that God has cast off Israel forever and there is no restoration in the last days, but that is to deny the whole body of Scripture.

This verse speaks of Israel being cut off at that time. They were going into captivity to Syria and to be dispersed throughout the world. All of the prophets, including Amos in the last chapter, speak of God's dealing and working with His people in restoring His love and favor in the last days.

God is going to raise her once again to a position of glory and honor, as He takes her once more as a bride that has been disobedient.

• **VERSE 3** The great decimation that would, and did take place, in Israel.

• **VERSE 8** The seven stars are the seven sisters, also known as the constellation of the Pleiades. Orion and Pleiades are two constellations of our winter sky.

• **VERSE 16** "Alas, alas" means we've had it. It's total despair.

The husbandman is the farmer.

There were professional wailers that you could hire for a funeral service.

• **VERSE 18** They were looking for the day of the Lord when God would reign and conquer all of their enemies, but they had become an enemy of God.

• **VERSES 21-23** They were supposed to come and fellowship with God on the feast days.

God is not interested in the outward observation, but a heart that is repentant toward Him. They were still offering the burnt offerings, the peace offerings, and the meal offerings, but no mention of sin offerings.

• **VERSE 27** They went into captivity beyond Damascus to Assyria.

CHAPTER 6:
WARNING TO THOSE AT EASE

• **VERSES 1-6** The northern kingdom trusted in the mountains of Samaria and felt their cities were well-defended.

• **VERSE 2** Calneh was the capital in the plains of Shinar. Hamath was the capital of Syria at that time, and Gath was the capital of the Philistines. They were no better than these pagan nations. They're just as evil, vile, and corrupt.

• **VERSE 7** Those who were living in the lap of luxury were going to be the first to go into captivity.

•**VERSE** 10 There were so many dead bodies that they weren't even buried— just cremated.

•**VERSE** 14 God raised up the Assyrians and the nation of Israel was wiped out.

CHAPTER 7:
WARNINGS TO WAKE UP

The Lord showed Amos things that are potential judgments or awakeners.

•**VERSE** 3 The word "repent" should be translated relented. The word "repent" means change, but the Bible tells us that "God is not a man that He should lie, nor the son of man that He should repent" (Numbers 23:19). God doesn't change (Malachi 3:6). God relented, for He did not bring the plague of locusts.

•**VERSES** 7-8 The plumb line makes a straight corner or a straight wall. God held the plumb line and He could see the crookedness and the perversity.

•**VERSE** 10 Bethel was one of the two cities where they had false worship. A priest of Bethel does not indicate a priest of God, but just one of the religious leaders.

•**VERSE** 12 The prophets were often called seers because of their visions and their ability to see into the spirit world.

HEBREW KEY WORD

chozeh = **seer or prophet (7:12).**

CHAPTER 8:
JUDGMENT IS COMING

•**VERSE** 5 The new moon was a Sabbath day. They were so greedy for gain, they became upset when they had to close on the Sabbath day.

The ephah was a bushel basket. They started making the basket smaller but still charged the same.

•**VERSE** 6 They put people into hock, buying them and making them slaves.

•**VERSE** 9 One day, during the Feast of Passover, it would turn dark at noon on a clear day. Passover takes place at full moon so it couldn't be an eclipse, for it's impossible to have an eclipse on a full moon. That was the day Jesus was crucified.

•**VERSE** 10 Baldness due to shaving the head in grief over the dead.

•**VERSE** 11 A famine for the Word of God.

•**VERSE** 14 The god in Dan was the calf.

CHAPTER 9:
JUDGMENT AND RESTORATION

•**VERSE** 1 Even though they try to flee during the great shaking of God, they're not going to escape.

•**VERSE** 8 God will not utterly destroy but will spare a remnant. He has yet a marvelous purpose for Jacob and for the people of Israel.

•**VERSES** 11-12 God never ends the story in darkness but He always brings you out into the light on the other side. The future is bright for God's people as He promised the restoration of the Davidic kingdom.

•**VERSE** 13 They'll still be reaping the abundant harvest when it's time to plow again.

STUDY QUESTIONS FOR AMOS

1. God is spelling out the judgments to come upon the neighbors of Israel. What was the reason given in Amos 2:4 for Judah's punishment?

_____

_____

_____

2. In Amos 4:6-11 we read of the various judgments God brought upon Israel over the years. Why did He have these judgments?

_____

_____

_____

3. Although Israel was continuing in her disobedience, what was God's plea in Amos 5:4?

_____

_____

_____

4. What did Amos say in response to Amaziah when he ordered him not to prophesy any longer? What does this tell you about the type of people the Lord uses? (Amos 7:14-15).

_____

_____

_____

5. The Lord declares in Amos 9:8 that He will judge Israel, but He will not utterly destroy it. What does He promise in Amos 9:14-15?

_____

_____

_____

THE BOOK OF
OBADIAH

AUTHOR OF THE BOOK:
Obadiah

PERIOD OF WRITING:
Unknown. Estimated from the 1000 BC to 400 BC.

TYPE OF BOOK:
Prophetic

THEME:
The coming judgment on Edom.

INTRODUCTION:
Obadiah had a vision of God's judgment against the nation of Edom.

The Edomites were descendants of Esau, the brother of Jacob. There was an animosity that seemed to exist between the brothers and continued on through the years, and the Edomites became the perennial enemies of Israel.

The Edomites had a vicious nature and took advantage of Israel's weaknesses. Every time Israel had a problem with an enemy, Edom would always attack them. It's because of this perennial attitude of hatred against God's people Israel that God judged Edom.

Though the book of Obadiah is basically addressed against Edom, it ends with Israel's final triumph and the day of the Lord when God blesses Israel once again, when the Deliverer is in Zion, and the Lord reigns.

CHAPTER 1:
THE PROPHECY AGAINST EDOM

•VERSE 1 A vision is a God-given capacity to view the spirit realm.

The Lord stirred up nations against Edom.

HEBREW KEY WORD

goy = heathen, nations, Gentiles (1:1).

•VERSE 3 A reference to Petra and the other cities that the Edomites had carved out of the rocks.

They felt very safe in cities such as Petra because of its narrow canyon entrance dwelling high in the rocks. They could easily stop an enemy by being up on the ledges and tossing rocks down on them.

•**VERSES 7-9** God predicts that though they feel secure and exalted in their position, He is going to utterly cut them off.

Teman was one of the major cities of Edom, which was known for its wise counselors. Eliphaz, one of the friends that came to comfort Job during his affliction, was a Temanite.

•**VERSE 10** The reason why Edom was to be cut off.

The violence began with Esau and Jacob. Later, Moses led the children of Israel through the wilderness and came to Edom. They sent a message to the king of Edom requesting passage through the land, promising that they would not eat of the food of the land unless they bought it, and they would provide their own water.

However, the king of Edom came down with his army and would not allow them passage. They had to take a circuitous route around Edom.

•**VERSE 11** Whenever a nation would come against Judah, Edom was there to support and encourage the enemies, and join in the plunder. This happened many different times in their history.

•**VERSE 12** Edom was rejoicing in the judgment of God against the nation of Israel. God, like a father, reserves the right to punish His own children, but doesn't let anybody else interfere.

God was chastising His own child Israel, but Edom was there cheering Him. This is God's indictment against them.

•**VERSE 14** When Israel was being attacked, the Edomites would stand at the borders and turn the children of Israel back, or turn them over to their enemies if they escaped.

•**VERSE 15** "Be not deceived; God is not mocked: for whatsoever a man soweth, that shall he also reap" (Galatians 6:7).

•**VERSE 17** "For blindness has happened to Israel in part until the fullness of the Gentiles be come in, and then all Israel shall be saved as saith the scripture. There shall be a deliverer in Zion" (Romans 11:25-26).

In the last days, God will take back His bride Israel and bestow again His blessing and His favor upon it, for the Deliverer shall come and establish the kingdom of God.

In God's covenant with Abraham, he was given all of the land from the River Euphrates to the Nile River. But they never took all of the land that God gave them nor drove out all of the enemies as they were commanded.

God had promised them much more than what they claimed. They became satisfied and content, and didn't press on to complete victory.

God has promised to you, His child, a glorious life of victory, power, peace, glory, and rest. But many Christians never fully take hold of all that God has provided.

God has made provision but we never fully possess the possessions.

•**VERSE 19** "They of the south" refers to the descendants of Jacob.

•**VERSE 21** God doesn't leave us in the darkness of judgment, but brings us to the glorious reign of our Lord Jesus Christ.

HEBREW KEY WORD

Obadiah = **servant of Yahweh (1:1).**

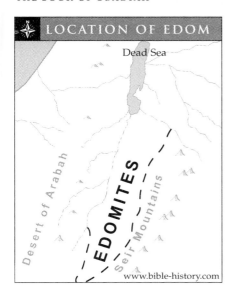

LOCATION OF EDOM

Dead Sea

Desert of Arabah

EDOMITES

Seir Mountains

www.bible-history.com

STUDY QUESTIONS FOR OBADIAH

1. Who were the Edomites?

_____

_____

_____

2. According to verse 3, why were the Edomites so prideful?

_____

_____

_____

3. God is declaring in verse 10 that the Edomites will be cut off forever. Why? (verses 10 and 11).

_____

_____

_____

4. The Lord is slow to anger and full of mercy, but the day of judgment will come. Compare verse 15 with Galatians 6:7 and write your discovery.

_____

_____

_____

5. In verse 17 the Lord declares that the house of Jacob will possess their possessions. Explain this in your own words.

_____

_____

_____

THE BOOK OF
JONAH

AUTHOR OF THE BOOK:
Most likely Jonah, though it is not identified.

PERIOD OF WRITING:
8th century BC.

In 2 Kings 14:25, we discover that Jonah was a prophet to Israel during the reign of Jeroboam II. Somewhere around 826 BC, Jonah prophesied in Israel.

TYPE OF BOOK:
Prophetic

THEME:
The reluctant servant and the compassion of God.

INTRODUCTION:
Nineveh was the capital of Assyria, and Jonah was a patriot who knew Assyria was a threat to his nation. Because the Assyrians were very wicked and cruel, he did not want to preach to them as God had called him to do. He didn't want the Ninevites to repent. He wanted to see them destroyed. Jonah was determined to escape the call and commission of God to go to Nineveh.

The book of Jonah is an interesting story with a lot of lessons. We learn of God's mercy and kindness, and we see His sovereignty, as Jonah learned that if God is taking you to Nineveh, then you are going. There is an easy way to learn and a hard way, but God will accomplish His purposes. The important truth is don't fight God, don't run from the call of God, because you're only running from what's best.

CHAPTER 1:
RUNNING FROM GOD

•VERSE 2 Nineveh was the capital of the Assyrian Empire, which finally conquered the northern kingdom of Israel, moved against the southern kingdom, and surrounded Jerusalem. The Assyrians historically were extremely cruel. When God told Jonah to go to Nineveh, Assyria was only ascending in power and had not yet become the world-dominating power.

The city of Nineveh was one of the oldest cities in the world and was mentioned in the book of Genesis, established by Nimrod. Nineveh was such a great city that it took three days to walk through it.

•**VERSE 3** Jonah knew Nineveh was a threat to his nation.

Nineveh was northeast from Israel. Trying to run from the call of God, Jonah caught a ship going west to Tarshish, probably in Spain, and it was the last outpost of civilization at that time. Jonah was determined to go as far as he could to escape the call of God.

HEBREW KEY WORD

barach = flee, to bolt, run (1:3).

•**VERSE 15** There are miracles before the great fish appeared: the storm itself, his sleeping in the middle of that kind of a storm, the lot falling upon him, and the sea becoming calm as soon as he was thrown in.

•**VERSE 17** The book of Jonah has come under a lot of criticism by those who do not believe in God.

God can do anything.

The God that I believe in and worship is He who created the universe and all of its life forms. God was able to prepare a fish—or in some translations, a sea monster—that was able to do what the Bible says was done. If man can make a submarine that can take men under the sea, God can surely prepare a great fish.

Jesus attested to the authenticity of Jonah's story. His death and resurrection after three days is similar to Jonah.

Jesus confirmed Jonah's experience and effectiveness of Jonah's ministry in Nineveh (Matthew 12:40-41).

CHAPTER 2:
JONAH'S PRAYER

•**VERSE 1** Jonah was so stubborn that he waited three days and nights before he began to pray.

•**VERSE 2** It must be very dark inside the stomach of the great fish. He might have thought he had died and had gone to hell. If it was a mammal, the heat and humidity would be horrendous at 98.6°F, with gastric juices sloshing and seaweed wrapping around his head.

•**VERSE 3** Psalm 42:7. There are about five quotations from the Psalms in his prayer, indicating that he had a good knowledge of them.

•**VERSE 4** Psalm 31:22. He's turning to God, broken and repentant.

•**VERSE 5** Psalm 69:1.

•**VERSE 8** Jonah learned the hard way, but shares his valuable lesson so we can learn the easy way.

It is a lying vanity to think that one can escape from the presence of God, and that we can work a better plan in our life than God's plan. God loves us and wants to bless us.

•**VERSE 9** He couldn't offer a lamb to God so he offered the sacrifice of thanksgiving. In Hebrews 13:15 we are encouraged to offer the sacrifice of praise, which is well accepted by Him.

"Salvation is of the Lord" because he knew that he was helpless and couldn't save himself out of the circumstance. It is an important lesson to learn that salvation is not of our own works and efforts.

•**VERSE 10** The fish was a more obedient servant than Jonah. Where it vomited Jonah is not stated but most commentators think it's in Joppa. If so, God brought him back to the place from where he tried to run. God often brings us right back to the place of failure to start over again.

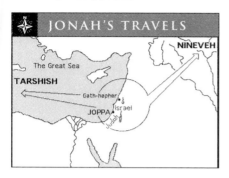

CHAPTER 3:
NINEVEH REPENTS

• **VERSE 3** It would take three days to walk from one end to the other.

• **VERSES 4-5** In his message there was no hope laid out, no call to repentance, no loving exhortations, just a message of judgment. The miracle and the amazing thing is that the people believed and repented.

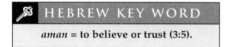

HEBREW KEY WORD

aman = to believe or trust (3:5).

• **VERSES 7-9** The proclamation of the king to fast, to pray, to put on sackcloth, and to afflict their souls was all on the basis of "Who knows, maybe God will change, and we will not be judged." There was no promise.

Over and over God promises that if we repent and turn from our sin, He would have mercy and pardon our sin. Therefore condemnation on us will be much greater than on the men of Nineveh, for they repented on the slim hope of "Who knows?"

Talking to the scribes and Pharisees, Jesus said, "The men of Nineveh will rise in judgment with this generation and they will condemn it. For they repented at the preaching of Jonah and behold a greater than Jonah is here" (Matthew 12:41).

The men of Nineveh repented at the preaching of an angry prophet who only preached the judgment of God. Jesus, the Son of God, had come encouraging people to come and experience God's love, yet they did not repent.

• **VERSE 10** Seeing their changed hearts and repentance, God relented from the judgment that was promised. He always knew that they were going to repent, and that's why Jonah was sent. God knows the end from the beginning.

CHAPTER 4:
JONAH'S ANGER—GOD'S COMPASSION

• **VERSES 1-2** Jonah was angry at God because of the tremendous success in Nineveh.

• **VERSE 7** The Lord had prepared a great fish, a gourd—and now a worm.

• **VERSE 8** God prepared the wind. He has charge of the elements.

• **VERSES 10-11** The Lord points out the inconsistency. Jonah was angry because the gourd died, yet he had nothing to do with its existence.

God created the Ninevites and they have eternal souls. God shows His great compassion and interest for the little children.

STUDY QUESTIONS FOR JONAH

1. After God called Jonah to go to Nineveh, he ran the other way. Why?

_____

_____

_____

2. Jonah took three days to humble himself and repent. What did he offer to the Lord according to Jonah 2:9? What did he learn?

_____

_____

_____

3. We can be assured that God is omnipotent and in control of all things. Report your findings from Jonah 1:4, 1:17, 2:10, and 4:6-8.

_____

_____

_____

4. Jonah only preached a message of judgment to the people in Nineveh, offering no hope at all. On what premise did Nineveh repent according to Jonah 3:9?

_____

_____

_____

5. Although God greatly used Jonah, what was his response in Jonah 4:1?

_____

_____

_____

THE BOOK OF
MICAH

AUTHOR OF THE BOOK:
Micah

PERIOD OF WRITING:
His ministry was in the 8th century BC, during the reigns of Jotham, Ahaz, and Hezekiah, the kings of Judah.

TYPE OF BOOK:
Prophetic

INTRODUCTION:
Micah was a contemporary to Isaiah the prophet, prophesying during the time that Isaiah was prophesying to Hezekiah the king. Micah's prophecies are centered on the northern kingdom of Israel, yet he does bring in Jerusalem and Judah into the prophecies as well.

Prophesying during this time meant that he was prophesying when the northern kingdom of Israel fell to the Assyrians, who then invaded the southern kingdom at the time of Hezekiah. Of course, they were defeated by God's intervention.

So Micah's prophecy is against Samaria and also against Jerusalem.

CHAPTER 1:
PROPHECIES AGAINST ISRAEL

•VERSE 1 Samaria was the capital of the northern kingdom, while Jerusalem was the capital of the southern kingdom of Judah. The majority of the prophecies will be toward Samaria.

•VERSE 2 Micah began with a broad prophecy not limited to just Samaria and Jerusalem, but to all of the inhabitants of the earth.

•VERSES 3-4 The judgment of God is coming upon the whole earth, looking toward the great tribulation period, described in Revelation 6-18.

•VERSE 5 These capital cities were the centers of government for Israel and Judah. The corrupted governments opened the door for an immoral nation. He was speaking out against the centers of government.

•VERSE 6 Today most of Samaria is covered by olive trees, but it's ruined and desolate. The valleys that once were filled with the great buildings are filled with rocks. The judgment of God came because of their transgressions.

•VERSE 8 The reaction of Micah over the vision of the destruction of Samaria.

•**VERSE 9** Samaria's illness was incurable as the southern kingdom worshiped in the groves and high places.

A reference to the Assyrian king who conquered the northern kingdom and destroyed Samaria, and will come to the very gates of Jerusalem.

•**VERSE 10** Gath was one of the capital cities of the Philistines. They hated to have their enemies rejoicing over their misfortunes.

Here is a remarkable play on words. "Gath" means weeping, and may be rendered as, "Weep not in weep town." "Aphrah" means dust, as "In dust town, roll thyself in the dust."

•**VERSE 11** "Saphir" means beautiful, as that which is beautiful shall be stripped naked and be ashamed. "Zaanan" means march, so the inhabitants of march did not march.

•**VERSE 12** "Maroth" is bitterness. We know from the prophecies of Isaiah that when the Assyrians came to Jerusalem, God intervened and destroyed the Assyrian army.

•**VERSE 13** Lachish was the fortified city of the northern kingdom near Mount Hermon taken by Sennacherib. "Lachish" means horse town, so it can be translated, "Bind the chariot to the horse, O inhabitant of horse town."

•**VERSE 14** "Achzib" means lies. "The house of lies will be a lie to the kings of Israel."

•**VERSE 15** A prophecy of Jesus Christ in the future. He was pronouncing judgment and devastation that is to come, but then he moves beyond to the glorious day of the Lord. God always brings us out to the light.

•**VERSE 16** The shaving of the head was done at the death of a loved one. The delicate children are the children that had been slain. Those that are not slain had been carried away captive. A time of mourning for them.

HEBREW KEY WORDS

Gath = weeping
Aphrah = dust (1:10)
Saphir = beautiful
Zaanan = march (1:11)
Maroth = bitterness (1:12)
Lachish = horse town (1:13)
Achzib = lies (1:14).

CHAPTER 2:
OPPRESSORS

•**VERSE 2** God is opposed to those who take advantage of others.

•**VERSE 5** The land that God gave and divided by lot under Joshua is now going to be taken away because of corrupt practices.

•**VERSE 6** Because he was exposing their evil, Micah was commanded not to prophesy to the people. They were not ashamed of what they were doing.

•**VERSE 7** God wants us to be honest, upright, and pure. Cheating, coveting fields, and taking them by violence are not of God.

•**VERSE 12** God promises the faithful remnant the day that the nation of Israel is restored. His hand will be upon them, and they will be restored to their land.

•**VERSE 13** The breaker goes before them to break up the walls so that they can pass through the gate. Their King, Jesus Christ, will pass before them and will lead them.

CHAPTER 3:
RULERS REBUKED

•**VERSES 1-2** It's tragic for a nation when the leaders and lawmakers hate good and love evil.

•**VERSE 3** The Lord speaks against the rulers who were taxing the people and taking advantage of them.

•**VERSE 5** Their prophets were saying "Peace," but were causing the people to err. There was no peace with God.

•**VERSE 6** God is declaring that these false prophets will come to their doom.

•**VERSE 10** The rulers over God's people were building beautiful public buildings with blood money from the destitute people.

•**VERSE 11** They were ready to take a bribe. The ministry had become a profession.

They felt that the temple was magical in that as long as they had the temple, God was dwelling with them, and no evil could harm them.

CHAPTER 4:
THE LAST DAYS

•**VERSE 1** Though the temple is to be destroyed and desolate, in the last days there will be glorious spiritual activity when the Lord shall rule and reign.

•**VERSE 2** He is talking about the kingdom age when Jesus reigns again.

•**VERSE 3** This will only happen when Jesus comes as the King of kings and Lord of lords, and we have one Ruler over the whole earth.

•**VERSE 6** God is prophesying the regathering of the Jews, a renewing of His Spirit in His people.

•**VERSE 7** Isaiah 9:7.

•**VERSES 9-10** This speaks of the coming captivity, not to Assyria, but to Babylon, which was not a military threat or power at that time.

•**VERSES 11-12** Micah skips from one era to another. Here he is speaking of the last days, the regathering of the people, and how the nations will come against her.

It's possibly a reference to Ezekiel 38 when the confederacy of Moslem nations: Iran, Ethiopia, Libya, Turkey; and the nations from the north gather together in an invasion against Israel (Zechariah 12:2-4; 14:1-4).

•**VERSE 13** Brass is a symbol of judgment. Iron is a symbol of strength.

CHAPTER 5:
THE RULER BORN IN BETHLEHEM

•**VERSE 1** A prophecy relating to Jesus Christ that was fulfilled in Matthew 27:30. He was smitten with a rod.

•**VERSE 2** A prophecy that Bethlehem would be the birthplace of the Messiah. "Whose goings forth have been from old, from everlasting" referring to the prophecy that Christ has always existed from everlasting, which could only be said of God.

This word "everlasting" in the Hebrew literally means the vanishing point. The eternal God stepped out of eternity and into time, and He dwelt as a man among men (John 1:1-3).

"And the Word became flesh, and dwelt among us" (John 1:14).

> ### HEBREW KEY WORD
> *olam* = everlasting;
> the vanishing point (5:2).

•**VERSE 3** The Messiah was cut off, therefore He will give them up. Israel was given up by God.

Now is an age when God is dealing with the Gentiles until Israel again begins to travail, seeking their Messiah. Jesus said, "You will not see Me again until you are saying, 'Blessed is He who comes in the name of the Lord'" (Matthew 23:39).

They will be praying for His coming. Israel is going to go through the great tribulation along with the rest of the world, and during this time they will turn to the Lord.

•VERSE 4 This is a prophecy concerning Christ and His relationship to Israel in the kingdom age. They shall then see the sign of the Son of Man coming with great glory to rule, to reign, and to establish God's kingdom.

•VERSE 5 Isaiah 9:6 tells us that His name will be "The Prince of Peace." Paul says of Christ in Ephesians 2:14, "He is our peace." Jesus said to His disciples, "Peace I leave with you, My peace I give unto you" (John 14:27).

He's not prophesying about the immediate threat from Assyria, but about the future threat when the company of Russia and mostly Moslem nations shall come and invade them in the last days.

•VERSE 7 Those of Jacob, wherever they are during this period, will be a blessing. God is going to bless them again.

•VERSES 8-15 God is declaring that in the great tribulation, He will execute vengeance in anger and fury upon the heathen such as they have never experienced or dreamed. It is a comfort to know that God has not appointed us unto wrath.

CHAPTER 6:
THE LORD'S CONTROVERSY WITH ISRAEL

•VERSE 3 They are still His people after all of this.

God was calling for them to lay out their cause.

•VERSE 5 Balak hired Balaam to curse; instead, he blessed them greatly. He spoke of the glory of Jacob and the star that would rise, and the king became angry with the prophet. God turned the curses into blessings.

•VERSE 8 As Samuel said to Saul, "Behold, to obey is better than to sacrifice, and to hearken better than the fat of rams" (1 Samuel 15:22).

God wants us to be merciful instead of vengeful. God hates a proud look and the pride of men. He wants us to walk humbly with Him.

•VERSES 10-11 They used false weights. When selling, they used the heavier weights; when buying, they used the lighter weights. God is rebuking them for their crooked practices.

•VERSES 14-15 They were going to lose everything, and the land was going to become desolate. Someone else will reap the benefits of all of their efforts and work.

•VERSE 16 Omri and Ahab were two wicked kings of Israel that led the people into abominable practices and sins.

CHAPTER 7:
ISRAEL WILL RISE

•VERSE 3 Bribery was everywhere in the government.

The great man gets whatever he wants—even his mischievous desires—because of his prominence.

•VERSE 4 They're flaunting the Law of God now, but their day is coming.

•VERSE 6 Total disorder within the nation. Family, the last faction of strength within a nation, has broken down completely.

•VERSE 7 The whole situation was so desperate and void of God's work, power, love, mercy, grace, and truth. The only hope is to look to the Lord.

•VERSE 8 The wonderful thing about walking with the Lord is that I may fall, but I will rise. There may be darkness, but the Lord will be a light to me.

You are to be a light in this dark world. There is no sin in falling—everybody does. The sin is lying there. Get up and start over again.

•VERSE 9 This is not the end. God's truth will triumph and His kingdom shall be established. Righteousness shall cover the earth as the waters cover the sea.

•VERSES 11-13 God's judgment will come from Assyria and other nations who will invade the land. This is allowed by God because they are reaping what they have sown.

•VERSE 15 Even as God delivered them by parting the Red Sea, so God is going to work again among the people with marvelous miracles.

•VERSE 16 Those nations that seek to come against Israel will be amazed at the power of this little nation with the power of God.

•VERSE 17 During the great tribulation, they will hide in the caves, crying unto the rocks and the mountains (Revelation 6:16-17).

•VERSE 18 As the prophet Isaiah said, "Come now, let us reason together, though your sins are as scarlet, they can be as white as snow."

He pardons iniquity to those who will call and repent. God will pardon your iniquities. It doesn't matter what you have done. The blood of Jesus Christ will cleanse a man from all sin.

•VERSE 19 God is going to take these people back. They are still His people and He will restore them unto Himself.

He conquers those things that have conquered us. He subdues the iniquity and the havoc that's destroying you. He destroys Satan's power in your life and He sets the captive free.

•VERSE 20 He promised to Abraham that from his seed, Jesus Christ, all the nations of the world shall be blessed.

The kingdom of God shall come, and Jesus shall reign, and they that are His shall live and reign with Him. That's our hope and His promise to us.

STUDY QUESTIONS FOR MICAH

1. As a prophet of God, Micah exposed evil. What was the response of the people in Micah 2:6? What would they rather hear according to Micah 2:11?

_____

_____

_____

2. In Micah 3:4, the Lord declares He will hide His face from the rulers because of their evil deeds. What were their deeds recorded in Micah 3:2-3?

_____

_____

_____

3. Micah prophesied about the future kingdom age when Jesus will reign. From Micah 4:2-7, describe this wonderful time.

_____

_____

_____

4. In 1 Samuel 15:22 we read, "Behold, to obey is better than to sacrifice, and to hearken better than the fat of rams." Micah also touches on this subject in Micah 6:6-8. What pleases God?

_____

_____

_____

5. Despite this desperate time for Israel, what is Micah's attitude in Micah 7:7?

_____

_____

_____

THE BOOK OF
NAHUM

AUTHOR OF THE BOOK:
Nahum

PERIOD OF WRITING:
The time of Nahum's prophecy is a matter of speculation. There are those Bible scholars who feel that he prophesied at the time Hezekiah was king in Judah, around 713 BC, a contemporary to Isaiah the prophet.

There are others who put his prophecies a little later, right around 620 BC just before Assyria was destroyed.

TYPE OF BOOK:
Prophetic

THEME:
God's final judgment on Nineveh.

INTRODUCTION:
Nahum prophesied against the city of Nineveh, declaring the judgment of God— 150 years after Jonah had visited the city.

When Jonah had been called to Nineveh, the people repented at his preaching and Nineveh was spared. But now God is proclaiming the destruction that is going to come against an unrepentant Nineveh and against Assyria.

Because Nineveh was completely destroyed, the Bible critics declared that it was a mythological city that never existed. But archeologists have discovered the ruins of Nineveh, finding palaces and a tremendous library containing the records of the Assyrians, listing ten different kings of Israel by name.

CHAPTER 1:
GOD IS HOLY, JUST, AND POWERFUL
•**VERSE 1** This prophecy is about the burden of Nineveh. Nineveh was the capital of Assyria.

The Assyrian Empire ruled the world from around 800-600 BC.

The Assyrians were very cruel, heartless people. They made a practice of seeking to terrorize their enemies.

Most of the scholars conclude that Nahum came from the region of Galilee. There is a village on the shores of the Sea of Galilee that is called Capernaum.

HEBREW KEY WORDS

Nahum = comforter
Capernaum = the home of Nahum (1:1).

•**VERSE 2** Every man has a god, even the man who claims to be an atheist. A person's god is the master passion that governs his life, and God wants to be the master passion of your life. If you allow anything else to be a substitute for Him, He is displeased and this displeasure is described in our human term of jealousy.

God is jealous for you because He loves you so much. He wants nothing but the best for your life. He knows that if you have any other love or passion above Him, you're not going to achieve or attain that which is best for you.

"Vengeance is Mine, I will repay," saith the Lord. There is a day of judgment coming. You cannot sin with impunity against God and think that you'll never have to answer for it.

The Assyrians conquered and destroyed the northern kingdom of Israel and took them captive. They were cruel in their treatment of Israel, and so the time of God's revenge against Assyria has come.

•**VERSE 3** God is slow to anger and is longsuffering, which often causes people to feel a security in their wickedness. But God will punish the wicked.

•**VERSE 7** In the midst of describing the awesome power of God in judgment, the prophet declares that the Lord is good. This is a basic foundation of theology that must be incorporated into our understanding.

God doesn't promise that you'll never have trouble. But whenever trouble comes, the Lord is a stronghold and a place to run for strength and protection.

•**VERSE 8** An overwhelming flood wiped out the defense and took down some of the great walls, and the city of Nineveh fell.

•**VERSE 9** The destruction of Nineveh was so great that for hundreds of years they questioned whether it was a mythological place or not, until the archeologists discovered it.

•**VERSE 10** The Assyrian king attacked the Babylonian and Mede troops that had besieged the city.

When the king celebrated his victory and they began to get drunk, the forces of the Medes and the Babylonians regrouped, attacked again, and caught them in their drunken state and destroyed them.

•**VERSE 11** A reference to Rabshakeh who came with his letter from Sennacherib, blaspheming God whom the Israelites were trusting (2 Kings 18:28-35).

•**VERSES 12-13** God is speaking to Judah. He has destroyed the Assyrian army that had come to capture Jerusalem. 185,000 of the Assyrian troops were slain by the angel of the Lord in one night.

•**VERSE 14** He's speaking to the Assyrians again.

•**VERSE 15** Nineveh had fallen and the Assyrians weren't going to come back again; they had been utterly cut off.

CHAPTER 2:
THE FALL OF NINEVEH

•**VERSE 1** He was describing the siege and the fall of Nineveh by the Babylonian and Mede confederacy, referring to these men as those that dash in pieces.

•**VERSE 6** A tremendous storm came which caused the Tigress River to flood the city of Nineveh and undermined the foundations of the walls.

A great portion of the walls of Nineveh were destroyed, and as soon as the flood receded, the armies came through the breach.

• **VERSE 8** Panic will overtake them and they will flee.

• **VERSE 9** The Assyrians had robbed other nations, so it was an extremely vast treasure store in Nineveh. Now it became the booty for the Babylonians.

• **VERSES 11-12** Where is that city of Nineveh that was like a lion conquering all?

• **VERSE 13** Nineveh shall be no more. They were completely destroyed.

CHAPTER 3:
NINEVEH'S UTTER DESTRUCTION

• **VERSE 4** The reason Nineveh had to be destroyed.

• **VERSE 6** People looked in wonder at the utter destruction that had taken place of this once powerful kingdom that was the terror of the whole world.

• **VERSE 8** No-amon was Thebes in Egypt, up in the Nile River about 400 miles from Cairo. It was conquered by Assyria and was once a very wealthy, opulent place.

• **VERSE 15** When the city of Nineveh was taken, it was torched and left in ashes.

• **VERSE 19** Assyria was utterly and completely destroyed, and there was nothing but rejoicing among the nations because of its cruelty and fierceness.

The annals of history record it just as Nahum had predicted. The destruction of Nineveh came 100 years later. The Word of God again was confirmed and fulfilled.

STUDY QUESTIONS FOR NAHUM

1. Nahum 1:2 says that God is jealous. What are your thoughts concerning this Scripture?

_____

_____

_____

2. God is just and will punish the wicked. Why do you think some people feel a sense of security in their wickedness? (Nahum 1:3; Psalm 103:8).

_____

_____

_____

3. History confirms the fulfillment of prophecies in the Bible. Read Nahum 1:8 and 2:6 and describe how Nahum prophesied the means by which Nineveh was destroyed.

_____

_____

_____

4. Why was Nineveh completely destroyed as stated in Nahum 3:4?

_____

_____

_____

5. In Nahum 3:19, the Lord declares that Nineveh's wound would be incurable. What actually happened to Nineveh?

_____

_____

_____

THE BOOK OF
HABAKKUK

AUTHOR OF THE BOOK:
Habakkuk

PERIOD OF WRITING:
During the final days of the southern kingdom, 7th century BC.

TYPE OF BOOK:
Prophetic

THEME:
Lament concerning the sin of Judah.

INTRODUCTION:
Habakkuk prophesied during the reign of Manasseh, the evil son of King Hezekiah, who had Isaiah put to death. During the reign of Manasseh, the nation of Judah had sunk lower into depravity than at any previous time in their history. Habakkuk had spoken against the corruption of the government and the nation and cried out to the Lord. Habakkuk prophesied of Babylon's coming invasion and of them being used as a rod of God to punish God's people.

The people of Judah didn't feel any threat at this time from the Babylonian Kingdom, as it had not yet become a major world power. Yet, there is the prophecy that God will use the Chaldeans as His instrument of judgment against Judah.

The key verse is Habakkuk 2:4, declaring, "But the just shall live by faith." The conditions were going to get worse until the nation would be conquered by the Babylonians. Habakkuk is going to need to trust God and have faith in God, because there will be nothing else.

CHAPTER 1:
HABAKKUK'S COMPLAINT

•VERSE 1 Habakkuk began with a prayer unto the Lord, complaining against the tremendous spiritual declension.

🔑 HEBREW KEY WORD

Habakkuk = embracer (1:1).

•VERSE 2 He was praying, but it seemed as though God did not answer his prayer. Things weren't changing for the better.

• **VERSE 4** There's a lack of enforcement of the law and justice in the judicial system. The wicked control the nation and the government, thus wrong judgment proceeds and unfair laws.

• **VERSE 6** The Lord reveals His plan of using the Babylonians as an instrument of judgment against these wicked people. They're going to come and possess this land.

• **VERSE 11** Habakkuk predicts the impending invasion and victory of Babylon over Judah and that they will attribute the victory to their god.

• **VERSE 12** The Lord revealed the plan which creates a greater problem in Habakkuk's mind. He prays the second time, expressing his lack of understanding of the ways of God.

• **VERSE 13** God sees iniquity but He cannot condone it. He cannot look upon it with approval.

Habakkuk didn't understand why God would use the Babylonians as instruments of judgment, and stand back as they consume a people that are more righteous than they were.

CHAPTER 2:
THE LORD ANSWERS HABAKKUK

• **VERSE 1** Knowing that he has challenged God, he is expecting God to reprove.

• **VERSE 4** This is probably directed at Nebuchadnezzar who was Babylon's leader when they conquered the land and fulfilled the prophecy.

Nebuchadnezzar was lifted up with pride, parading around Babylon.

The prideful ones shall be cut down, but in contrast the just will survive and live by faith. This glorious truth is proclaimed three times in the New Testament (Romans 1:17; Galatians 3:11; Hebrews 10:38).

Justification is through faith in Jesus Christ and not of works.

CALVARY DISTINCTIVE

"...but the just shall live by faith" (Habakkuk 2:4).

This is a theme we find throughout the New Testament, and therefore it's a theme we emphasize. The books of Romans and Galatians become very significant because they both set forth the grace of God and righteousness through faith.

• **VERSE 5** The more one indulges in the flesh, the more the flesh demands, rather than being satisfied.

• **VERSES 6-13** This is directed to Babylon and to subsequent nations that would seek to gain by war, to conquer by war, and to use bloodshed and iniquity to establish themselves.

• **VERSE 14** A beautiful prophecy of the future glorious kingdom age when Jesus comes to establish His kingdom upon the earth. The whole earth will be filled with the knowledge of the glory of the Lord.

• **VERSE 18** "Dumb idols" would be mute idols who can't speak.

• **VERSES 19-20** These idols cannot help in times of calamity. They can't speak nor breathe, but the living God is in His holy temple.

CHAPTER 3:
GOD'S DELIVERANCE

• **VERSE 2** "Revive Thy work" is literally, "keep alive Your work." This is a position of faith: trusting God when you don't understand.

• **VERSE 3** This is a glorious prophetic description of the second coming of Jesus Christ.

He'll be coming from the south and east of Jerusalem to the Mount of Olives.

•VERSE 4 Horns are always a symbol of power.

•VERSE 5 The great tribulation will precede Jesus coming for the church.

•VERSES 6-7 The cataclysmic changes will take place geographically upon the earth during the great tribulation. Cushan is Ethiopia. Midian is Saudi Arabia.

•VERSE 8 Rivers will be turned into blood.

•VERSE 12 Indignation is a word in the Old Testament that is commonly used for the period of the great tribulation. God does not thresh the church, His children, or His people. That's inconsistent with God. The great judgment is directed against the heathen.

•VERSE 13 Salvation for God's people, for He did not appoint us unto wrath according to the Scriptures.

•VERSES 14-16 The day of judgment is coming. It's a day of trouble that will come upon the people, as they invade with their troops.

In prophecy there is what they call the near and the far fulfillment. It applies to a local, present situation, but also has a secondary application for the future.

•VERSE 17 A total lack of supplies described.

•VERSE 18 The word "rejoice" in Hebrew is literally leap for joy. The word "joy" is to spin around under the influence of a great joyous emotion. "I'll jump for joy in the Lord and spin around in the God of my salvation." It is a hilarious and exuberant joy. Not only smiling and happy, but jumping up and down, spinning around in excitement in joy in the Lord—not in circumstances.

HEBREW KEY WORDS

alaz = rejoice; leap for joy
giyl = joy; to spin around in joy (3:18).

•VERSE 19 His trust was in the Lord, not in his resources or abilities.

Hinds' feet are deer's feet.

He's going to lift me up above the calamities and the distresses that are coming upon the earth.

In Hebrew, this is a poem to be sung with a cry using stringed instruments in the background.

It could be memorized and sung by the people to remind them that God reigns, and that the purposes of God are established.

God's kingdom shall come. The earth will be filled with the knowledge of the glory of the Lord after God has judged the earth and purged it from the wicked. The righteous shall reign in His everlasting kingdom.

STUDY QUESTIONS FOR HABAKKUK

1. Like Habakkuk, sometimes we feel as if God doesn't hear our prayers. How does the Lord comfort us in Habakkuk 1:5?

_____

_____

_____

2. Once the Lord reveals that He is going to use the Babylonians to judge Judah, why does Habakkuk question God in Habakkuk 1:12-13?

_____

_____

_____

3. What encouraging words do you find by the Lord expressed in Habakkuk 2:4?

_____

_____

4. Although Habakkuk is afraid and does not understand what the Lord is doing, what is his prayer in Habakkuk 3:2? What does this reveal about his relationship with the Lord?

_____

_____

_____

5. Habakkuk realizes that very difficult times are coming. What is the attitude of his heart? (Habakkuk 3:18-19).

_____

_____

_____

THE BOOK OF
ZEPHANIAH

AUTHOR OF THE BOOK:
Zephaniah

PERIOD OF WRITING:
During the reign of Josiah in the late 7th century BC.

TYPE OF BOOK:
Prophetic

THEME:
A call to repent, and ultimate joy when God establishes His kingdom on earth.

INTRODUCTION:
Zephaniah and Jeremiah were the last of the pre-exilic prophets—prophets before the Babylonian captivity. Haggai, Zechariah, and Malachi were the post-exilic prophets who prophesied after the captivity. The prophecy of Zephaniah is during the reign of Josiah but before the fall of Nineveh, the capital of Assyria.

Zephaniah takes his lineage back to King Hezekiah, his great, great grandfather. He was born during the reign of Manasseh and prophesied during the reign of Josiah, who had a fairly successful spiritual reign in Judah. Some commentators suggest that perhaps Zephaniah had an influence on Josiah.

Zephaniah also prophesied of the future and the great battle of Armageddon, when God will assemble the nations and the kingdoms into the Valley of Megiddo, that He might pour His indignation and His fierce anger upon them. He also declared God will establish His kingdom after the judgment, and it will be a day of rejoicing and shouting.

CHAPTER 1:
THE DAY OF JUDGMENT ON JUDAH

•**VERSES 2-3** In Zephaniah's prophecy there is the double aspect of fulfillment: the destruction that came from Babylon and Nebuchadnezzar, and the time of the great tribulation.

•**VERSE 4** This prophecy is against Jerusalem and Judah. It was fulfilled within 25 years from the time it was given.

The idolatrous pagan priests wore black robes. God is going to cut them off, as well as the priests who stood in the temple of God but were no longer His representatives.

HEBREW KEY WORD

Chemarim = black-robed (1:4).

•VERSE 5 Astrology is the worship of the host of heaven, an ancient cult from the Babylonian period when people believed the stars had influences over their lives.

The people had divided hearts; they swore by the Lord, but also swore by the god of pleasure, Molech.

•VERSE 7 Revelation 19 speaks of the great day of the Lord's wrath when He invites the birds to come and feast on the carcasses of kings.

•VERSE 9 The idea of leaping on the threshold is for the purpose to break into a house and steal, that they might fill their master's house with loot from the violence and deceit.

•VERSE 10 The fish gate was to the north, where the Babylonian army actually invaded.

•VERSE 11 Maktesh is the area where they did all the selling (the bazaar).

•VERSE 12 Those who are living a life of ease, not concerned about the Lord or the things of righteousness.

CHAPTER 2:
JUDAH'S ENEMIES JUDGED

•VERSES 2-3 Seek the Lord before the judgment comes. There's still opportunity to turn to God to save you.

•VERSE 4 Major cities of the Philistines.

•VERSES 5-6 The Philistines were tough and were enemies of the Israelites. But even the powerful Philistine cities are going to fall to the Babylonian army that will sweep through the land.

This once populated area will become desolate, and the shepherds will keep their sheep in the caves and in the ruins of these cities.

•VERSE 8 Moab was a descendant of Lot, as was Ammon, and they were enemies of the children of God.

Though they were related, as Abraham was Lot's uncle, yet these descendants of Lot were constantly battling against Israel. There was a lot of bitterness and enmity between them.

When Israel was weakened by the invasion of the Babylonians, they moved into the territory to take some of the land for themselves.

•VERSE 11 "Every knee shall bow, every tongue shall confess that Jesus Christ is the Lord" (Philippians 2:10).

•VERSE 13 When Zephaniah was prophesying, Nineveh still existed and had not yet been destroyed by the Medes and the Babylonians.

•VERSES 14-15 Within ten years of this prophecy, Nineveh was conquered and destroyed by Babylon.

Even as the city was being taken, they were still celebrating, thinking they could not fall since their defenses were so powerful, and that no one could stand up against them.

CHAPTER 3:
THE FUTURE OF ISRAEL

•VERSE 1 The Lord speaks against Jerusalem as the city that has become spiritually and morally filthy.

•VERSE 5 God rebuked them, but they knew no shame. Not only were they wicked and vile in their practices, but they were proud. They flaunted their wickedness before man.

•VERSE 7 God often brings judgment in the form of chastisement into our lives to correct us and turn us back to Him.

Even so, many still rebel against the Lord, and their condition worsens.

•**VERSE 8** The prophecy turns to the future to the great battle of Armageddon.

•**VERSES 10-13** The sequence here: God's judgment and the indignation, followed by the new age with one language—the restoration of the earth to God's order and God's plan.

•**VERSES 14-15** The glorious day when Jesus comes and reigns and dwells in the midst of His people.

•**VERSES 16-20** The future blessing upon the nation of Israel in the glorious kingdom age.

STUDY QUESTIONS FOR ZEPHANIAH

1. The book of Zephaniah speaks of God's approaching judgment. According to Zephaniah 1:4-6, 8, 9, and 12, to whom is God going to stretch out His hand against?

_____

_____

_____

2. Zephaniah knew that the Lord was merciful. What was he exhorting the people to do in Zephaniah 2:3?

_____

_____

_____

3. Zephaniah prophesied the coming judgment upon Moab and Ammon. What was God's reason for judgment? (Zephaniah 2:8, 10).

_____

_____

_____

4. In chapter 3 the Lord is speaking against the city of Jerusalem. According to verses 1 and 2, why is Jerusalem guilty?

_____

_____

_____

5. Although the Lord must bring judgment on sin, He always gives a reminder of hope and restoration. Describe from Zephaniah 3:15-20 some of the promised future blessings upon the nation of Israel.

_____

_____

_____

THE BOOK OF
HAGGAI

AUTHOR OF THE BOOK:
Haggai

PERIOD OF WRITING:
520 BC

TYPE OF BOOK:
Prophetic

THEME:
Correction and encouragement.

INTRODUCTION:
In the year 536 BC, Cyrus, the king of Persia, signed a decree allowing the Jews to return to the Holy Land and commissioned the Jews to rebuild the temple. Zerubbabel led 50,000 Jews back to Jerusalem. As they started rebuilding, there arose an immediate opposition from the people in the area. Letters were sent back to the Persian government warning that the Jews were a defiant people who would rebel against the government of Persia. As a result, they received a cease and desist order from the government about 534 BC, only two years after they began.

Haggai begins his prophecy in the second year of Darius the king. This is not the Darius of Daniel, but the one who came 16 years after they began to rebuild the temple. Haggai rebukes the people and calls them to repentance. Later he encourages the people to obey the Lord and get back to work in rebuilding the temple.

CHAPTER 1:
A CALL TO REBUILD THE TEMPLE

• **VERSE 1** The word of the Lord came to Haggai the prophet. It was addressed to Zerubbabel, the governor, and one of the leaders in the rebuilding, and also to Joshua the high priest.

• **VERSE 2** The people procrastinated.

• **VERSE 9** Jesus said to His disciples, "Don't worry about tomorrow, what you're going to eat, what you're going to drink, what you're going to wear. Seek ye first the kingdom of God, and His righteousness; and all these things shall be added unto you" (Matthew 6:31, 33).

Seek first the kingdom of God and He'll take care of these other things if you have the right priority.

•**VERSE 13** "I am with you" is the answer to any fears, doubts, or apprehensions.

When the task seems to be overwhelming and you don't know how you are going to do it, the word of the Lord is sufficient.

•**VERSE 15** He brought the first message on the first day of the month, and by the twenty-fourth of the month they are busy again rebuilding the temple.

CHAPTER 2:
ENCOURAGEMENT FOR THE BUILDERS

•**VERSE 1** The next message came from the Lord unto Haggai almost a month later.

•**VERSE 3** The book of Ezra says that there was tremendous excitement as they laid the foundation of the new temple and the people were thrilled. But the older people who remembered the glory of Solomon's temple were weeping.

•**VERSE 7** A prophecy of the great tribulation period when God is going to shake the world. "For the Lord said, 'And once again I am going to shake the world like it has never been shaken before. So that everything that can be shaken will be brought down, and only that which cannot be shaken shall remain'" (Hebrews 12:26-27).

Jesus Christ will come again and the glory of God will once more fill the temple.

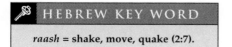

HEBREW KEY WORD

raash = shake, move, quake (2:7).

•**VERSE 10** It appears that Haggai's whole ministry was completed in three months.

•**VERSE 12** God gave many laws in Leviticus concerning holy and unholy things. There were many ways by which you could defile yourself, and the things you touched would become defiled.

•**VERSE 14** The people are unclean as they neglected God and His house. They're only concerned about their own welfare, and thus everything they touch is unclean and can't be accepted by God.

•**VERSES 15-19** As they began to build the temple again, the prophet came and said, "Mark this day. Things are going to change and you're going to have plenty. God will now take care of you and provide for you because you have put Him first."

This is a universal truth and law that is timeless. Put God first in your life and He will take care of the rest of the things in your life. Put the things of your life first, and you're always going to be running short.

•**VERSE 21** Another reference to the great tribulation period.

•**VERSE 23** In Revelation 11, God sends two witnesses to the Jews in the days of the great tribulation. One of the witnesses will be Elijah in fulfillment of the prophecy of Malachi. The identity of the other witness is unknown.

Some have suggested John the Baptist, Moses, or Enoch. The book of Revelation describes the two witnesses as two olive trees, referring to the prophecy of Zechariah, in which the olive trees were Zerubbabel and Joshua.

Here God said He will make Zerubbabel a signet in that day, which makes him another candidate.

STUDY QUESTIONS FOR HAGGAI

1. Why is Haggai correcting and exhorting the people?

_____

_____

_____

2. Haggai gave the people a message from the Lord. What was the incredible message that Haggai gave to the people? (Haggai 1:13). How do you think this comforted them?

_____

_____

_____

3. As with many people today, the Israelites worked hard yet didn't see much fruit from their labor. What was the Lord's explanation for this? (Haggai 1:6-9).

_____

_____

_____

4. Because some of the elders were discouraged at the modest appearance of this new temple, the Lord encouraged them by giving a glorious hope for the future. According to Haggai 2:7-9, what did the Lord promise?

_____

_____

_____

5. In Haggai 2:19 the Lord told the people that He would begin to bless them again. What had changed? (Haggai 2:15-19).

_____

_____

_____

THE BOOK OF
ZECHARIAH

AUTHOR OF THE BOOK:
Zechariah

PERIOD OF WRITING:
Approximately 520 BC.

TYPE OF BOOK:
Prophetic

THEME:
Focus on eternity.

INTRODUCTION:
Zechariah has the clearest insight concerning the coming of Jesus Christ than any of the other minor prophets combined. He prophesies of both the first and the second coming of Jesus Christ.

This period had been a time of intense dealings of the Lord with His people. They were discouraged and demoralized. The task of the rebuilding of the temple seemed more than what they could really do in their own energies.

The prophet Haggai had explained that their hard times were a result of placing God second. They had put their own interests before God.

Now Zechariah picks up this same theme, and as the people renew their efforts to rebuild the house of God, Haggai and Zechariah both encourage the people to keep up the good work and finish building the temple. Whereas Haggai was work-oriented, Zechariah had his eyes on heaven and the future.

CHAPTER 1:
THE HOUSE WILL BE REBUILT

•**VERSE 3** God's message through the ages. God has given the invitation. You can have fellowship with God if you will come to Him. But the Lord does not force Himself on the people nor force them to love Him.

HEBREW KEY WORD

shub = **turn or return (1:3).**

•**VERSES 4-5** Learn the lesson. Your fathers perished and were carried away to Babylon because they did not turn to Me.

•**VERSE 6** What the prophets had warned them happened. They were defeated and carried away captive.

•**VERSE 8** Zechariah had a series of visions that are like dreams. A dream comes when a person is in a state of sleep, and a vision comes when a person is awake but sees things in the spirit realm that are taking place or are going to take place. In the realm of the spirit, you move into the timeless dimension of eternity.

He begins by describing the one riding on the red horse as "the man," then calling Him "my lord." He then refers to Him as "the angel that talked with me." He ultimately identifies Him as "the angel of the Lord" in verse 11.

In the Old Testament, the angel of the Lord is often the pre-incarnate Jesus Christ.

•**VERSE 11** In the book of Job when the sons of God were presenting themselves to God, Satan also presented himself. God said to Satan, "Where have you been?" He said, "I have been walking to and fro throughout the earth, up and down in it." Here angels have been going throughout the earth observing, and their report is, "We have walked to and fro throughout the earth, and behold, the earth sitteth still, and is at rest."

•**VERSE 12** The angel of the Lord is now interceding.

•**VERSE 15** God was using the nations as an instrument of judgment against Israel, but they went beyond what was intended.

•**VERSE 16** The Lord promises that the house will be built. Those who had been working on the temple were convinced at this time that it wouldn't. Here the Lord is declaring that it will.

•**VERSE 17** There is a future for Jerusalem. There is a purpose of God yet to be accomplished. It has not yet been fully accomplished but will be accomplished in the kingdom age when Jesus comes and establishes God's kingdom upon the earth.

His throne will be on Mount Zion, and Jerusalem will be the capital of the earth during the reign of the Lord.

•**VERSE 18** The second vision. Horns are always used as symbols of power in the Bible. The four horns represent four kingdoms.

•**VERSE 20** The third vision. Carpenters are literally hewers or carvers.

CHAPTER 2:
THE APPLE OF HIS EYE

•**VERSE 1** The fourth vision.

•**VERSE 4** The young man referred to here was Zechariah.

Jerusalem is going to grow far beyond the boundaries of the walls. Today Jerusalem has expanded her borders tremendously. The walled city is now just a small portion in the center.

•**VERSE 5** His glory in the midst of her will not take place until Jesus comes again.

•**VERSE 6** This speaks of their dispersion. The Jews have been spread abroad through every part of the world. When the Soviet Union broke up, hundreds of thousands of Jews were able to return to Israel. This particular prophecy has been fulfilled in very recent history.

HEBREW KEY WORD

paras = spread abroad, break apart, disperse (2:6).

•**VERSE 8** If you touch the Jewish people, you touch the apple of God's eye, or the pupil of His eye.

God told Abraham that He would bless those that blessed him and He would curse those that cursed him. There should not be any kind of anti-Semitism, especially within the church.

•**VERSES 9-10** A glorious prophecy of the second coming of Jesus Christ.

•**VERSES 11-12** Jesus is going to come again and dwell upon the earth for 1,000 years. He will reign over the earth and will be worshiped. Judah will be His portion and He will set His throne in Jerusalem.

CHAPTER 3:
NEW GARMENTS

•**VERSE 1** In the fifth vision, the Lord showed him Joshua, the high priest, who was in charge of rebuilding the temple with Zerubbabel.

Satan is seeking to resist whatever work you may desire to do for the Lord (Ephesians 6:12).

•**VERSE 2** Michael the archangel said unto Satan, "The Lord rebuke you." It's better to let the Lord stand between you and Satan.

Satan is like a brand, a live coal that's been plucked out of the fire.

•**VERSE 3** In Scripture, garments are representative of a person's righteousness. Filthy garments represent self-righteousness, or righteousness that you have created for yourself by good works.

•**VERSE 4** The Bible says that our works are like filthy rags in the eyes of God (Isaiah 64:6).

Your goodness, your righteousness, your good works are not accepted.

The Lord changes our lives by our faith in Jesus Christ, and now we are clothed in the righteousness of Jesus Christ.

•**VERSE 8** The sixth vision is a prophecy of Jesus Christ. In Jeremiah and Isaiah Jesus is referred to as the righteous Branch that shall come out of the root of Jesse.

•**VERSE 9** Another title for Jesus, "The stone which the builders rejected has become the chief cornerstone" (Psalm 118:22).

In Revelation 5:6, seven eyes are the seven spirits of God that were resting upon the Lord, as in Isaiah 11:1-2.

•**VERSE 10** Speaking of the day of peace that will come, every man living in peace and unafraid according to the prophecies of Isaiah and Micah.

CHAPTER 4:
GOLDEN LAMPSTAND & TWO OLIVE TREES

•**VERSE 1** The seventh vision.

•**VERSES 2-3** This candlestick was probably similar to the one in the tabernacle that Moses constructed.

In Revelation 1, John saw seven lampstands and Jesus walking in the midst of the seven golden candlesticks. The Lord tells John that the candlesticks are the seven churches. Thus there is the beautiful symbolism of Jesus walking in the midst of His churches. It symbolizes that the church now is to be the light of Jesus to the world.

In Zechariah's vision, there were pipes that led to the golden bowl which kept it continually filled with oil. There was a constant supply of oil flowing from the trees into the bowl and into the cups, whereby there was constant light.

•**VERSE 6** When used in allegories, parables, dreams, or visions in Scriptures, oil is always a symbol of the Holy Spirit.

The work of God is not to be accomplished by might, nor by power, but can only be accomplished by the Spirit of the Lord.

CALVARY DISTINCTIVE

"Not by might, nor by power, but by my spirit, saith the LORD of hosts" (Zechariah 4:6).

God will go to tremendous lengths to make certain that His chosen leaders rely on the Spirit and not on their own power and wisdom.

• **VERSE 7** This was a word of encouragement to Zerubbabel.

He had been discouraged in the building of the temple, but by the Spirit of God the job will be done, and this mountain will be leveled.

• **VERSE 9** In Ezra, the temple was finished in the sixth year of Darius the king. The prophecy came to pass.

In less than four years they completed the job and the temple was rebuilt and dedicated again as a place for the people to come worship the Lord.

• **VERSE 10** These seven eyes are the seven spirits which stand before the throne of God in Revelation 5:6.

• **VERSE 14** God's two witnesses in the last days in Revelation 11.

CHAPTER 5:
THE FLYING SCROLL

• **VERSE 1** The eighth vision.

• **VERSE 2** Approximately 30 feet long and 15 feet wide.

• **VERSE 3** The Torah was placed in a scroll, and within the Torah is the law of Moses. The law of Moses gives blessings to those who are obedient and consequences to those who disobey.

• **VERSE 4** The warning of the judgment of God that was going to come. The world will be judged by the Law of God.

• **VERSE 5** The ninth vision.

• **VERSE 6** The ephah was the largest dry measure that the Hebrews had. It was a basket of about six or seven gallons.

• **VERSE 7** The covering was made of lead.

• **VERSE 8** The ephah is a symbol of commercialism. God views it as wickedness.

• **VERSES 9-11** God's rebuke against the commercial system that was headquartered in Babylon. It also speaks of the modern day commercial system that will be destroyed in Revelation 18.

CHAPTER 6:
THE CROWN FOR JOSHUA

• **VERSE 1** It doesn't tell us which two mountains they were.

• **VERSES 2-8** In Revelation 6, when the Lord opens the first seal, there are the four horses of the apocalypse. Here are four horses, but these are drawing chariots.

Red, symbolic of war and bloodshed; black, symbolic of famine; white, symbolic of power; and the bay horses are symbolic of strength.

We don't have a clear enough interpretation to know for certain what these various colored horses are.

• **VERSES 11-13** "Joshua" means Jehovah is salvation. Translated into Greek, the name is Jesus. He's to take this crown and put it upon Joshua's head, the high priest from the tribe of Levi.

Today Jesus fulfills both roles as the King and High Priest. The Branch who is going to build the true temple of God is none other than Jesus Christ.

• **VERSE 14** The crowns in the temple would be a reminder to the people of the future glory that would come to Israel.

CHAPTER 7:
MERCY INSTEAD OF FASTING

•VERSE 1 The work of rebuilding the temple has now been going on for approximately two years, and it will be another two before it is completed.

•VERSE 2 "They" are probably the people who were still in Babylon. The Jews from that area sent these men to Jerusalem to inquire of the Lord whether or not they should continue their fasting in the fifth month.

•VERSE 3 During the 70 years of captivity, in the fifth month there was an appointed fast commemorating the destruction of the temple. The question is, should they continue fasting now that they are rebuilding the temple?

•VERSES 5-6 The Lord's response was that He never ordered these fasts to begin with.

There was only one fast that was inaugurated by God in the Old Testament under the law, and that was Yom Kippur, the Day of Atonement. All of the other holidays were feasts, similar to Thanksgiving.

Spiritual exercises can become routine and meaningless. It was more like a holiday than a true fast for the Lord.

•VERSE 7 It is better to obey God than to fast.

•VERSE 9 What God wants is for you to be fair and to treat one another with sincere mercy and love.

•VERSES 10-11 These were the things the prophets were telling their fathers, but they wouldn't listen.

•VERSE 12 Their hearts became hardened to the commands of God.

•VERSE 14 They should have grieved over the fact that their fathers had closed their ears unto God. They were only mourning over the consequences, but not their evil.

CHAPTER 8:
THE FUTURE BLESSING

•VERSE 3 This is a promise of the future age when Jesus comes and establishes His kingdom upon the earth, and will reign from Mount Zion over the earth.

•VERSE 5 God sees the kingdom age in perfection, when boys and girls can play together safely in the streets. The Lord used this to describe a utopia because He loves children.

•VERSE 7 During the dispersion from the Babylonian and Assyrian captivity, they were spread to the north (Assyria and Babylon), and to the south (Egypt).

After the destruction of the temple by Titus and the Romans, they were also scattered to the east and to the west. God is going to gather them and save them from the east and west country.

•VERSE 9 They're in the middle of rebuilding the temple, so God was encouraging them to continue the work even as Haggai did when they laid the foundation.

•VERSE 10 It was dangerous to go out in the streets because of the strife, violence, joblessness, and poverty.

•VERSE 12 Your crops are going to be blessed. You've got your priorities right again. Because you've put God back in the proper place in your lives, God is going to bless you.

Haggai said, "Your barns are going to be full. You're going to be blessed of the Lord, because you've now taken on again the task of building the house of the Lord" (Haggai 2:18-19). They are completing the task, and Zechariah is pointing out that they are being blessed once again.

•VERSE 19 Make your days of fasting into days of feasting; cheerful days instead of days of affliction.

CHAPTER 9:
JUDGMENT ON THE ENEMIES OF ISRAEL

•**VERSES 1-2** Hadrach and Hamath were areas near Damascus in Syria.

•**VERSES 3-4** At the time of this prophecy, Tyre was a wealthy city on the island. Alexander the Great would move into this area and conquer the island city of Tyrus and destroy it completely.

•**VERSES 5-7** When Alexander the Great came, he destroyed the Philistine cities.

•**VERSE 8** When he came back through the area, he came to Jerusalem but respected the holy city. He was very superstitious and had a respect for spiritual things, so he did not violate the city.

The latter part of the prophecy refers to the kingdom age.

•**VERSE 9** Prophecy of the coming King. He is lowly and riding on a colt. This was partially fulfilled through the triumphant entry of Jesus into Jerusalem (Psalm 118).

In His first coming, Jesus did not establish the kingdom. In the second coming, He will establish His throne and gather together the nations of the earth for judgment.

•**VERSE 10** The Lord has given a message of peace to us.

The word "heathen" is the same word for nations or Gentiles. Through Him, we have entered into peace with God. His kingdom shall be from sea to sea, from the river to the ends of the world.

HEBREW KEY WORD

shalom = peace, rest, safe (9:10).

•**VERSE 11** Jesus established the "blood of thy covenant" through His death. The prisoners who were in the pit (*gehenna*) were freed.

•**VERSE 12** Jesus is the stronghold for every child of God.

•**VERSES 13-17** "How great is His goodness, and how great is His beauty!" is declared when the Lord reigns in the glorious kingdom age.

CHAPTER 10:
GOD WILL BLESS JUDAH

•**VERSE 2** People seeking to find guidance from fortunetellers or diviners.

•**VERSE 4** Out of Judah, in future tense (Isaiah 22:22-25; 28:16).

•**VERSE 7** They will return to God.

•**VERSE 8** "Hiss" is to call by whistling.

•**VERSE 10** They'll come back in such numbers that it will be hard to place them.

CHAPTER 11:
THE BROKEN STAFF CALLED BEAUTY

•**VERSE 1** When the Roman armies came against Jerusalem, they actually traveled through Lebanon and down into the upper Galilee region.

They first conquered the area of the Galilee, and then moved on and set siege against Jerusalem in AD 70.

•**VERSES 3-5** Over a million Jews in Jerusalem were slaughtered in AD 70 when Titus took the city.

The Jews that survived were taken back to be sold as slaves.

•**VERSE 9** This was literally fulfilled in the siege according to Josephus as they turned to cannibalism within the city because they were so hungry.

•VERSE 10 The staff "Beauty" is Jesus Christ who was crucified and cut off.

•VERSE 11 With the crucifixion and death of Jesus Christ, God's covenant with the nation Israel was broken. Their place of standing in divine favor was cut off.

Paul said, "Inasmuch as you've judged yourself unworthy of eternal life, I'm going to the Gentiles." God allowed blindness to happen to Israel at that point.

The covenant of the law whereby Jews were able to relate to God was broken. You can only come to God now on the basis of faith—and the Jew has to come like the Gentile at the present time.

God will not accept their offerings under the old covenant.

•VERSES 12-13 What a remarkable prophecy concerning the betrayal of Jesus Christ by Judas for 30 pieces of silver (Matthew 26, 27). The prophecy of Zechariah was literally fulfilled. The Lord spoke of the details 500 years before the event.

Under the law, if you had an ox and it gored your neighbor's servant to death, you would pay your neighbor 30 pieces of silver to pay for the slave that was lost. Jesus was sold for the price of a slave gored by an ox.

•VERSE 14 God broke bands, the union of brotherhood that He had between Judah and Israel.

•VERSE 15 Here Zechariah predicts the coming of the Antichrist (John 5:43).

•VERSES 16-17 They will receive the foolish shepherd, the Antichrist, but he will not care for them.

He will make a covenant with them, and after three and a half years, he will come to the rebuilt temple and profane it by going into the Holy of Holies and demanding to be worshiped as God.

There will be an assassination attempt against him, and he will be mortally wounded. His miraculous recovery will cause the whole world to look with awe upon him (Revelation 13:3).

CHAPTER 12:
JUDAH'S VICTORY AND MOURNING

•VERSES 2-3 This condition exists today in Israel. Israel as a nation is a burdensome stone to all the nations around it. They are totally surrounded by antagonistic forces.

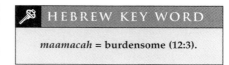

HEBREW KEY WORD

maamacah = burdensome (12:3).

•VERSES 4-5 God intervenes and gives Israel a complete victory over these opposing forces (Ezekiel 38, 39).

•VERSE 6 "In that day" refers to the day when God brings them a great victory.

•VERSE 8 He speaks of the power that God would give to them as a fighting force. The least of them would be as David, who was almost invincible conquering his enemies.

•VERSE 10 When this is all completed, Jesus will return and set His foot upon the Mount of Olives having the spirit of grace and supplication.

Zechariah declared, "And they shall look upon Me whom they have pierced" 500 years before Jesus' crucifixion.

There will be a great consternation because they will realize that for all of these years they have rejected God's true Messiah (Revelation 1:7).

•VERSE 11 There will be a great mourning in Jerusalem, as when Josiah was killed in the battle near Megiddo.

•**VERSES 12-14** All these people will mourn when they realize their suffering and misery through the years was caused by their blindness.

CHAPTER 13:
FALSE PROPHETS AND IDOLS CAST OUT

•**VERSE 1** The veil that has been covering their eyes will be taken away, and they will recognize Jesus as Lord.

There are many things that will transpire in that "day," which is not a 24-hour day but a period of time.

This "day" has already begun—because Israel is a nation, and God has defended them from their enemies—but it will culminate in the glorious appearing of Jesus Christ.

•**VERSE 2** Today mosques that were built in honor of the false prophet Mohammed stand on the Temple Mount where the holy temple was. There are statues, idols, and imagery in these holy sites. God is going to cleanse that area in that day.

•**VERSE 3** Under the law in the book of Deuteronomy, if a person would prophesy and it did not come to pass, they were branded as a false prophet and stoned to death.

In that day, the parents will be the ones who will take action against their children who are falsely prophesying.

•**VERSE 4** False prophets often wore camels' hides because this is how Elijah dressed—a rugged man in camel skins.

•**VERSE 6** We come to the true Shepherd, the one who was pierced.

•**VERSE 7** In Matthew 26:31, Jesus declared that this prophecy was about Himself.

•**VERSE 8** During the great tribulation, the population of the world will be almost decimated.

In Revelation we are told that one third of the earth's population will be destroyed by the plagues that come forth from the four horsemen of the Apocalypse.

As further judgment comes, another third of the remaining population of the world will be destroyed. Only one out of three in the nation of Israel will survive.

•**VERSE 9** God's unfailing love for His people and their beautiful restoration.

CHAPTER 14:
THE LORD IS KING OVER ALL

•**VERSES 1-3** Prediction of the coming day when Jerusalem will be destroyed by the Antichrist. The Lord is going to fight against this power.

•**VERSE 4** It will be an awesome cataclysmic experience when Jesus sets His feet upon the Mount of Olives and a new great valley is formed.

•**VERSE 5** "Behold He cometh with ten thousands of His saints," Enoch prophesied and was quoted by Jude.

The Lord will come again with His church, with His saints, setting His feet upon the Mount of Olives and setting up His kingdom in Jerusalem (Colossians 3:4; Revelation 19).

> ### ✝ CALVARY DISTINCTIVE
>
> "... and the LORD my God shall come, and all the saints with Thee" (Zechariah 14:5).
>
> The rapture can take place at any time. There are no prophecies that have yet to be fulfilled before the rapture occurs. It could happen before you're through reading this, and we would be thrilled if it did!

•**VERSES 6-7** Some type of phenomenon by which it will not be either light or dark; but likened unto a twilight.

•**VERSE 8** The former sea would be the Dead Sea. The hinder sea would be the Mediterranean.

Ezekiel tells us that when this river gets down to the Dead Sea, it will be healed so that there will be a lot of fish in it. And the area of Engedi will be a place where the fishermen will actually dry their nets (Ezekiel 47:10).

•**VERSE 9** Jesus shall be King over all the earth (Psalm 2:7-8).

•**VERSE 10** Describing the city limits of Jerusalem at that time.

•**VERSE 12** In its description this plague sounds like what happens through ultra radiation. It is a hint that there will be nuclear destruction.

•**VERSE 13** A civil war, turning against each other.

•**VERSE 20** Around the mitre of the high priest was inscribed, "Holiness unto the Lord." Now, even on the horses, the bells will be inscribed, "Holiness unto the Lord." Everything will be sanctified unto God at that time.

•**VERSE 21** A purity of worship will be returned when people will come freely to worship God with no pressure and no merchandising.

OLD TESTAMENT STUDY GUIDE

STUDY QUESTIONS FOR ZECHARIAH

1. What is God's message to the people written in Zechariah 1:3?

2. In one of Zechariah's visions he saw a flying scroll. What was this scroll as identified in Zechariah 5:3-4?

3. The Lord loves His children so much that He often reminds them of a future hope. What is the promise in Zechariah 8:3?

4. The Lord speaks about the staff called Beauty that is broken in Zechariah 11:10-11. What does this staff represent, and what is the result of breaking it?

5. God has promised that He will return and defeat all of Israel's enemies. What will happen subsequently? (Zechariah 12:10-11).

THE BOOK OF
MALACHI

AUTHOR OF THE BOOK:
Malachi

PERIOD OF WRITING:
Approximately 400 BC.

TYPE OF BOOK:
Prophetic

INTRODUCTION:
Malachi means "my messenger," and that is exactly what he was. He was the last messenger of the Old Testament.

Malachi prophesied when the children of Israel had returned from their Babylonian captivity and were starting to rebuild the nation. Nehemiah was leading the people in the rebuilding of the city while Malachi was providing messages from God. They read the Law of God to the people, but they had begun to put away their wives and began to marry Moabite women from the cities of Ashdod and Ammon.

After his prophecy, we have approximately 400 years of silence when God did not speak to man. It is interesting that the very last words of Malachi are a prophecy concerning the coming of Elijah before the great and dreadful day of the Lord (4:6). John the Baptist, coming in the spirit and the power of Elijah, was the voice of God to man after this long period of silence (Luke 1:17).

CHAPTER 1:
GIVING GOD CASTOFFS

•**VERSE 2** God's first word of the final word is, "I have loved you." That isn't in past tense, but past and present, "I continue to love you." God's love never ceases.

This is basically a book of God's rebuke, but it begins with an affirmation of God's love.

•**VERSES 3-4** "Wherein does God love us?" God answers by pointing out that He chose Jacob over Esau. According to tradition, the blessings should have gone to Esau because he was born first. But God reversed things and Jacob received the birthright, the blessing, and the promise.

HEBREW KEY WORD

Malachi = my messenger (1:1).

357

Being descendants of Jacob rather than Esau was the proof of God's love for Israel.

Both the descendants of Esau and Jacob were destroyed by Nebuchadnezzar and carried away as captives to Babylon.

However, the prophecy here is that Esau will go there endeavoring to rebuild, but Edom will not be rebuilt. Their area is going to be wasted and desolate, and they're not going to recover; whereas God is going to reclaim Jacob and Israel in the land.

To the present day the area of Edom is barren wilderness as God declared—a testimony to the faithfulness of the Word of God.

• **VERSE 5** The fate of Israel was much different; they were to abide. They are yet to experience their days of greatest glory in the coming kingdom of God.

• **VERSE 7** It was their attitude toward God that made everything they did unacceptable to God.

Men who were supposed to be leading the people spiritually had a negative attitude toward the Lord and the things of the Lord.

• **VERSE 8** According to the law they were to bring the best to offer unto the Lord, but they were bringing the blind, lame, and sickly animals. God deserves the best that we have but it's amazing how many times God gets the castoffs.

• **VERSE 13** Thinking the things of God were wearisome or boring was their attitude toward the ministry; an attitude that God detests.

• **VERSE 14** Under the law they were to offer only male animals as sacrifices. They weren't to offer a female unless they had no male at all. Here they were saying that they didn't have any male animals in their flock, so they were vowing and sacrificing unto the Lord a corrupt and deceitful thing.

CHAPTER 2:
MESSAGE TO THE PRIESTS

• **VERSE 1** A message directed now to the spiritual leadership.

• **VERSES 4-6** God had established the priesthood with the tribe of Levi because of the reverence that he had toward God.

• **VERSE 7** The ministers are the messengers of the Lord and their ministry should bring people the knowledge of God.

Paul said, "That which I have received from the Lord, I also delivered unto you" (1 Corinthians 11:23).

That should always be the means of communication to the church—God, through His servant, proclaiming His word and truth to His people.

• **VERSE 8** There are many people today who are turned away from the Lord because churches and ministers fail to proclaim the truth of the Lord.

• **VERSE 10** We should not have the divisions within the church because of competition, fighting, jealousy, and strife. We all serve the same Lord.

• **VERSE 11** The men of Judah, who had returned to rebuild the nation, were leaving their wives and marrying young women from foreign nations—strangers to God and His covenants.

• **VERSE 15** God commanded them not to marry outside of the race because He was seeking to preserve a godly seed for the nation Israel, in order that they might bring forth His Son into the world.

• **VERSE 16** God hates divorce.

• **VERSE 17** God will judge the wicked, and He is wearied by the false philosophy that everyone is good and that He delights in all men.

CHAPTER 3:
ROBBING GOD

•**VERSE 1** A prophecy of the coming of John the Baptist as the forerunner of Jesus, preparing the way for Him.

Jesus is the messenger of the covenant (Matthew 26:28).

•**VERSE 2** The prophecy jumps at least 2,000 years to Jesus' second coming. As Malachi writes, there is a co-mingling of both the first and the second comings of Jesus Christ.

John the Baptist came as the forerunner, proclaimed the coming of the Lord, and bore testimony of Christ (John 1:27, 29).

Jesus came to the temple and cleansed it by driving out the moneychangers and those that were selling doves. Although He was rejected, He is coming again, and this time Elijah shall precede Him and prepare the hearts of the people for His coming. So part of this was fulfilled in His first coming while much of it remains to be fulfilled in His second coming.

Malachi and the prophets did not see the two aspects of the coming of the Messiah. Peter said that they wrote of things they didn't really understand, earnestly desiring to understand them (1 Peter 1:10-12).

They were prophesying that He would reign as King and Lord forever upon the throne of David and establish the kingdom forever, and yet, they were saying, "and He was despised and rejected of men, a man of sorrow, acquainted with grief, cut off from the land of the living" (Isaiah 53:3). "The Messiah shall be cut off, but not for Himself" (Daniel 9:26), or without receiving the kingdom.

They wrote, honestly obeying the voice of the Spirit that was speaking to their hearts, though they themselves did not understand the things they wrote.

•**VERSE 5** This is referring to the second coming of Christ. The first activity when He returns to the earth is that of gathering the nations together for judgment.

The reason why they were doing these things is because they didn't have the fear of the Lord.

•**VERSE 6** God promised Jacob there would arise the morning star, and God keeps His word. God does not change. Immutability is one of His divine attributes.

•**VERSE 7** God still reaches out and calls to them even though they had failed so miserably.

•**VERSE 8** They were robbing God by holding back.

The word "tithe" means a tenth. God claims that a tenth of the increase belongs to Him. Actually, everything we have is His, but all He asks for is ten percent.

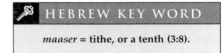

HEBREW KEY WORD

maaser = tithe, or a tenth (3:8).

•**VERSE 10** The only place that God challenges us to prove Him is in our giving.

"Give, and it shall be given unto you. Measured out, pressed down, and running over, shall men give into your bosom" (Luke 6:38). That's a spiritual City of David of God. The more you give, the more you will receive.

Paul expressed it by saying, "He who gives sparingly will receive sparingly, but he who gives bountifully will receive bountifully" (2 Corinthians 9:6).

•**VERSE 14** The benefits of walking with the Lord and living a life for Christ must be measured in eternal values, not temporal benefits.

Many times there are no temporal benefits but always great eternal value.

As Paul said, "The present suffering is not worthy to be compared with the glory that is going to be revealed" (Romans 8:18; 2 Corinthians 4:17).

It is for those eternal blessings that we commit our lives to serve the Lord and live a life of holiness.

•**VERSE 15** These people are in contrast to those who were robbing God, who were saying stout things against the Lord and would be judged by God.

The Bible says the fear of the Lord is the beginning of wisdom and knowledge, and the fear of the Lord is to hate evil.

•**VERSE 16** The Lord eavesdrops on every conversation concerning Him. God loves it when you talk about Him. He keeps this book of remembrance and records those who fear Him and who think upon His name.

•**VERSE 17** He's going to gather together all of His treasure, and you are one of His jewels. He prizes you more than silver, gold, diamonds, and rubies.

Your eternal salvation is so important to God that He gave His only begotten Son to redeem you from an empty life in sin. We are redeemed by the precious blood of Jesus Christ, God's only begotten Son—that's how much God values you.

CHAPTER 4:
ELIJAH AND THE DAY OF THE LORD

•**VERSE 1** The great day of God's judgment is coming, but those who fear the Lord and think upon His name will be His jewels, and will be written in His book of remembrance.

They will be spared from the day of judgment that is coming to destroy the wicked.

•**VERSE 2** The glorious promise of the coming of Jesus Christ: the Sun of Righteousness with healing in His wings to establish God's glorious kingdom upon the earth.

•**VERSES 5-6** This prophecy was partially fulfilled in the first coming of Christ in John the Baptist, but the complete fulfillment is yet future.

After the church is removed, after the Israelites realize their error, the two witnesses will come. A real revival will take place among the nation of Israel before the Lord comes in His judgment upon the earth.

STUDY QUESTIONS FOR MALACHI

1. God makes it very clear that He loves His children. In what ways were they showing their true feelings toward God in Malachi 1:7-8, 12-13?

_____

_____

_____

2. Malachi 2 is addressed to the priests. Describe their ministry as you read Malachi 2:7-8.

_____

_____

_____

3. God is letting the people know in Malachi 3:8-10 that they have been robbing Him. What does God ask from us, and what is His promise in return?

_____

_____

_____

4. Although much of the book of Malachi speaks of God's judgment to come, it is also a wonderful promise to those who love Him. What promises do you find in Malachi 3:16-17?

_____

_____

_____

5. What does God say He is going to do before the great and dreadful day of the Lord? (Malachi 4:5-6).

_____

_____

_____

STUDY NOTES

STUDY NOTES

STUDY NOTES

BIBLE COMMENTARIES BY CHUCK SMITH

NEW TESTAMENT STUDY GUIDE

Master the New Testament quickly and easily using this verse-by-verse overview. Includes introductions, explanations, study questions, Greek word origin definitions, biblical maps, charts, and diagrams.

STANDING UP IN A FALLEN WORLD

Based upon the book of Daniel, this book by Chuck Smith inspires today's young adults to take a stand for righteousness, and to seek to overcome this fallen world and its evil ways.

THE GOSPEL ACCORDING TO GRACE

A clear and enlightening commentary on the book of Romans. Chuck Smith reviews Paul's epistle, one of the most important books in the Bible, on a verse-by-verse basis. Study guide included!

WHAT THE WORLD IS COMING TO

This book is a complete commentary on the book of Revelation and the scenario for the last days. Our world is coming to an end fast, but you don't have to go down with it! Recently updated and revised.

TO ORDER CALL 1-800-272-WORD

THROUGH THE BIBLE COMMENTARY C-2000 SERIES ON MP3

Using an MP3 format, The Word For Today compiled Pastor Chuck Smith's entire C-2000 series on a set of eight CDs. You can now fit the complete audio of Pastor Chuck's Bible commentary into your pocket.

GOSPEL OF JOHN AUDIO COMMENTARY

The Gospel of John is one of the greatest testaments of God's unfailing word for a Christian, as well as for the unbeliever. In this fascinating verse-by-verse commentary, Pastor Chuck Smith illustrates the Gospel of John with simplistic understanding.

GALATIANS INDEPTH AUDIO COMMENTARY

All may come freely unto God on the basis of God's love and grace, and not on the grounds of our good merit or works. In this in-depth Bible study, Pastor Chuck Smith teaches the importance of justification by faith, the position of liberty, and the fruit of the Spirit.

EPHESIANS INDEPTH AUDIO COMMENTARY

It was the apostle Paul's desire that we might know the hope of God's calling, the glorious riches of God's inheritance in the saints, and the availability of God's great power. Join Pastor Chuck Smith as he teaches verse-by-verse in-depth on this great epistle.

For information about additional products
or to be added to our e-mail list
for product updates,
please contact:

THE WORD
FOR TODAY

P.O. Box 8000, Costa Mesa, CA 92628
800-272-WORD (9673)
www.twft.com • E-mail: info@twft.com